Growth Divergences

Growth Divergences
Explaining Differences in Economic Performance

Edited by

José Antonio Ocampo, Jomo K. S. and Rob Vos

Orient Longman

Zed Books
London and New York

TWN
Third World Network

Published in association with the UNITED NATIONS

Growth Divergences was first published in 2007.

Published in association with the United Nations

Published in the Indian Subcontinent, South East Asia (except Malaysia and Singapore)
and Africa by
ORIENT LONGMAN PRIVATE LIMITED
Registered Office: 3-6-752 Himayatnagar, Hyderabad 500 029 (A.P.), India
Email: info@orientlongman.com *Website:* www.orientlongman.com
Other Offices: Bangalore, Bhopal, Bhubaneshwar, Chennai, Ernakulam, Guwahati,
Hyderabad, Jaipur, Kolkata, Lucknow, Mumbai, New Delhi and Patna

Published in the UK, Europe, USA, Canada and Australia by
ZED BOOKS LIMITED
7 Cynthia Street, London N1 9JF, UK and
Room 400, 175 Fifth Avenue, New York, NY 10010, USA
www.zedbooks.co.uk
Distributed in the USA on behalf of Zed Books by
Palgrave Macmillan, a division of St Martin's Press, LLC
175 Fifth Avenue, New York, NY 10010, USA

Published in Malaysia and Singapore by
THIRD WORLD NETWORK
131 Jalan Macalister, 10400 Penang, Malaysia
www.twnside.org.sg

Published worldwide by the United Nations and distributed worldwide
via the UN specialized network of agents
United Nations Publications
2 United Nations Plaza Room DC2-853, New York, NY 10017, USA
https://unp.un.org *Email:* publications@un.org

United Nations' sales number: E.07.IV.7
ISBN: 978 81 250 3362 2 Pb (Orient Longman)
ISBN: 978 1 84277 880 7 Hb (Zed Books)
ISBN: 978 1 84277 881 4 Pb (Zed Books)

A catalogue record for this book is available from the British Library
US CIP data is available from the Library of Congress

Cover and book design by Orient Longman Private Limited 2007
Typeset in Minion Pro 10.5/13 by OSDATA, Hyderabad 500 029, India
Printed in India by Graphica Printers, Hyderabad 500013

Contents

Acknowledgements

The United Nations' *World Economic and Social Survey 2006* was on the theme of *Diverging Growth and Development*. To prepare for the survey, over a dozen background papers were commissioned, many of which have since been issued as working papers by the Department of Economic and Social Affairs (DESA). In response to popular interest in the novel theme of the survey, we have abridged or significantly revised versions in this volume.

This book would not have seen the light of day if not for the contributions and revisions of the authors themselves as well as the untiring efforts of Dominika Halka, Suzette Limchoc and Ivan Foo. Zehra Aydin, Saroja Douglas, Mary Jane Holupka, Mary Nolan, Cheryl Stafford and Lauralea Banks worked conscientiously to copy-edit these chapters for publication.

We are grateful to all of them for their respective contributions.

The editors

Overview

The chapters in this volume were all prepared as background papers of the *World Economic and Social Survey (WESS) 2006* and to help better understand and explain the major divergences in economic growth performance since the first United Nations Development Decade in the 1960s. The selection and abridging of these papers for inclusion in this book have been based on the criterion of their relevance to understanding the two major divergences in economic growth performance since the 1960s and especially during the last quarter century.

Unrestricted international movement of goods, services and factors of production has always been one of the principal aims of economic liberalization and has been regarded by many as the essence of globalization since the 1980s. The deregulation of domestic markets and their opening up to international firms and market forces has certainly dominated policy discussions in many developing countries, helping to create a world with fewer countervailing pressures from governments than at any time since the late 1920s. This was not only expected to accelerate growth across the world economy, but to favour, in particular, growth prospects in poorer countries and, as a result, help close the income gap with richer countries.

Chapter one provides a concise summary of the main findings of *WESS 2006*. It begins with a survey of post-war growth trends, showing a growing gap in income per capita between the North and the South as well as between some high growth economies in the South in contrast to other developing countries. Clearly, there is no strong or sustained global trend towards economic convergence, especially during the last quarter century of greater international economic integration, often referred to as globalization. Instead, growth spurts as well as collapses have been the norm, except for a few economies able to achieve high and sustained growth over extended periods of time. Most of the chapter summarizes various trends considered at greater length in the rest of this volume, including structural change, productivity growth, international trade, foreign direct investment (FDI), private capital flows, pro-cyclical macroeconomic policies, investments in infrastructure and human resources, aid effectiveness, the impact of institutions and good governance, and their implications for global inequality, international development and security.

More recent convergence predictions lack the analytical conviction that comes from core economic theory, introducing instead a more open-ended empirical dimension to the discussion of global growth and distribution. Accordingly, in chapter two Richard Kozul-Wright considers whether or not the shift to more liberal policy regimes has given rise to a growth accelerating investment-export nexus in poorer countries and one particular, one that is built around attracting FDI. He begins with a discussion of the convergence concept and raises some initial doubts about its suitability for understanding global growth and distribution dynamics. This is followed by a comparative description of those dynamics over the past two decades, which suggests that a strong and uniform convergence trend has not emerged. Rather uneven and episodic growth performances, combining spurts, collapses, stagnation and intermittent stellar performances have been the norm. Next, he suggests some reasons why international economic forces associated with increased trade and FDI flows may have contributed to this uneven playing field. The final section asks if international inequality will become a concern at the multilateral level, and what kind of changes to current rules and arrangements might be needed to help create a fairer system of global governance.

In chapter three, Lance Taylor and Codrina Rada review the growth and development performance of developing countries in the latter part of the 20th century. Sustained growth among 'successful' countries was accompanied by structural changes – in terms of output and labour share shifts, trade diversification, sustained productivity growth – with some strong reallocation effects due to movements of labour from low to high productivity sectors. Neither the widely accepted "twin deficits" nor the "consumption-smoothing" behaviour views of macroeconomic adjustment seem to apply, though macroeconomic flexibility may be very important. Finally, neither human resource development nor foreign direct investments are sufficient by themselves to stimulate growth.

In chapter four, José Antonio Ocampo and María Angela Parra argue that developing countries are more likely to experience growth successes and collapses together, clustering in specific time periods. They suggest that this can be explained by the existence of a global development cycle. This cycle reflects common external factors that affect all or many developing countries, and thus enhances or constrains their growth possibilities. Nonetheless, country-specific factors, particularly economic specialization, significantly shape their growth dynamics. The authors observe a very large gap in the economic growth performance of developing countries diversifying into higher technology manufacturing exports and of successful raw material producers.

Sanjay Reddy and Camela Minoiu (2006) have examined the phenomenon of real-income stagnation in a large cross-section of countries during the last four decades. They define stagnation as negligible or negative growth extending over a number of years, and find that it affected 103 out of 168 countries under consideration. Stagnating countries were more likely to have been poor, in Latin America or sub-Saharan Africa, conflict-ridden and dependent on primary commodity exports. Stagnation tends to be recurrent: countries that had stagnated in the 1960s had a 75 per cent likelihood of stagnating in the 1990s.

Empirical growth research routinely assumes that growth is a linear and separable function of underlying determinants. The key policy implication of this assumption is that the effects of policies on economic growth are independent of a country's structural as well as institutional features. In chapter five, Francisco Rodríguez argues that this assumption is theoretically and empirically untenable using appropriate non-parametric tests; both hypotheses are strongly rejected by commonly used growth data sets. The data requirements needed to make meaningful inferences about growth effects typically exceed the number of observations available, casting doubt on the validity of cross-country regressions commonly used in policy analysis.

Helen Shapiro highlights how the rationale for and instruments of industrial policy has changed since the 1960s in chapter six. She argues that theories of industrialization have come full circle, as many assumptions behind the market failure paradigm have regained currency, though the earlier policy implications of these theories have not made a similar comeback. She compares the strategies of East Asia and Latin America, reviews the explanations for their divergent industrial performance and suggests a "back to the future" Latin American situation, noting the region's balance of payments constraints and dependence on commodity-like industrial products.

Francisco Rodríguez then explores the relationships among openness, poverty and inequality in Africa in chapter seven. He reviews social development on the continent since 1980, and then examines poverty and inequality in the context of the macroeconomic policy framework that has guided African policymaking over the last three decades. He highlights the major factors underpinning openness and social development, and concludes with policy recommendations.

Financial development and economic growth are clearly related. However, as pointed out by Valpy FitzGerald in chapter eight, the channels and even the direction of causality have remained unresolved in both theory and practice. Moreover, the wide range of organizational forms involved preclude any clear conclusion as to what kind of financial institutions might maximize economic growth. Nonetheless, strong causality from particular forms of financial institutions to rapid economic growth has recently become a central axiom of economic theory, strengthened by apparent support from empirical cross-country studies of the relationship between indicators of financial development and observed rates of growth. Specifically, greater financial depth would be associated with higher levels of productivity, and thus, income per capita and higher levels of development would be associated with a more advanced financial structure, involving evolution from banks to non-bank financial intermediaries, and from both of these to stock markets.

FitzGerald argues further that the dismantling of the traditional development finance model (based on bank-based systems, directed credit, public development banks, closed capital accounts, capped interest rates, and active monetary intervention) has become a core element of the economic reform and structural adjustment process led by international financial institutions. These reforms were expected to raise savings and investment levels, increase the rate of growth and reduce macroeconomic instability. FitzGerald shows that these objectives have been far from achieved. The series of financial crises that have erupted since the mid-1990s have been most heavily debated, but the decline of funding for large firms in productive sectors, and for small and medium enterprises in general, is also a major problem and potentially even more significant to sustainable growth and poverty reduction in the long run.

This is not to say that the potential contribution of financial development to economic growth would not be considerable, but that it cannot be taken for granted and depends on the construction of appropriate institutional structures. One key implication of the analysis is that the development of a long-term bond market should be a priority of financial reforms in developing countries. Bond markets not only provide long-term capital for (public) investments and growth at reasonable real costs, but also help stabilize exchange rate expectations and enable the monetary authorities to intervene effectively to dampen macroeconomic cycles caused by external shocks.

In chapter nine, Sanjay Reddy and Camela Minoiu analyze the growth impact of official development assistance to developing countries. Their approach differs from those of previous studies in two key ways. First, they disentangle the effects of developmental, growth-enhancing aid from politically-motivated aid, which may even be growth-depressing. Second, their specifications, allowing for the effect of aid on economic growth to occur over longer time-lags, robustly show that developmental aid promotes long-run growth.

In chapter ten, Francisco Rodríguez explores whether the post-1980 decline in infrastructure investment in developing countries has been a source of growing disparities in world per capita GDP. After reviewing earlier discussions of the infrastructure-productivity link, he argues that the literature points to a significant effect of infrastructure provision on productivity. However, his own study of whether reduced infrastructure provision can explain growing growth disparities using data for 121 countries since 1960 suggests that infrastructure investment appears to only be a minor cause of growing divergence in per capita incomes.

In chapter eleven, Mushtaq Khan argues that the differences of views between economists regarding governance have to do with the types of state capacities that determine the critical governance capacities necessary for the acceleration of development and with the importance of governance relative to other factors at early stages of development. On the first issue, there is an important empirical and theoretical controversy between liberal economists, who constitute the mainstream consensus on good governance, and statist and heterodox institutional economists, who agree that governance is critical for economic development, but argue that both theory and evidence show that the governance capacities required for successful development are substantially different from those identified by the 'good governance' literature. The second area of disagreement concerns the relative importance of governance reforms in accelerating development in countries with low levels of development. His review of theory and evidence addresses these two major questions, as well as debates in contemporary literature on the role of governance in explaining differences in development performance since 1960, with particular emphasis on the period after 1980.

Finally, according to Mansoob Murshed in chapter twelve, a lack of growth prevents poverty reduction, while poverty increases conflict risk because individuals have less to lose from violence. The causes of long-term growth failure are similar to the causes of civil war, the most obvious being institutional failure. Diverging average incomes between rich and poor countries also exacerbate global insecurity. Both the 'greed' and 'grievance' hypotheses have some explanatory power, as both imply the breakdown of conflict management institutions and social contracts leading up to civil war.

The idea of greed as an explanation for conflict, mainly based on cross-country econometric claims, has recently been seriously challenged. The abundance of extractable mineral resources or illicit drugs can perpetuate existing civil wars, while the prevalence of conflict seems greater among mineral, coffee and cocoa exporters, compared to other agricultural and manufactured goods exporters, who also seem to experience higher growth rates. The grievance explanation for contemporary civil wars has been explored in detailed case studies. Inter-group or horizontal inequalities seem to have considerable explanatory power, but low per-capita income, implying growth failure, is the most robust explanatory factor for conflict risk. Post-war economic reconstruction should therefore be broad-based and address the horizontal *inequalities* that helped engender conflict in the first place.

1
Explaining Growth Divergences

JOSÉ ANTONIO OCAMPO, JOMO K.S. AND ROB VOS

In 1950, a person living in Europe, Japan or the United States had an average income 16 times greater than a person residing in Ethiopia. Half a century later, this ratio has more than doubled, to 35 times, with most of the world's poorest nations falling similarly behind their wealthier counterparts. Steady growth in industrialized nations coupled with inconsistent, if not negative, growth in developing countries has driven this divergence in global equity over the last fifty years. Only a few developing countries have sustained rapid growth in recent decades, and included among these are the world's two most populous states – China and India. Since these two countries alone account for more than a third of the population, global trends show that inequality among the world's people may have declined. However, when these same countries, especially China, are excluded from consideration, trends reveal that international income inequality has, in fact, risen from already high levels (United Nations, 2006a; Jomo with Baudot [eds], 2007).

Figure 1.1 shows that income disparities between countries are large and widening. Rising inequality is a trend at odds with conventional economic wisdom on how income differentials among countries should change given greater global economic integration. During the 1980s and 1990s, there was a belief that international market integration would close the income gap between poor and rich countries. While a small number of countries achieved some significant income convergence in recent decades, many others that opened up their trade and financial systems to global markets have lost ground.

FIGURE 1.1

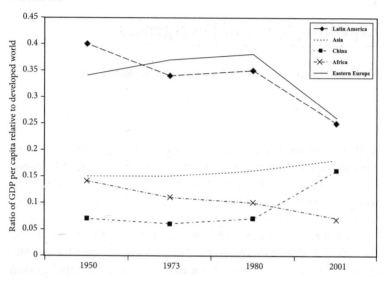

Source: UN/DESA based on Maddison (2001).

DIVERGENCE MATTERS

High income inequality, which prevails in many countries, not only signals injustice, but in developing countries particularly, unequal opportunities, and the resulting unutilized economic potential makes it much more difficult to achieve basic development goals, such as those outlined in the Millennium Development Goals (MDGs). In addition to internal inequality, divergences among countries are critical. The *World Economic and Social Survey (WESS) 2006,* in examining the causes and implications of growth, focused on average income divergences among countries with primary attention given to rising income inequality (United Nations, 2006a). Accordingly, about 70 per cent of such global income inequality can be explained by differences in incomes among countries (Milanovic, 2005). While this does not make the disparities within countries any less important, it implies that average economic welfare or living standards, to a very large extent, appear to be set by where one lives.

World markets are far from equitable and there are several conditions which do not favour a narrowing of the income divergences among countries. Richer countries have better 'endowments', which give them preferential access to capital markets and make them less vulnerable to shifts in international commodity markets. Global investors generally prefer to invest in countries with greater wealth and better developed institutions, which are presumed to ensure lower investment risk. Poorer countries have less diversified economies and exports, making them much more vulnerable to shifts in commodity prices and shocks in international financial markets. Developing countries also have little voice in the negotiation processes setting the rules governing global markets.

Widening global disparities, in turn, may be harmful to growth itself. Reduced access to stable sources of international finance and weaker bargaining positions in international trade will leave some of the economic potential of poor countries underutilized, implying a welfare loss for the world economy at large. Lower growth further slows efforts to eradicate poverty. In some cases, low growth and high inequality have also exacerbated emerging regional conflicts, civil wars and social instability. Ignoring the growing world income inequality implies ignoring all this. To redress this will require both domestic and international policy efforts.

Diverging Patterns of Economic Growth

Rising inequality among countries is mainly the result of differences in economic performance over decades. Broadly speaking, the income gap between the industrial and developing countries was already very large before World War II, and has continually widened since the 1980s. At the same time, however, growth experiences among emerging economies have varied greatly, with the sustained growth of a limited number of success stories, mostly in East Asia, partly accounting for increased income disparities among developing countries.

In other parts of the world, a much larger number of countries have seen erratic or declining growth with long-lasting impacts on living conditions. In the 1960s and 1970s, nearly 50 out of a sample of 106 developing countries experienced one or more prolonged episodes of sustained and high per capita income growth of more

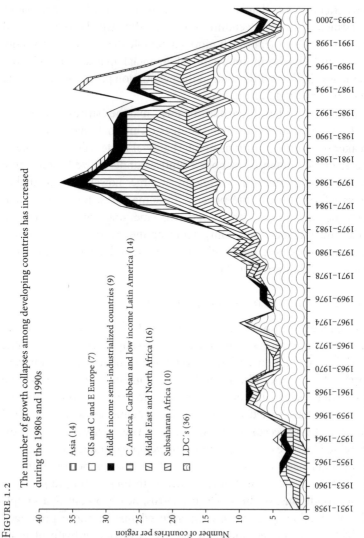

FIGURE 1.2

The number of growth collapses among developing countries has increased during the 1980s and 1990s

□ Asia (14)

□ CIS and C and E Europe (7)

□ Middle income semi-industrialized countries (9)

■ C America, Caribbean and low income Latin America (14)

▨ Middle East and North Africa (16)

▨ Subsaharan Africa (10)

▨ LDC´s (36)

Number of countries per region

1951-1958
1953-1960
1955-1962
1957-1964
1959-1966
1961-1968
1963-1970
1965-1972
1967-1974
1969-1976
1971-1978
1973-1980
1975-1982
1977-1984
1979-1986
1981-1988
1983-1990
1985-1992
1987-1994
1989-1996
1991-1998
1993-2000

Source: UN/DESA, based on Maddison (2001).

than 2 per cent per year (see Figure 1.2). Since 1980, however, only 20 developing countries have enjoyed periods of sustained growth. In contrast, no less than 40 developing countries have suffered growth collapses, or periods of five years or longer during which there was no growth or a decline in per capita income. During the 1980s and 1990s, this phenomenon increased, and the cases of successful growth diminished with some notable exceptions, mainly in Asia. Such growth failures have been most frequent among the least developed countries (LDCs) and in sub-Saharan Africa, although such episodes also affected the transition economies during the 1990s. This was unlike preceding decades, when growth collapses rarely happened, affecting less than ten countries.

Developing countries have, of course, done better recently. Indeed, recent trends since 2002 show fairly widespread growth in emerging economies, a pattern not seen since the late 1960s and early 1970s. During 2004–2006, the per capita income of developing countries should have grown, on average, at a rate of more than 4 per cent yearly, with the LDCs performing even better (United Nations, 2006b). Whether this recent performance signals a longer-term trend remains unclear. A few key factors behind this latest upturn include a combination of high commodity prices, low interest rates, and increasing official development assistance and debt relief to the poorest countries. Since these favourable conditions are not permanent, the continuation of strong growth will depend critically on the ability of developing countries to use current assistance for investments that ensure long-term economic development.

Economists have no consensus on the precise causes of growth successes and failures, with recent studies reiterating the complexities of economic growth. The searches for answers should not merely focus on economic factors, but should also take into account each country's history and institutional setting. Analysis should focus on the binding constraints on growth such as the limitations to mobilizing sufficient domestic or foreign finance, low levels of human resources and technological capabilities, insufficient basic and social services, weaknesses in governance, and poor market regulation. The importance and relevance of these obstacles tend to vary with context. Global markets affect the sources of growth and influence the space for domestic policy making to overcome such constraints. Success in development thus depends both on country level efforts to create dynamic sources of growth and on an enabling international environment.

Productivity Growth and Structural Change

Productivity growth in developed countries mainly relies on technological innovation. For developing countries, however, growth and development are much less about pushing the technology frontier and much more about promoting productive activities with higher levels of productivity. Such structural change can be largely achieved by adopting and adapting existing technologies, substituting imports, entering world markets for manufactures and services, and through the rapid accumulation of physical and human resources.

The industrial sector typically contributes more dynamically to overall output growth, because of its potential higher productivity growth, which results from increasing returns to scale and gains from innovations and learning-by-doing. Manufacturing's greater dynamism is also derived from its capacity to forge greater vertical integration among different sectors of the economy by processing raw materials and intermediate industrial inputs. Modern services are also a source of productivity gain and often essential for industrialization. The growing international trade in services offers new opportunities for export development. Besides the growth of industry and modern services, the ability to continue to generate new dynamic activities is crucial for rapid economic progress.

Over the past four decades, such dynamic transformations have clearly characterized the fast-growing East and South Asian countries. Economies experiencing relatively little structural change have lagged behind, particularly in Africa. Sluggish long-term growth in the middle-income countries of Latin America and the Caribbean as well as in Central and Eastern Europe, the Middle East and the former USSR have, in fact, been associated with deindustrialization. In these countries, growth has been limited to low-productivity services, with agriculture and industry remaining nearly stagnant. Fast growth in East and South Asia, by contrast, has been linked to strong expansions of both the industrial and service sectors, and a rapid decline in the importance of agriculture.

These economies also show sustained increases in labour productivity as labour shifts from low- to high-productivity sectors, including modern services. Nonetheless, low growth performance has also seen employment shifts to services. However, in contrast to Asia, services in sub-Saharan Africa, Latin America and the former USSR have experienced modest productivity growth, as many have sought employment in informal services due to lack of sufficient job creation in other parts of the economy. Dynamic structural change thus requires strengthening economic linkages within the national economy as well as productivity improvements in all major sectors. The degree of integration of the national economy also influences the likelihood of net gains from international trade and investment.

INTERNATIONAL TRADE, FOREIGN DIRECT INVESTMENT AND DIVERGENCE

Export 'quality', not just 'quantity'

Increased integration into the world economy seems to have exacerbated divergences in growth performance among countries. Trade can help stimulate growth, but it is not just a matter of how much countries export, but rather of what they export. Faster overall economic growth driven by trade is associated with more dynamic export structures (see Figure 1.3). This is understood as the export mix that allows countries not only to participate in world markets for products with greater growth potential (most often, high-tech products with a high income elasticity of demand), but also to help strengthen productive links with the rest of the domestic economy and generate increased value added for a wider range of services and products.

Some East Asian countries managed to diversify their exports in this manner, reflecting the pattern of structural change. In contrast, the slower-growing developing countries have relied on export activities with less value added or rooted in a less integrated domestic economy. Many of these countries remain heavily dependent on exports of primary commodities, and have often lost market shares in world trade. They have also suffered from larger adverse trade shocks. For instance, primary commodity prices have been more volatile than those of other export products, and the terms of trade for non-oil commodity exports declined by almost 40 per cent between 1980 and 2003. The recent recovery in commodity prices has only partially offset this decline; by the end of 2005, average non-fuel commodity prices were still below 1980 levels in real terms.

FIGURE 1.3

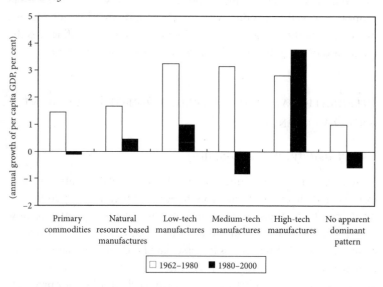

Source: UN/DESA, based on World Development Indicators 2005, and Feenstra and others (2005).

Diversifying into high-technology exports may not be immediately feasible for many developing countries. Low-income countries typically lack adequate basic manufacturing capacity, infrastructure and human resources, as well as international trading capacity to develop dynamic export activities. However, these countries do have some capacity to compete in world markets for primary goods. To begin with, they should pursue industrial strategies to diversify exports by processing natural resources and agricultural products as well as producing other light manufactures.

Foreign Direct Investment Should Foster Domestic Linkages

The impact of foreign direct investment (FDI) on economic growth depends on the role it can play in strengthening domestic linkages in the economy. Since the 1980s, FDI grew at a faster pace than both world output and trade, though by the 1990s, four-fifths consisted of 'brownfield' rather than 'greenfield' FDI mergers and acquisitions. Developing countries witnessed a tenfold increase in average annual FDI inflows, though over two-thirds of it remained concentrated in developed countries. FDI to developing countries has also been heavily concentrated, with well over 80 per cent of the flows to emerging economies moving to only a dozen (mostly middle-income) countries, including China and India. This trend has been fostered by the development of international production networks in manufacturing industries and modern services, as well as the reduced restrictions on capital flows and privatization in developing countries.

FDI brings finance and, often, technology, new management and market access, and can thus contribute significantly to long-term growth in developing countries. Clearly, however, flows go mostly to countries with higher incomes, larger markets and infrastructure. In this sense, FDI appears to have contributed to growth divergences. Also, countries with substantial FDI increases have not always experienced strengthened economic growth. Even though all major Latin American countries and some larger African economies saw higher FDI shares in the 1980s and 1990s, overall investment rates stagnated or declined.

In order to gain from FDI, domestic firms and institutions need to have the necessary absorptive capacities. Countries that made significant investments in building domestic infrastructure and human resources to more effectively target investors (e.g., Singapore, Ireland) have been the most successful in leveraging inward FDI. Conversely, there seems to be limited scope for long-term benefits from FDI when it is attracted with tax incentives or temporary market access advantages (such as the Multifibre Arrangement [MFA] and the subsequent Agreement on Textiles and Clothing [ATC]) without a complementary build-up of local capabilities and linkages between foreign affiliates and local firms.

Trade Liberalization not Necessarily Good for Growth

Trade liberalization has been the main policy trend associated with globalization in recent decades. In most parts of the world, this has led to an expansion of export volumes, but not necessarily to higher economic growth. Countries able to diversify and to develop higher productivity activities have seen more visible growth gains. Fostering greater economic and export diversification is a major challenge, requiring both active domestic policies and a more enabling trading environment for developing countries.

Most developing countries that have witnessed sustained high growth since the 1960s have used active industrial policies to support the economic diversification and technological upgrading of their economies. Successful export-led growth strategies have involved varying combinations of supportive macroeconomic policies, (selective) infant industry protection, export subsidies, directed credit schemes, local content rules (no longer allowed under the WTO) and large investments in human resources, as well as strategic alliances with multinational companies. Developing country governments thus need to adopt active production sector development strategies.

Support measures have often been tied to specific performance criteria. The space for conducting this type of active production sector development policy has been narrowed by greater international economic integration, new international economic agreements, reduced macroeconomic policy space and policy conditionalities imposed as new 'conventional wisdoms'. Developing countries, particularly the least developed countries, still have some 'special and differential treatment' as defined under GATT during the Uruguay Round. In practice however, aside from the poorest LDCs, developing countries have been subject to rules similar to as the now developed countries, which enjoyed such policy space for much longer periods.

Developing countries need a much better international trading environment. Better trading opportunities should involve improved market access for exports of both primary commodities and light manufactures by developing countries, and reduced domestic support for and protection of agricultural production in developed country markets. This also implies better opportunities to participate in world markets for services, including those requiring mobility of low-skilled labour.

Developing countries also need to be able to pursue policies to build the supply capacities needed to succeed in global markets and achieve dynamic structural transformation of their economies. Middle-income countries in particular need rules that facilitate export diversification, especially into manufacturing and services that encourage domestic market integration. This will probably require special measures in support of infant industries with export potential as well as a much more developmentally oriented international intellectual property regime.

PRIVATE CAPITAL FLOWS AND PRO-CYCLICAL MACROECONOMIC POLICIES

Volatile Capital Flows Harm Growth

There is no evidence that private financial flows have consistently led to increased investment and growth in developing countries over the past forty years. Since the 1970s, developing countries, mostly middle-income countries, have gained greater access to short- and long-term private financing, but these flows have largely marginalized the poorest countries. Meanwhile, commercial bank lending and portfolio investments have proven to be highly pro-cyclical for developing countries. Both the availability and cost of external financing ease during periods of economic expansion, and tighten to become more expensive during economic downswings.

Thus, private external financing has exacerbated economic volatility. During the 1980s and 1990s, surges or sudden reversals and the flight of private capital flows primarily caused the major currency and financial crises. Economic volatility creates greater uncertainty, with adverse effects for long-term investment and growth. The costs of the currency and banking crises have been massive and, according to some estimates, have lowered the incomes of affected developing countries by 25 per cent or more. The challenge for developing countries is therefore to reduce reliance on volatile short-term flows and to ensure long-term financing for desired productive investments.

Macroeconomic Stability and Policy Flexibility both Important for Growth

Macroeconomic stability strongly influences long-term growth performance and should be seen more broadly than as a tool for preserving price stability and sustainable fiscal balances. Macroeconomic stability is also about avoiding large swings in economic activity and employment, in addition to maintaining sustainable external accounts and avoiding exchange-rate overvaluation. The frequency of financial crises in developing countries indicates that macroeconomic stability also involves maintaining well-regulated domestic financial sectors, sound balance sheets in the banking system and sound external debt structures.

Most developing countries enjoyed robust growth and a relatively stable macroeconomic environment in the 1960s. In the decades thereafter, the fast-growing East Asian economies managed to achieve much greater macroeconomic stability than the much slower-growing developing countries elsewhere. Macroeconomic stability and growth mutually reinforce each other. Stronger growth makes it easier to achieve greater macroeconomic stability, among other things by enhancing the sustainability of domestic and foreign public debt. Conversely, greater stability, in its broad sense, reduces investment uncertainty and hence is supportive of higher long-term growth.

Stabilization policies, as implemented in many developing countries since the 1980s, have mostly emphasized lowering inflation and restoring fiscal balance. While moderating inflation and fiscal prudence are sensible macroeconomic policy objectives, countries have often pursued these goals at the expense of other dimensions of macroeconomic stability. Price stability has often been achieved at the cost of exchange-rate overvaluation and unsustainable external debt burdens. Meanwhile, macroeconomic policies in much of the developing world have been highly pro-cyclical over the past two decades. This has been particularly costly during economic slowdowns, when such policy stances have led to lower employment and waning economic growth.

FIGURE 1.4

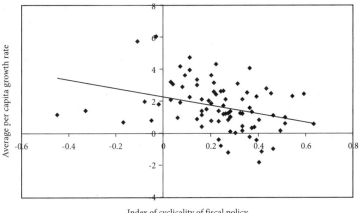

Pro-cyclical fiscal policy negatively influences long-term growth

Index of cyclicality of fiscal policy

Source: UN/DESA, based on data by Kaminsky, Reinhart and Vegh (2004); and World Bank, World Development indicators 2005 database.

Note: The index is constructed as a weighted average of indicators of fiscal policy cyclicality, which include public expenditure, a proxy for changes in tax rates and changes in expenditure over the business cycle in developing countries. Positive figures denote higher pro-cyclicality; and negative numbers, the level of counter-cyclicality. Further details may be found in Kamisnky, Reinhart and Végh (2004).

Macroeconomic volatility tends to be much higher at lower levels of development, not only because of greater vulnerability to external shocks, but also owing to more constrained macroeconomic policy space. Generally, the fiscal policy stance in most developing countries has been highly pro-cyclical and often exacerbated by pro-cyclical capital flows. For a large sample of developing countries, there exists a strong negative correlation between pro-cyclical fiscal behaviour and long-term growth (see Figure 1.4). In East Asia, for instance, fiscal policies have been more neutral or even counter-cyclical, suggesting that counter-cyclical macroeconomic adjustment policies may be beneficial for growth, especially for developing countries.

Counter-cyclical Macroeconomic Policies

For many developing country governments, the space for counter-cyclical macroeconomic policies is limited, as available fiscal and foreign exchange resources tend to be small relative to the magnitude of the external shocks they face. International action mitigating the impact of private capital flow volatility can help broaden this policy space. Governments can take measures to enhance the scope for counter-cyclical policies by improving the institutional framework for macroeconomic policy making.

First, the institutional setting for fiscal policy should strike a balance between fiscal prudence and fiscal flexibility to ensure both policy credibility and fiscal sustainability. Setting fiscal targets that are independent of short-term fluctuations in economic growth (so-called structural budget rules) can be effective in forcing a counter-cyclical policy stance. Some developing countries, such as Chile, have been able to manage such fiscal rules successfully. Furthermore, fiscal stabilization funds could help smooth, over time, revenues from unstable tax sources, such as those based on primary export production.

The experiences of such funds in various parts of the world have varied. They do not provide an easy panacea, and careful management of such funds is required. Nonetheless, fiscal stabilization funds can form an effective instrument to resolve inter-temporal trade-offs in fiscal spending by also protecting growth-enhancing long-term public investment in infrastructure and human development during times of lower tax revenue caused by external shocks and economic downturns.

Second, a certain degree of discretionary power should be retained. Since the 1980s, governments of many developing countries have moved from discretionary macroeconomic policy arrangements to rule-based ones. This shift was founded on the belief that the latter would avoid policy-generated macroeconomic instability. More than 20 economies have adopted inflation targeting as their framework for monetary policy. Under this monetary regime, an independent central bank commits itself to price stability by publicly announcing the level of inflation it will permit. This kind of policy arrangement has the potential of enhancing central bank policy transparency and credibility.

At the same time, however, the narrow focus of monetary policy on a strict inflation target biases macroeconomic stabilization against growth and employment objectives. Rule-based policies may function well for some time, especially when the economy does not suffer major shocks. As the structure of the economy changes over time, so will its vulnerability to external shocks. For instance, financial shocks may become more important than terms-of-trade shocks. In such a changing context, predetermined policy rules are more likely to become less relevant or turn out to be too rigid. Moreover, as the risks and uncertainties facing an economy never present themselves in exactly the same way or to the same degree, a certain amount of space for discretionary policies will always be needed to make adjustments that will minimize macroeconomic losses.

Third, macroeconomic policies should be well integrated with other areas of economic policy making. In the fast-growing East Asian economies, for example, macroeconomic policies were part of a broader development strategy, contributing directly to long-run growth. Fiscal policies in these economies have given priority to development spending, including investments in education, health and infrastructure as well as subsidies and credit guarantees for export industries. Monetary policy has been coordinated with financial sector and industrial policies, including directed and subsidized credit schemes and managed interest rates to directly influence investment and saving, whereas exchange-rate policies have generally had a pro-export bias. In contrast, macroeconomic policies in many Latin American and African countries since the 1980s have focused on much more narrowly defined short-term stabilization objectives.

Policies to Dampen International Financial Volatility

The challenge for multilateral financial institutions is to help developing countries mitigate the damaging effects of volatile capital flows and to provide counter-cyclical financing mechanisms to compensate for the inherently pro-cyclical nature of private capital flows (see also Ocampo, Kregel and Griffith-Jones [eds], 2007). A number of options can help dampen the pro-cyclicality of capital flows.

A first set of measures would include the adoption of financial instruments that reduce currency mismatches and link debt-service obligations to the capacity to pay (for instance, through GDP- or commodity-linked bonds). These can then be accompanied by public loan guarantees with counter-cyclical features issued by multilateral development banks and export credit agencies. A third area would involve support for developing country governments to strengthen regulatory frameworks that provide disincentives to short-term capital inflow volatility as well as sound domestic financial private and public sector structures.

In addition, multilateral surveillance – primarily by the International Monetary Fund (IMF) – should remain at the centre of crisis prevention efforts. Enhanced provision of emergency financing at the international level in response to external shocks would reduce unnecessary costs of adjustment and of maintaining large reserve balances. For both middle- and low-income countries, appropriate facilities would include enhanced liquidity provisions to smoothen fluctuations in export earnings, particularly those caused by unstable commodity prices and natural disasters. Better and easier access to official (international) liquidity during capital account crises should be facilitated commensurate with the potentially large needs of countries that may surpass normal lending limits based on the IMF quotas of members.

Public Investments Necessary for Growth

Part of the observed growth divergences is attributable to gaps in public investment and spending on infrastructure and human development.

Need for Improved Infrastructure

Adequate infrastructure is necessary for firms to be productive, and countries often need to build up a threshold or minimum level of infrastructure (e.g., a port and road network) to attract private investments and achieve productivity growth. Countries often also require sustained and substantial public investment to maintain investment and growth. Failure to do so is part of the reason why Latin America and sub-Saharan Africa have fallen behind the East Asian countries, which have protracted infrastructural investment. Latin America has experienced a decline in infrastructural investment since the 1980s due to increased fiscal austerity and greater reliance on private investments.

Differences in investment lead to significant variability in the quality and availability of infrastructure. Since the 1960s, road density in Latin America and sub-Saharan Africa barely increased, whereas it tripled in East Asia. Also, the availability of telephone lines in East Asia is now double that of Latin America and ten times that of sub-Saharan Africa. The evidence suggests that lagging infrastructural development could account for as much as a third of the widening income differentials between East Asian and Latin American economies.

The evidence also suggests important complementarities between public and private investments. Where governments have cut public investment in infrastructure or have privatized infrastructural services, private investors have generally failed to fill the gap. This outcome in many countries in Latin America and Africa is clearly at odds with the initial expectations from such privatization programmes.

Human Development

Some empirical studies suggest that developing countries could catch up with the developed world if only they increased their levels of human development. The links between growth and human development are complex, however. The high income inequality among countries is paralleled by large disparities in other human development indicators, such as life expectancy and educational attainment. Unlike per capita incomes though, the world has seen more convergence among countries in terms of improvements in health and education outcomes. Countries with successful economic growth performances all had relatively high levels of human development when growth took off and substantially improved their education and health indicators as average incomes rose (United Nations, 2006a). But not all countries with relatively higher levels of human development have managed to sustain high long-term economic growth rates (see Ocampo, Jomo and Khan [eds], 2007).

Human development is, of course, an objective in its own right. However, it seems to be a necessary, but not sufficient, condition for sustained economic growth. Lifting other constraints on economic growth and structural change will be necessary to create opportunities for a better-educated population. The dynamic promotion of full, decent and productive employment is crucial in this regard.

Long-term Investment in Infrastructure and Human Development

Improvements in human development and infrastructure require adequate and sustained levels of public spending. Infrastructure growth requires large-scale investments, which take time to generate returns. Improvements in education and health are also part of longer-term efforts requiring sustained financing of social services. Good infrastructure, education and health can provide important social gains, thus justifying the crucial role of government in ensuring sufficient investment. In many countries, a lot can be gained by improving the cost-effectiveness of public education, health programmes, and infrastructure investment.

Countries with significant gaps will have to substantially increase fiscal commitments for expenditures in these areas. As discussed earlier, counter-cyclical fiscal policies can help sustain adequate government social spending and public investment, thereby limiting cuts in critical areas during economic downswings. Additionally, improved financing schemes and less corruption in the contracting of infrastructure works could help reduce costs and boost cost-effectiveness. Strengthening the tax base will often be essential, particularly in countries with low government revenues. For the poorest countries, substantial additional resources from abroad will be required to make the necessary investments. More development aid will be needed and should be allocated through budget support for investments in infrastructure and human development.

INCREASING AID AND AID EFFECTIVENESS

When the United Nations embarked on its first development decade in the 1960s, it was generally understood that an intensified effort to mobilize internal and external resources would be necessary if growth targets were to be met. Most of these resources would have to be allocated to infrastructure and human resources to overcome development bottlenecks. Increased aid flows were seen as critical to surmounting growth constraints and providing developing countries with a much needed 'big push'.

The target of 0.7 per cent of the gross national income (GNI) of developed countries for official development assistance (ODA) emerged in this context. In the decades that followed, this target for aid transfers has not been met, and aid flows from the member states of the Development Assistance Committee of the OECD fell to less than a third of that target, with much of this serving political, rather than economic, priorities. At the International Conference on Financing for Development in Monterrey in 2002, the international community reiterated the target of 0.7 per cent of GNI for ODA by donor countries, and identified the Millennium Development Goals (MDGs) as tangible criteria against which to assess ODA effectiveness. Aid moved back to centre stage in the development debate and renewed proposals for big pushes — as in the early 1960s — emerged. Aid has since picked up again, though actual flows to the poorest countries have not risen due to one-time debt- and disaster-relief commitments, including the Iraq debt write-off.

The effectiveness of international development assistance has become heavily disputed. According to some views, aid has not contributed to economic growth, and has done little to reduce poverty. In contrast, *WESS 2006* as well as Reddy and Miniou's chapter contend that aid has been positive for long-term development once politically-motivated aid is factored out. In this sense, ODA has helped counter the factors contributing to the income divergences of the past four decades.

However, since the magnitude of aid transfers has remained limited, the contribution of ODA to reducing international income disparities has been weak. In this sense, the deterioration of aid commitments has exacerbated divergence, particularly since it was more difficult for the poorest countries to adjust to the economic shocks of the 1980s and 1990s. Of course, ODA has not always been supportive of economic growth; in particular, politically-motivated assistance has had weak returns in terms of human or economic development in the recipient countries.

These findings provide some support for the renewed idea of a big push for developing countries fuelled by aid. In this regard, the MDGs could be viewed as a set of targets requiring substantial investment to improve infrastructure and social services. Well-designed programmes supported by aid could put the poorest nations on a path of faster growth. Such an approach assumes not only that enough is known about how best to channel such resources efficiently in specific country contexts, but also that recipient governments have the capacity to manage the resource flows in a way that generates cumulative income and boosts welfare and productivity gains.

INSTITUTIONS AND GOOD GOVERNANCE

It is now widely acknowledged that institutions and governance matter for economic growth and explain widening global income disparities. As their importance has been extensively examined in recent years, it has become increasingly difficult to identify what institutional 'quality' and forms of 'good governance' should be pursued to support sustained growth processes. Such qualities appear to be inherently context specific. Policy makers need to know whether significant economic opportunities can be generated by focused changes in existing institutions and governance.

Economic and institutional history suggests that improving institutional frameworks in specific areas can reduce constraints to growth. For instance, China's reform of rural and agricultural institutions during the late 1970s helped pave conditions for its subsequent economic success. In 1978, China introduced the household responsibility system, under which households obtained rights under long-term leases to collectively-owned land. In exchange, farmers were obliged to supply a pre-determined share of output to meet the collectives' production quotas, but the remaining output could be sold on the free market or to the government at negotiated prices. Viet Nam also introduced land reform with a limited transfer of cultivation rights to tenants to motivate increases in agricultural productivity. In contrast, the Republic of Korea and Taiwan Province of China enacted full transfers of land ownership to farmers shortly after World War II, to improve agricultural incentives. In all cases, the significant ensuing agricultural output growth contributed to the industrial take-off several years later, while introducing compensatory measures to minimize the social and economic costs associated with redistributive reforms.

Such successes go beyond reforms of rural and agricultural institutions. Several countries, such as the Southeast Asian countries and Mauritius, have successfully attracted foreign investment into export processing zones (EPZs) and licensed manufacturing warehouses (LMWs) in order to diversify production and exports, and foreign financial institutions with new discriminatory regulatory frameworks for the financial sector.

These experiences suggest two important conclusions. First, several types of governance restructuring can be effective in lifting binding constraints to economic growth. Success was largely determined by institutional reforms appropriately tailored to prevailing socio-economic conditions. Second, the relatively limited reforms in China and Viet Nam suggest that acceleration of economic growth does not require immediate, large-scale and comprehensive institutional reforms or 'shock treatment'. Fairly minor institutional changes can have profound results if such changes are appropriate and signal further desired reforms. Third, institutional reforms should involve much more than creating markets and strengthening property rights. They should also entail adequately regulating markets, providing public goods, ensuring the fairness of rules and equitable outcomes, building consensus and avoiding social conflict.

Growth failures in many poorer countries have been exacerbated by violent conflicts. Institutional weaknesses and civil strife cannot be analyzed in isolation from the economic conditions in these countries. Both growth failures and armed conflicts seem greater among countries that are mineral, coffee and cocoa exporters, compared to other agricultural and manufactured goods exporters. Growth collapses and conflicts are not directly caused by dependence on natural resource revenues, but require other mechanisms, such as a weakened social contract and diminished state capacity.

The availability of easily lootable mineral resources or illicit drugs can help start and perpetuate civil wars and armed conflicts. Wealth that can be generated quickly by resource exploitation can exacerbate social inequalities, political conflicts, and even violence, including between the central government and the local authorities where the resources are located. WESS 2006 and Murshed's chapter in this volume suggests this 'natural resource curse' can be mitigated and avoided by strong pre-emptive institutional initiatives, which can curtail conflicts.

Implications for Governance Reform Policies

While governance reform is intrinsically difficult, WESS 2006 analysis suggests little cause for pessimism that certain countries will be mired in low growth and shackled by institutions that will impede their growth. Sustained growth can begin with imperfect institutions, but it is important for the government to be credibly committed to removing institutional and other obstacles to growth. Governance reform should therefore be about creating legitimate, well-functioning public institutions. International cooperation can help, but only by supporting domestic processes that are appropriately context sensitive, gradual and non-disruptive.

For the international community, this finding has particular relevance for countries emerging from conflict or 'failed states'. In many cases, the most important consideration is fostering the resumption of economic activity, which usually means agricultural recovery, an often essential step towards subsequent economic development. Further investment in this sector raises farmers' incomes and thus, aggregate demand in the economy. If shared, agricultural recovery can help create a stable and just society. With overall economic recovery, more opportunities to reform institutions and improve governance arise, generating a virtuous circle.

Improvements in governance – particularly in such areas as ensuring transparent budgetary processes, building a better civil service and improving social service delivery – can thus be crucial for enhancing development performance. What really works at the country or local level however does vary. Thus, externally defined governance pre-conditions and conditionalities to aid flows, a recent and growing requirement of donor agencies, may not produce the desired outcomes in terms of better quality public services.

GLOBAL INEQUALITY, SECURITY AND THE INTERNATIONAL DEVELOPMENT AGENDA

A country's growth performance is not only determined by factors within state geographical boundaries, especially in today's integrated global economy. Countries with isolated domestic economies, weak institutions and low infrastructural and human development, have less opportunity to gain from international trade and investment. They will also find it difficult to 'take off' and reduce their vulnerability to external shocks, in turn, increasing the likelihood of growth collapses and social conflicts as 'vertical' and 'horizontal' inequalities rise. Rising international inequalities therefore have important impacts on the implementation of the United Nations development agenda. Inequities make achievement of the MDGs and the other internationally agreed development goals more difficult, especially by undermining global security. Failure to redress the trend of growing world inequality could therefore have wide-ranging impacts on global economic and human development.

REFERENCES

Feenstra, Robert C., and others (2005). World trade flows: 1962–2000. NBER Working Paper, No. 11040. Cambridge, Massachussetts: National Bureau of Economic Research, January.

Jomo, K. S., with Jacques Baudot [eds] (2007). *Flat World, Big Gaps: Economic Liberalization, Globalization, Poverty and Inequality.* United Nations Publications, New York, with Zed Books, London, Orient Longman, Hyderabad, Third World Network, Penang.

Kaminsky, Graciela, Carmen M. Reinhard and Carlos A. Vegh (2004). When it rains, it pours: procyclical capital flows and macroeconomic policies. NBER Working Paper, No. 10780. Cambridge, Massachusetts: National Bureau of Economic Research. September.

Maddison, Angus (2001). *The World Economy: A Millennial Perspective.* Development Centre Studies. Paris: Organization for Economic Cooperation and Development Centre.

Milanovic, Branko (2005). *Worlds Apart: Global and International Inequality, 1950–2000.* Princeton University Press, Princeton, NJ.

Ocampo, José Antonio, Jomo K. S. and Sarbuland Khan [eds] (2007). *Policy Matters: Economic and Social Policies To Sustain Equitable Development.* United Nations Publications, New York, with Zed Books, London, Orient Longman, Hyderabad, Third World Network, Penang.

Ocampo, José Antonio, Jan Kregel and Stephany Griffith-Jones [eds] (2007). *International Finance and Development.* United Nations Publications, New York, with Zed Books, London, Orient Longman, Hyderabad, Third World Network, Penang.

United Nations (2006a). *World Economic and Social Survey 2006: Diverging Growth and Development.* United Nations, New York.

United Nations (2006b). *World Economic Situation and Prospects 2006.* United Nations, New York.

2
Mind the Gaps: Economic Openness and Uneven Development

RICHARD KOZUL-WRIGHT

A system of unrestricted international flows of goods, services and factors of production, has always been one of the principal aims of economic liberalism and, since the late 1970s, has been regarded by many as the essence of globalization. Following the lead set by advanced countries, the deregulation of markets and their opening up to international firms and market forces has come to dominate policy discussions in many developing countries, helping to create a world with fewer countervailing pressures from governments than at any time since the late 1920s. This was not only expected to raise incomes significantly across the world economy, but to favour growth prospects in poorer countries and, as a result, to close income gaps separating them from the richer countries.

The win-win logic behind this promise of convergence draws its intellectual authority from the text book theory of international trade whereby specializing according to comparative advantage allows countries to reap efficiency gains from moving to a production and trading profile that uses their relatively abundant resources to the full and importing goods that embody otherwise relatively scarce resources. Even countries which lag behind in all sectors benefit by following this path. This has been described as "the deepest and most beautiful result in all of economics" (Findlay, 1991: 99).

While this model is much admired for its counter-intuitive elegance, it rests on a set of severely restrictive assumptions whose distance from reality has troubled generations of leading economists beginning with Adam Smith, no less, who not only insisted that a universal system of free international trade was more utopian ideal than policy blueprint, but also that the costs of adjusting to openness required that it be done "only by slow gradations, and with a good deal of reserve and circumspection". Both Smith and David Ricardo were fully aware of how, in the absence of these assumptions, freer trade might very well lead to widening income gaps, i.e. to economic divergence. With a good deal of supporting historical evidence, divergence models have become a staple of the development literature (Darity and Davis, 2005).

Conventional economists have responded by pointing to distortions that could have impeded the levelling influence of market forces and by identifying new sources of convergence that could complement and augment those associated with trade. Increased capital mobility, a defining feature of the current phase of globalization, is one such contender to help close income gaps in a more open world economy, given that the "principles of international factor movements do not in their essentials differ from those underlying trade in goods" (Krugman and Obstfeld, 1997: 159). However, economists have been reluctant to embrace unreservedly the idea of efficient international financial markets as a source of convergence (Bhagwati, 1998) preferring instead, to identify "grey area sources of dynamic efficiency", including the most productive use of entrepreneurial resources (Bhagwati and Srinivasan, 1999) and to the "collateral benefits" (Rogoff and others, 2006) from hosting foreign firms. In this vein, Robert Lucas (2000) has concluded that the diffusion of technology and ideas generated by leading industrial economies is already narrowing income gaps across the globe and will make everyone "equally rich and growing" by 2100.

Such convergence predictions lack the analytical conviction which comes from sticking to core theory, accepting instead a more open-ended empirical discussion on global growth and distribution. Accordingly, this chapter will consider whether or not the shift to more liberal policy regimes has given rise to sustained growth-acceleration and poverty reduction in poorer countries as well as income convergence with the developed countries. It begins with a discussion of the convergence concept and raises some initial doubts about its suitability for understanding global growth and distribution dynamics. This is followed by a comparative description of those dynamics over the past two decades, which suggests that a strong and uniform convergence trend has not emerged. Rather, uneven and episodic growth performances, combining collapses, stagnation and intermittent but unsustained growth spurts, have been the norm. Next, it suggests some reasons why international economic forces associated with increased trade and FDI flows have contributed to this uneven playing field. The final section asks how a fairer system of global governance might tackle the challenge of rising international inequality better.

CONVERGENCE: A DEAD END?

Conventional economic wisdom describes the ideal environment for maximizing economic welfare, at the local as well as the global levels, as an open, flat and predictable landscape where market prices are left alone to guide the allocation of economic resources. A comprehensive package of liberalization and deregulation measures is expected to bring about this environment by releasing two big levelling forces; one is international trade, working through the exploitation of comparative advantage, the other, pro-poor growth, working through decreasing returns to scale and technological spill-overs. The discrepancy between this theory and the empirical record of uneven economic development has usually been explained by the presence of countervailing and distortionary political influences, usually associated with the rise of nation states. Globalization, by rolling back the state and unleashing cross-border private capital flows, is seen, at long last, as holding out the prospect of a truly level economic playing field (Wolf, 2004).[1]

On some assessments, liberalization measures have helped launch industrial take-offs across the developing world and triggered factor price convergence.[2] But there is a growing recognition that rapid trade liberalization by itself is unlikely to bring about income convergence (Winters, 2004), and that financial liberalization may unleash capital flows that work in the opposite direction (Bhagwati, 1998).[3] Instead, attracting FDI has been made the catalyst of a new growth regime because it is expected both to open up new export opportunities and to bring "collateral benefits", in particular technological spill-overs (Rogoff and others, 2006), that raise productivity performance. As this export-FDI nexus becomes more firmly established in developing countries, global income convergence is expected to follow (World Bank, 2002).

Reviving the convergence framework in light of new trends in the global economy has required some methodological amendments to the earlier generation of growth models which had identified a steady state on which all countries would converge in the long run, albeit more quickly in poorer countries thanks to a faster pace of capital accumulation.[4] In particular, the idea of "conditional" convergence has been distinguished from this earlier "absolute" variant by introducing a broader notion of capital, along with different technological and behavioural parameters, which together allow for a variety of possible steady states. Backward areas still have the potential to grow faster than advanced areas, but this potential will only be realized if they satisfy certain conditions, which are more open to policy influence than was the case with traditional models. Where these conditions are not satisfied, the growth rate in backward areas may be as slow, or even slower than in advanced areas.

This approach has opened new pastures for growth accounting. In particular, a plethora of cross-country regression exercises has suggested that among all the possible conditioning variables, the most fundamental is how open an economy is to international market forces. A seminal paper in this tradition was by Sachs and Warner (1995), who introduced a five point system to classify countries into "open" and "closed". After controlling for other variables and initial income levels, they find that open economies grew faster than closed economies. They also reported strong evidence of beta-convergence (catching-up) amongst open economies, but no sign of it amongst closed economies. On the basis of these and related findings, the IMF (1997: 84–85) concluded that open trade and capital account policies were among the most important factors promoting economic convergence.[5]

But despite the impressive show of empirical force, these efforts to revive the convergence argument have encountered a good deal of criticism. Critics have pointed to various methodological difficulties in trying to capture a process as complex as economic convergence in a simple econometric equation.[6] In particular, and even assuming that a positive statistical association between trade or FDI and economic growth was established, this still leaves open the direction of causation,[7] and even if the finding that poorer countries tend to grow faster than rich countries was perfectly correct, indicating some kind of causal relationship whereby poor countries have a genuine growth advantage over rich countries, this still does not automatically imply that international dispersion of per capita incomes or productivity levels will fall in the course of time.

A second line of criticism has suggested that conditional convergence is a distraction, on the grounds that ascertaining how far each country is from its own steady state ignores the more fundamental question why some countries are rich and some are poor.[8] This has much less to do with missed (static) efficiency gains from misguided policy interventions, and much more with the effectiveness of institutional and policy responses to market failures, particularly those linked to technological development. Because, first-mover advantages linked to technological leadership are likely to be a major source of divergence, the catch-up challenge throws up many more policy challenges than recognised in convergence models. Indeed, these models like their predecessors are seriously compromised by assuming technology is a public good or that it automatically spills over from FDI.[9]

A final criticism of the convergence thesis concerns the idea that competitive markets are the default position of socio-economic organization. This strips the catch-up process of any historical or social frame of reference in deference to the requirements of an axiomatic model-building exercise. This is reflected in a general unwillingness to contemplate the influence of asymmetric power relations in shaping economic outcomes, including in international trade (Gomory and Baumol, 2000). But it is also visible in the tying of distribution dynamics to a steady state and balanced growth path, which bears little resemblance to unsteady, unbalanced and structurally fragmented economies undergoing discontinuous changes associated with industrialization, urbanization and a demographic transition. Insofar as price signals emerge from an institutional framework that incorporates a prior set of social values and preferences, it follows that there will be no single, ideal market structure that will generate optimal outcomes for all the population groups participating in the international economy. From this perspective, market forces are not pre-programmed to generate stable equilibria, let alone social harmony. Rather, as Toner (1999: 21) notes, "successive rounds of increasing returns, real price reductions, demand and output expansion, investment, and increasing returns, act not to equilibrate supply and demand but to perpetuate disequilibria". Thus, growth, as Albert Hirschman recognized, should be viewed as "a chain of disequilibria . . . that nightmare of equilibrium economics, the endlessly spinning cobweb, is the kind of mechanism we must assiduously look for as an invaluable aid in the development process."

In a world economy permeated by processes of circular and cumulative causation, it would be surprising to expect a reduction of income inequalities, within and between countries, to come about as a result of market liberalization *unless* it also led to a marked acceleration in the rate of capital investment, in both physical and human assets, in the poorer countries, and to accompanying changes in economic structure. What seems more likely is that countries at different levels of development can experience different growth dynamics, and that convergence pressures from external integration only become apparent once various economic thresholds, in terms of industrial development, infrastructure development, skill accumulation, etc., are crossed. From this perspective, diversity in growth experiences is the norm, and only surprises those who believe that "all economies are the same, and that the complex interaction of external conditions, non-economic factors and peoples' beliefs have no real causal importance in explaining growth experiences" (Kenny and Williams, 2001: 15).

The Stubborn Persistence of International Income Inequality

The gap in real incomes per head between developing countries and the advanced countries has grown significantly over the past 40 years

(Figure 2.1), the simple product of the higher starting income of the latter and their faster average annual per capita growth rates (Table 2.1).

FIGURE 2.1
Divergence big time: Real GDP per capita, 1960–2005 (constant 2000 $)

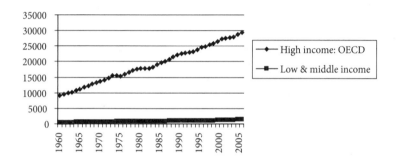

Source: World Bank, World Development Indicators on line.

Aggregate figures can, of course, be misleading and there are some important differences within the developing world, with Asia maintaining a much stronger growth performance than other regions and with catch-up growth a feature of the East Asian experience. Indeed, given that, among developing countries, Latin America began this period with the highest per capita income, subsequent growth trends have generated convergence across the developing world, even as they have diverged from advanced countries (Figure 2.2). There have also been differences in growth performance over time. Developing countries outpaced advanced countries for a number of years in the 1970s and again since the mid 1990s. However, even making a simple extrapolation from recent performance, it would still take around 175 years for developing country incomes to converge on those in advanced countries.

Table 2.1

Income levels and growth rates, 1950–2001, selected regions and countries

	GDP per capita (1990 international dollars)				Annual average per capita compound growth rates		
	1950	1973	1980	2001	1950-73	1973-80	1980-2001
Developed	6,298	13,376	15,257	22,825	3.3	1.9	1.9
Eastern Europe	2,111	4,988	5,786	6,027	3.8	2.1	0.2
Former USSR	2,841	6,059	6,426	4,626	3.3	0.8	-1.6
Latin America	2,506	4,504	5,412	5,811	2.6	2.7	0.3
Argentina	4,987	7,973	8,245	8,137	2.1	0.5	-0.1
Brazil	1,672	3,882	5,199	5,570	3.7	4.3	0.3
Mexico	2,365	4,845	6,289	7,089	3.2	3.8	0.6
Peru	2,263	3,952	4,205	3,630	2.5	0.9	-0.7
Asia	918	2,049	2,486	3,998	3.6	2.8	2.3
China	439	839	1,067	3,583	2.9	3.5	5.9
India	619	853	938	1,957	1.4	1.4	3.6
Japan	1,921	11,434	13,428	20,683	8.1	2.3	2.1
Pakistan	643	954	1,161	1,947	1.7	2.8	2.5
Africa	894	1,410	1,536	1,489	2.0	1.2	-0.1
South Africa	2,535	4,175	4,232	4,208	2.2	0.2	0.0
Egypt	718	1,022	1,641	2,992	1.5	7.0	2.9
Ghana	1,122	1,407	1,172	1,311	1.0	-2.6	0.5
Kenya	651	961	1,029	1,016	1.7	1.0	-0.1

Source: United Nations (2006), Table 1.1.

What is more telling is that relative to their own past, the growth performance of developing countries' has deteriorated in recent years. Of a total of 124 developing countries, growth in 95 of them (i.e., over three-quarters) was faster in the period 1960–1978 than between 1978 and 1998 (Milanovic, 2002) and only a handful of countries have been able to hit the kind of growth target needed to address their economic and social deficits.[10] Since 1980, countries at the very bottom of the income scale have been particularly hard hit leading to a 'twin peaks' global income distribution (Quah, 1996), with a "hollowing out" of the middle-income range of countries (United Nations, 2006: 8). Milanovic and Yitzhaki (2001) estimate that just 8 per cent of the world's population now fall under the latter classification.

FIGURE 2.2
GDP per capita in selected developing countries and regions compared to the G-7, 1970–2000

Source: World Bank, World Development indicators, on line.

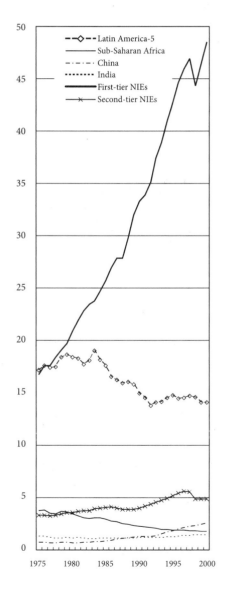

Polarization has taken place against a general slowing of global growth over the past two decades which has hit poorer countries particularly hard (Figure 2.3). But that slowdown has coincided with a more widespread stalling of industrial dynamism in many countries, retardation of social progress, and a dearth of star performers posting catch-up growth rates.[11] Together these factors have pressed down on the ratio of developing country incomes to those in the developed world, with countries in East Asia the notable exception (Table 2.2).

FIGURE 2.3

Slowdown and meltdown: average per capita growth in the world and Sub-Saharan Africa, 1961–2005

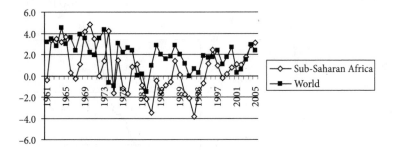

Source: World Bank, World Development Indicators, on line.

Income gaps and ratios are not the only way of measuring international inequality. The Gini coefficient is often used as a more integral measure that aims to take all members of a chosen set into account. On this measure a number of studies have reported a reduction in international inequality since 1980. However, as Sutcliffe (2006) has noted, there is little agreement on how significant this has been, and more importantly, it is a result that hinges on the performance of a single outlier; removing China from the country set reverses the trend back to one of rising international inequality, and even more sharply than before 1980. The Theil decomposition of international inequality shows a similar result (United Nations, 2006: 14). Given its size, China's performance is obviously central to the analysis of global trends. However, from a comparative perspective what happens in a single country (however large) should not be used to obscure what is in fact a highly variegated picture (Berry and Serieux, 2003).

TABLE 2.2
Ratio of per capita income to developed countries

	1950	1973	1980	2001
Eastern Europe	0.34	0.37	0.38	0.26
Former USSR	0.45	0.45	0.42	0.20
Latin America	0.40	0.34	0.35	0.25
Argentina	0.79	0.60	0.54	0.36
Brazil	0.27	0.29	0.34	0.24
Mexico	0.38	0.36	0.41	0.31
Peru	0.36	0.30	0.28	0.16
Asia	0.15	0.15	0.16	0.18
China	0.07	0.06	0.07	0.16
India	0.10	0.06	0.06	0.09
Japan	0.31	0.85	0.88	0.91
Pakistan	0.10	0.07	0.08	0.09
Africa	0.14	0.11	0.10	0.07
South Africa	0.40	0.31	0.28	0.18
Egypt	0.11	0.08	0.11	0.13
Ghana	0.18	0.11	0.08	0.06
Kenya	0.10	0.07	0.07	0.04

Source: United Nations (2006), Table 1.1.

Economists still have no conclusive explanations as to the precise causes of growth spurts and collapses. However, their willingness to admit as much has at least allowed bits and pieces of a new consensus to emerge in which the historical, geographical and institutional setting of each country matters; and where structural and technological changes are difficult to disentangle from the process of adding more and more inputs.

What is known is that most sustained growth spurts have been in East Asia, led by Japan in the 1950s, and followed by a series of neighbouring episodes beginning in the 1960s and the 1970s. All established macroeconomic regimes with a very fast rate of capital accumulation was a feature of all these stories (Table 2.3). Avoiding sharp slowdowns or contraction has also been a common feature, although the late 1990s proved a traumatic period for some previously recognized strong performers.[12] The fact that South Asian economies also avoided the severe shocks of the early 1980s appears to have been an important factor in their subsequent accelerating growth, and the handful of success stories in Africa (most notably, Botswana and Mauritius) and Latin America (Chile) since the early 1980s exhibit a similar tendencies.

TABLE 2.3
Growth rates of fixed capital stock (per cent per year changes)

	Japan	Korea	China	India	Brazil
1960s	12.5	8.9	1.9	4.5	5.8
1970s	8.5	14.6	7.2	4.1	9.6
1980s	6.1	11.2	8.4	4.9	4.1
1990s	4	9.6	10.9	6.2	2.2

Source: Glyn (2006).

Still, there is clearly more to long-term success than simply avoiding shocks. A strong productivity performance is generally recognized as key to fast and sustained economic growth (Baumol and others, 1989). For most developing countries, that means putting more work through a rapid pace of capital accumulation and changing the structural change towards activities with higher levels of productivity. Developing the industrial sector is key to overall output growth because of its proclivity to rapid productivity growth, which results from increasing returns to scale, specialization, large rents from innovations and learning-by-doing. Its greater dynamism also derives from its capacity to forge strong links within and between different sectors of the economy by processing raw materials and semi-industrial inputs by diversifying the supply of intermediate inputs and by providing a market for ever more specialized capital goods. These features have been well documented for advanced countries, but developing countries continue to show faster growth as the industrial and service sectors increase and as the agricultural sector decreases (United Nations, 2006: 32–36). Still, structural change involves more than just industrial growth, particularly at the lowest levels of development where raising the productivity of the agricultural sector is likely to be key. There is, moreover, considerable room for diversity in the timing and pace of industrial development across countries, reflecting differences in resource endowments, size and geographical location.

The challenge of linking accumulation to structural change has certainly not become any easier in recent decades: not only is the quality of investment more difficult to gauge in an interdependent world, but the amount of resources committed to investment by successful catch-up economies is just as great, and perhaps even greater, than ever before. Looking at patterns of structural change over the past four decades, the fastest growing East Asian economies have, through an effective mixture of rapid capital accumulation, growth in industrial employment, and strong export performance, created diversified economies and have reached a level of maturity consistent with their employment structures tilting towards modern services.[13] Beginning later than their north-easterly neighbours, and still lagging some way behind, fast growth in South East and South Asia has also been associated with a rapid decline in the importance of agriculture and strong expansions of both industrial and service sectors, largely centred around upgrading from resource-based and labour-intensive activities to middle-range technology products. China has entered this path recently while on the other hand, economies which have struggled to effect systematic structural changes have lagged behind, particularly in Africa, where mounting debt and premature liberalization have tightened the constraints on domestic resource mobilization, leading to deindustrialization and declining public investment. But sluggish long-term growth and weak structural change have also co-existed in many middle-income countries of Latin America and the Caribbean as well as countries in Central and Eastern Europe, the Middle East and the former USSR.

In these countries, growth has often been concentrated in the services sector, with agriculture and industry remaining nearly stagnant and often shedding jobs. Indeed, the two big structural trends in these economies over the past two decades—the informalization of economic activity and premature de-industrialization—have had a particularly damaging effect on longer-term productivity and output growth.

TRADE, FDI AND INTERNATIONAL INEQUALITY

The broad picture of the last two decades is one of erratic growth around a trend rate that was lower than that before the debt crisis. In some cases, principally in much of SSA, the trend in per capita GDP growth has been negative, although there have been a small number of economies (most notably, China and India) that rose significantly above earlier performances.[14] This has led to income divergence between most developing countries and their richer counterparts for the period since 1980, a trend that has been exaggerated by very uneven structural and social changes. This is not what was promised by the proponents of market-driven globalization.

Understanding the diversity of growth patterns certainly requires sensitivity to specific local conditions and histories. But institutional and policy choices have also mattered. In particular, as in the case of Latin America and much of Africa, there have been pronounced discontinuities due to the rapid switch from an inward to an outward-oriented development strategy. In light of the cumulative nature of economic development, a key question must be whether the workings of the international economy over the past two decades or so have made it more or less difficult for virtuous development circles to be established in countries that have rapidly opened up to international market forces and firms.

Trading More, Earning Less

Trade matters for a country's economic health and well being for all kinds of reasons. However, its long-term development impact is principally about whether it can help trigger and sustain the kind of cumulative growth processes that propels a country across the income and productivity thresholds that define economic maturity, by releasing scale economies, technological externalities and learning opportunities of one kind or another. There is certainly plenty of evidence to suggest that faster overall growth is associated with more dynamic export profiles (see introduction). However, because this is closely linked to industrialisation, trade relations are shaped as much by increasing returns, monopoly conditions, externalities and incomplete markets as by given factor endowments. There is nothing in theory to suggest that this world will be a converging one.

The emergence of virtuous growth circles depends on there being a strong and sustained accumulation drive of the kind that underpinned Western European and Japanese growth after World War II, and that was repeated from the early 1960s in the first-tier NIEs, and from the mid-1970s in the second-tier NIEs.[15] But while these examples confirm the possibility of a virtuous circle between investment, exports and growth - investing in sectors with significant productivity and market potential, and using export proceeds to finance the imports of capital goods and intermediate inputs required for further productivity increases - the links do not emerge automatically. A good deal hinges on the policies and institutions devised to help raise the rate of capital accumulation and deepen technological linkages. As suggested in the previous section, most success cases have used a variety of policies to ensure that profits are used to increase productive capacity and employment, and to encourage industrial upgrading, including credit rationing, subsidised credit, fiscal concessions, targeted industrial policies and active labour market measures (Vartianen, 1995, Wade, 1995).

But there is another less advertised trend, which touches even some of the most successful trading economies in the past twenty five years, whereby increased trade has generally failed to translate into commensurate increases in income. In a recent study of 127 developed and developing countries, Dowrick and Golley (2004) found that between 1960 and 1980, increased trade helped productivity to grow in poorer countries at double the rate in richer countries, but that this gain was reversed in the period of more open trade between 1980 and 2000, when the marginal impact of trade on productivity growth favoured the richer countries, and actually turned negative for poorer countries. A similar conclusion is reached by Wacziarg and Welch (2003) who, based on the Sachs-Warner methodology, found that the results were period sensitive, with openness having little impact on growth in the 1990s, and more open economies actually benefited less than relatively closed economies. Developing countries, it seems, have been trading more in a liberalized world, but earning less from doing so.

A clear indication of the contingent links between trade liberalization, trade structure and development is that increases in the developing countries' share of world manufactured exports during the past two decades have not been matched by a corresponding rise in their share of global value added (Figure 2.4). Indeed, in a number of cases, shares of global manufacturing income have actually fallen over the past decade or so, while for others, it has risen by much less than their share of world exports of manufactures (Table 2.4).

These trends appear to contradict a basic tenet of post-war development thinking, which recommended that developing countries should diversify from primary products to manufactures in order to ensure a more balanced integration into the trading system together with sustained improvements in productivity growth and rising living standards. These were all strongly and positively related in the three decades after 1945, both in the developed countries and in newly industrializing economies such as Korea and Taiwan (Glyn, 2006: 92-94). By contrast, in a number of the countries that have pursued more export-oriented policies since the debt crisis of the early 1980s, real wages have been stagnant or falling, as in Argentina, Egypt, Mexico, Morocco and Turkey, and/or currencies have been sharply devalued, as in Chile, Ghana, Malaysia and Pakistan, all of which have seen rising shares of manufactured exports (UNCTAD, 2003: 111).

One of the problems seems to lie with a lopsided reliance on external demand as the basis of sustained growth, a reliance which carries with it the familiar dangers of overproduction and resulting adverse price movements (Heintz, 2003). On its own, a small country can rapidly expand its exports in a given market with negligible impact on overall supply and prices – the "importance of being unimportant" – but once a large number of countries, or just a few large economies (such as India and China) follow the same route there

FIGURE 2.4
Trade in manufactures and value added in manufacturing for selected groups of economies, 1981–2003

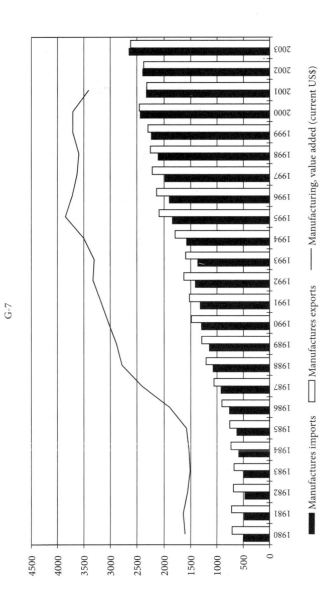

G-7

■ Manufactures imports   □ Manufactures exports   —— Manufacturing, value added (current US$)

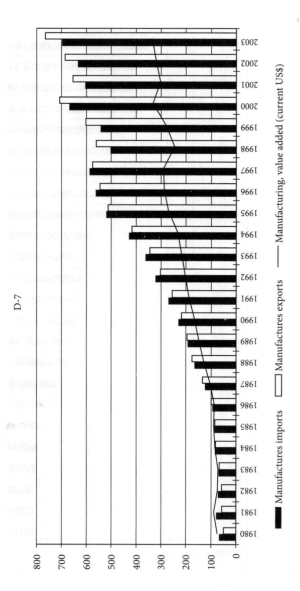

D-7

■ Manufactures imports   □ Manufactures exports   — Manufacturing, value added (current US$)

Source: WB WDI 2005 Database

will be an increased risk of oversupply and declining terms of trade for the exporters. This increased risk of falling prices, resulting from a "fallacy of composition", now seems to be facing exporters of some manufactured goods as a result of widespread efforts to replicate the successful experience of the Asian NIEs. And as previously the case with primary commodities, such a risk becomes all the more likely if there is an asymmetry in the structure of global markets.[16]

TABLE 2.4
Share of selected regional groups and developing economies in world exports of manufactures and manufacturing value added, 1980 and 2001

	Share in world exports manufactures		Share in world value added manufactures	
	1980	2001	1980	2001
High income	81.4	79.5	—	77.6
Low & middle income	15.4	20.0	16.1	22.5
Latin America & Caribbean	1.4	4.1	4.7	5.3
Argentina	0.1	0.2	0.8	0.8
Brazil	0.6	0.7	2.6	1.2
Chile	0.0	0.1	0.2	0.2
Mexico	0.2	2.8	1.4	2.0
South Asia, East Asia & Pacific	0.6	9.9	5.2	11.5
NIEs	3.4	8.8	0.7	2.7
Hong Kong, China	1.5	3.8	0.2	0.2
Korea, Rep.	1.2	2.8	0.5	2.2
Singapore	0.7	2.2		0.4
ASEAN-4	0.4	3.8	1.1	2.2
Indonesia	0.0	0.7	0.4	0.7
Malaysia	0.2	1.5	0.2	0.5
Philippines	0.1	0.6	0.3	0.3
Thailand	0.1	1.0	0.3	0.7
China		4.9	2.7	7.5
India	0.4	0.7	1.0	1.2
Turkey	0.1	0.5	0.3	0.4

Source: WDI database 2005

Evidence on the evolving market structure of some key developing country exports, such as clothing and electronic and electrical goods, tends to confirm this risk (UNCTAD, 2002: 121–124). These involve internationally standardized goods vunlerable to oversupply in highly competitive markets with declining price trends which, in some cases such as electronic goods, are also more volatile than those for similar goods traded among the developed countries. Indeed, such trends are already having an impact on the terms of trade of those developing countries most dependent on exports of manufactures and leading some observers to revive the idea of "immiserizing growth", i.e. increased economic activity resulting in lower standards of living through declining income terms of trade.[17]

In this respect, the apparent change in the structure of exports to more dynamic products by developing countries can be misleading as for the most part developing countries' involvement in skill and technology intensive products is confined to the labour-intensive parts of vertically integrated production networks (see below).[18] This is most obviously true in the electronics sector where high-tech final products embody a number of low-tech activities involving the assembly of imported parts. But the production of medium-technology automobiles and even low-technology clothing also comprise a range of activities of differing technological sophistication and capital intensity, allowing for the separability and reorganization of the various components of the value-added chain.

What seems clear (Figure 2.5) is that rapidly opening up to the international trading system has not encouraged the kinds of dynamic linkages between capital accumulation, industrial upgrading and export performance that have been a hallmark of successful performers in the past.

In fact, a weakening of the linkage between investment and exports has been particularly noticeable in some middle-income countries, whose combination of (relatively) high wages and low productivity levels has, in the face of growing competition, squeezed profits (UNCTAD, 2003; Rodrik, 2006). In a number of these countries, particularly in Latin America, the resulting weakening of investment has held back productivity growth and upgrading in the more labour-intensive industries, such as textiles and clothing, and at the same time, has arrested the process of diversification to more dynamic areas of manufacturing. Indeed, in almost all cases where a substantial change occurred in the investment pattern, with the exception of the transport sector in some countries, it was towards resource-based or labour-intensive products (UNCTAD, 2002: 115–17). Alice Amsden (2001: 260–68) provides further evidence that the capital goods sectors commonly associated with successful industrial

FIGURE 2.5
Changes in manufacturing value added in relation to changes in exports of manufactures: 1990–2000 compared to 1980–1990.

Source:
World Bank, World Development Indicators on Line.

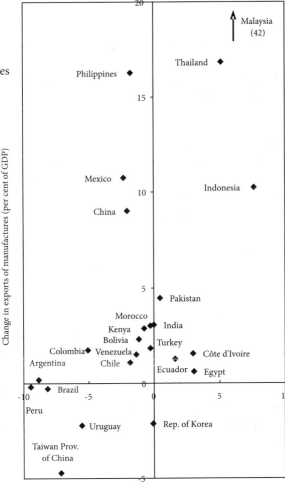

Change in manufacturing value added (per cent of GDP)

diversification and upgrading have grown particularly slowly in Latin America. Indeed, on her chosen measure of structural change, the economies of Latin America struggled between 1980 and 1994 and some fell further further behind East Asia. She attributes this, in part, to a slow growth environment biased towards the destructive rather than the creative forces of market-led structural change.

Attracting FDI: The Economics of Putting the Cart Before the Horse

Since the early 1980s, FDI has grown at a much faster rate than both output and trade (Figure 2.6), in part facilitated by changes in manufacturing production processes and in corporate governance, by innovations in financial markets, by increased liberalization of FDI regimes and privatization, among others.[19] As a consequence of the rapid growth in flows, the stock of world FDI has increased almost twenty fold since the early 1980s, reaching close to a quarter of world GDP. In light of this growth, there has been growing enthusiasm among policy makers at the national and international levels for attracting FDI. Indeed, as was noted earlier, the idea of harnessing global business through good policies and good governance to attract FDI has become central to efforts to salvage the promise of convergence in a more open global economy.

To date however, increased FDI flows have remained highly concentrated in the developed economies (Figure 2.7), continuing a trend that began after 1945 when the axis of international production shifted to the overseas expansion of large manufacturing firms from the United States and Western Europe. The resulting increase in FDI, often by firms in the same sector, i.e. intra-industry flows, was principally the product of strong growth prospects, large market size and technological sophistication.[20] Because many of these same economic forces are behind the rapid expansion of FDI in the modern service sectors, including banking and distribution, this bias towards advanced countries has continued since 1980, through surges in mergers and acquisitions.

FIGURE 2.6
The expansion of trade and FDI, 1970–2003 (index 1980=100)

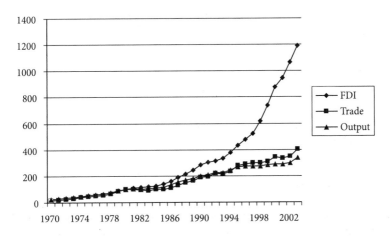

Source: World Bank On Line Data Base and UNCTAD FDI database.
Note: FDI figure is for the stock of FDI, from 1980.

FIGURE 2.7
Geographical composition of global FDI flows, 1970–2003

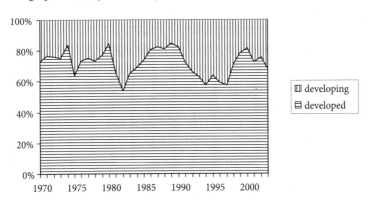

Source: UNCTAD, FDI database.

TABLE 2.5
FDI as a share of gross fixed capital formation

	1970s	1980s	1990s	2000s
World	2.2	3.1	6.5	12.3
Developed countries	2.1	3.1	5.9	12.3
Developing Countries	2.8	3.0	8.2	12.0
Africa	3.3	2.2	6.5	13.9
Latin America and Caribbean	3.8	3.9	11.4	16.7
Asia	1.8	2.9	7.2	10.3

Source: UNCTAD FDI database.

Still, developing countries have experienced a fifteen-fold rise in average annual inflows since the mid-1980s, including a rise in the share going to the service sector. This rise in FDI flows has translated into a significantly higher share of capital accumulation in most developing countries and regions (Table 2.5), maintaining hope of a new growth dynamic. However, again these increased flows have been marked by a persistently high level of concentration, with just 12 countries accounting for over 80 per cent of total flows albeit with a distinct shift in the geographical pattern of flows towards East Asia (and away from Latin America), dominated in recent years by the emergence of China as a host economy whose inward stock of FDI increased from 1.1 per cent of the global FDI inward stock in 1990 to over 6 per cent since the late 1990s. Indeed, Asia is the only developing region that has seen its share of global flows rising over the past three decades. This is important because FDI dynamics appear to be cumulative, with the size of the existing stock of FDI having a strong bearing on the size of subsequent flows, and suggesting that the recent FDI surge to developing countries is likely to have been a source of economic divergence rather than convergence (Mody, 2004: 1201–1205).

For reasons discussed earlier, FDI into export-oriented manufacturing has received a good deal of attention in terms of its potential for breaking with past patterns of international economic relations. Between 1990 and 2003, the share of manufacturing in the FDI stock by the group of developing countries rose from 25 to 37 per cent, while the share of developing countries in the global stock of manufacturing FDI increased from one-fifth to close to one-third during the same period.

The shift is particularly pronounced in those sectors, notably clothing, electronics and automobiles, which, as discussed earlier, are among the most dynamic in the trading system. However, FDI in these sectors has not necessarily acted as a catalyst for this industrialization. Rather, the existence of a vibrant industrial base, robust local markets and a dynamic enterprise sector are preconditions for attracting (and benefiting from) FDI in manufacturing. Countries where growth has stalled or collapsed, or where the manufacturing base has been eroded, have little chance to participate in and benefit from the most dynamic elements of the international production system. Thus, the recent rapid expansion of export-oriented manufacturing activities linked to FDI has been heavily biased towards a handful of countries in East Asia, with China the single largest recipient of FDI into the manufacturing sector. Pockets of industrial FDI are spattered across all regions, however, FDI has been more attracted into services, through privatization (as in much of Latin America) or into natural resource activities (as in most of Africa and Latin America).

A good deal of industrial FDI has been linked to participation in international production networks (IPNs), in which corporations slice up their value chain, relocating or outsourcing the different parts, from product design to final delivery, in a way that enhances overall profits.[21] In some cases, production is organized by large TNCs producing a standardized set of goods in several locations (as in electronics and transport industries). In others, production involves groups of small and medium-sized enterprises located in different countries and linked through international subcontracting (as in clothing).

A key test of whether increased FDI is likely to reduce global income inequalities is the establishment of the kind of dynamic investment-export nexus formed earlier in East Asia and which led to a steady diversification of production away from those activities requiring only unskilled labour. In fact, evidence from the macroeconomic level does not suggest that FDI has brought a general improvement in the investment climate in host economies, including crowding-in domestic investment. If anything domestic capital formation and FDI have actually become disconnected in recent years (UNCTAD, 2003: 76–78) and links to job creation have been tenuous (Spiezia, 2004).[22] Thus a good deal depends on whether FDI organized through production networks brings increased technological and organizational spill-overs to developing countries along with positive effects on the balance of payments. To date, the evidence is mixed and does not support the claim that such a nexus is taking hold in other developing economies.

The fact that, in the context of production networks, parts of the same final product may cross and re-cross national boundaries more than once somewhat inflates the gross value of trade (Krugman, 1995). But more importantly, there is strong evidence suggesting a very high import elasticity from participation in IPNs. In the case of Mexico, for example, it has been estimated that over the past two decades, imports for further processing constitute as much as one half to two thirds of total sales of affiliates of United States TNCs in certain industries (UNCTAD, 2002). Similar patterns are discernable in some North African economies, in Central America and in parts of Asia, including Cambodia, and the Philippines.[23] Under these circumstances, the contribution to value added from participating in production networks is determined by the cost of the most abundant and least mobile factor, that is, labour, whereas the rewards to internationally mobile factors such as capital, management and know-how are reaped by their foreign owners. The overall impact of FDI on the balance of payments of the host country is likely to vary considerably with the sectoral pattern of FDI inflows, the share of TNC profits in value-added, the degree of import dependence, external debt servicing by TNCs and the proportion of the final goods sold in domestic markets (Akyuz, 2004). Certainly the danger exists that as profit remittances and other capital outflows linked to FDI begin to take place the longer-term impact on the balance of payments will will not be favourable (UNCTAD, 2003: 143–144).

There is nothing new about FDI being attracted into enclaves of export-oriented production using a good deal of imported inputs and technology and with limited linkages to the rest of the economy; this has been a long-standing feature of commodity chains in the primary sector (Singer, 1950). However, the degree of disintegration is likely to be even greater for manufactures though its extent is difficult to judge. In the absence of comprehensive national input-output tables the significance of enclave production is difficult to reassure but can be indirectly gauged by a country's GDP (a measure of the value of output generated within national boundaries) being much higher than its GNP (a measure of national income actually earned by national citizens), by a high ratio of export earnings to value added, by the presence of a large informal economy and by periodic profit surges in the capital account. All have certainly been apparent across parts of . the developing world in recent years.

Several studies suggest that the combination of increased capital mobility and rapid entry into the global labour force of unskilled labour has greatly weakened the bargaining position of poorer countries, reinforcing highly asymmetric relations between oligopolistic market structures at the top of the value chain and competitive market structures at the bottom (UNCTAD, 2002; Milberg, 2004). It seems doubtful under these conditions that IPNs are likely to generate many opportunities for strong spill-over effects.[24] In the first place, participation in the labour-intensive and low-skill parts of the value chain of production networks is unlikely to attract FDI with a high level of technological sophistication. Therefore, it is not clear what kind of spill-overs should be expected from these arrangements.[25] Additionally, the potential for spill-overs from engaging in IPNs is reduced, not only because the package of technology required at any one site become narrower, but also owing to cross-border linkages being strengthened at the expense of domestic ones. As a result, technological upgrading can be more difficult for economies used by TNCs primarily as bases for exports to third markets than for economies where FDI is of a more traditional horizontal type seeking markets.[26] Whether, under these circumstances, FDI triggers a "race to the bottom", as some have suggested (Stiglitz, 2002), or reintroduces "immiserizing growth" (Kaplinsky and Morris, 2002), it is certainly difficult to see how it can act as a force for income convergence.

Thus despite the talk of a new growth regime led by global business, in order to profit from FDI, countries still need to have the necessary absorptive capacity among domestic firms and institutions. Growth effects from hosting FDI seem to be highly conditional and non-linear, where threshold levels, in income, human capital, technological know-how and enterprise development, must be crossed before a significant positive impact can be identified.[27] Countries where an inflow of FDI has been paralleled by significant investments in building domestic capabilities (e.g., in Singapore and Ireland) have been the most successful in leveraging inward FDI. Conversely, when FDI is attracted in response to major tax incentives, or as a result of trade policy distortions (such as textile and clothing quotas), without a simultaneous build-up of local capabilities and without the creation of linkages between foreign affiliates and local firms, there is limited scope for long-term benefits from FDI and little evidence that it acts as an independent accelerator of growth.[28]

IS INCREASING INTERNATIONAL INEQUALITY AN INTERNATIONAL POLICY ISSUE?

There is little in the pattern of international trade and FDI flows to suggest that separately or together their expansion will automatically generate the kind of growth dynamics consistent with a converging global economy. Indeed, as we have seen in a world permeated by processes of circular and cumulative causation, it would be surprising to expect a reduction of income inequalities between countries to come about as a result of market liberalization *unless* it also led to a marked acceleration in the rate of accumulation, in both physical and human assets and in technological know-how, in poorer countries. In many cases, that has simply not happened.

But should international income inequality be the concern of multilateral institutions? There are lots of reasons why domestic policy makers worry about the level of inequality within their countries. Not only does a high level of income inequality usually signal a wider set of social and economic injustices, but it can also be detrimental to growth, whether by fuelling political resentment and instability, or through the potential misuse and waste of resources. And the likelihood is that instability and waste will get worse when markets respond to and reinforce the power and advantages of those already at the top. Segmented labour markets will likely hold back wages and provide little rationale for workplace training; weak local consumer markets will stunt enterprise growth and prevent scale economies from emerging, financial markets that cater exclusively to a privileged strata of firms and households will hamper capital formation, etc. While success cases have handled the inequality predicament in light of particular local circumstances, the broad sweep of history suggests that all have used a judicious mix of markets, regulation and public action to bring together the forces of social justice, growth and economic efficiency in ways that strengthen the development process.

All these have parallels with the challenges of an increasingly interdependent world economy in which income distribution is far worse than for almost any individual country. Growing income gaps among countries raise questions of social injustice, which readily spill across borders, whether through the rise of illegal immigration or the decisions of elites in developing countries to invest their resources in financial assets in rich countries. But there are also potentially troublesome links to the economic dynamism and stability of the global economy. Given existing gaps, the kind of cross-border cumulative feedback mechanisms, whether through trade and financial flows or knowledge and technology spill-overs, that could add to global dynamism will not materialize, or will be confined to the regional or sub-regional levels, adding to further divisions and tensions. The earlier discussion of trade and FDI seems to bear this conclusion out. Moreover, the absence of trust among countries, by parallel with domestic trends, is likely to accompany a more unequal global economy is also likely to have a major bearing on the effectiveness of multilateral rules and arrangements. In a market economy, income accrues to those who possess and have secure title to such assets and the distribution of endowments helps to explain the distribution of incomes. If such inequalities persist, the danger is for an increasingly disorderly international economic system.

The danger is likely to be exacerbated if economic leverage is reinforced by asymmetric political influence. Multilateral rules and arrangements have of course been devised, in part, to address such asymmetries. However, developing countries have, since the creation of Bretton Woods, had a much weaker voice in the process, and in many respects changes to those rules and arrangements over the past three decades have seen their concerns relegated even further. In particular, while the post-war arrangements were founded on the belief that adverse influences emanating from trade, finance and debt should be countered through measures that preserved growth and development, under present arrangements and policies, developing countries almost invariably find themselves obliged to adjust to international imbalances through domestic retrenchment at the same time as their obligations in the trade and financial systems have moved closer to those demanded of the developed countries, and in some respects have actually become more onerous.

The Monterrey Consensus recognized this weakness in international economic decision-making processes and gave a clear mandate to the international community to improve the participation of developing countries. The Doha Round of trade negotiations also signalled an intention to move in much the same direction by making development a priority in the negotiations. However, progress on increasing the voice of poorer nations in the Bretton Woods institutions has been slow, and within the World Trade Organization (WTO), each country has one vote, negotiation processes are nonetheless perceived to be unfair because of the imbalances in commercial interests that weigh unevenly on what is ostensibly a consensual process.[29]

Taking international justice more seriously requires giving greater room to the idea of "adaptive efficiency", the capacity to develop institutions that provide a stable framework for economic activity but, at the same time, are flexible enough to provide the maximum leeway for policy choices at any given time and in any given situation in response to specific challenges (North, 1993). Historically, the evolution of today's successful economies has certainly been marked by such adaptive efficiency. An emphasis on flexibility and the need to experiment reflect the realities of operating in an uncertain world where our knowledge of the best ways to promote economic growth and development is limited, and what we do know suggests that success is characterized by diversity, contingent on national political and social cultures, on historically determined path dependencies, and on the qualities of the ruling elites. Experimentation, together with rules and conventions to ensure that failed experiments are dropped rather than retained to avoid embarrassment, is thus crucial for raising the probability of success.

Adaptive efficiency was, of course, a hallmark of the original Bretton Woods system, and there is an eminently sensible agenda looking for a similar balance between global integration, democratic politics and economic policy sovereignty, although there are differences on what should be rolled back and what areas brought under new rules and surveillance.[30] Exactly how much institutional reform might be needed or is possible at the international level to rebalance the multilateral system is ultimately a political question involving trade-offs among the major powers (Rogoff, 1999: 28).

The basic policy issue facing most developing countries seeking to integrate with the global economy is not fundamentally one of more or less trade liberalization or more or less controls on FDI, but how best to extract, from their participation in that system, the elements that will complement their efforts at domestic resource mobilization and structural change. Here the counterpart of "adaptive efficiency" is the idea of sufficient "policy space" for developing countries to manage the interface between external and internal integration (Kozul-Wright and Rayment, forthcoming). What that might mean in terms of existing multilateral arrangements has been recently set out by the German Development Minister:

> Development institutions, in particular the Bank and the Fund, should actively advise on a range of policy alternatives and thus create "policy space" for the countries. Here it is not so much a question of "policy advice" in the classic sense. Rather, the role of the IFIs is to identify trade-offs, show possible alternatives policy options, make experience from other countries accessible and contribute to the establishment of national analytical capabilities. A further streamlining of conditionality and focusing performance criteria on output indicators would also contribute to ownership (Wieczorek-Zeul, 2004)

Extending this perspective to the tracking system, trade policy is essentially one policy instrument among several with which countries can pursue their objectives for economic growth and development, and the key question is whether and under what conditions it is effectual. There is growing recognition that trade liberalization will not bring about desired changes independently of a wider set of strategic policy initiatives and institutional conditions, particularly those that effect investment in many developing countries. But the sensible policy conclusion -- that if the benefits of free trade and international capital movements are contingent on a number of crucial pre-conditions, there is no logic in giving priority to liberalization until those conditions are satisfied -- is still resisted. Since, on closer examination, these pre-conditions include the existence of institutions appropriate for a market economy, effective domestic markets and infrastructure, the capacity to pursue sound macro-economic-policies in a market-based environment, and so on, the implication is that opening up to global market forces should follow success, or at least sufficient progress, in meeting these basic challenges of economic development and internal integration.

All developing countries that experienced sustained successful economic growth since 1960 have used active industrial polices to support the economic diversification and technological upgrading of their economies. Successful export-led growth strategies have also involved supportive pro-growth macroeconomic policies, (selective) infant industry protection, export subsidies, directed credit schemes, local content rules, large investments in human resources, as well as strategic alliances with multinational companies. Support measures often were clearly tied to specific export or other performance criteria. The space for conducting this type of active production sector development policies has narrowed in the context of recent multilateral trade agreements, but has not disappeared completely (UNCTAD, 2006b). Still, it is important that greater flexibility be restored for this purpose in World Trade Organization (WTO) negotiations.

It is also important that the governments of host countries can adopt a strategic approach to FDI, carefully evaluating net gains and preserving a range of policies to ensure that it supports the objectives of domestic development. This requires policy makers to ask different questions from those concerned simply with attracting FDI. Is FDI likely to raise the production costs and lower the profitability of domestic firms? What is the likely extent of positive spill-overs and linkages from FDI, and are domestic firms likely to benefit from them? What is the likely scale of increased import dependence and future profit repatriation? What are the potential problems of nurturing new domestic firms in sectors where TNCs have gained an early dominance? There are no easy answers to these questions and no hard and fast rules for striking the right balance between nurturing domestic enterprises and attracting foreign ones. What is clear is that policies have to be adapted to individual circumstances. Sometimes they may need to include restrictions on entry to certain sectors, prior approval for joint ventures, domestic content agreements, and so on. At other times it may be advisable to have an open-door policy with few restrictions, and sometimes it may be desirable to provide incentives to attract FDI to preferred sectors. A key point is that spill-overs and other benefits from FDI are unlikely to occur without the presence of strong local firms able to take advantage of them. This goes against the more conventional strategies which continue to give a leading role in the development process to FDI and TNCs, and against the policy stance of most developed countries which deplores any restriction on the free movement of foreign investment. Nevertheless, countries which have adopted policies to guide FDI within a national development strategy do not appear to have had much difficulty in attracting it – coherent national policies and good prospects for growth seem to be the key attractions for TNCs while at the same time increasing the bargaining power of the host country.

CONCLUSION

In today's increasingly interdependent world economy, the growth performance of a country is determined by factors that operate both within and outside its geographical boundaries. Conventional economic models predict that the growing influence of international market forces should automatically generate convergence, i.e. a narrowing of income gaps between rich and poor countries, as long as a liberal policy regime is maintained. This paper has argued that there is little in the experience of the past three decades to suggest that the principal vectors of globalization – liberalized trade and capital markets along with international production – have generally worked in this direction or has led to a significant re-distribution of the global stocks of productive assets.

International trade and foreign capital movements remain largely dominated by transactions among the already-rich countries, and though developing countries have been trading more, all too often they have been earning less from those these activities. FDI has rarely flowed to the poorest countries where economic growth and accumulation have failed to take off or have remained weak and uncertain. By definition, FDI means that ownership of capital assets remains in foreign hands and so, the initial returns will accrue to them. The key test of FDI as a contributing force for sustainable development and a reduction in income inequalities is therefore whether it has a positive, catalytic effect on domestic investment. The evidence on this, as we have seen, is very mixed, and where liberalization policies have been most energetically pursued, the effect is often negative. Moreover, we have also shown that although FDI can incorporate a developing country into internationally integrated production chains, it often confines it to those functions requiring unskilled labour, often the assembly of imported components. In principle, this is not necessarily a bad place to start, but if the backward linkages to the domestic economy are weak or non-existent, and the evidence suggests this is usually the case, FDI will not contribute to a reduction of inter-country inequalities and is likely to exacerbate income differences within the host country. The finding that despite a rising share of world exports of manufactures, the developing countries' share of global value-added (i.e. gross factor incomes) in manufacturing has been falling points to FDI as widening, rather than narrowing, the income gap between the rich and the poor.

In other words, the economies of a more dispersed and specialized international division of labour have tended to accrue disproportionately to advanced countries and to the foreign owners of capital. This has not ruled out some catch-up performances, most recently and notably in China and India, albeit in both cases, coming from a very long way behind the leading pack. However, in neither case can a strict diet of opening up explain successful growth performance. Rather, local "policy heresies" appear to have helped successfully manage the interface between internal and external integration in a way that has helped perpetuate virtuous growth circles. The paper suggests that repeating these experiences elsewhere in the developing world will probably require changes in global governance to allow more room to countries to experiment with institutions and policies in order to discover what will be effective in a particular national context where history, culture and initial economic conditions all have important influences on the possibilities for growth and development.

Notes

[1] There is a vast literature seeking to measure how far globalisation has actually gone; see Glyn (2004) for a recent assessment.

[2] Wood, 1994; Baldwin and others, 1998; Bhagwati, 2005.

[3] Economic historians are familiar with the divergence properties of international finance from the pre-1914 globalization era, see Kozul-Wright (2006).

[4] The original model is associated with Robert Solow and Trevor Swan. For a review of the early growth literature including its empirical shortcomings, see Scott (1991). Mankiw and others (1992) and Barro and Sala-I-Martin (1992) were seminal contributions to reviving and revising this work.

[5] Various authors have refined the openness-growth argument by examining the role of other conditioning variables, including country size (Frankel and Romer, 1999), geographical proximity (Ben-David, 1993; 1996); technological spill-overs (Edwards, 1998), and good governance (Winters, 2004). For further discussion of this literature, see chapter 8 of this book.

[6] Rodriguez and Rodrik (1999) and Kenny and Williams (2001) examine some of the methodological problems with the cross-country econometric literature. See also the chapter 6 in this volume.

[7] Plenty of studies report the direction running from domestic success in raising productivity to increased trade, rather than the reverse; see, for example, Clerides and others (1998) Aw and others (1998) and Bernard and Jensen (1998). Harrison (1996) reports two-way causation.

[8] See, for example, Quah (1996).

[9] As, for example, in Lucas (2000); for criticisms, see Bernard and Jones (1996) and Temple and Johnson (1998).

[10] Obviously in light of what has already been said, it would be wrong to identify any hard and fast benchmark for all developing countries. Still, many regard a 6-8 per cent target as what is needed to tackle those deficits that and to visibly close income gaps with the more developed countries.

[11] See UNCTAD, 2003 and the chapters by Taylor and Rada, Ocampo and Parra and Shapiro. The social situation is discussed extensively in Jomo, ed. 2006. Given that there are important social thresholds that impact on growth performance, stalling in social areas has almost certainly contributed to vicious growth circles in a number of developing countries.

[12] On the links between the shift towards a more liberal policy regimes and financial crises, see UNCTAD, 1998; Chang and others (ed.), 2001. Avoiding sharp shocks was also a feature of success stories on the European periphery, most notably Ireland.

[13] The intertwining of export diversity and industrial development as part of a progressive growth dynamic has been stressed by Imbs and Wacziarg (2000). Significantly they report a shift from a diversified to a more specialized trading profile at much the same income level as others have found "positive deindustrialization" (Rowthorn and Wells, 1997).

[14] Some small island economies, such as Barbados, Mauritius and Seychelles, also enjoyed faster growth after the debt crisis, although again, their recoveries began earlier. Indeed, outside Asia, perhaps only Chile sustained a significant improvement over its past performance, beginning in the mid-1980s, albeit still failing to match Asian rates of growth.

[15] Their large tradeable goods sectors and substantial industrial capacity built up during the 1960s and 1970s, was a key factor enabling these economies to recover quickly from the shocks of the late 1970s and early 1980s.

[16] In the case of commodities, the Prebisch-Singer hypothesis assumed that technical progress in the developed countries led to higher wages and living standards of those employed but not to lower prices, including those for goods exported to developing countries; in contrast, in the developing countries increased productivity tended to result in lower prices for the goods exported to developed countries rather than to better real wages. Hence, there was a secular tendency for the terms of trade to move against developing countries and especially for those exporting primary products..

[17] For empirical evidence on this trend, see UNCTAD, 2002; Maizels and others, 1998; and Maizels, 2000. On immiserizing growth, see Kaplinsky and Morris, 2002.

[18] The classification of internationally traded goods by relative factor intensity and other characteristics is generally based, because of data limitations, on the characteristics of those products in developed countries, usually the United States. Applying the same classification to other countries implicitly assumes that the categories are homogeneous with respect to the characteristics in question and that there are no factor intensity reversals among countries. In practice it is the heterogeneity of the standard product categories rather than factor intensity reversals that limits the usefulness of applying such classifications to other countries.

[19] There is a vast literature on the various factors driving the recent surge in FDI; for a useful textbook treatment, see Dicken (2004).

[20] The classic statement is Hymer (1960); see also Rowthorn(1992), Driffield and Love (2005). Most developing countries were peripheral to these trends, offering only marginal investment for TNCs, and then usually in the protected markets of larger countries. Up to the mid-1970s, Mexico and Brazil accounted for well over half of developing country flows in manufacturing. For a useful discussion of the nature and impact of such investments with reference to the Brazilian experience, see Evans (1979).

[21] Such networks are not a new development, dating back to the 1960s in parts of East Asia, and becoming a more prominent feature of the international division of labour in the 1970s, see Helleiner (1973) and Henderson (1991).

[22] On the mixed evidence for FDI crowding in or out domestic investment, see Agosin and Mayer (2000) and Khumar and Pradhan (2002). According to Ghosh (2004) the tendency of FDI to crowd out local investment rose in all developing regions, including SSA, in the period 1990-1997 compared with 1983–1989 which may well be due to the growing share of M&As in FDI flows. More detailed analysis needs to look at individual country cases, and while these are few to draw on, those that have been undertaken also confirm a mixed picture, see Harrison and Macmillan (2002) for one such study on Cote d'Ivoire, and Braunstein and Epstein (2004) on China.

[23] A recent study of the Latin American experience by ECLAC has concluded that "...many countries that improved their international competitiveness through FDI in manufactures not based on natural resources generated very weak linkages between the local economy and the export platforms. In general, the lack of linkage promotion strategy was highlighted, especially in the cases of Mexico, Costa Rica and Honduras, where the success in exports has not been followed by a similar development of the local industrial base" (UNCTAD/ECLAC, 2002). For a discussion of the Cambodian experience with FDI, see Rasiah (2006), and on doubts about China's experience with FDI, see Braunstein and Epstein (2004).

[24] Spill-overs are essentially defined as productivity benefits accruing to domestic firms, either in the same sector or other sectors; for general reviews of the evidence, see Aitken and Harrison (1999), Gorg and Greenaway (2001), Blomstrom and Kokko (2003).

[25] It is worth noting here that the evidence on FDI among advanced countries that are responding to factor cost differences does not bring spill-overs to the host country, see Driffield and Love.

[26] Indeed, because market-seeking FDI is more dependent on the domestic economy, it gives the host country government greater bargaining power for using FDI selectively to ensure that it will create spill-overs and linkages with domestic industry.

[27] See, inter alia, Borenszstein and others 1995, de Mello, 1997; Lim, 2001. Employment figures point in much the same direction, with little evidence of positive employment effects from hosting FDI in low-income countries but stronger gains in higher-income countries, see Spiezia, 2004.

[28] For evidence on the lagged nature of FDI in the growth process, see Carkovic and Levine (2002), Mody (2004) Nunnenkamp and Spatz (2004), and on its dependence on country characteristics, see Rodrik (1999).

[29] Changes are underway however. Since the turn of the millennium, ODA has not only increased, after falling sharply during the 1990s, but there is a push to cut back the conditionalities on aid and to strengthen donor coordination. Arguably what is still needed is a stronger multilateral profile for the aid architecture to ensure that political interference is kept to a minimum (UNCTAD, 2006a). There have also been tentative moves to extend the representation of developing countries in the Bretton Woods institutions and to extend surveillance to the big economic powers. However, movement has been slower in other areas. Mechanisms to deal with international bankruptcy are being discussed as are rules on some aspects on the workings of international financial markets though facing considerable resistance. On labour mobility, there has so far been little discussion.

[30] See, for example, Helleiner (2000); Rodrik (2002); Nayyar (2002); and Stiglitz (2006).

REFERENCES

Agosin, M., and R. Mayer (2000). Foreign investment in developing countries: Does it crowd in domestic investment? UNCTAD Discussion Paper No. 146, UNCTAD, Geneva.

Aitken, B., and A. Harrison (1999). Do domestic firms benefit from foreign direct investment? Evidence from Venezuela. *American Economic Review,* 89 (3).

Akyuz, Y (2004). Trade, growth and industrialisation in developing countries: Issues, experience and policy challenges. Penang, Malaysia. UNDP Asia-Pacific Conference on Trade.

Amsden, A (2001). *"The Rise of The Rest": Challenges to the West from Late Industrializing Economies.* New York, Oxford University Press.

Aw, B.Y. and others (1998. Productivity and the decision to export: Micro evidence from Taiwan and South Korea. NBER Working Papers 6558, National Bureau of Economic Research

Baldwin, R. and others (1998). Global income divergence, trade and industrialization: The geography of growth take-offs, NBER Working Paper No. 6458, March , National Bureau of Economic Research

Barro, R., and Sala-I-Martin (1992). Convergence. *Journal of Political Economy,* 00 (2).

Baumol, W., and others (1989). *Productivity and American Leadership.* MIT Press. Cambridge.

Ben-David, D (1993). Equalizing exchange: Trade liberalization and income convergence. *Quarterly Journal of Economics* 108.

Ben-David, D (1996). Trade and convergence among countries. *Journal of International Economics, 40,* , May.

Bernard, A and J. Jensen (1998). Exporting and productivity. paper presented at the 1998 Summer Institute, NBER, Cambridge, MA, August

Bernard A. and C. Jones (1996). Comparing apples to oranges: Productivity convergence and measurement across industries and countries *American Economic Review* 86 (5

Berry, A. and J. Serieux (2004). All about the giants: Probing the influences of world growth on income distribution at the end of the 20th century. *CESifo Economic Studies,* 50 (1.

Bhagwati, J (1998). The capital myth. *Foreign Affairs* May-June: 7–12.

Bhagwati, J. (2005). From Seattle to Hong Kong. *Foreign Affairs,* December.

Bhagwati, J. and T. Srinivasan (1999). Outward orientation and development: Are revisionists right? Yale University Economic Growth Center Discussion Paper 806.

Blattman, C., and others (2003). The terms of trade and economic growth in the periphery, 1870–1983. NBER Working Paper Series No. 9940 (National Bureau of Economic Research)

Blomström, M., and A. Kokko (2003). Human Capital and Inward FDI. CEPR Working Paper, no. 167, London, CEPR.

Borensztein, E. and others (1995). How Does Foreign Direct Investment Affect Economic Growth?" NBER Working Paper 5057. Cambridge, National Bureau of Economic Research.

Braunstein, E. and G. Epstein (2004). Bargaining Power and Foreign Direct Investment in China: Can 1.3. Billion Consumers Tame the Multinationals? In W. Milberg, ed., *Labor and the Globalization of Production: Causes and Consequences of Industrial.* New York: Palgrave Macmillan.

Carcovic, M. and R. Levine (2002). Does foreign direct investment accelerate economic growth?" mimeo, Minneapolis, MN, University of Minnesota, May.

Chang, H-J. and others (2001). *Financial Liberalization and the Asian Crisis*. London: Palgrave.

Clerides, S. and others (1998). Is learning by exporting important? Micro-Dynamic evidence from Columbia, Mexico, and Morocco. *Quarterly Journal of Economics* 113.

Darity W and L. Davis, (2005). Growth, trade and uneven development, *Cambridge Journal of Economics*, 29 no.1.

Driffield, N. and J. Love (2005). Intra-industry foreign direct investment, uneven development and globalisation: The legacy of Stephan Hymer. *Contributions to Political Economy*, 24.

de Mello, L (1997). Foreign direct investment in developing countries and growth: A selective survey. *Journal of Development Studies* 34 (1).

Dicken, P. (2004). *Global Shift: Transforming the World Economy*. 4th ed. London: Paul Chapman.

Dowrick, S. and J. Golley (2004). Trade openness and growth: Who benefits? *Oxford Review of Economic Policy*, 20, Spring.

Edwards, S (1998). Openess, productivity and growth: What do we really know? NBER Working Paper no. 5978, Cambridge, National Bureau of Economic Research

Evan, P (1979). *Dependent Development: The Alliance of Multinational, State and Local Capital in Brazil*. Princeton: Princeton University Press,

Findlay, R. (1991). Comparative advantage. *Palgrave Economic Dictionary*. London: Macmillan.

Frankel, J. and D. Romer (1999). Does trade cause growth? *American Economic Review* 89 (3), June.

Ghosh, A (2004). Capital inflows and investment in developing countries. *Employment Strategy Papers* November, Geneva, ILO.

Glyn, A (2004). The assessment: How far has globalization gone?. *Oxford Review of Economic Policy*. Oxford University Press, 20(1).

Glyn, A (2006). *Capitalism Unleashed. Finance, Globalization, and Welfare*. Oxford: Oxford University Press.

Gomory, R. and W. Baumol (2000). *Global Trade and Conflicting National Interests*. Cambridge, MA.: MIT Press.

Gorg H and Greenaway D (2001). Foreign direct investment and intra-industry spillovers. Paper prepared for the UNECE/EBRD Expert Meeting Financing for Development. Geneva, 3 December.

Harrison, A (1996). Openness and growth: A time-series, cross-country analysis for developing countries. *Journal of Development Economics*, 48.

Harrison, A., and M. Macmillan, (2003) Does direct foreign investment affect domestic credit growth? *Journal of International Economics* Volume 61, 1.

Heintz, J (2003). The new face of unequal exchange: Low-wage manufacturing, commodity chains and global inequality. *Political Economy Research Institute, Working Paper Series* (59), Amherst, University of Massachusetts.

Helleiner, G (1973). 'Manufacturing exports from less developed countries and multinational firms, *Economic Journal*, 83.

Helleiner, G (2000). Markets, politics and globalization: Can the global economy be civilised? Tenth Raúl Prebisch Lecture, Geneva UNCTAD.

Henderson, J (1991). *The Globalisation of High Technology Production*. London: Routledge.

Hymer, Stephen (1960). *The International Operations of National Firms: A Study of Direct Foreign Investment*. Cambridge: MIT Press (1976).

IMF (1997). *World Economic Outlook*. Washington DC, IMF.

Imbs, J. and T.R. Wacziarg, (2000). Stages of diversification, CEPR Discussion Paper no. 2642, London CEPR.

Jomo K.S. ed. (with Jacques Baudot), (2006). *Flat World, Big Gaps: Economic Liberalization Gobalization, Poverty and Inequality*. London, Zed Press.

Kaplinsky, R. and M. Morris (2002). The globalization of product markets and immiserising growth: Lessons from the South African Furniture Industry. *World Development*, 30 (7).

Kenny, C. and D. Williams (2001). What do we know about economic growth? Or, why don't we know very much? *World Development*, 29.

Kumar, N. and J. P. Pradhan, (2002). Foreign direct investment,externalities and economic growth in developing countries: Some empirical explorations and implications for WTO negotiations on investment, RIS Discussion Paper 27, RIS, New Delhi.

Kozul-Wright, R (2006). Globalization now and again, in Jomo K.S. ed., *Globalization under Hegemony: The Changing World Economy*, New York, Oxford University Press.

Kozul-Wright, R. and P. Rayment, forthcoming, *The Resistible Rise of Market Fundamentalism: Rethinking Development Policy in an Unbalanced World*. London, Zed.

Krugman, P (1995). Growing World Trade: Causes and Consequences. *Brookings Papers on Economic Activity*, 1.

Krugman, P. and M. Obstfeld (1997). *International Economics: Theory and Policy*. Reading: Addison-Wesley.

Lim, E-G (2001). Determinants of, and relation between foreign direct investment and growth: A summary of the recent literature. IMF Working Paper 175, Washington D.C. IMF.

Lucas, R (2000). Some macroeconomics for the 21st century: *Journal of Economic Perspectives*, 14 (1).

Maizels, A (2000). The manufactures terms of trade of developing countries with the United States (1981–1997). Working Paper 36, Queen Elizabeth House, Oxford University.

Maizels, A. and others (1998). The Prebisch-Singer hypothesis revisited. In D. Sapsford, and J. Chen (eds). What is the title of this book? London: Macmillan Press.

Mankiw, G. and others (1992). A Contribution to the Empirics of Economic Growth. *Quarterly Journal of Economics*, May, 107

Milanovic, B (2002). True world income distribution 1988 and 1993: First calculations based on household surveys alone. *The Economic Journal* 112.

Milanovic, B. and S. Yitzhaki (2001). Decomposing world income distribution: Does the world have a middle class? World Bank Policy Research Working Paper No. 2562, February.

Milberg, W. ed (2004). *Labour and the Globalisation of Production: Causes and Consequences of Industrial Upgrading*. New York,Palgrave.

Mody, A (2004). Is FDI Integrating the World Economy? Paper presented at the XIII World Congress of the International Economics Association in Lisbon, Portugal, September 2002. Forthcoming in *World Economy*.

North, D (1993). Economic performance through time. The Alfred Nobel Lecture, Oslo, Norway.

Nunnenkamp, P and J. Spatz (2004). FDI and economic growth in developing countries: how relevant are host-economy and industry characteristics? *Transnational Corporations*, 13 (3).

Nayyar, D. ed (2002). *Governing Globalization: Issues and Institutions*, Oxford: Oxford University Press.

Quah, D (1996). Twin peaks: Growth and convergence in models of distribution dynamics. *Economic Journal*, 106.

Rasiah, R (2006). Sustaining development through garment exports in Cambodia. Processed, Faculty of Economics and Administration. Kuala Lumpur, University of Malaya.

Rodriguez, F., and D Rodrik (1999). Trade policy and economic growth: A skeptic's guide to the cross-national evidence. NBER Working Paper no. 7081, National Bureau of Economic Research.

Rodrik, Dani (1999). *The New Global Economy and Developing Countries: Making Openness Work*. Washington DC: Overseas Development Council.

Rodrik, Dani (2002). Feasible globalizations. NBER Working Papers 9129, National Bureau of Economic Research.

Rodrik, Dani (2006). Understanding South Africa's Economic Puzzles. NBER Working Paper No. 12565 National Bureau of Economic Research

Rogoff, K (1999). International institutions for reducing global financial instability. *Journal of Economic Perspectives*, 13, fall.

Rogoff, K. and others (2006). Financial globalization: A reappraisal. NBER Working Paper no 12484, National Bureau of Economic Research

Rowthorn, R (1992). Intra-industry trade under oligopoly: the role of market size. *Economic Journal*, vol.102.

Rowthorn, R., and J. Wells (1987). *Deindustrialisation and Foreign Trade*. Cambridge: Cambridge University Press.

Sala-I-Martin, X (1996). The classical approach to convergence analysis . *The Economic Journal* 106.

Sachs, J., and A. Warner (1995). Economic reform and the process of global integration. *Brookings Papers on Economic Activity* 1.

Scott, M.F (1991). *A New View of Economic Growth*, Clarendon Press, Oxford.

Singer, H (1950). The Distribution of Gains between Investing and Borrowing Countries. *American Economic Review* 40 (2).

Smith, A (1976). *The Theory of Moral Sentiments*. Oxford: Clarendon Press.

Spiezia, V (2004). Trade, foreign direct investment and employment: Some empirical evidence. In E. Lee and M. Vivarelli (eds). *Understanding Globalization, Employment and Poverty Reduction*. New York: Palgrave Macmillan.

Stiglitz, J (2002). *Globalization and its Discontents*. London: Penguin Books.

Stiglitz, J. (2006). Making Globalization Work, WW Norton, New York.

Sutcliffe, B (2006). A converging or diverging world? In Jomo K.S ed., *Flat World, Big Gaps: Economic Literalization, Globalization and Inequality*. London: Zed Books.

Taylor, L (1994). Hirschman's strategy at thirty-five. In L. Rodwin and D. Schon, eds. *Rethinking the Development Experience: Essays Provoked by the Work of Albert O. Hirschman*. Washington, DC: Brookings Institution.

Temple, J. and P. Johnson (1998). Social capability and economic growth. *Quarterly Journal of Economics*, 113 (3).

Toner, P (1999). *Main Currents in Cumulative Causation: The Dynamics of Growth and Development*. London, Macmillan.

UNCTAD (2002). *Trade and Development Report 2002*. New York and Geneva: United Nations.

UNCTAD (2003). *Trade and Development Report 2003* . New York and Geneva: United Nations.

UNCTAD (2005). *Economic Development in Africa: Performance, Prospects and Policy Issues.* New York and Geneva: United Nations.

UNCTAD (2006a). *Economic Development in Africa: Performance, Prospects and Policy Issues.* New York and Geneva: United Nations.

UNCTAD (2006b). *Trade and Development Report 2002.* New York and Geneva: United Nations.

UNCTAD/ECLAC (2002). Summary and conclusions. Joint Regional Seminar on FDI policies in Latin America, Santiago, Chile, 7–9 January.

United Nations (2006). *World Economic and Social Survey 2006: Diverging Growth and Development*, United Nations, New York.

Vartianen, J (1995). The state and structural change: What can be learnt from successful Late Industrializers. In H-J Chang and R. Rowthorn eds., *The Role of the State in Economic Change.* Oxford: Clarendon Press.

Wacziarg, R. and K. Welch (2003). Trade Liberalization and Growth: New Evidence. NBER Working Papers 10152, National Bureau of Economic Research

Wade, R (1995). Resolving the state-market dilemma in East Asia. In H-J Chang and R. Rowthorn, eds. *The Role of the State in Economic Change*, Oxford, Clarendon Press.

Wieczorek-Zeul, H (2004). Statement to Development Committee, October 2.

Winters, L. A (2004). Trade liberalization and economic performance: An overview. *The Economic Journal* 114 (February: F4–F21).

Wolf, M (2004). *Why Globalization works.* New Haven and London: Yale University Press.

Wood, A (1994). *North-South Trade, Employment and Inequality: Changing Fortunes in a Skill-Driven World.* Oxford: Oxford University Press.

World Bank (2002). *Globalization, Growth and Poverty: Building An Inclusive World Economy.* Oxford: Oxford University Press.

World Bank (2003). *Global Economic Prospects*, Washington D.C.: World Bank

3

Productive Structure and Effective Demand during the Great Divergence: Regional Contrasts

CODRINA RADA AND LANCE TAYLOR[*]

This study is about the growth and development performance of non-industrialized countries in the latter part of the twentieth century, in particular about a "great divergence" of their growth rates of per capita Gross Domestic Product (GDP) since around 1980. Our goal is to explore the factors underlying this pattern, and trace out plausible lines of causation for its diversity. The analysis follows Kuznets (1966) in attempting to organize the data in such a way as to highlight salient relationships, or the lack thereof, among key economic variables.

Changes in growth trends and widening income inequality among developing countries and between developed and most developing countries coincided with important changes in views on economic policies. A major shift occurred worldwide after the 1970s and 1980s when, under the tutelage of World Bank and International Monetary Fund (IMF), most developing countries moved to liberalize their external current and capital accounts along with domestic labour and financial markets. They also privatized public enterprises, de-emphasized industrial policy interventions, and encouraged a greater private sector role in general. Emphasis was placed on supply-side "accumulation" processes, for physical and human capital and foreign direct investment (FDI). Fiscal austerity figured in many programs sponsored by the Bretton Woods Institutions. More than a quarter of a century has passed since the first versions of IMF and World Bank macro reforms became the conventional wisdom. Data are now available for a long enough time to enable policy analysts to sort their implications out.

At best, the new orientation had mixed results in either reversing the slowdown in growth that many countries encountered in the last quarter of the twentieth century (details below) or helping them break away from their poverty and low level development traps (Taylor, 2001, 2006; Vos, Taylor and Paes de Barros, 2002). Indeed, income gaps have widened over time.

We begin by investigating economic evolution for the period 1970–2003, studying several indicators to see how they relate to the growth or non-growth of per capita GDP. The policy background is then brought in, with emphasis on ideas emanating from the Bretton Woods institutions. Suggestions are offered about other approaches to policy that may help generate more sustained and equitable development than has been the case in the recent past.

To keep the discussion within bounds, the data are organized in terms of 12 regional groups including 57 developing and transition countries: rapidly growing East Asian economies (or the "Tigers"), Southeast Asia, China, South Asia, semi-industrialized "Latin America" (including South Africa and Turkey with economic structures similar to their counterparts in the Western Hemisphere), the Andean countries, Central America and the Caribbean, Central and Eastern Europe, Russia and Ukraine representing the former USSR, "representative" and "other" countries in sub-Saharan Africa[1], and the Middle East. The nations in each group are listed in the Appendix.

DIVERGENCE IN THE 20TH CENTURY

To set the discussion, Figure 3.1 shows the GDP and sectoral per capita output growth rates by region in constant 1990 US dollars.[2] We identify three cohorts of regions and countries that had similar patterns of growth:

There was *sustained growth* in the Tigers, China, Southeast Asia, and South Asia (dominated by India). Relative to the other regions, South Asia had less robust expansion and Southeast Asia did not bounce back as strongly from the 1997 crisis as did the Tigers. These regions "diverged upwardly" from the rest of the developing world.

The second, *late recovery* group includes semi-industrialized Latin America, Central America and Caribbean, and Central and Eastern Europe. All the regions showed somewhat faster growth late in the century, although formerly socialist Europe is in an ambiguous situation. Over the period 1970–2003 it grew slightly faster in per capita terms than South Asia (2.7 per cent vs. 2.6 per cent per year) but because of the transition shock around 1990 it seemed more appropriate to call its case one of "late recovery."

Finally, the two African regions with other Africa dominated by Nigeria, the Andean group, the Middle East, and Russia and Ukraine were either *stagnant* throughout the period or experienced volatile economic expansion. Data for the last decade suggest that Representative Africa and Russia and Ukraine have been enjoying growth which if is continues could advance them into the late recovery group.

IDENTIFYING STRUCTURAL CHANGE

Sustained growth in successful regions was associated with changes in economic structure in several dimensions. The slow growers did *not* generate such changes. Economists trained in the structuralist tradition hold that development requires economic transformation or the "ability of an economy to constantly generate new dynamic activities" (Ocampo, 2005) characterized by higher productivity and increasing returns to scale. Our evidence supports this point of view. Recognizing the structural shifts that occurred in the regions with sustained growth can help chart future directions that other developing economies may be able to take. Needless to say, any economy is a unique entity with its own characteristics that require its own policies. But stylized facts show that there are dynamic movements of key macro variables that show up in connection with sustained output growth across different economic systems.

Throughout this chapter we analyze these movements from several angles, in terms of formalized decomposition exercises (for the algebraic details, see Taylor and Rada, 2006a: Appendix II) and more informal analysis of data on foreign trade patterns.

FIGURE 3.1
Sectoral growth rates, 1970–2003

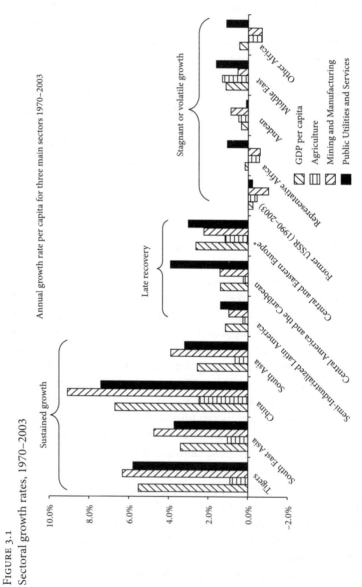

Annual growth rate per capita for three main sectors 1970–2003

Source: World Development Indicators 2005 database

One decomposition breaks down labour productivity growth between agricultural, industrial, and service sectors. Overall productivity growth comes out as an average of own-rates of growth, weighted by output shares, for all sectors along with "reallocation effects" which are positive for sectors with relatively low average productivity in which employment falls or for high-productivity sectors in which employment rises.[3]

A second exercise focuses on growth rates of the economy-wide employment to population ratio which is decomposed into an average of growth rates of the ratio by sectors weighted by employment shares. At both the national and sectoral levels, the ratio of employment to total population will rise if the growth rate of output per capita exceeds growth of labour productivity.[4] An economy can be considered to be performing well if it has both sustained productivity growth and a stable or rising employment–population ratio.

Thirdly, we examine the association between capital stock and output growth. We also contrast growth rates of labour and capital productivity and ask how they feed into widely used but fundamentally misleading calculations of "total factor productivity growth." The two inputs' productivity growth rates turn out to be linked by a simple accounting identity, which helps explain the "Asian" pattern of falling capital productivity over time.

Finally, we look at net borrowing flows – incomes minus expenditures – over time for the government, private, and rest of the world "institutional sectors", normalized by GDP.[5] As an accounting identity, borrowings must sum to zero:

(Private investment – saving) + (Public spending – taxes) + (Exports – Imports) = 0,

with a positive entry indicating that a sector is a net contributor to effective demand. Changing sectoral roles in this equation can be important aspects of the growth process. For example, as shown below, mutually offsetting co-movements of government and foreign net borrowing occurred sporadically at most. In other words, the widely accepted "twin deficits" view of macro adjustment does not seem to apply. Nor do the data suggest that "consumption-smoothing" behaviour – an important feature of mainstream Ricardian equivalence growth theory – is empirically relevant. Macroeconomic flexibility, on the other hand, may be very important. Strong fluctuations in private and foreign net borrowing did not derail growth in the upwardly diverging Tigers and, to a lesser extent, Southeast Asia.

OUTPUT GROWTH PATTERNS

The contrast in Figure 3.1 between Asia and Eastern Europe and the other regions is striking. The Asian regions (even South Asia) had very high growth rates in industry. Service sector growth was strong in Central and Eastern Europe and, to a lesser extent, in Latin America and Central American and the Caribbean.

Figure 3.2 presents scatter plots of per capita GDP growth in the agriculture and industry vs. the percentage changes in their respective sectoral shares (again for 1970–2003). The rapidly growing Asian countries identified in Figure 3.1 showed substantial shifts in shares, in the classic movement from primary toward secondary and tertiary sectors.

The agricultural share shows a negatively sloped regression line for the whole 12-region sample. But contrast the results for the five fast-growing regions with those for the others. While the former show a clear relationship between faster output growth and a decreasing share, the lagging seven regions generate a random scatter – a result that will repeat itself for several other indicators of structural change. Among the rapid growers, China's agricultural share fell by an astonishing 34 percentage points over the period. In South and Southeast Asia, agriculture saw its output share decline 19 and 17 percentage points respectively. The rising agricultural shares in the Andean and Middle Eastern regions are anomalous as is the decrease accompanied by negative growth in Russia and Ukraine.

Similar observations apply to the industrial sector and service sectors with clear associations emerging for the rapid growers and ill-defined data clouds for the other regions. Growth is associated with structural change and the absence of growth is not.

The growing regions had rising industrial shares as can be observed in the northern quadrant of Figure 3.2. Four slow growers suffered

FIGURE 3.2
Growth performance and structural change in industry and agriculture

Annual GDP per capita growth and changes in Industrial and agriculture output shares (1970–2003)

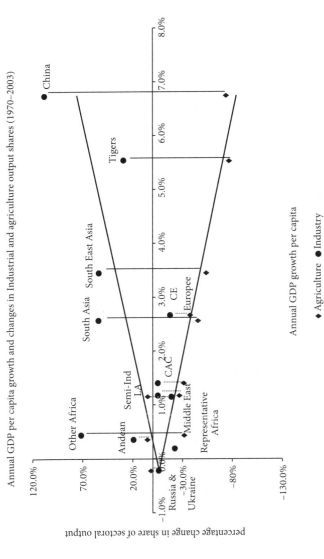

Source: UN National Accounts.

long-term deindustrialization, while the industrial share in Russia and Ukraine scarcely budged. Big shifts in industrial shares in the Middle East and other Africa (with Nigeria as the largest economy included) were driven by developments in the petroleum sector.

The fast growers had predictable increases in the service sector share as well (details not shown here). The Tiger region service share rose to 64 percent by 2003, and supported strong job creation as reported below. There was no apparent relationship for the lagging regions.

Labour Productivity Growth

Historically, labour productivity increases have been the major contributing factor to growth in real GDP per capita. At the same time, faster productivity increases cut into employment growth unless they are offset by rising effective demand. The five rapidly growing regions had productivity growth rates exceeding – some greatly exceeding – the rich country norm of two per cent per year. The others fell well short, and the former USSR had negative productivity growth.

In terms of phasing over time, more detailed results show that Russia/Ukraine suffered an enormous productivity collapse (-9.7 per cent per year) in 1991–1995, but then recovered to 5.6 per cent (1999–2003). Central and Eastern Europe showed a similar though far less violent pattern. The Tiger region rapidly recovered its productivity growth rate of 4–5 per cent per year after the 1997 Asian crisis. Southeast Asia also had 4–5 per cent annual productivity growth prior to the 1997, but rates tailed off thereafter. The other regions had growth rate fluctuations over time but no clear trends.

Figures 3.3 (a–d) summarize direct and reallocation contributions by sector to overall productivity increases. Agriculture in Figure 3.3a evidently did not play a crucial role in the process. In several countries agriculture's reallocation effects were negative. The meaning is that this sector, with its relatively low average productivity, had positive employment growth. This finding is not surprising in countries such as China, South Asia, and Africa where agriculture's share in total employment is significant but the result is slightly discordant in the Middle East.

FIGURE 3.3 (a–d)
Contribution of main sectors to productivity growth and sectoral shifts in employment/population ratios

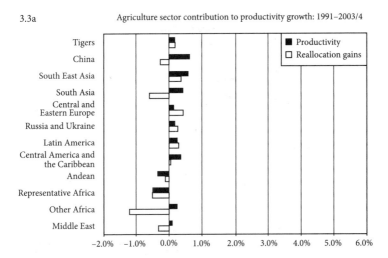

3.3a   Agriculture sector contribution to productivity growth: 1991–2003/4

3.3b   Industrial sector contribution to productivity growth: 1991–2003/4

3.3c

Service sector contribution to productivity growth: 1991–2003/4

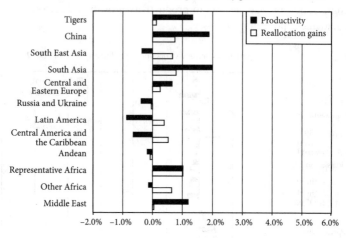

3.3d

Sectoral contribution to employment 1991–2003/4

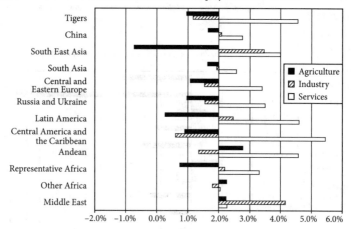

Sources: International Labour Office, GET database, for employment and World Bank, *World Development Indicators 2005* database, for output.

The industrial sector's own productivity growth made a substantial contribution to the total in four of the rapidly growing regions (Figure 3.3b) and there was a strong reallocation contribution in Southeast Asia, the outlier. The direct contribution of nearly six per cent per year in China is striking. Industry made a visible contribution in the two poorer Western Hemisphere regions but detracted from overall performance in Russia and Ukraine and the Middle East, with the latter gaining from reallocation.

Services in Figure 3.3c also added to the total in the rapid growers: as with industry, a negative direct but positive reallocation contribution in Southeast Asia. In other regions, the direct contribution from services was typically negative with modest positive contributions from reallocation. This distinction among regions has implications for job creation, as taken up below.

Finally, from an alternative data set we were able to do decompositions for the period 1980–2000 for the four Asian regions, with 1986 as the starting year for South Asia (not shown here). The same general pattern holds as in Figures 3 (a–c), with services playing a more important role in the Tigers.

The bottom line on productivity growth is that the two non-agricultural sectors made solid contributions to the total in the fast-growing regions, even as their overall importance in the economy rose. Elsewhere the results were a mixed bag, with no clear patterns emerging. Insofar as it is measured by average labour productivity growth, technological advance was evident in the growing regions and absent or, at best, sporadically present in other corners of the world.

EMPLOYMENT GROWTH PATTERNS

Figure 3.3d summarizes our results regarding shifts in sectoral employment to population ratios in terms of their contributions to changes in the ratio economy-wide. Regional growth rates of the overall ratio hovered around zero, with more positive than negative values. As noted above, at both the sectoral and national levels, the ratio(s) will grow when the growth rate of output per capita exceeds labour productivity growth. The ratio(s) will also tend to rise when population growth is negative, as was the case in Eastern Europe and the former Soviet Union.

The most striking outcome in Figure 3.3d is the apparent *similarity* of all 12 regions in the sense that services showed a rising employment to output ratio everywhere, rather strongly except in Other Africa, the Middle East, and (to an extent) South Asia. The details, however, differed between fast- and slow-growing regions.

For the rapid growers, the positive contribution of services to employment growth shows that output per capita grew faster than the sector's rising productivity levels that underlie its positive contributions to growth overall (darkened bars in Figure 3.3c). Positive reallocation gains were due to the fact that services have relatively high average productivity. In the slower growing regions, direct contributions of services to economy-wide productivity were weak but rising demand still created jobs. Productivity did not increase rapidly within the sector but via reallocation effects the shifts in employment toward it (reflected in Figure 3.3d) added to overall productivity growth.

Relative to total population, agriculture was a source of employable labour in nine regions, very strongly in Southeast Asia, and a sink only in the Middle East, Other Africa, and (especially) in the Andean region. Only in the Middle East and Southeast Asia was the industrial sector a strong provider of jobs (a fact explaining Southeast Asian industry's strong reallocation contribution to overall productivity growth in Figure 3.3b). Consistent with Figures 3.1 and 3.2, industry's rate of productivity growth tended to exceed its growth in demand per capita. An old structuralist observation in development economics is that the industrial sector is the main motor for productivity increases but not for job creation.

Capital Productivity and Total Factor Productivity Growth (TFPG)

The next topic is the role of capital accumulation in growth. We computed capital stock growth rates for the regions by cumulating real gross fixed capital formation over time from a postulated initial level of the capital stock (capital-output ratio of 2.5) with a depreciation rate of 0.05. As discussed more fully in Taylor and Rada (2006a: Appendix II), after a decade or two such estimates of the capital growth rate should be insensitive to the parameters because capital stock growth tends to converge to investment growth over time.[6]

Figure 3.4 compares growth rates of output and the capital stock. In contrast to most other indicators discussed herein, there is a clear positive association between the two growth rates across *all* regions – a standard empirical result. This relationship is usually thought to emerge from the supply side as discussed immediately below, but it also could be attributed to demand. In a simple model based on effective demand, if investment grows at a certain rate then output and (as just indicated) the capital stock will ultimately grow at that rate as well. The fact that the slope of the putative relationship between the two growth rates in Figure 3.4 is close to one argues more for a demand- than supply-side story. In the latter, the slope would exceed 45 degrees, with a less than one-for-one partial impact of faster capital growth on output growth.[7]

FIGURE 3.4
Output and capital stock growth rates, 1990–2004

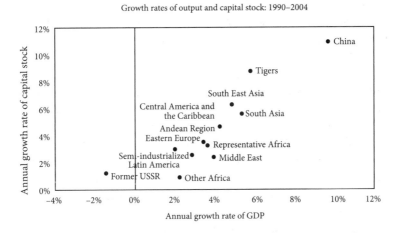

Growth rates of output and capital stock: 1990–2004

Also note that the capital growth rate exceeded output growth in the Tigers, China, Southeast Asia and the former USSR. These regions had *falling* capital productivity. Such an outcome can be expected in the rapidly growing Asian regions where industrial restructuring took place towards capital-intensive industries. Nevertheless these findings can also be said to be the outcome of accounting requirements As demonstrated in Taylor and Rada (2006a: Appendix II), the difference between labour and capital productivity growth rates must be equal to the difference between capital and labour growth rates as a "theorem of accounting". If capital grows faster than labour, then labour productivity has to grow faster than capital productivity.[8] If the capital to labour ratio rises very rapidly, then capital productivity growth may even have to be negative. This outcome is sometimes said to characterize an "Asian" pattern of growth, or a "Marx bias" in technical progress. It can also result from negative labour force growth as in the former USSR and Eastern Europe.

Capital and labour productivity growth rates are plotted in Figure 3.5. Again note the contrast between regions. The rapid growers all had negative or nearly zero capital productivity growth rates and rising labour productivity which could have resulted from better technology "embodied" in new capital goods. Detailed data show that China's capital productivity fell more rapidly over time. The former USSR lost on both fronts and the rest had small, mostly positive, growth of both indicators.

Instead of asking whether capital stock growth impacts directly on labour productivity (a question we could not directly address with our data set), much of the productivity literature focuses on "total factor productivity growth" (TFPG) or the "residual." TFPG turns out to be a weighted average of labour and capital productivity growth rates, with the weights being the labour and non-labour income shares of value-added at factor cost. The question then becomes: what is the labour share? In developing countries, the share of *remunerated* labour income in GDP is likely to be less than 40 per cent. Most economically active people are not paid wages but rather toil within unincorporated proprietorships such as urban petty commerce, as labourers on peasant farms etc. The market value of their work must be imputed in one way or another, with all the calculations being extremely dubious.

Figure 3.5 shows estimates of TFPG for labour shares of 0.4 (realistic?) and 0.7 (the standard number) respectively. Either way, because of their negative capital productivity growth, TFPG in the

FIGURE 3.5
Capital and labour productivity growth rates and TFPG

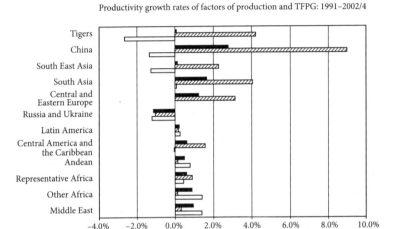

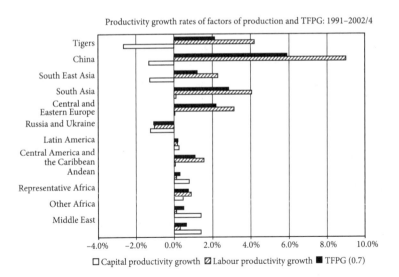

Sources: GFCF and GDP data comes from World Development Indicators 2005 database; employment data is from International Labour Office, GET database.

rapidly growing regions fell well short of labour productivity growth. For the lower labour share, TFPG in the Tigers and Southeast Asia was close to zero. Such findings are often used to portray the failings of the "Asian model," but mostly they reflect an accounting identity and the arbitrary nature of the TFPG indicator.

DIVERSIFICATION OF TRADE

Regional diversity persists when we take up changes in patterns of foreign trade which accompany structural changes of the economy. We examine the technological composition of exports and changes in sectoral composition of exports and imports. For the sake of space we present visually only the changes in sectoral composition of exports in Figure 3.6.[9]

Fast-growing regions generally had increases in the shares of manufactured exports. The same trend is observed in the composition of imports with manufactures taking a greater role in regions such as Southeast Asia in which assembly operations are important. The rapid growers typically also had rising technological content of exports, the most impressive being the Tigers where high-tech exports represented 48 per cent of total exports in 2002 compared to 16 per cent two decades before. Technological upgrading was less evident in slow-growing regions. In fact several slow growers such as the Andeans maintained or even enhanced traditional patterns of specialization in mining products and/or agriculture.

OPEN ECONOMIES AND THEIR PATTERNS OF NET BORROWING

Next, we take up interactions between demand and supply. The focus is on the balance of payments, often the fulcrum for both short- and long-term limitations on growth in developing economies. There are at least three incompatible contemporary doctrines regarding how open macro-economies operate. Twin deficits (TD) and Ricardian equivalence (RE) dogmata are widely spread in mainstream literature,

FIGURE 3.6
Composition of exports by commodity, 1980 and early 2000s

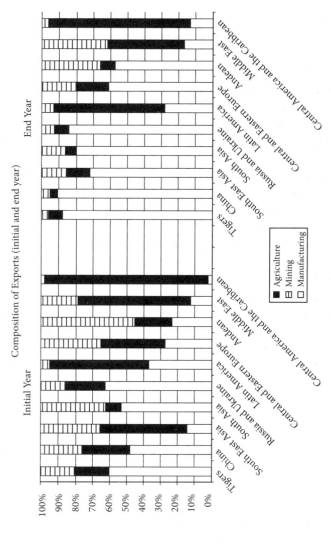

Source: World Trade Organization database.

while development and heterodox economists often favour a structural gap (SG) explanation of external balance.

In development macroeconomics, the twin deficits hypothesis traces back at least to the IMF economist Jacques Polak's (1957) blueprint for the "financial programming" exercises that to this day are the linchpin of the Fund's stabilization packages worldwide. The recipe for action is to cut the fiscal deficit, which is supposed to improve the economy's external position. Polak, of course, was drawing on a long tradition of monetarist analysis of the balance of payments. In one variant, unless the private sector chooses to increase its saving – or, more precisely, reduce its net borrowing as discussed below – then a higher fiscal deficit must be paid for by domestic money creation. Aggregate demand consequently goes up. Under tacit assumptions that all resources are fully employed and the domestic price level is tied to foreign prices by arbitrage in foreign trade (purchasing power parity or PPP applies), the higher demand has to spill over into a bigger trade deficit.

Ricardian equivalence (Barro, 1974) emerges from dynamic optimal savings models postulating that all resources are fully employed and that households smooth their consumption (or, more generally, expenditure) over time. It plays a far more central role in contemporary mainstream macroeconomics than Polak's somewhat dated monetarism[10]. Along the lines of Say's Law, RE broadly asserts that a change in fiscal net borrowing will be offset by an equal shift in private net lending. In an open economy context, any one country's external position then has to be determined by inter-temporal trade-offs between consumption and saving with all countries in the world producing the same good (Obstfeld and Rogoff, 1997). In this context, traditional counter-cyclical fiscal policy does not play a role.

However TD and RE stories are not compatible because they assign different roles to private and foreign net borrowing. Under TD, private borrowing is "neutral" in that it does not respond to shifts in the foreign or fiscal positions. Under RE, the current account is neutral with regard to fiscal shifts while private and government borrowing dance the trade-offs.

Finally, causality can also be interpreted as running the other way – from the foreign to the fiscal and/or private sector financial gap. Perhaps the external deficit is "structural" and will persist in the face of plausible domestic policy changes. In this sense, structure is built into foreign trade. Within "reasonable" ranges of real exchange rate values and the level of economic activity, the trade deficit – or surplus, say for China or Germany – will not change by very much. It need not be close to zero because of lacking or excess competitiveness of domestic producing sectors.

SG analysis resembles full employment RE in that its binding external gap imposes a supply constraint on the system. Particularly in a developing country context, the question becomes how does effective demand adjust to meet the commodity supply permitted by available imports? To hold demand stable, any shift in the private or public sector net borrowing position has to be reflected into an offsetting change in the other domestic gap, as under RE. Mechanisms that can make this happen are sketched below. If private net borrowing is neutral, then fiscal deficit will reflect a shift in the external gap: TD with causality reversed. It becomes interesting to see what patterns emerge from the data.

FIGURE 3.7

Resource gaps by institutional sectors in the Tigers, China and South East Asia

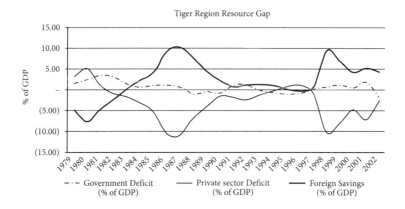

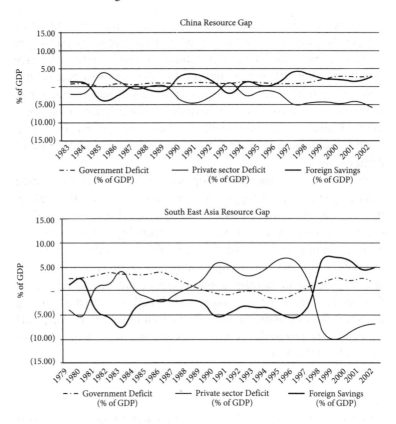

Source: United Nations Common Database

Several borrowing styles can be identified. In the Asian regions in Figure 3.7, the fiscal role was rather passive, with major adjustments taking place between private and foreign net borrowing. The private and foreign co-movements were relatively large, with swings up and down exceeding 10 per cent of GDP in the Tigers and Southeast Asia. Big reductions in external deficits were forced from abroad in the 1997 crisis, but upswings tended to be associated with falling private saving and rising import propensities. Maintaining very high per capita income growth over a 25-year period with the macro economy subject to such extreme fluctuations is a feat perhaps unprecedented historically.

FIGURE 3.8
Resource gaps by institutional sectors in South Asia and semi-industrialized Latin America

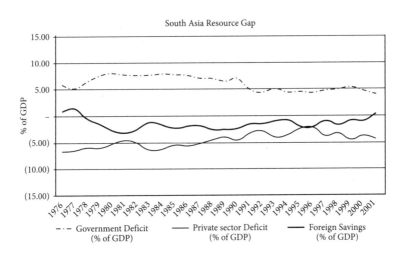

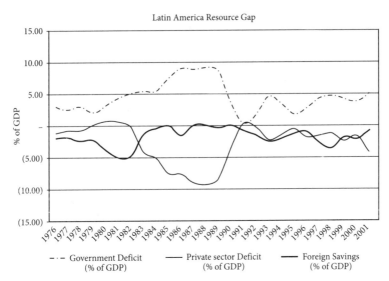

Source: United Nations Common Database

Figure 3.8 shows the history for two regions with persistently high levels of government net borrowing – rapidly growing South Asia and economically stagnant middle income Latin America. South Asia's private net lending share resembles China's, except that the private surplus financed a fiscal deficit while China's external account was in surplus. The large fiscal deficit (largely driven by India) did not create an equally large external gap because along SG lines hard currency was not available (until very recently) to pay for expanded imports. The private sector was the only possible source of finance for the government's net borrowing. Except for the latter part of the recessionary "lost decade" of the 1980s, Latin America appeared to have a more or less structural external deficit. Note the wide offsetting swings in the government and private borrowing flows along East Asian lines, unfortunately associated with a long period of economic stagnation as opposed to the other region's rapid growth. A massive dose of fiscal austerity in the late 1980s courtesy of the IMF had a very modest impact on the external deficit but was met by increased private borrowing, in a pattern that later partially reversed.

In Figure 3.9, the Andean economies, Central America and the Caribbean, Eastern Europe, and representative Africa appear to have structural external deficits. In all cases the fiscal deficit was cut back (in the 1980s in Latin America and Africa and the 1990s in Eastern Europe) as IMF-sponsored stabilization programs were wheeled into place. Rather than reductions in external deficits, there were increases in the private net borrowing, with subsequent oscillations between private and government positions.

In the Middle East (not shown here) from around 1980 until the mid-1990s, a trend reduction in the fiscal deficit was accompanied by a falling foreign deficit. A similar pattern showed up in the former-USSR after the mid-1990s. In both regions, the "structural" factor was almost certainly the external position, with the fiscal accounts accommodating. In other words improvements in the fiscal position as in Russia/Ukraine and the Middle East were probably driven by a better balance of payments, rather than the opposite.

FIGURE 3.9
Resource gaps by institutional sectors in Central and Eastern Europe, Central America and the Caribbean, Andean region and Representative Africa.

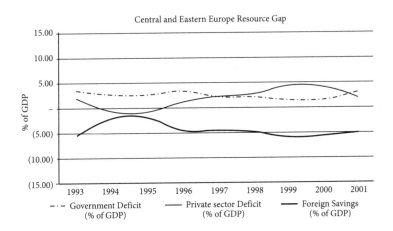

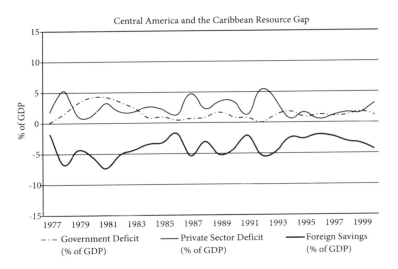

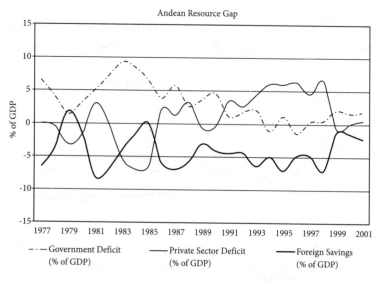

Andean Resource Gap

- - —Government Deficit   ——Private Sector Deficit   ——Foreign Savings
(% of GDP)   (% of GDP)   (% of GDP)

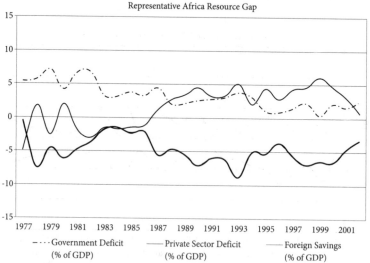

Representative Africa Resource Gap

- - · ·Government Deficit   ——Private Sector Deficit   ——Foreign Savings
(% of GDP)   (% of GDP)   (% of GDP)

Source: United Nations Common Database.

Crowding-out of private demand by higher public demand under a binding external constraint that holds output roughly constant is a familiar story. Harking back to Polak's monetarist stance, if prices are *not* stabilized by PPP then they may begin to rise in response to higher effective demand. Inflation tax and forced saving mechanisms can kick in, reducing real demand by the private sector (Taylor, 2004). In Figures 3.8 and 3.9, such processes also appeared to work in reverse. Austerity relaxed the squeeze on the private sector, and its demand went up by enough to keep output close to the limit imposed by a structural external gap.

With regard to RE, there is scant evidence suggesting the presence of consumption-smoothing in the sense of rising private sector net lending in response to higher output. In four of the five rapidly growing regions, private net borrowing went up as a share of GDP and net lending fell during periods of sustained, rapid growth. The exception is China after the mid-1980s, but there it is at least plausible to argue that the rising external surplus drove the observed rise in private net lending than the reverse.

The Policy Background

As noted at the outset, a major policy shift occurred worldwide beginning in the 1970s and 1980s – a move on the part of most countries to deregulate or liberalize their external current and capital accounts along with domestic labour and financial markets. Our empirical results help trace out its implications.

As Figure 3.1 illustrates, growth performances deteriorated after 1980 in many parts of the world. Clear success cases at the country level – various Tigers, China, Vietnam in Southeast Asia, and more recently India – are scarcely paragons of neo-liberalism. Some Eastern European policy-makers think of themselves in that way but many vestiges of the old order remain.

Moreover, the fact that structural change in several dimensions – output and labour share shifts, trade diversification, sustained productivity growth with strong reallocation effects in some cases – showed up strongly in the fast-growing economies, and sporadically elsewhere, carry an implicit message that intelligent sector-level policies can facilitate the development process. To an extent, structural change can be planned.

In macro terms, austerity was supposed to lead to improvement in external balances along IMF financial programming lines. The decompositions described just above show clearly that was not the common outcome. Even falling government deficits and rising external surpluses in the Middle East and Russia are better explained from the external than domestic side. More typical were co-movements of private and government or, less frequently, private and foreign borrowing flows. These patterns have to be examined in terms of the specific macro behaviour of each economy concerned.

Macroeconomic flexibility, although difficult to define and probably even harder to attain, also appears to be important. Witness the wide swings in net borrowing flows between 1980 and 2000 in the Tigers and Southeast Asia. Through it all, they continued to grow.

Stated goals of the liberalization package were to enhance labour productivity and employment growth. Outside the consistently expanding economies, this did not happen. Productivity movements across sectors differed in detail across slow-growing and stagnant regions but did not add up to very much. Employment to population ratios rose in the Andean and Middle Eastern regions.[11] Elsewhere, liberalization did not help create jobs – industrial jobs in particular.

Privatization and financial deregulation were followed by financial crises in many countries, sometimes more than once. They were associated with vulnerability and under-regulation of the financial sector which promoted speculative behaviour on both sides of the market. National balance sheets became dangerously short on foreign assets and long on domestic holdings including real estate and equity – usually newly created through privatization – and cycles of real exchange rate appreciation. The crises help explain the erratic performances in Latin America, Eastern Europe, and Russia. As noted above, Southeast Asia did not recover as strongly as the Tigers from the 1997 crisis. China and India to a large extent evaded its impacts by maintaining capital controls.

Finally, the supply-side emphasis of the new policy package – austerity supposedly leading to higher saving and investment rates, an emphasis on human capital accumulation, and opening economies to foreign direct investment – did not seem to bear fruit outside the rapidly growing regions. There was a clear association between capital stock growth and output growth across all regions, but here the supply-side interpretation is not compelling. The results in Figure 3.4 can just as well be explained by rapid capital stock growth contributing to labour productivity growth and driving output growth from the side of demand with savings adjusting endogenously, rather than by higher savings leading to more capital which fed into output via some sort of aggregate production function.

Results across the regions *differed*. Fast-growing regions were less zealous about applying the liberalization philosophy, and performed better. Elsewhere, there was enough variety to suggest that specific aspects of each region and its economies were important in shaping outcomes. *Structure matters*. The policy analysis challenge is to figure out just how and why.

How Should Policy Change?

An idea tracing back to Adam Smith and recently restated by Reinert (2006) and formalized by Rada (2007) is that the economy can usefully be viewed as a combination of dynamic increasing returns sectors and more plodding constant or decreasing returns activities. The goal is to stimulate the former while shifting resources, especially labour, from the latter. Figures 3.2 and 3.3 illustrate how the rapidly growing regions succeeded at this task. The question is how to design policies that will facilitate similar processes elsewhere.

Indeed, charting institutional changes that could open up degrees of freedom for the pursuit of developmental policies may be a fruitful approach. Some examples:

Does the open economy "trilemma" really bind? That is, can independent monetary/fiscal policies, exchange rate programming, and open capital markets all be combined? In the land of textbooks it is straightforward to show that they can be, or in other words that the Mundell-Fleming "duality" between a floating exchange rate and control of the money supply does not exist. In principle, a central bank has enough tools at its disposal to control monetary aggregates and interest rates regardless of the forces determining the exchange rate.[12]

In practice, however, arbitrary changes in monetary and exchange rate policies may be attacked by markets. As emphasized by Nayyar (2005), the question then becomes one of how other policies may be deployed to widen the boundaries on feasible manoeuvres. Frenkel and Taylor (2006) argue that under appropriate circumstances a weak exchange rate can be desirable for developmental reasons. The "circumstances" include a productive sector which is responsive to price signals; a monetary authority willing and able to maintain a weak rate for an extended period of time, perhaps supported by capital market and other interventions); and, political willingness to bear the, conceivably high, initial costs of devaluation including potential inflation and output contraction. Getting away from the recent obsession with using the exchange rate for "inflation targeting" could be a useful step toward making it a more useful development policy tool.

In the area of industrial and commercial policy, the impact of the WTO has been to rule out interventions involving tariffs and trade while up to a point different forms of subsidies (witness Airbus vs. Boeing!) are still considered kosher. How can developing and transition economies operate effectively in this new environment? The Smithian prescription to stimulate increasing returns sectors did not cease to apply when the WTO was born. The question is how to implement it under present circumstances.

At the macro level, a question implicit in Figure 3.3 is also relevant: how can economies avoid the "jobless growth" that has been characteristic of the liberalization period? Evidently, productivity growth must be positive for per capita incomes to rise but demand growth must be stronger to create employment. It remains to be seen in many countries whether they will be able to program rapid growth in demand under a regime of liberalized international capital markets.

APPENDIX: COUNTRIES IN THE REGIONAL GROUPS

1. Representative Africa: Ghana, Kenya, Uganda and Tanzania
2. Other Africa: Cameroon, Ethiopia, Ivory Coast, Mozambique, Nigeria, Zimbabwe

3. Central America and the Caribbean: Costa Rica, Dominican Republic, El Salvador, Guatemala, Jamaica
4. Andean Region: Bolivia, Ecuador, Peru
5. Semi-Industrialized Latin America (with Turkey and South Africa as additions): Argentina, Brazil, Chile, Colombia, Mexico, Venezuela, Turkey, South Africa
6. South Asia: Bangladesh, India, Pakistan, Sri Lanka
7. China
8. Southeast Asia: Indonesia, Philippines, Thailand, Viet Nam
9. Tigers: Korea, Malaysia, Singapore, Taiwan
10. Middle East: Algeria, Egypt, Morocco, Tunisia, Iran, Iraq, Jordan, Saudi Arabia, Syria, Yemen
11. Former-USSR: Russian Federation, Ukraine
12. Eastern Europe: Bulgaria, Czech Republic, Hungary, Poland, Romania, Slovakia

NOTES

[*] Research support from DESA and the Ford Foundation and suggestions by José Antonio Ocampo, Jomo K. S., and Rob Vos are gratefully acknowledged. For a more complete version of this paper, please see UN-DESA Working Paper no. 34. http://www.un.org/esa/desa/papers/2006/wp34_2006.pdf

[1] The representative group is made up of four countries often discussed in the development literature, and the others are included essentially on grounds of data availability.

[2] It is customary to make international income comparisons in terms of purchasing power parity (or PPP). However, as explained in Appendix II, PPP estimates distort the macroeconomic relationships that are at the heart of our analysis. When it comes to policy formation, it is far more useful to think about macro relationships in traditional "real" terms.

[3] The approach follows Syrquin (1986).

[4] The original insight is Pasinetti's (1981).

[5] The approach followed here is a variant on a demand decomposition proposed by Godley and Cripps (1983).

[6] A caveat: our capital stock series for the former-USSR and Eastern Europe begin in 1990, which means that the estimated growth rates are less reliable than those for other regions where the base year was 1970.

[7] That is, the 45-degree slope would not fit a neoclassical aggregate production function. It could be "explained" by a constant capital-output ratio, but that in turn is inconsistent with the "Asian" pattern of falling capital productivity discussed immediately below.

[8] This sort of "decreasing returns" to more capital is built into many mainstream and heterodox growth models, which mostly serve to rationalize the accounting identity described in the text.

[9] The initial and final years for export compositions are 1980 and the early 2000s.

[10] Although, as we will see below, Polak sans PPP can help explain recent interactions between public and private sector deficits in several developing regions.

[11] A rise of the ratio in Russia/Ukraine can be discounted because of negative population growth.

[12] For the gory textbook details, see Chapter 10 in Taylor (2004). Frenkel and Taylor (2006) present a more institutionally nuanced discussion.

References

Barro, Robert J. (1974). Are government bonds net worth? *Journal of Political Economy*, 82: 1095–1117.

Frenkel, Roberto, and Lance Taylor (2005). Real exchange rate, monetary policy, and employment. Paper prepared for the High-Level United Nations Development Conference on the Millennium Development Goals. New York.

Godley, Wynne, and T. Francis Cripps (1983). *Macroeconomics*. Fontana, London.

Kuznets, Simon (1966). *Modern Economic Growth*. Yale University Press, New Haven.

Lucas, Robert E., Jr. (2000). Some macroeconomics for the 21st century. *Journal of Economic Perspectives*, 14: 159–168.

Maddison, Angus (2001). *The World Economy: A Millennial Perspective*. Organization for Economic Co-operation and Development, Paris.

Nayyar, Deepak (2005). Development through globalization? Paper presented at the WIDER conference on 'Thinking Ahead: The Future of Development Economics', Helsinki.

Obstfeld, Maurice, and Kenneth Rogoff (1997). The intertemporal approach to the current account. In Gene M. Grossman and Kenneth Rogoff (eds). *Handbook of International Economics* (Vol. 3). North-Holland, Amsterdam.

Ocampo, J. A. (2005). The quest for dynamic efficiency: Structural dynamics and economic growth in developing countries. In José Antonio Ocampo (ed.). *Beyond Reforms, Structural Dynamics and Macroeconomic Vulnerability*. Stanford University Press, Stanford, CA.

Pasinetti, Luigi L. (1981). *Structural Change and Economic Growth*. Cambridge University Press, Cambridge.

Polak, J. J. (1957). Monetary analysis of income formation and payments problems. *International Monetary Fund Staff Papers*, 6: 1–50.

Rada, Codrina, and Lance Taylor (2006a). Empty sources of growth accounting, and empirical replacements à la Kaldor and Goodwin with some beef. *Structural Change and Economic Dynamics,* 17(3), 486–500, December 2006.

Rada, Codrina, and Lance Taylor (2007). A Growth Model for a Two-Sector Economy with Endogenous Employment. *Cambridge Journal of Economics*, forthcoming.

Reinert, Erik S. (2005). Development and social goals: Balancing aid and development to prevent 'welfare colonialism'. Paper prepared for the High-Level United Nations Development Forum on the Millennium Development Goals, New York.

Syrquin, Moshe (1986). Productivity growth and factor reallocation. In Hollis B. Chenery, Sherman Robinson, and Moshe Syrquin (eds). *Industrialization and Growth*. Oxford University Press, New York.

Taylor, Lance (ed.) (2001). *External Liberalization, Economic Performance, and Social Policy.* Oxford University Press, New York.

Taylor, Lance (2004). *Reconstructing Macroeconomics: Structuralist Proposals and Critiques of the Mainstream.* Harvard University Press, Cambridge MA.

Taylor, Lance, and Codrina Rada (2007). Can the Poor Countries Catch Up? Guarded assessments on mainstream assumptions for the 21st century. *Metroeconomica* 58(1), pp. 127–154, February 2007. Schwartz Center for Economic Policy Analysis, New School for Social Research, New York.

Taylor, Lance (ed.) (2006). *External Liberalization in Asia, Post-Socialist Europe, and Brazil.* Oxford University Press, New York.

Vos, Rob, Lance Taylor, and Ricardo Paes de Barros (eds) (2002). *Balance of Payments Liberalization in Latin America: Effects on Growth, Distribution, and Poverty.* Edward Elgar, Northampton, MA.

4

Explaining the Dual Divergence: The Role of External Shocks and Specialization Patterns

JOSÉ ANTONIO OCAMPO AND MARÍA ANGELA PARRA*

The traditional focus of the literature on economic growth is the determinants of long-term trends. This approach makes sense for industrial economies, where a stable long-term growth pattern is discernible, as in the United States, or where major historical breaks can be identified, as in Western Europe (Maddison, 1991). However, as a growing literature has shown, long-term growth patterns in the developing world are not independent of economic fluctuations. Even for industrial economies, as a leading theorist of growth has pointed out, 'it is impossible to believe that the equilibrium growth path itself is unaffected by the short-to medium-run experience' (Solow, 2000: xvii).

Breaks or instability of long-term patterns are thus of the substance, not a marginal feature of growth patterns in developing countries. In turn, major external shocks play an essential role in explaining breaks in growth patterns. This underscores the need to look carefully at the interaction between external and domestic factors in the macroeconomic dynamics of developing countries. Specialization patterns create another critical interaction between external and domestic factors, and also play an essential role in explaining growth performance in the developing world.

This chapter explores the impact of external shocks and specialization patterns on long-term growth in the developing world over the past four decades. It is divided into five sections. The first section succinctly presents major analytical issues involved in understanding growth in the developing world. The second looks at developing countries' performances, underscoring the widening income gap between developed and developing countries, but also the divergent performances of developing countries, which jointly generate a pattern of 'dual divergence'. The third section explores the interaction between external and domestic macroeconomic factors, and the fourth considers the role of changes in specialization patterns. The last section draws conclusions and major policy recommendations.

CRITICAL ANALYTICAL ISSUES FOR UNDERSTANDING GROWTH IN THE DEVELOPING WORLD

Fluctuations and changes in the trend are an essential component of 'long-term' growth patterns in the developing world. The experience of developing countries indicates, indeed, that growth does not take place in steady flows, but involves a mix of episodes of stable growth with spurts and collapses of different frequency, magnitude and duration. The typology of growth experiences is thus diverse: it includes a few experiences of persistent convergence vis-à-vis industrial countries, but also (and more commonly) truncated convergences, growth collapses and development traps (Ocampo, 2005; Pritchett, 2000; Ros, 2005).

External factors, particularly terms of trade shocks and fluctuations in international capital markets, play a central role in explaining breaks in long-term growth patterns. In one of the best known studies on economic growth instability in the developing world, Easterly and others (1993) show that a large part of the variance of growth rates of developing countries, even in periods as long as a decade, can be directly explained by shocks – in the terms of trade, debt crises and sharp changes in net external transfers – and by wars. These factors have been, for a long time, the focus of the structuralist tradition.

In economies experiencing substantial shocks, which countries can only, to a limited extent, counteract with counter-cyclical macroeconomic policies, it may be impossible to insulate long-term trends from short-term trajectories. The major explanation for this is the path dependence due to dynamic economies of scale: the close association between technological learning and production experience (i.e., 'learning by doing' in a broad sense) as well as similar processes related to the development of marketing networks and the growth of firm reputation (goodwill). This means that both negative shocks (an external crisis, a natural disaster, or a war) and positive shocks (the discovery of new natural resources) may have long-term implications.[1] In a related way, the formation of macroeconomic expectations in economies facing recurrent shocks necessarily involves a learning process (Heymann, 2000).

The important role of external factors means that the traditional focus of the growth literature on the domestic factors that explain individual countries' growth performances may be misplaced. Indeed, relevant domestic factors may not be independent of external conditions. This view is clear in Astorga, Bergés and FitzGerald's (2005) analysis of the performance of six major Latin American economies in the twentieth century. As they show, terms of trade volatility, trade fluctuations and interest rate shocks were major obstacles to sustained economic growth in these economies over the century, and it is difficult to assess whether they were more important than domestic shocks, as the latter were often associated with the former. Furthermore, shocks had, on several occasions, indirect influences on growth, by inducing policy changes.

Domestic factors, as well as regional factors (usually captured by regional dummies in cross-country econometrics) also play a role in determining long-term growth. However, their effect is not independent and must thus be understood in terms of interactions with the external economic environment – e.g., factors that allow countries to benefit from favourable external conditions or reduce vulnerability to negative shocks, or that explain why a country or a region fails to experience rapid growth during periods of growth success in the developing world, or allow them to mitigate or entirely avoid growth collapses. Nonetheless, this way of viewing the role of domestic factors is entirely different from traditional growth analysis. It implies that short-term factors may be more important for long-term dynamics than usually recognized. It also means that relevant country- and region-specific factors, which depend on global and regional trends, may be time-bound. It finally implies that long-term determinants of ('necessary conditions' for) growth – such as institutions, or the level of human capital and infrastructure – may play a rather passive role, as 'framing conditions', rather than as direct determinants of the rhythm of economic growth.

Among domestic factors that interact with external conditions, specialization patterns have been generally ignored in orthodox analyses. Seen in this light, the major pattern over the past quarter century has been the rapid transformation of the structure of developing country exports: primary goods and natural-resource intensive manufactures fell relative to low-, mid- and high-technology manufactures. All developing country regions diversified into the more dynamic components of world trade, but East and South Asia diversified much faster (including into low-technology manufactures). The success stories of these countries have been related to their achievements in entering external markets, profiting from dynamic economies of scale and transforming their production structures accordingly.

GROWTH PATTERNS IN THE DEVELOPING WORLD

The widening income gap *between* regions and countries has been a feature of the world economy for the past two centuries. The story of the developing countries is one of 'divergence, big time' vis-à-vis the industrial world (Pritchett, 1997), with a few exceptions so far in history. History has also shown considerable growth divergence among developing countries.

A *dual divergence* has thus been in place in the world economy over the past few decades: between developing countries and the industrial world, on the one hand, and among developing countries, on the other. This has been a result of several patterns. First, several success stories ('miracles') have occurred at different times in various parts of the developing world (China and India being the most recent). There are, however, very few instances of 'peripheral' countries that have joined the industrial 'centre' (Japan and the Republic of Korea being the notable exceptions in this regard, perhaps with some of the other 'first-tier' Asian NIEs). This implies that growth spurts have been more commonly followed by either stagnation at middle- or even low-income levels or by outright collapses. And, worst of all, a not insignificant number of poor countries have never really experienced growth for extended periods of time, indicating that they have never broken out of (under)development traps.

Table 4.1 helps to underscore some basic 'stylized facts' about the post-war development experience. The post-World War II 'golden age' (1950–1973) was characterized by fairly widespread growth in the developing world. This was also the case in what turned out to be the transition phase, delimited by the two oil shocks, 1973–1979. Except for Africa, the developing world did not initially follow the slowdown most of the industrial world experienced. This is, furthermore, the only long period where there was some convergence of the average real incomes of developing countries with the industrial world. The period since 1980 saw again divergence between the industrial and the developing world. The dominant feature of this period was the high frequency of growth collapses in the developing world outside Asia (see Figure 1.2 in the first chapter of this volume). This has been followed recently by broad-based growth in the developing world (United Nations, 2006b), but it is still too early to say whether this period represents a new phase of convergence.

Table 4.1 also indicates that divergence among developing countries increased in the mid-1960s and has remained high since then. As we show in this chapter, the opportunity to benefit from growing markets for manufacturing exports from developing countries was fundamental for the initial surge in divergence, but vulnerability to external shocks became critical after the first oil shock. The transition period, covering the years between the two oil shocks of the 1970s, seems to have seen the peak of divergence among developing countries, largely due to the poor performance of sub-Saharan Africa.

These findings suggest that *growth successes and collapses tend to cluster in specific time periods* (Ocampo and Parra, 2006a) and *also in space* (United Nations, 2006a), as major regional deviations from average developing country patterns in different periods suggest: Africa (negatively) in 1973–1980, and East and South Asia (positively) in 1980–2002. It is unlikely that the domestic factors in the growth literature can explain such clustering. Thus, we have to rely on common external factors, as well as regional and domestic factors that transmit their effects.

TABLE 4.1
Annual average per capita GDP growth, 1950–2005

	Maddison (2003)				United Nations		
	1950–65	1965–73	1973–80	1980–2001	1973–80	1980–2002	2002–05
Developed countries							
Weighted average	3.6%	4.0%	1.9%	2.0%	1.8%	2.0%	2.0%
Simple average	3.8%	4.2%	2.1%	2.0%	2.0%	2.0%	1.7%
Western Europe	4.0%	4.3%	2.2%	2.1%	2.1%	2.0%	1.6%
United States	2.3%	2.8%	1.5%	2.0%	1.5%	2.0%	2.5%
Developing countries							
Weighted average	2.6%	3.1%	2.5%	2.4%	3.0%	1.9%	4.5%
Standard Deviation	2.0%	3.1%	3.4%	2.5%	3.9%	2.5%	3.2%
Simple average	2.4%	2.6%	1.4%	0.4%	1.9%	0.5%	2.9%
Africa	2.2%	1.6%	0.6%	-0.1%	0.9%	0.1%	2.3%
Latin America	1.9%	2.6%	2.0%	0.2%	2.0%	0.1%	2.8%
Western Asia	3.0%	4.0%	1.9%	-1.0%	2.9%	-1.6%	1.8%
South Asia	1.4%	2.0%	0.7%	2.5%	1.1%	2.2%	4.1%
Eastern Asia	3.3%	5.2%	3.9%	3.7%	4.1%	4.0%	5.0%
Central and Eastern Europe	4.0%	3.9%	1.6%	0.3%	2.7%	1.5%	3.3%

Source: Authors' calculations based on Maddison (2003) and UN/DESA database.

The clustering of both successes and collapses implies that a global development 'cycle' or 'trajectory' has influenced the growth patterns of developing countries (Figure 4.1). This trajectory approximates the average growth performance of developing countries resulting from external factors that affect all or large clusters of them, and thus constrains each country's growth possibilities. Given the leading role of the industrial world in determining growth in the developing world, it is not surprising that this trajectory coincides, to some extent, with that of industrial countries. In particular, the end of the Keynesian 'golden age' in industrial countries also marked the end of the 'golden age' of development. Nonetheless, other determinants of the average trajectory are more specific and relate to trade and financing patterns that strongly affect developing countries, particularly the effects of commodity price instability on the large number of developing countries dependent on primary exports, and boom-bust cycles in international financing, particularly to 'emerging market' economies. These determinants increasingly encompass the *global* effects of events originating in developing countries with systemic importance–particularly the effects of China on world commodity markets in recent years. Such determinants may have diverse effects on different countries and regions. In this sense, the average growth trajectory is not inconsistent with variable performance within the developing world and, particularly, with strong regional dimensions.

The major break in the experience of the developing world took place in the 1980s, which became the 'lost decade' in most parts of the developing world, to draw a term that was originally coined for Latin America. Indeed, although the 1973 oil shock disturbed the normal functioning of developed economies, and had important effects in developing countries as well (directly and through the recycling of petrodollars), it had diverse effects on different developing countries. To explain why 1980 turned out to be a more important break in long-term growth patterns in developing countries, we must turn to two major and largely unexpected shocks that severely affected much of the developing world.

FIGURE 4.1
The growth trajectory of developing countries

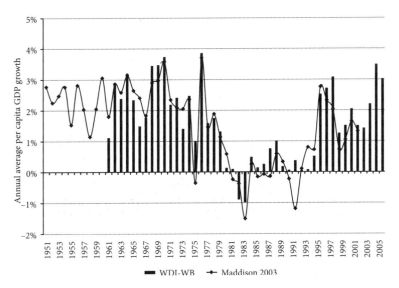

Source: Authors' calculations based on Maddison (2003) and World Bank, World Development Indicators (WDI) online.

The first was the *permanent effect of the 1979 interest rate shock* (Figure 4.2), which had no historical precedent. As inflation promptly receded, real interest rates in the U.S. (using the 10-year Treasury note rate as a benchmark) increased from –1.8 per cent in 1979 to 3.6 per cent in 1981, reaching a peak of 8.2 per cent in 1984. The interest rate effectively faced by developing countries was even higher, as the average risk premium paid by developing countries added to the LIBOR rate rose from 2.5 per cent in 1979 to 22 per cent in 1981 in real terms. Having profited from the recycling of petrodollars, developing countries suffered a substantial shock that implied, for many of them, significant balance of payments' distress.

FIGURE 4.2

Debt/GNI ratio, interest rate and spreads

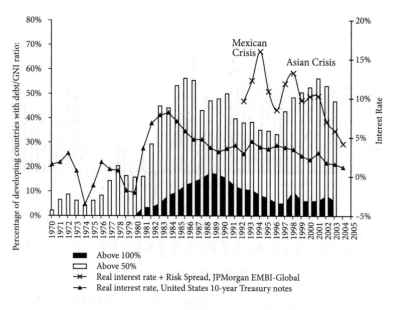

Source: Authors' calculations based on World Bank, Global Development Finance, online and JP Morgan database.

The debt dynamics of developing countries turned explosive *after* the interest rate shock and had both short-term and long-term effects. The proportion of low to middle income non-HIPC (heavily indebted poor countries) developing countries with moderate debt ratios (over 50 per cent of GDP) was low prior to the shock, and the proportion with critical debt ratios (over 100 per cent of GDP) was nil (Figure 4.2). It rose rapidly after the interest rate shock, with a two-year lag. The situation began to normalize in the late 1980s and early 1990s, again following trends in international interest rates. The 1997–1998 Asian and Russian crises, and their contagion effects, interrupted the recovery of the 1990s, but these crises had weaker and more temporary effects than the debt crisis of the 1980s. A major reason was the sharp fall in interest rates experienced in recent years, the joint effect of falling US interest rates *and* risk spreads. In the case of HIPC (not shown in Figure 4.2), the worsening trend pre-dated the 1979 interest rate shock, largely due to the poor performance of Africa after the first oil shock. However, it accelerated after the shock, particularly in terms of the countries for which debt exceeded GNI, and debt ratios remained high even in the face of falling interest rates.[2]

Overall, debt ratios in the developing world remained at high levels for the next quarter century after the 1979 interest rate shock. Three basic reasons explain this. The first is that real interest rates remained high, at over 4.5 per cent for almost twenty years; in fact, they only returned to low real levels in the early 2000s, together with a sharp reduction in risk spreads. The second was the lack of international institutions to manage debt overhangs, in sharp contrast to the 1930s, when broad-based moratoria was the only such 'institution' available. Eventually, a few solutions emerged, but only had weak effects (the Brady Plan of the late 1980s) or took a long time to fully materialize (the HIPC Initiative of the mid-1990s, which took a decade to become a debt write-off and has still not been fully implemented). Third, together with the hike in interest rates, net financial resource transfers became negative, both in the 1980s and after the Asian crisis.

The second shock experienced after 1980 was the *structural drop in the terms of trade* (Figure 4.3). In contrast with the evolution of interest rates, the non-oil commodity terms of trade shock did have precedents, but only in the distant past (the 1920s). Real non-oil commodity prices experienced a structural downward shift of over 30 per cent, breaking the long essentially trend-less period since the 1920s (Ocampo and Parra, 2003). The price index of manufactures exported by developing countries, relative to manufactures exported by developed countries, also experienced a sharp downturn during the 1980s.

The depth and duration of the unprecedented interest rate and terms-of-trade shocks explain the unexpectedly large magnitude of ex-post risks that the developing world had to confront, and thus, the large number of growth collapses that followed. Table 4.2 shows that, by themselves, high initial debt ratios or high commodity dependence help to explain little of the growth slowdown and the growth divergence among developing countries in the 1980s, but the interaction between

FIGURE 4.3
Terms of trade

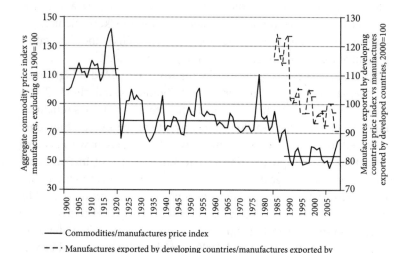

—— Commodities/manufactures price index

- - - Manufactures exported by developing countries/manufactures exported by
developed countries price index (right scale)

Source: Authors' calculations based on Grilli and Yang (1988), Ocampo and Parra
(2003) and United Nations (2003).

these two factors was important. Countries experiencing both factors
grew about two to three percentage points less than those countries
that did not experience that combination. However, other factors
clearly played an important role. Some are common to the developing
world: even under the best combination (low debt, low commodity
dependence, larger size and middle income), developing countries
performed poorly.[3] So, the conditions prevailing throughout the 'lost
decade' turned out to have depressive effects well beyond what can be
explained by the relevant 'initial conditions' of each economy.

Interestingly, the two factors that caused the 'lost decade' may, at
long last, be waning. Low real interest rates and the HIPC Initiative
seem to be finally reducing long-term debt overhangs, while Chinese-
led growth has strengthened commodity markets. It is still unclear,
however, if these recent trends will be sustainable, as the disturbance
in global financial markets associated with the correction of current
global imbalances may lead to higher interest rates or risk premia,

interest rates are rising again and commodity prices may already have reached a peak (United Nations, 2006b).

TABLE 4.2
Interaction between indebtedness level and commodity dependence in the 1980s

	Primary com. share of total exports <20%	20%< Primary com. share<50%	50%< Primary com. share	Total
External debt/GNI 1980<30%				
Number of countries	8	8	8	24
Average per capita GDP growth	0.3%	2.2%	0.4%	
Standard deviation p.c. GDP growth	3.1%	2.8%	3.3%	
30%< External debt/GNI 1980<50%				
Number of countries	7	7	8	22
Average per capita GDP growth	0.3%	0.2%	−1.9%	
Standard deviation per capita GDP growth	3.6%	1.8%	2.9%	
External debt/GNI 1980>50%				
Number of countries	6	10	6	22
Average per capita GDP growth	−0.4%	−1.1%	−0.9%	
Standard Deviation per capita GDP growth	1.7%	2.7%	2.4%	
Total	21	25	22	68

Source: Authors' calculations based on data from Maddison (2003), and WB-WDI.

THE INTERACTION BETWEEN EXTERNAL AND DOMESTIC MACROECONOMIC FACTORS

The central role played by the international environment does not render regional and country-specific factors insignificant. But it changes the nature of the relevant issues. It particular, it emphasizes the crucial role that interaction between domestic and external factors play in explaining why a country or region departs from the average trend in different phases of the global development trajectory–i.e., why they fail to experience rapid growth during phases of growth success in the developing world as a whole, or why they can mitigate or entirely avoid growth collapses.

Two issues are particularly important in this regard. The first are those associated with macroeconomic performance in the face of adverse external shocks. Given the central role it played in determining the cluster of growth collapses in the 1980s, we will focus on this period here, but similar remarks can be made for other conjunctures. Particularly, a voluminous literature on the Asian and Russian crises has shown the role that dependence on short-term flows and capital account liberalization played in determining the growth performance of different countries. In the following section, we will focus on a second set of interactions between domestic and external factors resulting in specialization patterns.

The degree of trade liberalization, as measured by the levels of tariff and non-tariff protection, did *not* play a role in the relative performance of different countries during the 1980s (see, for example, UNCTAD, 1992, Part II: Ch. I). But the mix between commodity dependence and external debt did have a role, as we saw in the previous section, as did the degree of macroeconomic instability, defined in orthodox terms, such as inflation or black market exchange rate premia. As Rodríguez and Rodrik (2001) show, this is the correct interpretation of the effects of several measures of 'openness' used in cross-country econometrics.

Variance in performance among developing countries during the 'lost decade' has been analyzed from two different angles. The first is through characteristics of the macroeconomic adjustment mechanism. This approach has underscored the virtues of a broader set of macroeconomic instruments, including mixing orthodox with less orthodox instruments (see, for example, Taylor, 1988). The second is through the institutional capacity to manage such shocks. In this regard, for example, Rodrik (1999) has argued that institutional capacity to manage conflict may help explain why, in the face of the same adverse circumstances, some countries were able to avoid high inflation. This argument gives strong indirect backing to the old Latin American structuralist idea that distributive conflicts underlie inflation.

Other structural factors may have been at work, too. A typical debate in the Latin American literature of the 1980s focused on the 'domestic transfer problem' – i.e., on how to transfer resources to the government to service the external debt. This transfer was made more difficult in those countries in which the government did not have direct access to foreign exchange (i.e., did not directly or indirectly control the foreign exchange generated by exports), and thus had to guarantee access to foreign exchange through indirect means (see, for example, ECLAC, 1996). Inflationary crises were more common in countries where the internal transfer was more difficult.

The point that we want to underscore, however, is that the relevant domestic factor in this context (inflation) was not independent of external factors. This is reflected in the frequency of episodes of high inflation in the developing world during the 'lost decade' (see Figure 4.4). Such frequency resulted mainly from the broad-based foreign exchange gaps that developing countries faced, which had direct and indirect impacts on nominal exchange rates and thus, on domestic inflation. It is hard to accept that the clustering of high inflation episodes can be explained other than as a result of common external (global and regional) factors.

These arguments indicate that external factors have direct, as well as indirect, effects on performance in developing countries. The direct impacts are related to vulnerability factors: commodity dependence and high debt. The indirect effects are associated with the capacity of individual countries to manage such shocks. But the relevant domestic factors are not independent of the source of the shock. So, in this case, they are associated with the capacity to manage the strong foreign exchange shocks the economies faced, by managing to avoid high inflation as well as large distortions in the foreign exchange market. We will concentrate in the next section on an additional link between domestic and external conditions, highlighted in the structuralist literature, but generally ignored in mainstream growth analysis–the role of specialization patterns.

FIGURE 4.4

Incidence of high inflation in the developing world

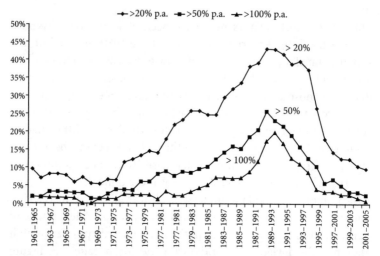

Source: Authors' calculations based on World Bank, World Development Indicators online.

SPECIALIZATION PATTERNS

Viewed from the point of view of the domestic production structure, long-term growth can be understood as a sequence of sector-specific growth spurts. Its dynamics are determined by the nature and intensity of the innovations that underlie them and the domestic linkages they generate (Ocampo, 2005). Long-term growth is thus the result of a successful sequence of innovations in the production structures and thus essentially a *micro*economic and, particularly, *meso*economic process. These sectoral dynamics are ignored or assumed to play a passive role in growth analyses that concentrate on institutional or macroeconomic features and policies. In contrast, it plays a central role in the 'structuralist' tradition of economic thinking, broadly defined, which has focused its attention on the dynamic transformation of production structures.

Innovations must be broadly understood in this context, as the development of new activities and new ways of doing previous activities. It is thus equivalent to Schumpeter's (1961) concept of 'new combinations', which encompass not only the development of new production methods and the introduction of new goods and services or of new qualities of goods and services (the two concepts most usually associated with technological innovation), but also new marketing strategies, the opening up of new markets, the discovery of new sources of raw materials or the exploitation of previously known resources, and the establishment of new industrial structures.

In developed countries, innovations are primarily associated with technological waves, but in developing countries, they are more closely linked to the attraction of sectors, activities and technologies previously developed in the industrial world. Historically, success stories have involved import substitution, export promotion or a mix of both strategies. In a globalized world economy, exports obviously play an increasingly important role. They may generate productivity gains through different channels emphasized in the economic literature. In the neoclassical tradition, faster productivity growth is associated with resource transfers from non-competitive to more competitive outward-oriented sectors. Here, the quantity of exports and the magnitude of the initial 'distortions' generated by protection policies are the relevant variables. From the 'structuralist production link' tradition, the 'quality' of exports is more important. This means that the capacity of exports to generate rapid economic growth depends crucially on the type of products exported. In particular, rapid growth is associated with manufacturing exports, and particularly with exports of goods and services with higher technological content.

There is growing evidence for this second view. One of the most important recent contributions on this issue is that of Hausmann, Hwang and Rodrik (2005), which indicates that the quality of exports, as indicated in the 'income level' of a country's exports (i.e., an estimate of the weighted average income of countries exporting specific products, which may be seen to reflect their technological content), is an independent determinant of economic growth.

In this regard, a developing country may be seen as choosing between either of two broadly defined export strategies: increasing market shares in sectors where it has an established position (static comparative advantage) or diversifying into higher technology products (building new comparative advantages). Both strategies may succeed, but the latter is more likely to be a winning strategy for two different reasons. First, it responds to and builds capacity to adapt to changes in international market conditions, which change drastically over time, thus creating new, but also destroying old export opportunities. Second, diversification towards 'dynamic products' in world trade is also important, because it limits the risk that the export market will get rapidly saturated and prices may decrease due to a large number of developing countries exporting the associated goods and services–a phenomenon known as the fallacy of composition (Mayer, Butkevicius and Kadri, 2002).[4]

In the last forty years, international trade has experienced an important expansion. Although developed economies still dominate the manufacturing trade, developing countries have rapidly expanded their share. Developing countries now export almost one third of total world manufacturing exports, compared to one-eighth in 1980 and one-twentieth in 1962. The structure of developing country exports has also been changing rapidly: the share of primary goods and natural-resource intensive manufactures in total non-oil exports fell relative to low-, mid- and high-technology manufactures. In this sense, there has been an upgrading in developing countries' exports in general.

It is worth noting that the involvement of developing countries is often limited to labour-intensive stages in the production process of technology-intensive goods in the context of international production chains. This diminishes the growth potential of these exports. Unfortunately, this cannot be shown well with available trade data. This issue and the related influence of multinationals are certainly important topics for further research.

All developing country regions diversified into the more dynamic components of world trade, but East Asia diversified much faster (including into low-technology manufactures), followed by Latin America (see Figure 4.5). Sub-Saharan Africa and other least developed economies (LDCs) diversified more slowly away from primary commodities and into natural resource based manufactures, and their total export growth has not been rapid. The Middle East and North Africa continue to be specialized in oil exports (which still account for 75 per cent of their total exports), but some diversification towards

FIGURE 4.5
Patterns of specialization per region[a]

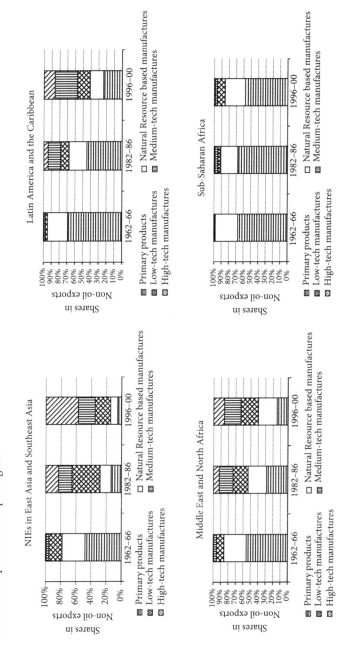

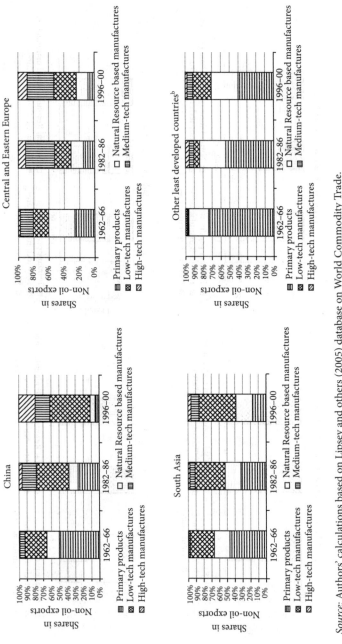

Source: Authors' calculations based on Lipsey and others (2005) database on World Commodity Trade.

a. Total regional exports are a simple average for the period of the individual country's exports in each category.

b. LDCs excluding Ethiopia, Mozambique, Uganda, Tanzania and Yemen, already included in the other groups.

non-natural resource manufactures has also taken place. Central and Eastern Europe have diversified to medium-tech manufactures. These four regions continue to be small players in the world trade in manufactures (less than 4 per cent).

Over these forty years, the more dynamic markets for developing countries' manufacturing exports have been those with relatively high technological content (United Nations, 2006a). Those markets have been clearly dominated by a particular group of developing countries, namely the newly industrialized economies (NIEs) in East Asia and South Asia. Coincidentally, those countries have been the only ones that have achieved some degree of catch up to developed economies per capita GDP. As we will see, although there are cases of countries able to grow rapidly while further specializing in primary products or natural resource based manufactures, those were the exceptions, rather than the rule.

The simple correlation between specialization patterns and growth presented in Figure 4.6 shows that, during the period 1962–2000, per capita GDP growth in the developing world was negatively correlated with continued reliance on the exports of primary goods and natural resource-intensive manufactures, but positively correlated with diversification into mid- and high-tech manufactures. Standard regression analysis (not reported) captures that, but cannot reflect significant differences in performance around the average pattern.

Table 4.3 provides evidence of the interaction between success in increasing market shares and specialization patterns, differentiating two phases in this process: 1962–1980 and 1980–2000.[5] The countries are sorted according to the pattern of specialization relevant to describe a specific country's exports. Thus, a country is classified in the sector for which the change in the share in its total exports, multiplied by the share the country has in developing countries' exports in that sector, has increased the most. This measure shows diversification over time, combined with the relative importance of the country in developing countries' total exports in each category in the final period. So, if a country had an important increase in its share of high-tech manufactures relative to total exports, but still represented a relatively small share in developing countries' exports, this measure will be relatively small at the end of the period.[6]

FIGURE 4.6

Patterns of specialization and growth, 1962–2000

(a) Reliance on primary commodities and natural resource based manufactures

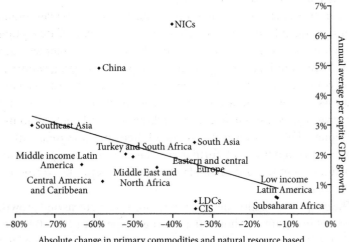

Absolute change in primary commodities and natural resource based manufactures share in total non-oil exports

(b) Diversification towards medium and high-tech manufactures

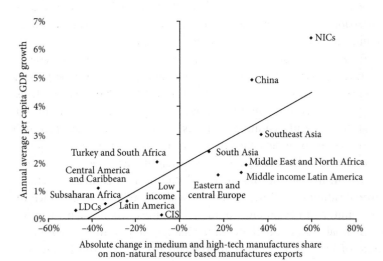

Absolute change in medium and high-tech manufactures share on non-natural resource based manufactures exports

Source: Authors' calculations based on Lipsey and others (2005) database on World Commodity Trade and Maddison (2003).

TABLE 4.3
Economic growth according to the trade specialization indicator

A. 1962–1980

Primary commodities	Per capita GDP average annual growth	Natural resource based manufactures	Per capita GDP average annual growth	Low-technology manufactures	Per capita GDP average annual growth	Middle-technology manufactures	Per capita GDP average annual growth	High-technology manufactures	Per capita GDP average annual growth
Average	1.5%		1.7%		3.2%		3.1%		2.8%
Standard deviation	1.7%		1.3%		2.0%		2.3%		2.4%
Paraguay	3.9%	Malaysia	4.6%	South Korea	7.5%	Oman	7.6%	Singapore	7.4%
Cote d'Ivoire	2.6%	Indonesia	3.3%	Taiwan	7.4%	Saudi Arabia	6.3%	Israel	4.2%
Nigeria	2.6%	Ecuador	3.2%	Thailand	4.5%	Libyan Arab J.	6.2%	Mexico	3.8%
Burundi	2.6%	Guatemala	2.6%	Tunisia	4.3%	Hong Kong SAR	6.0%	Fm USSR	2.5%
Bolivia	2.5%	Albania	2.5%	China	3.7%	Algeria	4.5%	Philippines	2.4%
Bahrain	2.3%	Cameroon	2.0%	Egypt	3.7%	Iraq	4.2%	Gabon	2.0%
Rwanda	1.8%	Sri Lanka	2.0%	Iran (Islamic R. of)	3.2%	Brazil	4.1%	El Salvador	1.1%
U.R. of Tanzania	1.3%	Honduras	1.7%	Turkey	3.2%	Romania	4.1%	Niger	-0.9%
Sierra Leone	1.3%	Myanmar	1.7%	Morocco	2.9%	Trinidad and Tobago	3.6%		
Madagascar	-0.4%	Cuba	1.4%	Pakistan	2.9%	Panama	3.6%		
Ghana	-1.1%	Guinea	1.3%	Colombia	2.8%	Bulgaria	3.4%		
Angola	-1.8%	Chile	1.3%	Hungary	2.6%	Costa Rica	3.2%		
		Peru	1.3%	Czechoslovak	2.3%	Poland	3.1%		
		India	1.2%	Uruguay	1.7%	Syrian Arab R.	3.0%		
		Jamaica	0.8%	Mauritius	1.7%	Jordan	3.0%		
		United Arab E.	0.7%	Haiti	1.1%	Dominican R.	3.0%		
		Senegal	-0.7%	Afghanistan	-0.2%	Congo	2.4%		
		Vietnam	-0.9%			Argentina	2.1%		
						Lebanon	1.9%		
						South Africa	1.8%		
						Zimbabwe	1.8%		
						Venezuela	0.6%		
						Liberia	-0.3%		
						Kuwait	-3.8%		

B. 1980–2000

Primary commodities	Per capita GDP average annual growth	Natural resource based manufactures	Per capita GDP average annual growth	Low-technology manufactures	Per capita GDP average annual growth	Middle-technology manufactures	Per capita GDP average annual growth	High-technology manufactures	Per capita GDP average annual growth
Average	-0.1%		0.5%		1.0%		-0.8%		3.8%
Standard deviation	1.1%		2.3%		1.9%		1.8%		2.1%
Mozambique	0.8%	Equatorial Guinea	8.8%	Mauritius	4.6%	Mexico	0.7%	South Korea	6.4%
Benin	0.8%	Chile	2.7%	Vietnam	4.4%	Panama	0.6%	China	6.0%
Senegal	0.5%	Oman	2.7%	India	3.6%	Hungary	0.6%	Taiwan	5.3%
Mauritania	0.1%	Seychelles	2.0%	Sri Lanka	3.5%	Trinidad and Tobago	0.5%	Thailand	4.6%
Zimbabwe	-0.1%	Iran (Islamic R. of)	0.9%	Indonesia	2.7%	Argentina	0.2%	Singapore	4.6%
Peru	-0.7%	Uruguay	0.9%	Pakistan	2.5%	South Africa	-0.3%	Malaysia	3.9%
Cote d'Ivoire	-2.3%	Bahrain	0.7%	Myanmar	2.5%	Jordan	-0.5%	Hong Kong SAR	3.6%
		Ghana	0.5%	Turkey	2.5%	Venezuela	-0.9%	Israel	1.9%
		Brazil	0.3%	Nepal	2.3%	Kuwait	-1.3%	Costa Rica	1.2%
		Mongolia	0.1%	Dominican R.	2.2%	Liberia	-1.5%	Philippines	0.0%
		Lebanon	-0.2%	Tunisia	2.2%	United Arab E.	-2.5%		
		Cameroon	-0.3%	Egypt	1.7%	Libyan Arab J.	-5.5%		
		Congo	-0.4%	Lao People's D. R.	1.5%				
		Cuba	-0.5%	Poland	1.2%				
		Paraguay	-0.5%	Cambodia	1.1%				
		Gambia	-0.7%	Colombia	0.9%				
		Central African R.	-0.9%	Morocco	0.8%				
		Angola	-1.0%	El Salvador	0.7%				
		Ecuador	-1.4%	Syrian Arab R.	0.7%				
		Zambia	-1.5%	Jamaica	0.6%				
		Gabon	-2.7%	Albania	0.6%				
				Czechoslovakia 1/	0.4%				
				Honduras	0.1%				
				Guatemala	-0.4%				
				Bulgaria	-0.6%				
				Romania	-1.6%				

Primary commodities	Per capita GDP average annual growth	Natural resource based manufactures	Per capita GDP average annual growth	Low-technology manufactures	Per capita GDP average annual growth	Middle-technology manufactures	Per capita GDP average annual growth	High-technology manufactures	Per capita GDP average annual growth
				Nicaragua	−1.6%				
				Former USSR 2/	−1.9%				
				Madagascar	−2.0%				
				Haiti	−2.3%				
				Saudi Arabia	−2.5%				

Source: United Nations (2006a).
1/: since 1993, Czech Rep and Slovakia.
2/: since 1992, Russian Federation and Ukraine.

In the period 1962–1980, the most successful countries in terms of per capita GDP growth moved from natural resource based sectors to manufacturing exports in general. There were cases of high growth related to natural resource based sectors (Malaysia, Indonesia and Ecuador in natural resource based manufactures, and Paraguay in primary goods), but the core of the high growth group diversified to low- and medium-tech manufactures.[7] In 1980–2000, rapid economic growth was achieved only by countries specializing in high-tech exports and, to a much lesser extent than in the previous period, in low-tech manufactures, while exports of mid-tech manufacturing exports ceased to be a source of dynamic growth. In turn, specialization in natural resource based sectors became a source of negligible economic growth. While there are cases of relatively high growth in the natural resource based (NRB) manufactures sector (Equatorial Guinea, Chile, Oman and Seychelles), there is none in the primary commodities sector in this period.

The success stories of the East Asian countries have been commonly related to their achievements in entering external markets, profiting from dynamic economies of scale and transforming their production structures accordingly. Their superior growth performance, even in a period in which developing countries were, in general, stagnating or collapsing, is closely associated with the continuous effort, both by the State and the corporate sector, to upgrade export production capacities, which have lead to sustained industrialization. As indicated in the voluminous literature on East Asian industrialization, the strategy followed by these countries has been quite different from trade liberalization, in the traditional sense of the term (see, for example, Amsden, 2001; Wade 1990).

In contrast, in sub-Saharan Africa, the share of manufacturing in GDP fell in the 1980s and stabilized in the 1990s at relatively low levels. South America experienced premature deindustrialization during these decades, while Mexico and Central America avoided this trend by specializing in high-import intensive manufacturing exports, but with limited benefits in terms of growth, due to weak internal linkages and low capacity to capture a larger share of the value added in the production chains in these sectors (see, in this regard, ECLAC, 2004; Ocampo and Martin, 2004; Palma, 2005).

Activities with limited domestic value added (e.g., maquila) are also likely to be footloose. In the terms used by Palma (2004), unless the industries are firmly 'anchored' in the domestic economy, their growth-enhancing capacity evaporates. Ocampo (2005) refers to these specialization patterns as 'shallow'. This is also linked to the relationship the country establishes with FDI: if the strategy to attract FDI is focused, not on creating assets (by providing human resources and infrastructure), but on offering special incentives to multinational investments, the process can ultimately be counterproductive (Mortimore and Peres, 2001).

UNCTAD (2003) has argued that the impact of integration into the world economy largely depends on the circumstances under which it takes place and on the policies pursued during the phase of closer integration into the global economy. This helps to link the structural transformation process and the macroeconomic dynamics generated by global shocks analyzed in previous sections. Integration of Latin America and Africa (as well as Central and Eastern Europe) marked a sharp shift in development strategy, occurring in a 'big-bang' manner and following the debt crisis (i.e., a period of weakness). This contrasts with the integration process in East Asia, which occurred from a position of relative strength and was characterized by a continuous and purposeful strategy of gradual opening up. Expressing it in the Schumpeterian terminology used by Ocampo (2005a), in East Asia, the 'creative' elements prevailed ('creative destruction'), while in other regions of the world, the 'destructive' components of the restructuring process were stronger ('destructive creation'), reflecting the destruction of many import-substitution activities and the weak domestic linkages generated by new export sectors.

CONCLUSIONS AND SOME POLICY RECOMMENDATIONS

This chapter argues that, contrary to industrial countries, 'long-term' growth patterns in developing countries have been characterized by large elements of discontinuity: fluctuations and changes in trends, associated with spurts and collapses of different frequency, magnitude and duration. Major breaks in the growth process in the developing world tend to cluster around specific time periods, and are associated with major external shocks.

A central feature of stable growth dynamics in developing countries is thus their capacity to manage vulnerability to external shocks and to productively use favourable external environments. The relevant domestic variables, and their interaction with external factors, are contingent on the circumstances of a specific period, and their joint effect may have long-term implications associated with path dependence. Furthermore, the evolution of the relevant 'domestic' variable (e.g., domestic inflation) may be largely determined by external factors.

The transformation of export and production structures is another critical link between domestic and external factors that determine growth in developing countries. In the 1960s and 1970s, growth was associated with the capacity to move from natural resource based sectors in general to manufacturing, while in the 1980s and 1990s success has been mainly associated with high-tech and, secondarily, with low-tech manufacturing exports.

The success of East Asian countries has been related to their capacity to conquer external markets, profit from dynamic economies of scale and transform their production structures accordingly. Their superior growth performance, even in a period in which developing countries were generally stagnating, is closely associated with the continuous effort, both by the State and the corporate sector, to upgrade export production capacities, which has sustained industrialization.

Some major policy implications follow from the analysis. The first is that the capacity to manage major external shocks is critical to avoid adverse breaks in growth trajectories. Developing countries can take measures by themselves ('self-insurance'), but they will have limited effects or success in only a few countries. Managing global adverse factors facing developing countries is thus critical.

Similarly, designing pro-active strategies to diversify exports and upgrade export capabilities is critical, but so is the need to maintain the 'policy space' for developing countries to do so. This is not only true in multilateral agreements, but also in bilateral trade agreements, which have been most restrictive in this area (Shadlen, 2005).

Entering high technology manufacturing and services is the best option, but may not be available to most developing countries. Indeed, most developing countries would have to compete in primary goods and natural resource or low-tech manufacturing exports, where they are likely to face 'fallacy of composition' effects. For those countries, improving the volume and quality of primary exports, processed and unprocessed, is certainly a good alternative (Bonaglia and Fukasaku, 2003), but success for them as a group would clearly depend on the continued opening of markets for these products by industrial countries. In the long term, all developing countries should be aware of the risk of 'fallacy of composition', while promoting a process of export diversification that creates dynamic comparative advantages and 'climbs the ladder' towards more technologically advanced products.

NOTES

[*] This chapter draws upon Ocampo and Parra (2006a). The authors are grateful to Cornelia Staritz for her excellent research assistance in the preparation of this chapter.

[1] See, for instance, Easterly (2001: ch. 10), or the analysis of 'Dutch disease' by Krugman (1990: ch. 7), and van Wijnbergen (1984).

[2] Most of HIPC debt is concessionary official debt. The relevant interest rates are thus not market rates.

[3] According to conventional regression analysis not reproduced here.

[4] For an analysis of terms of trade and fallacy of composition effects, see Ocampo and Parra (2006b).

[5] This table provides the detailed information used for Figure 1.3 in chapter 1 of this volume.

[6] For a full description, refer to United Nations (2006a: Appendix to Chapter 3).

[7] There were also declines in per capita GDP related to non-natural resource based exports, but these countries are mainly mineral fuel exporters (Afghanistan, Liberia, Niger and Kuwait), which suggest other dynamics (Dutch disease, for example) underlying their bad performance in that period.

REFERENCES

Amsden, Alice (2001). *The Rise of the Rest: Non-Western Economies' Ascent in World Markets*. Oxford University Press, New York.

Astorga, Pablo, Ame R. Bergés, and Valpy FitzGerald (2005). Endogenous growth and exogenous shocks in Latin America during the twentieth century. Discussion papers in economic and social history no. 57, March. University of Oxford, UK.

126 • Growth Divergences

Bonaglia, Federico, and Fukasaku, Kiichiro (2003). Export diversification in low-income countries: An international challenge after Doha. OECD Development Centre working paper no. 209, June, Paris.

Easterly, William (2001). *The Elusive Quest for Growth: Economists' Adventures and Misadventures in the Tropics*. MIT Press, Cambridge, MA.

Easterly, William, Michael Kremer, Lant Pritchett, and Lawrence Summers (1993). Good policy or good luck? Country growth performance and temporary shocks. *Journal of Monetary Economics* 32 (3), December: 459–484.

ECLAC (2004). *Productive Development in Open Economies*. United Nations Economic Commission for Latin America and the Caribbean, Santiago.

ECLAC (1996). *The Economic Experience of the Last Fifteen Years: Latin America* United Nations Economic Commission for Latin America and the Caribbean, Santiago.

Feenstra, Robert C., Robert E. Lipsey, Haiyan Deng, Alyson C. Ma and Hengyong Mo (2005). World trade flows: 1962–2000. NBER Working Paper 11040, National Bureau of Economic Research, Cambridge, MA; available at http://www.nber.org/papers/w11040

Grilli, Enzo R., and Maw Cheng Yang (1988). Primary commodity prices, manufactured goods prices, and the terms of trade of developing countries: What the long run shows. *The World Bank Economic Review* 2 (1): 1–47.

Hausmann, Ricardo, Jason Hwang, and Dani Rodrik (2005). It is not how much but what you export that matters. Working paper, December, John F. Kennedy School of Government, Harvard University, Cambridge, MA.

Heymann, Daniel (2000). Major macroeconomic upsets, expectations and policy responses. *CEPAL Review* 70, April: 13–29.

Krugman, Paul (1990). *Rethinking International Trade*. The MIT Press, Cambridge, MA.

Maddison, Angus (1991). *Dynamic Forces in Capitalist Development: A Long-Run Comparative View*. Oxford University Press, Oxford.

Maddison, Angus (2003). *The World Economy – Historical Statistics*. Development Centre Studies, Organisation for Economic Co-operation and Development, Paris.

Mayer, Jorg, Arunas Butkevicius, and Ali Kadri (2002). Dynamic products in world exports. UNCTAD discussion paper no. 159, May, United Nations Conference on Trade and Development, New York and Geneva.

Mortimore, Michael, and Wilson Peres (2001). Corporate competitiveness in Latin America and the Caribbean. *CEPAL Review* 74, August: 37–59.

Ocampo, José Antonio (2005). The quest for dynamic efficiency: Structural dynamics and economic growth in developing countries. In José Antonio Ocampo (ed.). *Beyond Reforms, Structural Dynamics and Macroeconomic Vulnerability*. ECLAC, Santiago, Stanford University Press, Stanford, and World Bank, Washington, DC: 3–44.

Ocampo, José Antonio, and Juan Martin (2004). *América Latina y el Caribe en la Era Global*. CEPAL, Santiago, and Alfaomega, Bogotá

Ocampo, José Antonio, and María Angela Parra (2006a). The dual divergence: Growth successes and collapses in the developing world since 1980. In Ricardo Ffrench-Davis and José Luis Machinea (eds). *Economic Growth with Equity: Challenges for Latin America*. Palgrave, London: 61–92.

Ocampo, José Antonio, and María Angela Parra (2006b). The commodity terms of trade and their strategic implications for development. In Jomo K. S. (ed.). *Economic Globalization, Hegemony and the Changing World Economy during the Long Twentieth Century*. Oxford University Press, New Delhi: 164–194.

Ocampo, José Antonio, and María Angela Parra (2003). The terms of trade for commodities in the twentieth century. *CEPAL Review* 79, April: 7–35.

Palma, Gabriel (2005). Four sources of 'de-industrialization' and a new concept of the Dutch Disease. In José Antonio Ocampo (ed.). *Beyond Reforms, Structural Dynamics and Macroeconomic Vulnerability*. ECLAC, Santiago, Stanford University Press, Stanford, and World Bank, Washington, DC: 71–116.

Palma, Gabriel (2004). Flying-geese and lame ducks: Regional powers and the different capabilities of Latin America and East Asia to 'demand-adapt' and 'supply-upgrade' their export productive capacity. Processed, August, Faculty of Economics and Politics, University of Cambridge, UK.

Pritchett, Lant (1997). Divergence, big time. *Journal of Economic Perspectives* 11 (3), Summer: 3–17.

Pritchett, Lant (2000). Understanding patterns of economic growth: Searching for hills among plateaus, mountains and plains. *World Bank Economic Review* 14 (2), May: 221–250.

Rodríguez, Francisco, and Dani Rodrik (2001). Trade policy and economic growth: A skeptic's guide to the cross-national evidence. In Ben S. Bernanke and Kenneth Rogoff (eds). *NBER Macroeconomics Annual 2000*. MIT Press, Cambridge, MA.

Rodrik, Dani (1999). Where did all the growth go? External shocks, social conflict and growth collapses. *Journal of Economic Growth* 4, December: 385–412.

Ros, Jaime (2005). Divergence and growth collapses: Theory and empirical evidence. In José Antonio Ocampo (ed.). *Beyond Reforms, Structural Dynamics and Macroeconomic Vulnerability*. ECLAC, Santiago, Stanford University Press, Stanford, and World Bank, Washington, DC: 211–232.

Schumpeter, Joseph (1961). *The Theory of Economic Development*. Oxford University Press, New York.

Shadlen, Kenneth C. (2005). Exchanging development for market access? Deep integration and industrial policy under multilateral and regional-bilateral trade agreements. *Review of International Political Economy* 12 (5), December: 750–775.

Solow, Robert M. (2000). *Growth Theory: An Exposition*. Second edition. Oxford University Press, New York.

Taylor, Lance (1988). *Varieties of Stabilization Experience: Towards Sensible Macroeconomics in the Third World*. Clarendon Press, Oxford.

United Nations (2006a). *World Economic and Social Survey 2006: Diverging Growth and Development*. United Nations, New York.

United Nations (2006b). *World Economic Situation and Prospects 2006*. United Nations, New York.

United Nations (2003). *International Trade Statistics Yearbook, Volume II: Trade by Commodity*. United Nations, Geneva and New York.

UNCTAD (2003). *Trade and Development Report 2003: Capital Accumulation, Growth and Structural Change*. United Nations, Geneva and New York.

UNCTAD (1992). *Trade and Development Report 1992*. United Nations, Geneva and New York.

van Wijnbergen, Sweder (1984). The Dutch disease: A disease after all? *Economic Journal* 94 (373), March: 41–55.

Wade, Robert (1990). *Governing the Market: Economic Theory and the Role of Government in East Asian Industrialization*. Princeton University Press, Princeton, NJ.

5

Growth Empirics in a Complex World: A Guide for Applied Economists and Policymakers

FRANCISCO RODRÍGUEZ[*]

Albert Einstein is often credited with stating that "everything should be made as simple as possible, but not simpler."[1] To a certain extent, the neoclassical theory of economic growth constitutes an effort to apply the first part of this dictum to the study of economic development. Going at least back to Solow (1956), modern growth theory has attempted to set up stylized models that can help us understand the long-run economic behaviour of developed and developing economies within the same analytical framework.

The empirical counterpart of modern growth theory is the cross-country growth regression. Although the application of statistical analyses to cross-national data in order to uncover the causes of development goes back at least to the work of Kravis (1970), the seminal contributions of Barro (1991) and Mankiw, Romer and Weil (1992) are commonly credited with the integration of neoclassical growth theory and regression-based international comparisons. These contributions spurred a voluminous literature attempting to find empirical evidence to support or rebut hypotheses emphasizing the role of factors as varied as education, colonial origins, institutions and fertility on economic development. In a recent comprehensive survey of the literature, Durlauf, Johnson and Temple (2006) counted 145 regressors that have been found to be relevant in existing statistical studies.

The cross-country growth regression has become by now a ubiquitous feature of development analysis. Its use is commonplace in policy reports of multilateral organizations, country-level analyses of economic performance, and informed policy discussions. A well-placed scatter plot of growth rates against a variable of policy interest is often an essential part of any attempt to convince policymakers of the virtues of a particular policy choice. At the same time, most of the profession has become less than sanguine about the validity of the growth regression approach to study problems of development. For just about every study claiming the existence of a positive relationship between a policy, institutional or structural variable and growth, there appears to be at least one claiming the contrary. After a decade of proliferation of empirical studies of economic growth, there appears to be nothing close to a consensus regarding the determinants of economic growth; whatever coincidence there is, in any case, does not seem to have come from the results of cross-country growth regressions.

There is by now an emerging consensus in the profession that a simple regression of growth on potential determinants is unlikely to be very informative about the possible effect of policy, structural or institutional reforms. The list of problems, which includes omitted variables, lack of robustness, measurement problems and reverse causation, is endless and can seem utterly confusing to applied economists and policymakers with an interest in the literature. Most of the academic empirical papers that have gained broad attention in recent years are credited with having given imaginative solutions to the most troubling of these problems. The new consensus in the growth literature could be summarized as stating that "we can't believe most cross-country growth regressions, but we can at least believe the good ones." We will discuss some of these papers in the second section.

At the same time that these empirical developments have attempted to rebuild the empirical basis of modern growth theory, the experience of the 1990s has led to a wholesale rethinking of the policy approaches to development policymaking. Most of the action of multilateral organizations and economic policy advisers during the last decade of the twentieth century appeared aimed towards providing developing countries with a list of policies that, if adequately implemented, would be able to generate sustained economic growth. Williamson's (1990) characterization of the "Washington Consensus" gyrates precisely around such a list, while more recent discussions about the consensus

– see, for example, Stiglitz (1999) and Williamson (2000) – have centred upon what was missing in that list. Few appeared to question whether such a list made sense.

In contrast, the growth experience of the 1990s shows striking diversities in the policy choices associated with successful outcomes. Although some of the highest growing countries in the world during the 1990s, such as Chile and Korea (whose growth rates of per capita GDP over the 1990–2003 period were respectively 3.7 per cent and 4.7 per cent), had relatively open free market economies, others, such as Lebanon and Lesotho (growth rates of 6.1 per cent and 4.8 per cent over the same period), clearly did not. As discussed elsewhere in this volume, there appears to be very little correlation between openness and growth in this period, with the groups of very open and very closed economies displaying economic performances which spanned the range of outcomes. Deeper analysis of development experiences has led to the identification of country cases – such as that of El Salvador (Hausmann and Rodrik, 2005) – that have done "everything right" in terms of following the Washington Consensus, yet have not seen payoffs in terms of economic growth. Perhaps one of the most surprising assessments has come from within the World Bank itself. In a recent comprehensive appraisal of the results of a decade of economic reforms published by that institution, the role of complex interactions is not only recognized, but made to play a central role. In their words:

> To sustain growth requires key functions to be fulfilled, but there is no unique combination of policies and institutions for fulfilling them... different polices can yield the same result, and the same policy can yield different results, depending on country institutional contexts and underlying growth strategies . . . Countries with remarkably different policy and institutional frameworks – Bangladesh, Botswana, Chile, China, Egypt, India, Lao PDR, Mauritius, Sri Lanka, Tunisia and Vietnam – have all sustained growth in GDP per capita incomes above the U.S. long-term growth rate of close to 2 per cent a year. (World Bank, 2005b: 12)

The academic literature has also seen renewed interest in understanding why similar economic policies appear to work differently in different countries. The importance of interactions among different dimensions of potential regressors has become the focus of recent attention in the academic literature, as is evident in the recent contribution by Hausmann, Rodrik and Velasco (2004). These authors have pointed to the relevance of understanding the role of non-linearities and non-separabilities among different variables in the growth process. The effect of variables like openness or competition is unlikely to be separable from a country's initial structural or institutional conditions. It may also be very difficult to predict *ex ante*, as policymakers are likely to live in a world of radical uncertainty regarding the consequences of policy actions within the historically specific settings in which they must take their actions.

These new modes of thinking about growth experiences suggest a different set of problems for the empirical and theoretical growth literature. The underlying complexity of economic outcomes automatically raises questions about the validity of using the same lens to view disparate growth experiences. If countries are structurally distinct, so that the effect of policy or institutional reforms must be conditioned on its historically specific conditions, is it appropriate to attempt to understand them through overarching theories that apply to all countries alike? Or, is a more situation-specific approach to theorizing the appropriate answer? What are the necessary conditions of similarity that are implicit in the decision to include more than 100 countries in an empirical comparison? Do we have any evidence that these conditions are satisfied?

We attempt to tackle these questions in the third section. As we show there, the conventional approach to cross-country empirical comparisons, which requires the running of linear or quasi-linear regressions on broad sets of developing and developed countries, is at odds with any but the most simplified version of the growth process. We argue that the underlying complexity basically renders existing data comparisons at best uninformative and at worst highly misleading.

This set of objections is fundamentally different from those dealt with in section 2. While the earlier set of objections admit to a set of "internal" solutions, in which the methodology can be adjusted to deal with existing problems, such solutions are unlikely to be of help if the underlying problem is one of structural complexity. Adequately dealing with unknown complexity requires information which far surpasses what is available at the cross-country level. Grappling with these problems requires the external solution of searching for data outside of the realm of cross-national growth comparisons.

• This chapter is an attempt to present the complex set of issues involved in empirically evaluating the cross-national framework in simple, non-technical language that can be digested by policymakers and applied economists. Therefore, I have made my best effort to keep the use of mathematics to a bare minimum. In my case, the bare minimum turned out to be two equations. Most of the results borrow heavily from a more technical paper (Rodríguez, 2005), to which interested readers are referred.

CONVENTIONAL PROBLEMS, CONVENTIONAL SOLUTIONS

The conventional empirical growth exercise entails fitting a linear regression to cross-sectional or panel data with a functional form such as:

$$\gamma_{Yit} = \alpha_0 + \alpha_1 y_{t-1} + \gamma_1 z_{1t} + \ldots \gamma_k z_{kit} + \varepsilon_t \tag{1}$$

where γ_{Yit} is the rate of per capita GDP growth, y_{t-1} is the log of initial GDP, and $z_{it1} \ldots z_{kit}$ refer to a set of country-specific controls that can include variables such as investment in physical and human capital, the rate of population growth and other potential production function shifters such as policies, institutions, and economic structure.

Fitting an equation of this type is of course the day-to-day work of most applied economists, both within and outside the field of economic growth. Whether doing so makes sense depends on whether such an equation is an adequate characterization of the data. If the equation embodies the "true" process generating the data, then estimating it should yield useful results, provided we have a sufficient number of observations to make valid inferences. Of course, if the regression is wrong, estimating it can give us just about any result. For this reason econometricians have developed a battery of specification tests that evaluate whether there are signals that the model being estimated is inadequate.

A great part of the reasons why (1) may be wrong have to do with the existence of a correlation between the residual term ε_{it} and the explanatory variables. In other words, if what we seek to explain is how much growth varies with changes in a given policy (for concreteness, let us call it z_1), it is difficult to know how to interpret (1) if the disturbance term also varies systematically when z_1 changes. Equation (1) tells us that we should be looking for the direct effect of changing z_1 by one unit, which is equal to its coefficient, γ_1. But if the disturbance changes whenever z_1 changes, then the regression will pick up both the direct effect and any indirect effects associated with the joint changes in the disturbance and the independent variable.

A simple example may suffice. Suppose that we are interested in examining the effect of openness on growth, but it just so happens that countries that tend to have more well-developed institutions also tend to be more open. Suppose that we do not introduce a measure of the quality of institutions into our regression. Then when we attempt to estimate (1) the coefficient on openness will pick up both the effect of openness on growth and the effect of institutions on growth. To make matters really extreme, suppose that openness has nothing to do with growth, but that it is strongly correlated with institutions – perhaps because, as suggested by Friedman and Friedman (1980), more liberal democratic societies also tend to be more market-oriented. Then estimating (1) will tell us that openness is significantly associated with growth even though it is not. The basic reason is that the regression confuses the effect of openness with the effect of institutions – a logical mistake, given that these vary together a lot.

The example just given constitutes a case of *omitted variable bias* and is the most common and well-known form of misspecification bias. Its label also suggests an obvious solution: put the omitted variable back into the equation. If the problem is that we incorrectly left institutions out of the estimated equation, then we should be able to fix it by putting them back in. The solution is nevertheless not always that simple. For one, we may not have an adequate measure of institutions – there is still widespread disagreement about exactly what constitutes an institution, how to measure it, and even more on how to construct a manageable numerical index. Any measure of institutions that we come up with is likely to be measured with substantial error, thus capturing only part of cross-country institutional differences. Whatever is not captured by this measure will remain in the disturbance term, thus clouding our estimates of both effects (that of institutions and that of openness).

Furthermore, one cannot really be sure of what one should do if, after controlling for institutions, the coefficient on openness becomes statistically insignificant. For one, if institutions and openness are highly correlated, statistical insignificance may simply be a signal of collinearity between the two variables. That is, the coefficients become insignificant not because they don't exist but because it's very hard to tell the difference between both variables. We are also likely to have lost observations when we go from running the regression on openness to running the regression on openness and institutions, so that our result may disappear because we got rid of the countries that were giving us valuable information about the relationship. Furthermore, suppose that the reason that institutions and openness are correlated is that greater openness *causes* changes in institutions, perhaps because defending authoritarian states is more difficult with greater flows of ideas. Then openness could still have an effect on growth which operates indirectly through institutional change, but by concentrating just on its direct effect we are underestimating its relevance.

One school of thought, going back at least to Levine and Renelt (1992), has emphasized the desirability of seeking for *robustness* in statistical results as a response to the problem of specification bias. In essence, if we do not know whether we are running the correct specification (i.e., if institutions should be included in the equation or left out), then we can only be certain that our variable of interest has an effect on the dependent variable if it comes out with a consistent sign in a great number of alternative specifications.

Omitted variable bias is not the only reason that (1) may fail. *Measurement error* in the independent variables can cause similar problems. Suppose that we have a rough proxy for openness. Then there is a part of the potential effect of openness on growth that will not be picked up by our rough measure, but that will rather form part of the residual. This effect will be proportional to the magnitude of our error in measuring openness. Therefore our imperfect measure of openness will be correlated with the residual, clouding our coefficient estimates. This type of error, called *attenuation bias*, will tend to bias our coefficient estimates towards zero. But the effect on the coefficient estimates of other regressors can be either positive or negative.[2] For example, if institutions are measured with error, our coefficient estimate on openness can be either overestimated or underestimated. The worst part of the story is that we don't know which of these will be the case.

A third type of reason why the explanatory variable may be correlated with the residual is *endogeneity*, also known as reverse causation. It is quite intuitive that any correlation between growth and an explanatory variable may run in the opposite direction than suggested by equation (1). Do more open economies become richer, or are richer economies more likely to liberalize trade, thus becoming open? Do liberalizations cause growth accelerations, or do countries that experience periods of high growth find it easier to institute more radical reforms? Or is it perhaps the case that countries take the decision to liberalize only under substantial pressure from multilaterals when they are undergoing economic crises? All of these possibilities suggest that we should not only be interested in (1) but also in an alternative equation which specifies openness as a function of growth. But if growth causes openness, this means that *any* change in growth – including those caused by the set of factors summarized by the residual term – will cause a change in openness. That is, openness will be correlated with the residual of (1), making it impossible to disentangle the effect of openness on growth from the effect of growth on openness without additional information.

The set of problems that we have just sketched may seem daunting, and they have indeed posed major hurdles for applied growth researchers. But even though they are difficult to deal with and shed considerable doubt on the results of the traditional growth regression, they have also given rise to an agenda of empirical growth research concerned with finding solutions to these problems. This agenda has by and large been of at the very least limited success in that it has been able to tackle these problems for the study of particular issues, giving rise to a subset of results that are generally perceived to be stronger than those of the first generation of the growth empirics literature. In what follows, we briefly discuss three examples.

Sala-i-Martin (1997) and Sala-i-Martin, Doppelhoffer and Miller (2004) have offered an intuitive way out of the problems of specification bias and omitted variables, based on the already mentioned robustness criteria originally suggested by Levine and Renelt (1992). Their solution is based on the following intuition: if we are uncertain as to what the correct specification of (1) is, why not just run them all? Modern computational methods allow us to run very large numbers of regressions and look at the average properties of the derived estimators.[3] If we observe that some variables consistently come up with a positive (or negative) sign regardless of the way in which the regression is specified, we can be confident that these coefficients are not particularly sensitive to specification problems. The authors have come up with an interesting and surprising result: a large number of variables are robustly associated with growth. Out of sixty-seven variables considered by them, eighteen are robustly associated with growth, with the strongest evidence favouring the relative price of investment, primary school enrolment, and the initial level of real GDP per capita.

Discussions regarding problems of measurement have been present in many subfields of growth empirics. One example is the case of trade policy, surveyed elsewhere in this book, where the discussion has dealt with the appropriateness of the summary indicators of trade policy constructed in the early nineties. As discussed in that chapter, most of the effort in the literature has been centred on developing new indicators. Generally, indicators of trade volumes (as a percentage of GDP) tend to be positively associated with growth, but indicators of trade policy (such as tariff rates) are not. Another example is the case of education, where most measures of stocks of education (as opposed to flow indicators such as enrolment rates) appear to be unrelated to growth (Pritchett, 2001; Easterly, 2001). Recent research, however, has unveiled that measures of the quality of education are correlated with growth, although they tend to be available for a smaller subset of economies (Hanushek and Kimko, 2000).

The state of the art method for tackling endogeneity problems is the use of instrumental variables estimators. The basic intuition behind these is simple. Suppose that we are worried that reverse causation is contaminating the estimate of our variable of interest on growth. For concreteness, suppose we are attempting to estimate the effect of institutions on growth but think that part of the positive correlation displayed by the data comes form the fact that richer countries tend to develop better institutions. A simple solution would be to find a subset of events in which institutions changed for reasons that had nothing to do with growth. In a statisticians' ideal world, we would have controlled experiments in which we could be sure that institutions had varied randomly, much as explanatory variables change in real laboratory settings. It is not clear that such an experiment is neither feasible nor desirable for anyone except those completely obsessed with growth econometrics. However, there may be cases in which history or nature is able to give us this type of exogenous variation, so that there is a source of change in our variable of interest which is so clearly exogenous to the process under consideration that if we do observe that it is associated with changes in growth, those cannot reflect a process of reverse causation.

An example of this type of research is given by Acemoglu, Johnson and Robinson's (2001) paper. The starting point of the analysis of these authors is the observation that differing patterns of colonization led to differences in institutions. In principle, these need not be exogenous because they could be a response to country characteristics, but the authors cogently argue that these patterns were caused to a great extent by differences in environmental conditions. Territories that were more hostile to colonial settlement were more likely to generate poor institutions. When settlers found appropriate conditions, they created "Neo-Europes" which transplanted European institutions. In other cases, they created extractive institutions. If this theory of institutional formation is correct, differences in European settler mortality rates generate exogenous variation in environmental conditions and patterns of colonization, and therefore in present day institutions.

Acemoglu, Johnson and Robinson do indeed find that European settler mortality rates help predict the quality of colonial institutions and that these in turn help predict the quality of institutions today. This opens up the possibility of taking an instrumental variables approach to estimating the effect of institutions on development. If the changes in institutions that are associated with differences in European settler mortality rates are also associated with higher levels of incomes today, then we can be certain that this association is not due to reverse causation, because today's level of development could not have been the cause of European settler mortality. The authors do indeed find that this is the case: using settler mortality rates as an instrument, they find a significant effect of institutions on growth.

None of the examples presented above are immune to criticism. They do, however, show that the discipline has been able to find ingenious solutions to difficult problems within the setting of the linear growth regression. All of the solutions have been framed as mechanisms through which we can restore (1) to be an adequate representation of the data, either because we can reinterpret it in terms of averages of a great number of specifications, because we can more accurately measure the dependent and independent variables, or because we can eliminate the source of correlation between the independent variable and the residual. We believe these can be characterized as *internal solutions* because they have been able to tackle these problems within the methodology of growth empirics, partly as a result of the fact that the objections did not fundamentally question the intrinsic appropriateness of (1). In the next section, we turn to a different set of questions.

COMPLEXITY AND GROWTH EMPIRICS

In order to introduce the second equation of this chapter, I will argue that two alternative assumptions that stand in stark contrast to (1) constitute reasonable characterizations of reality. First, I will argue that growth is a non-linear function of its determinants. Second, I will argue that the form of this function is unknown. In other words, in contrast to equation (1), I argue that we should be thinking in terms of the following equation:

$$\gamma_{Yit} = f(y_{t-1}, z_{1t}, \ldots z_{kit}) + \varepsilon_t \tag{2}$$

where the functional form of $f(.)$ is unknown.

None of these two cases is difficult to make. Note that the key distinction between the linear specification of (1) and that a general non-linear function such as (2) is that the former rules out situations in which the effect of the independent variable depends on its initial level or the initial level of other variables. Hypotheses that specify contingent relationships, such as openness being beneficial for growth when complementary institutions have been developed or when the economy has been able to build a competitive manufacturing base, cannot be evaluated under (1). From the standpoint of (1), the only valid hypotheses are that openness is equally good, equally harmful, or equally irrelevant for all countries.

As discussed in the introductory section to this chapter, recent reflections on the growth experience of the nineties have highlighted the substantial differences in the paths that countries have taken to achieve successful outcomes. The fastest growing economies in the world display remarkable differences in the growth strategies that they adopted. Furthermore, it is also the case that countries that adopted very similar development strategies experienced notably dissimilar growth performances. If anything, (1) appears completely inadequate to handle the complex type of relationships that appear to be driving these experiences.

Growth theory also suggests that (1) is an incorrect specification. Surprisingly, nonlinearities and policy complementarities in the growth process are an essential characteristic of even the most basic growth models. In Rodríguez (2005), I have revisited Mankiw, Romer and Weil's (1992) original derivation of the linear growth equation, which is commonly taken as a justification for equation (1). In that paper, I show that Mankiw, Romer and Weil's derivation of a linear growth equation *does not* extend to variables whose effect on growth operates through their capacity to shift the efficiency with which society uses resources. In other words, the linear specification arising out of the augmented Solow model applies only to initial GDP and the savings rates of physical and human capital.[4] This is particularly relevant because the theoretical justification for introducing variables like policies, institutions or economic structure in a growth regression is precisely that they affect the efficiency with which societies transform their inputs into outputs.

It is possible, however, to make much more than a theoretical or intuitive case for (2) against (1). The linearity hypothesis can be tested econometrically. Indeed, given that such tests are part of the econometricians' basic toolkit, it is surprising that they are almost completely absent from existing growth empirics. Table 5.1 presents the results of basic linearity tests, generated by approximating $f(.)$ by a Taylor polynomial expansion and testing the hypothesis that the non-linear terms are excludable. The table reports the results of 1000 regressions, using all 125 combinations of five indicators of policies, institutions, and structural conditions with alternative specifications of the linear part of the growth equation and alternative measures of GDP from World Bank (2005a) and the Penn World Tables (Heston, Summers and Aten, 2002).[5] Depending on the choice of specification, the linearity hypothesis is rejected between 90.4 per cent and 99.2 per cent of the time.

TABLE 5.1
Linearity Tests, Taylor Polynomial Expansions

Equation	1	2	3	4
Controls	1975 GDP	1975 GDP, Schooling	1975 GDP, Schooling, Investment Rate	1975 GDP, Schooling, Investment Rate, Population Growth
Penn World Tables, 1975–00				
Median F-Statistic	4.90	4.92	4.62	5.01
Median P-Value	0.00	0.00	0.00	0.00
Number significant (/125)	116	113	114	114
Percent Significant (5%)	92.80%	90.40%	91.20%	91.20%
World Bank, 1975–03				
Median F-Statistic	5.00	4.72	4.74	4.71
Median P-Value	0.00	0.00	0.00	0.00
Number significant (/125)	123	124	124	121
Percent Significant (5%)	98.40%	99.20%	99.20%	96.80%

A set of alternative nonparametric tests, discussed in detail in Rodríguez (2005) also produce strong rejections of the separability hypothesis. Depending on the choice of methodology, the percentage of times in which separability is rejected oscillates between 57.6 per cent and 98.4 per cent. In other words, the effect of policies, institutions and economic structure on growth depends on the levels of other variables and not just on their own level.

Those familiar with the empirical growth literature at this stage may argue that (1) is not an accurate characterization of all of it. Many recent contributions, in fact, have emphasized the role of non-linear effects. Some examples of this type of research are Barro (1996) on democracy, Borensztein, De Gregorio and Lee (1998) on inequality, Chang, Kaltani and Loayza (2005) and DeJong and Ripoll (2006) on openness. These contributions and others along those lines invariably make one or both of the following assumptions: (i) they assume that the effect of the variable of interest is non-linear, but that all other variables enter the equation linearly; (ii) they assume that the form of the linearity can be captured by a simple subset of quadratic and/ or multiplicative terms. Both of these assumptions are extremely difficult to justify. A direct implication of (1) is that if any of these specifications is correct, it follows that the rest are not. It is almost as if researchers in the field are willing to forget the nonlinearities they have just discovered as soon as they are ready to jump to a new one. Perhaps for this reason, nonlinear effects play a very minor role in the more general literature. To take an example, none of the 89 million regressions run by Sala-i-Martin, Doppelhoffer and Miller (2004) include nonlinear effects. Regarding (ii), presuming that the non-linearities can be captured by a small number of multiplicative or interaction terms is tantamount to asserting that one knows the functional form to be estimated (and that it turns out to be a very convenient one).

This brings us to our second contention: that $f(.)$ is unknown. Perhaps the simplest justification of this assumption is that growth economists have no clue as to what $f(.)$ looks like. As argued above, even the simplest approach based on the Solow model yields a function which is nonlinear in the usual variables of interest to growth analysts such as policies, institutions, and economic structure. Models of how to integrate these variables into the growth process abound, but there is nothing even remotely close to a consensus on even which subset we should be looking at. If anything, the huge theoretical literature on economic growth has served to show that it is possible to write a sensible model linking just about any variable with growth. There also may be a fundamental distinction between estimating a country-level aggregate growth function which is really a representation of an economy's complex dynamics and estimating a plant-level production function which is closer to a technological relationship. Positing that $f(.)$ is unknown is simply measuring our ignorance by the correct yardstick.

Once we agree to treat $f(.)$ as unknown, the unsatisfactory nature of simplified approaches to dealing with nonlinearities becomes evident. Using a quadratic term to control for a nonlinearity will not be valid if the underlying relationship is anything other than quadratic; the same reasoning applies to simple interaction terms. Both will yield biased and inconsistent coefficients unless we get the functional form right.

The adequate approach to dealing with unknown nonlinearities is to use nonparametric regression analysis. In Rodríguez (2005), I do precisely this, using a battery of nonparametric tests to evaluate commonly tested hypotheses about the effects of policies, institutions, and economic structure on growth. The results are discouraging: these tests are almost always inconclusive regarding the effect of these variables on growth. The confidence intervals around the estimated effects are almost always too wide to allow any type of inference on the sign of the relationship to be made.

The reason for these results can be traced back to a well-known result in non-parametric econometrics known as the *curse of dimensionality*, which, roughly speaking, states that as the relevant number of dimensions grow, the data requirements associated with estimating functions of variables aligned on these dimensions grow exponentially. For example, having 100 observations to estimate a one-dimensional relationship is tantamount to having 10 observations ($100^{1/2}$) to estimate a two-dimensional specification and to having 4.64 observations ($100^{1/3}$) to estimate a three-dimensional specification. To be consistent, a researcher should place the same faith on a regression estimate of a general non-linear function in three dimensions that is run with 100 observations than she should put on a correctly specified linear regression that was run with less than 5 observations.

A possible reaction to this result is to attempt to run back to linear regressions and take comfort in the fact that they appear to allow us to find significant associations between variables. But what the non-parametric tests tell us is that the *real* confidence intervals around these variables, once we take into account our ignorance of the actual model of the world, are extremely wide. The narrower confidence intervals of linear regressions are little more than a comfortable illusion caused by the adoption of an incorrect methodology.[6]

CONCLUDING COMMENTS

The simple argument posed in this chapter is that once we recognize the true multi-dimensionality of the growth process, existing cross-country data is insufficient to allow us to understand it in a statistical sense. It is one thing to try to distinguish between the hypothesis that openness is equally good for all countries and the hypothesis that openness is equally bad (or equally irrelevant) for all countries than trying to distinguish among a broad set of potential hypotheses that allow for complex interactions between openness and a host of country-specific characteristics such as its primary export dependence and the effectiveness of its government spending. In order to do the former one may be able to get away with using a small number of observations; this is unlikely to be feasible if one is attempting the latter. The problem is that if the latter specification is the better reflection of reality, attempting to use the former is likely to lead to results that are at best uninformative and at worst highly misleading.

What lessons can applied economists and policymakers take away from this discussion? First of all, I would like to emphasize that I do not claim that the empirical analysis of growth data sets is futile. What I have claimed is that growth economists are using this data to ask questions that it cannot answer. I do not think that we will ever be able to understand, say, whether institutions matter for growth – and much less *how* they matter for growth – using cross-national comparisons. These comparisons are simply too coarse to allow us to capture the complexity of the real world in this dimension. What we may be able to do is to test other types of hypotheses about the growth process. This chapter, for example, has shown that it is possible to decisively reject the hypothesis that growth is a linear function of its determinants. In other words, what the data says is that we do not seem to be in a world where any country can expect to have the same effect from a proportionate change in a particular policy, institution or structural characteristic irrespective of its starting level. This is an important conclusion in itself: it shows that we do not live in a world where the same rules can be use to design growth strategies in China and in Chile. In the dimension of policy, institutional and structural effects, the world does not seem to be very flat. Rather, it appears to be a pretty rocky place.

Policymakers should not interpret the results of this research as an "anything goes" justification to economic policy. The fact that we are uncertain as to the relationship between policies and growth does not mean that we can do anything with policies any more than the high unpredictability of a farmer's income can justify that he stop cultivating his land. What it does mean is that there is much to gain from deploying context-specific thinking to the analysis of policy decisions and that policymakers are unlikely to learn much about the likely effects of a policy in their country from looking at the aggregate patterns of reactions of other economies.

In my view, applied economists have a vast under-explored territory in the application of methods and modes of analyses which are suited to country-level analysis and which have been underexploited in the study of economic growth. Detailed microeconomic studies can exploit the availability of information in labour and industrial surveys to help us understand the causes of productivity and human capital accumulation. Time-series studies of macroeconomic interactions can help us make sense of an economy's reaction to monetary and fiscal policy shocks. Historical and institutional analyses can help us understand the complex links between political alliances and economic policy design.

Context-specific thinking about the growth process promises to be a difficult task. Putting the different pieces of a country's growth puzzle together will require joining efforts across subfields of economics as well as with other disciplines in the social sciences.[7] It will also require a more open dialogue between academics and the policymakers that are the main depositories of country-specific knowledge on the concrete effects of economic policies. Perhaps this effort can finally endow our analyses with the level of simplicity appropriate to the true complexity of the development process.

NOTES

[*] The author thanks María Eugenia Boza, Jomo K. S., Rob Vos, Codrina Rada, Mariángela Parra, Dani Rodrik, Ricardo Hausmann, Andrés Velasco, and Sanjay Reddy for valuable conversations that led to this chapter. I am particularly grateful to the United Nations' Department of Economic and Social Affairs for having supported the research that gave origin to this chapter.

[1] The statement appears to be itself a simplified paraphrasing of one given during the 1933 Herbert Spencer Lecture at Oxford, when he stated: "The supreme goal of all theory is to make the irreducible basic elements as simple and as few as possible without having to surrender the adequate representation of a single datum of experience" (Einstein, 1933: 10–11). The paraphrased version is very commonly cited (e.g. Frank (2001: 791) and it is unclear whether he actually made it or not.

[2] For a simple, intuitive explanation of this fact see Wooldridge (2006: 322–323).

[3] Actually, the total number of regressions contemplated by Sala-i-Martin, Dopplehoffer and Miller (2004) is 1.48×10^{27}, which is not computationally feasible. Their algorithm is based on randomly choosing a subset of "only" 89 million regressions.

[4] An additional term, which includes a non-linear transformation of the population growth rate, can be included linearly in the regression under additional assumptions. The intuition for this result is that, unlike human and physical capital, there is no law of accumulation of institutions that makes them sufficiently near to a point at which we can take a linear approximation to the underlying equation.

[5] Variable definitions are in Table 5.1. A linear part of the growth equation is maintained in order to keep consistency with the Mankiw, Romer and Weil specification.

[6] Some researchers appear tempted to use the linear specification because of the belief that it captures an "average effect" (Helpman, 2004: 73). This belief is incorrect. The conditions necessary for it to be true are particularly stringent and almost never satisfied in cross-country data (See Rodríguez, 2005, Proposition 1).

[7] For an attempt to do precisely this, see the essays in Hausmann and Rodríguez (2006).

REFERENCES

Acemoglu, Daron, Simon Johnson, and James A. Robinson (2001). The colonial origins of comparative development: An empirical investigation. *American Economic Review* 91 (5): 1369–1401.

Barro, Robert (1991). Economic growth in a cross-section of countries. *Quarterly Journal of Economics* 106 (2): 407–443.

Barro, Robert (1996). Democracy and growth. *Journal of Economic Growth* 1: 1–27.

Borensztein, Eduardo, De Gregorio, Jose, and Lee, Jong-Wha (1998). How does foreign direct investment affect economic growth? *Journal of International Economics* 45: 115–135.

Chang, Roberto, Linda Kaltani, and Norman Loayza (2005). Openness can be good for growth: The role of policy complementarities. Processed, World Bank, Washington, DC.

DeJong, D. N., and M. Ripoll (2006). Tariffs and growth: An empirical exploration of contingent relationships. *Review of Economics and Statistics* (forthcoming).

Durlauf, Steven N., Paul Johnson, and Jonathan Temple (2006). Growth econometrics. In P. Aghion and S. Durlauf (eds). *Handbook of Economic Growth*. North Holland, Amsterdam. 555–677

Easterly, William (2001). *The Elusive Quest for Growth: Economists' Adventures and Misadventures in the Tropics*. MIT Press, Cambridge.

Einstein, Albert (1933). *On the Method of Theoretical Physics*. Oxford University Press, New York.

Frank, Leonard Roy, ed. (2001) *Quotationary*. Random House, New York.

Friedman, Milton, and Rose D. Friedman (1980). *Free to Choose: A Personal Statement*. Harcourt Brace Jovanovich, New York.

Hanushek, Eric A., and Dennis D. Kimko (2000). Schooling, labor force quality, and the growth of nations. *American Economic Review* 90 (5), December: 1184–1208.

Hausmann, Ricardo, and Francisco Rodríguez (eds) (2006). Venezuelan Economic Growth: 1970–2005. Processed, Harvard University, Cambridge, MA.

Hausmann, Ricardo, Dani Rodrik, and Andrés Velasco (2004). Growth diagnostics. Processed, Harvard University, Cambridge, MA.

Hausmann, Ricardo, and Dani Rodrik (2005). Self discovery in a development strategy for El Salvador. *Economía* 6 (1): 43–101.

Helpman, Elhanan (2004). *The Mystery of Economic Growth*. Harvard University Press, Cambridge, MA.

Heston, Alan, Robert Summers, and Bettina Aten (2002). *Penn World Tables Version 6.1*. Center for International Comparisons at the University of Pennsylvania (CICUP), October.

Kravis, I. B. (1970). Trade as a handmaiden of growth: Similarities between the Nineteenth and the Twentieth Centuries. *Economic Journal,* 80: 850–72.

Levine, Ross, and David Renelt (1992). A sensitivity analysis of cross-country growth regressions. *American Economic Review* 82 (4): 942–963.

Mankiw, N. Gregory, David Romer, and David N. Weil (1992). A contribution to the empirics of economic growth. *The Quarterly Journal of Economics* 107 (2): 407–437.

Pritchett, Lant (2001). Where has all the education gone? *The World Bank Economic Review* 15 (3): 367–391.

Rodríguez, Francisco (2005). Growth empirics when the world is not simple. Processed, Department of Economics and Social Affairs, United Nations, New York.

Sala-i-Martin, Xavier (1997). I just ran 2 million regressions. *American Economic Review* 87 (2), May: 178–183.

Sala-i-Martin, Xavier, Gernot Doppelhoffer, and Ronald Miller (2004). Determinants of long-term growth: A Bayesian Averaging of Classical Estimates (BACE) approach. *American Economic Review*, September: 812–835.

Solow, Robert M. (1956). A contribution to the theory of economic growth. *Quarterly Journal of Economics* 70: 65–94.

Stiglitz, Joseph(1999). The World Bank at the millennium. *Economic Journal* 109 (459): F577–597.

Williamson, John (1990). What Washington means by policy reform. In John Williamson (ed.). *Latin American Adjustment: How Much Has Happened?* Institute for International Economics, Washington, DC. 5–20

Williamson, John (2000). What should the World Bank think about the Washington Consensus? *World Bank Research Observer*, August. 251–64.

Wooldridge, Jeffrey M. (2006). *Introductory Econometrics: A Modern Approach.* Thomson, Southwestern.

World Bank (2005a). *World Development Indicators.* Electronic Database. World Bank, Washington, DC.

World Bank (2005b). *Economic Growth in the 1990s: Learning from a Decade of Reform.* World Bank, Washington, DC.

6
Industrial Policy and Growth

HELEN SHAPIRO

The chapter will review the impact of industrial policy on growth in developing countries from the 1960s until the present. This is a propitious time to conduct such an assessment. Within policy-making and academic circles, extremely critical views of state intervention in general, and industrial policy in particular, are no longer as dominant, and have given way to more nuanced approaches. This opening allows for a reassessment of earlier policies from today's vantage point, as well as reflection about new challenges posed by global production and constrained policy options.

The chapter will make an explicit comparison between the strategies of East Asia and Latin America. These are the most industrialized regions within the developing world, accounting for 80 per cent of manufacturing value added (Lall, Albaladejo and Moreira, 2004: 9). East Asia's income and manufacturing growth rates have surpassed those of Latin America, and much of the literature on industrial policy engages in explicit comparison between the regions and offers explanations for their diverging performance.

Why Industrial Policy?

It is useful to recount briefly the motivating factors behind the push to industrialize, if only to place the subsequent policies in their historical context. The economic arguments pointed to the secular deterioration in the terms of trade for poor countries' raw material and agricultural exports, differing income elasticities of demand for agricultural and industry (Engel's curves), and more generally, how high productivity growth, considered the basis of rising per capita income, was only attainable through industrialization.[1] It also reflected the political pressures and interests behind economic autonomy following political independence in some countries, export pessimism from both the collapse of commodity prices and world trade in the 1930s, and the post-war protectionism in Europe and elsewhere. There was also a relatively hospitable international climate, in which US international agencies and multilateral institutions supported such initiatives. In this context, returning to a dependence on raw material exports was considered both economically unviable and politically problematic.[2]

In their arguments promoting government intervention, many early development economists focused on a "missing factor" – capital, technology, entrepreneurship – which was unlikely to emerge from market forces alone. Therefore, different methods were required to elicit these missing ingredients for growth. Imperfect capital markets, for example, were unlikely either to generate sufficient savings or allocate them efficiently without some form of market intervention. Technological and pecuniary externalities lead to underinvestment. In addition, investors' expectations were often based on past experience, requiring some kind of "inducement" mechanism to elicit investment in new industrial activities (Hirschman, 1958, 1977).

With respect to capital, some focused on low domestic savings rates and the need to harness foreign capital in the form of aid or direct investment (Lewis, 1955). Gerschenkron (1962) argued that the greater relative backwardness of modern less-developed countries, in contrast to previous industrializers, required a leap into the most modern, capital-intensive sectors. In the face of this challenge, and equipped with a weak private sector and scarce capital, only the state had the capacity to mobilize and allocate resources. Others saw the problem from a Keynesian perspective as one of motivating investors, rather than as one of scarce savings. Due to the prevalence of pecuniary externalities, Nurkse (1953), Rosenstein-Rodan (1943), and Scitovsky (1954) argued that governments need to coordinate investment decisions and promote a "Big Push."

Despite these differences, there was broad consensus around the basic assumption that development required non-marginal change that market forces alone could not generate.[3] The goal was to reallocate resources to industry from agriculture or raw materials. The strategy involved changing the incentive structure to redirect them.

There were two other implicit, but ultimately, questionable, assumptions that experience would later make apparent. The first had to do with the nature of technological change. The development process was typically portrayed as one of factor accumulation and technology, like labour and capital, was viewed as just another missing factor. Embodied in capital, it could be imported and, assuming fixed-technology production functions, applied in the same methods as in the country of origin. The second had to do with the state and technocratic omniscience. State planners, armed with input-output tables from industrialized countries, and given the assumptions about technology, could simply allocate resources accordingly and leapfrog into the modern industrial era.

NEOCLASSICAL BACKLASH[4]

The first neoclassical reaction to state-guided industrialization aimed at the associated costs. Using new analytical tools such as effective rates of protection and domestic resource costs, these authors showed that industrial policies were inefficient and tried to correlate 'distorted' policy regimes with poor economic performance (Little, Scitovsky and Scott, 1970; Balassa, 1982). Their critique was bolstered by the success of export-oriented countries such as South Korea and Taiwan which at the time were thought to have non-interventionist states. Their rapid growth in comparison to economies which followed inward-oriented strategies seemed to provide empirical validation that dynamic gains could be had from free trade (Krueger, 1984).

This debate between old-style development economists and more orthodox theorists, however, still centred on market failure and whether intervention was necessary. In the 1980s, a second wave of critique attacked the early development economists' implicit belief in the efficacy of government intervention. Various models of the interaction between the state and private actors pointed to the possibility that "bureaucratic failure" could be worse than "market failure." Krueger (1974) argued how quantitative restrictions on imports led firms to compete for import licenses and their attached rents, thereby squandering resources in unproductive, rent-seeking activities. This approach came to a different explanation for the relative success of East Asian newly industrialized countries (NICs) – the pressures of international competition mitigated against the worse sort of rent seeking observed in countries practicing more inward-oriented industrialization.

This literature was correct in its claim that state intervention does not necessarily lead to efficient outcomes. The lack of a theory of the state was less problematic for neoclassical theory, which at least assumed that markets function and presupposed a minimal role for government. In contrast, the omission of the state as an explicit actor is a fundamental flaw in the development theorists' argument, since they relied upon the state as an agent of change and presumed that it had the requisite political autonomy and administrative tools to carry out the task.

EMPIRICAL FINDINGS AND EMERGING CONSENSUS

Although early in this debate, some claimed that the East Asian NICs had relatively free trade and non-interventionist governments, it soon became clear that the governments were extremely interventionist. Subsequently, a huge literature has documented how all late industrializing countries followed quite similar strategies and relied on the same policy instruments to kick-start industrialization in the 1950s and 1960s. They all tried to substitute imports with domestic production and used government planning to target priority sectors. They used selective protection (tariffs, quotas, import licensing, and foreign exchange rationing), domestic content requirements, and subsidized credit. In her survey of twelve countries that had successfully moved into mid-technology industries, Amsden (2001) found that the public sector had a large role in capital formation in the 1960s that diminished over time; even where development banks per se were insignificant, government played a large role in credit allocation through the banking system. What's more, they each targeted the same group of basic industries.[5] Even sceptics of import substitution such as Bruton have concluded that with respect to policy instruments, their similarities outweigh their differences. Looking at effective rates of protection, he points out how high effective rates of protection were not necessarily correlated with poor results, as "a number of countries, later achieving outstanding success, showed the same sort of protection picture as did later failures" (Bruton, 1998: 912).

A key difference among these countries was how fast and how extensively they moved into manufacturing exports. While some inward-oriented countries such as Mexico and Brazil grew at fast rates during the 1960s and 1970s, the East Asian export-oriented countries grew even faster.[6] This challenged the long-standing export pessimism of development economists. Although Latin American manufactured exports also grew in the 1970s, they were a much smaller share of both total manufacturing value added and of gross domestic product (GDP). They also failed to keep up with imports, as the region entered into the balance-of-payments crisis of the late 1970s and early 1980s. In light of these performance indicators, East Asian export-led growth came to be seen as a more effective industrialization strategy.

Based on the conclusion that East Asian success was due to its outward orientation, and in the wake of the debt crisis in Latin America, countries were encouraged by the World Bank and others to liberalize trade. The assumption was that the anti-export bias of import-substitution policies, along with the lack of domestic competition, discouraged innovation and encouraged rent-seeking behaviours. These micro inefficiencies, in turn, had led to macro imbalances and slower growth rates. Exports and import competition would have dynamic effects through learning and innovation.

Subsequent work by Rodrik (1995a) and others point out how these assumptions about the gains from trade are open to question. The static efficiency costs of import substitution turn out to be relatively small and can't explain slower growth. The dynamic learning effects from trade in East Asia are also open to dispute. Rodrik argues that in the case of South Korea's innovative firms, causation may have been from efficiency to exporting, rather than the other way.

Additional work by Amsden (1994), Fishlow and others (1994) and Wade (1990) also countered the emphasis on outward orientation and focused on the efficacy of East Asia's selective interventions. In this framework, exports are a reflection of their governments' superior "reciprocal control mechanisms" (Amsden, 1994). All these governments required some kind of performance targets in exchange for special favours – ranging from exports, domestic content, research and development (R and D) spending, or financial arrangements – but they were not as extensive or effective.[7]

The conclusion that selective industrial policies led to East Asian success is by no means universally accepted (Nolan and Pack, 2003). However, to the extent that their contributions are seen as consequential, the conditions that allowed for their efficacy are seen as nonreplicable. The capacity of governments elsewhere to enforce reciprocity commitments is questioned; markets are therefore required to enforce this discipline on firms. The focus in policy-making once again shifted to state, rather than market, failure, just when the theoretical development literature began to move in the opposite direction.

THEORY AND PRACTICE DIVIDE

In contrast to the 1960s, a kind of schizophrenia began to emerge in the 1980s and 1990s as theory and practice moved in opposite directions. Governments in Latin America and elsewhere weakened or dismantled the public institutions associated with state-led industrialization and liberalized trade. Pressure mounted on East Asian countries to do the same, although they moved more slowly in this direction. Concurrently, various international trade agreements institutionalized these market-driven reforms by committing countries to free trade, and prohibiting industry-related policies such as trade-related investment measures and export subsidies.

Just as these reforms were being vigorously promoted, their theoretical foundations were being undermined. Many of the underlying assumptions about market failure which motivated industrial policies of the 1960s – and were subsequently dismissed as irrelevant in the 1980s – have made an astounding comeback in development economic theory. In addition, new approaches to technical change and innovation, some originating in the literature on firm competitiveness, have challenged previous assumptions about firm behaviour. Together, they have generated a huge literature documenting how market forces will not produce optimal results and that some kind of state intervention is necessary to promote industrialization. Based on these theoretical findings, this literature has also proposed new explanations for East Asia's success, and helps shed light on Latin America's relatively poor performance.

Although repackaged in formalized models, the arguments behind coordinating investment or a "Big Push" have changed little since first proposed by Rosenstein-Rodan, Nurkse and Scitovsky more than 50 years ago. In the presence of increasing returns, industrialization in one sector raises demand for other sectors and makes large-scale production in these sectors more profitable. The presence of these pecuniary externalities makes different firms' and industries' profits interdependent and thereby provides a rational for a government-coordinated investment strategy. As argued by Murphy, Shleifer, and Vishy (1989: 1024), "a program that encourages industrialization in many sectors simultaneously can substantially boost income and welfare even when investment in any one sector appears unprofitable."

The notion that countries can be stuck in a low-level equilibrium trap has also made a comeback, as it has been show that multiple equilibria can exist in the face of pecuniary externalities driven by increasing returns. Under these conditions, making the transition from so-called "cottage production equilibrium" to "industrialization equilibrium" (Murphy, Shleifer and Vishy, 1989: 1004), which entails specializing in different types of manufacturing, is the challenge countries face. This echoes a point made long ago by Gerschenkron, among others, about backwardness and inertia-that more than a market signal is required to displace the previous equilibrium in order to make non-traditional investment projects attractive (Shapiro and Taylor, 1990).

What this work suggests, in contrast to traditional models of comparative advantage, is that a country's specialization pattern determines its rate of growth (Ros, 2000, 2001). This literature also offers new explanations for the success of East Asia and the relative failure of Latin America that have focused not on prices or exports but on investment. As suggested by Murphy, Schleifer, and Vishy (1989: 1025), "countries such as South Korea that have implemented a coordinated investment program can achieve industrialization of each sector at a lower explicit cost in terms of temporary tariffs and subsidies than a country that industrializes piecemeal. The reason is that potentially large implicit subsidies flow across sectors under a program of simultaneous industrialization." Ros (2001) and others attribute East Asia's success to policy interventions which sped up the transition from one pattern of production to another.

The acknowledgement that sectors are not all equal in a world of differential returns to labour and capital reflects the insights from the literature on firm strategy and competitiveness. In contrast to the passive price-taking firms of comparative statics, this literature portrays successful firms as those that create and maintain barriers to entry and the rents associated with them. By exploiting "competitive" advantages based on innovation, firms are then not dependent on unsustainable cost advantages such as low wages or exchange rates. According to this logic, a firm's strategy must be to avoid price-competitive sectors, vulnerable to forces beyond its control (Porter, 1980).

By extension, a "competitive" nation does not specialize in these sectors, either. In explicit contrast to theories of comparative advantage, a country's competitive advantage is determined by innovation rather than factor endowments. For Porter (1990), this means that national policies should help create an environment of demanding consumers, domestic competition, strong supplier linkages, and good infrastructure.[8]

Amsden, focusing on late-developers, also puts firms and their technological capacity at the heart of development. Their ability to shift away from primary resources to knowledge-based assets – a set of managerial and technological skills that allow them to either produce a product "at above prevailing market prices (or below market costs)" – determines a country's long-term growth (Amsden, 2001: 3). In contrast to the standard emphasis on getting the macro right, the starting point for Amdsen and others[9] is the firm.

The treatment of technology also distinguishes this work from early development economists. Rather than a missing factor akin to capital or labour, knowledge or technology is portrayed as a learning process. As Lall (2003: 15) puts it, "industrial success in developing countries depends essentially on how enterprises manage the process of mastering, adapting and improving upon existing technologies. The process is difficult and prone to widespread and diffuse market failure." In this world of imperfect information and technology rents, the firm is not a competitive, price-taker implicit in most macro approaches. Moreover, public support is crucial to help build their technological capabilities. In recent decades, the competitive pressures to be near the technological frontier have only increased with the fall in trade barriers and transportation, communication and information costs (Amsden, 2001: 282).

This work on the firm and the assumption of imperfect information and information externalities, particularly with respect to technology, has challenged what has been the dominant view of rents since Krueger's classic 1974 article. Since then, rents and rent-seeking were portrayed as the main scourge of development and the trump card against any selective state interventions, even in the presence of market failure. Correspondingly, domestic barriers to entry and the lack of foreign competition, which enabled a rent-seeking environment, were seen as reducing the incentive to innovate.

Now, the acknowledgement that rents are at the heart of technological change and not simply politically derived is ubiquitous in the theoretical and empirical literature on the micro-foundations of development. Free trade, rather than forcing firms to innovate, may simply force them out of business if the productivity gap with foreign competitors is too large. Using the findings from endogenous growth models, in which R and D is a key factor in determining a firm's competitiveness, and the finding that losses from monopoly power may be secondary to losses associated with underinvestment in specialized goods and services, it provides a new twist to old infant industry arguments. For example, Traca (2002) argues that temporary protection, which would allow firms to maintain market share and increase returns, is warranted for firms if they are far from the technological frontier. Otherwise, they would not be able to maintain market share and returns necessary to sustain the costs of R and D necessary to become internationally competitive. Rodrik (2004) also makes the case that firms will invest in risky non-traditional activities only with the assurance that their rents will not dissipate from foreign or domestic competition.[10] These works are helpful in explaining the divergent performances of regions since liberalization.

PERFORMANCE

During the 1980s and 1990s, Latin America's total and per capita growth rates did not compare favourably with either East Asia or its own 1950–1980 performance. Some countries, such as Chile, Argentina, Bolivia, and Uruguay, did experience faster growth rates in the 1990s than during the import-substitution period, but the largest economies of the region, Brazil and Mexico, did not. Even when the analysis is refined to identify each country's particular years of crisis and recovery, as opposed to comparing only the 1980s with the 1990s, the overall annual growth rate of 4 per cent during recovery did not match the overall base period rate of 5 per cent (Hofman, 2000). With respect to investment, while the region regained its 1980 average rate of 21 per cent as a share of GDP by the late 1990s, neither Brazil nor Mexico had recovered its previous peak. Moreover, the region's average was no where near the average of East Asia, nor was it sufficient to reduce significantly unemployment and poverty levels (Stallings and Peres, 2000: 77–78). With the exception of Chile, the growth that has been achieved came largely from high rates of capacity utilization, raising questions about sustainability.

Latin America's performance in manufacturing was also relatively weak. From 1980 to 2000, manufacturing value added (MVA) in the developing world as a whole grew by 5.7 per cent, as compared to 2.3 per cent in the industrialized countries.[11] MVA grew by 9.1 per cent in East Asia, 6.5 per cent in South Asia, 4.8 per cent in the Middle East and North Africa, 1.7 per cent in Sub-Saharan Africa, and only 1.4 per cent in Latin America and the Caribbean. As a result, Latin America's share of the developing world's MVA fell from 48 per cent to 22 per cent, while East Asia's rose from 29 per cent to 58 per cent. On a per capita basis, the Latin American region is still the most industrialized, but that lead is diminishing. Even when only the 1990s growth rate is considered, if Mexico is excluded, the region's MVA grew at only 1.9 per cent. (Mexico grew at 4.4 per cent, which, according to Lall and others, was largely due to the trade benefits derived from NAFTA, rather than from liberalization per se.) Moreover, that growth rate is still lower than both the import-substitution period and that of East Asia. Indeed, manufacturing is no longer the engine of growth in the region, as its share of GDP has been falling.[12]

In contrast to its lagging performance in manufacturing, Latin America and the Caribbean did shift to exports at a fast rate. The region's manufacturing exports grew faster than MVA from 1981-2000, as did global manufacturing exports. Due to sluggish growth in the 1980s, the region's exports grew at 10 per cent, following East Asia at 13.4 per cent and South Asia at 11 per cent. It was the leader during the 1990s, however, growing at almost 15 per cent a year, compared to 11.6 per cent for East Asia. The share of developing country manufactured exports from Latin America and the Caribbean fell from 25 per cent to 19 per cent, while that of East Asia rose from 52 per cent to 69 per cent. East Asia's share of global manufactured exports increased from 7 per cent to 18 per cent over this period, while Latin America and the Caribbean saw its share fall from 3.2 per cent to 2.4 per cent. As a whole, the developing world's share of global exports rose from 13 per cent to 27 per cent.

The sectoral breakdown of manufacturing also diverged between the regions. In many Latin American countries, such as Brazil, Chile, Argentina, Colombia and Peru, the fastest growing industries are those that process natural resources. In Mexico and Central America, there has been a shift towards labour-intensive assembly operations, mostly for export. Generally, labour-intensive sectors geared for the domestic market fared poorly, as did capital goods and consumer durables. The motor vehicle industry is an exception. It was also industrial commodities and the automotive industry which saw the greatest improvements in productivity, approaching the technological frontier (Benavente and others, 1996; Katz and Stumpo, 2001).

This rise in resource-based activities is in contrast to global trends. In global manufacturing, the share of resource-based and low-technology activities in total manufacturing fell, as that of medium- and high-tech activities grew. In Latin America, resource-based activities, starting from a higher base than East Asia, increased their share to 40 per cent, while they declined to less than 30 per cent in East Asia. Medium- and high-technology sectors grew at 16 per cent in East Asia, as compared to 6 per cent in Latin America. As a result, the overall share of medium- and high-tech in manufacturing is almost 60 per cent in East Asia, as compared to less than 50 per cent in Latin America.

Likewise, developing countries overall have moved into high- and medium-technology exports, which are also the categories showing the highest growth rates. Resource-based exports showed the slowest growth rates, falling from 23 per cent of manufacturing exports in 1981 to 13 per cent in 2000. As put by Lall, Albaladejo, and Moreira (2004: 15), "Given the general rise in the share of HT (high tech) in trade, export success is now increasingly associated with the ability of countries to move into these products. This is as true of developing and industrialized countries, and the most competitive countries in the developing world are shifting rapidly into HT exports." In contrast, the structure of Latin America's exports reflects that of manufacturing more generally. The medium-tech automotive industry was the largest category, followed by natural resource processing industries, foodstuffs and primary commodities. High-tech exports followed.

Explanations for Performance

A variety of explanations has been put forth to explain the different rates of growth across regions. Some have suggested that liberalization hasn't gone far enough. Most have emphasized the need for complementary "second-generation" reforms which focus on institutions and regulations, rather than simply macro stabilization and liberalization. Many have argued that in regards to industrial performance, it is difficult to disassociate industrial policies or the lack thereof from the broader macroeconomic environment. In Latin America, for example, overvalued exchange rates combined with trade liberalization during the 1990s hit import-competing industries particularly hard.

The literature that emphasizes industrialization and firm capabilities suggests different causal factors. One is the relative decline in R and D spending in Latin America. According to a variety of indicators, the gap in technological capacity between Latin America and countries such as South Korea, China, Taiwan, and India, is growing. These include R and D spending in manufacturing, and the private sector's share in R and D expenditure (Amsden, 2001: 277–278). In its comprehensive study of Latin American competitiveness in a global context, the Inter-American Development Bank supports Amsden's conclusions. It finds that East Asia (excluding China) spent 5 times more on enterprise-financed R and D than Latin America and the Caribbean, and that "the gap is likely to be rising sharply over time" (Lall, Albaldejo, and Moreira, 2004: 43).

The reasons behind this growing gap are hard to specify.[13] One may be the fact that governments in countries such as India, Korea, China, and Taiwan have historically promoted R and D and technology to a greater extent than those in Latin America, and have continued to do so. These programs have both supported capabilities for domestic firms and pressured foreign companies to invest in local R and D and to maximize spill-overs.[14] Lall (2003:21–22) suggests that this also explains differing performances within East Asia.

Latin America's R and D gap may also reflect how sectors with a relatively high level of technological content were hit hard by the combination of free trade and overvalued exchange rates. Those industries, which had spent more intensively on R and D, have had difficulty competing with imports from more industrialized advanced countries (Katz and Stumpo, 1995). Brazil is an exception to this regional trend, and may have been more successful in retaining industries with high engineering content precisely because it reduced its trade barriers relatively late. Benavente and others (1996: 62) conclude, "It is very likely that the high level of complexity reached by the metal product and machinery sectors, the scale of the domestic market and the higher level of protection maintained up to the early 1990s strongly influenced the fact that Brazil maintained an industrial structure more oriented towards dynamic and technologically advanced sectors than the other countries of the region." In short, this work suggests that Latin America suffered from too much liberalization, too soon, rather than too little, too late.[15]

In her survey of late developing countries, Amsden (2001) comes to a similar conclusion about how the timing of liberalization matters, particularly with respect to the relative strength of domestic and transnational firms. Countries outside of Latin America that opened relatively late and had supported domestic firms were more likely to retain medium- and high-tech industries. In the recent phase of mergers and acquisitions that has taken place in all of the late developing countries to enhance scale economies, Taiwan, China, Korea and India were more likely to have national firms strong enough to survive and/or to be viable as joint venture partners.

This raises the question of whether the greater role of foreign firms in manufacturing in Latin America has any implications for its relatively weak performance compared to East Asia. Interestingly, the theoretical literature cited above on the need to coordinate investment or to protect firms until they reach the technological frontier or generate adequate returns fails to mention ownership, implicitly assuming that the firms are independent and nationally owned. Much of the literature on competitiveness makes similar assumptions, and does not consider the ramifications of transnational firms' global strategies on national industrial development.[16]

In Latin America, foreign firms have dominated the most dynamic manufacturing sectors since their inception, and their control has increased since liberalization. According to Garrido and Peres (1998), sales by the biggest 100 industrial firms in Latin America broke down as follows for 1996: 40.2 per cent by private, national firms; 57.3 per cent by private, foreign firms; and 2.5 per cent by state-owned firms. The share held by private national firms had fallen from 45.9 per cent in 1990. Even large national conglomerates which held dominant positions in their local markets found themselves poorly positioned to confront trade liberalization.

Evidence suggests that transnationals invest virtually nothing in local R and D in developing countries (Amsden, 2001: 207). This may put even successful sectors at risk. According to Lall, Albaladejo and Moreira (2004: 13), "The few outstanding successes in LAC (Latin

America and the Caribbean) in manufactured exports face severe competitive challenges. Export activity is often de-linked from local industry and capabilities, and the competitive base will be eroded unless these links are greatly strengthened. While this is also true of some East Asian countries, others have built impressive local capabilities and even the weaker ones are acutely conscious of the need to develop local capabilities-and are investing in doing so more assiduously than the leaders in LAC."

Transnational firms also have the option of confronting new competitive pressures by integrating their subsidiaries into their global production networks. This can involve limiting national production to particular product lines and complementing them with imports, or importing parts and components for final assembly. In regard to Argentina, Kosacoff (2000: 188) writes: "In short, the data show that the manufacturing sector has itself utilized trade openness and economic deregulation to increase its imports not only of parts and components but of finished production, too. This is indicative of a trend towards the vertical de-integration of activities that affects both manufacturing activities... and commercialization activities. . . ."

As a result of these processes, intermediate and supplier industries are drastically shrinking. Even should relative comparative advantage indicators change, in some sectors there may be no domestic substitutes remaining to replace imports, and they are difficult to regenerate. Given the importance attributed to these sectors, the potential consequences for future development are dire. For example, Porter and others who have focused on the role of geographic agglomeration have emphasized the importance of strong supplier linkages for innovative firms (Porter, 1990; Krugman, 1991).[17] Ciccone and Matsuyama (1996: 57) suggest that new sources of innovation may be concentrated at the intermediate, rather than the final, output stage of production, and see "the proliferation of intermediate inputs and producer services as the essential part of economic development and growth."

This pattern has also led to balance-of-payments concerns. Numerous studies have shown that transnational firms in Latin America are leading an 'import-intensive' or 'deficit-prone' industrialization process. While exports of natural resource processing industries, foodstuffs, and primary commodities have grown fast, imports of capital goods and labour-intensive products are growing even faster, so the manufacturing trade balance is increasingly negative. Economic concentration has increased, as transnational subsidiaries and large national firms are in a better position to take advantage of the new environment; small and medium sized firms, many of which had been suppliers to big firms are now being replaced by imports.

Kosacoff (2000) argues that in Argentina, vertical de-integration and the increased dependence on imports explain why the costs of adjustment were higher, and growth in output, slower, than anticipated in the 1990s. Moreno Brid (2000) raises similar issues about Mexico. Using a balance-of payments-constrained growth model, he shows how Mexico's income elasticity of import demand has doubled over the last 15–20 years.[18] Looking at Brazil, Miranda argues that the intensive use of imported intermediate goods will not be sustainable.[19] As a result of these factors, Ocampo (2004–5: 296) concludes that "the multiplier effects and the technological externalities generated by the high-growth activities associated with exports and FDI have been weak."

In sum, in the context of a favourable international climate, domestic liberalization and macroeconomic stability, and rapid export growth, Latin America's GDP growth rates have been disappointing. They haven't matched earlier growth rates or those in East Asia. In addition, resource-based activities "*continue to dominate manufacturing and there has been a general downgrading of the technology structure*" in small and medium sized economies (Lall, Albaladejo, and Moreira, 2004: 31).

Moreover, the few successes in manufacturing cannot be attributed to liberalization per se. With the exception of maquila industries, all of these sectors were established under import-substitution regimes. In Latin America, natural resource processing industries received state support. This came in the form of financial and technical support to non-traditional agriculture and forestry, or as subsidies in the 1970s and 1980s to help firms invest in state-of-the art, capital-intensive processing plants.[20] To the extent that freer trade did not lead to large-scale restructuring in most of the late-industrializing countries, Amsden (2001: 266) concludes that "the resource allocation of the developmental state appears to have been efficient enough to withstand the market test."

In both East Asia and Latin America, exports were based on the productive capacity and expertise developed during import substitution.[21] The Latin American automotive industry is an obvious case in point. Transnational corporations initially invested so as not to lose potentially lucrative markets when most countries became closed to imports. They were first pushed into exporting through government programs. Moreover, the industry remains one of the key exceptions to liberalization, subject to special sectoral policies throughout the region.[22]

Indeed, the logic behind import-substitution policies was to force firms to make large investments that were not easily reversible. These investments constrained a firm's options; they were subsequently forced to consider the need to protect access to these markets and their past investments, which they did not treat as sunk costs (Shapiro 1994). Given the acknowledged importance of path dependence, and the fact that many of the successful sectors and firms got their start under import substitution, it is difficult to attribute growth in the recent period only to liberalization policies.

In addition, non-traditional exports that were distinct from products initially produced for the domestic market, and were therefore not the outcome of import-substitution policies per se, were usually produced by the same firms that did maturate under the import-substitution regime. To the extent that managerial and technological capabilities at the firm level are key to development, then acknowledging this continuity of major firms is critical.[23] Work by Roberts and Tybout (1995) on Colombian exports and Maloney and Azevedo (1995) on Mexico reinforces this point. Costs associated with entering export markets lead to path dependence, in that firms already exporting are more likely to continue doing so.

These issues raise the more general question of the appropriate time frame in which to assess industrial policy impact. This is true for both East Asia and Latin America. Indeed, some observers have begun to look to "initial conditions" that predate any industrial policies to explain relative success or failure.[24]

Finally, there is a peculiar "back to the future" quality with respect to Latin America's situation, similar to the trends in the theoretical literature. Liberalization was expected to increase efficiency at a micro level, which in turn would help address its macro balance-of-payments problems. Similarly, import substitution was adopted in part to overcome the region's chronic external imbalances by reducing its dependence on raw material exports and manufactured imports. As first noted by Diaz-Alejandro, import-substituting industrialization paradoxically made countries even more dependent on imports, at least in the short run, and therefore growth more vulnerable to an import constraint. Likewise, although exports have increased under liberalization, imports have risen even more, in part due to the vertical de-integration of the manufacturing sector. As discussed above, many observers today are concerned about an ever-more binding balance-of-payments constraint.[25] The restructuring processes underway also raise the question of whether what is good for the 'competitive firm' is good for national development more broadly, since what works for a subset of firms may make the national economy more prone to balance-of-payments crises and slower growth in the short to medium run.

Other characteristics are disturbingly familiar to an earlier phase. In the 1950s and 1960s, Latin America was concerned about finding itself in raw materials with low income and price elasticity of demand; today it still finds itself at the low-growth, commodity end of the industrial spectrum. While its export industries are no longer the raw material export enclaves of the past, they have become increasingly de-linked from the domestic economy as they move towards the assembly of imported parts and components while the design and technology intensive activities are done elsewhere.

Conclusion

In many ways, theories of industrialization have come full circle. Fifty years ago, the reigning paradigm considered market failure to be endemic. After years of being discredited or ignored, many of the assumptions behind this paradigm have been made a comeback. The policy implications of these theories, however, have not been similarly resurrected. In contrast to their predecessors, contemporary theorists of market failure have been reticent about policy recommendations. Given the acknowledged limitations of import-substitution policies, scepticism about government capacity, and a very different global economy, this is not surprising. Moreover, the challenge facing the more developed countries – making the existing industrial infrastructure more competitive, or upgrading technological capabilities – requires different approaches to that of kick-starting industrialization.

The default policy recommendation is still the market (see World Bank, 2002; Nolan and Pack, 2003).[26] The emphasis of reform has switched to institutions that will allow the market to perform more efficiently. Given the weakening theoretical and empirical foundations for market-based solutions, the assumption that state failure is always worse than market failure needs to be reconsidered.

NOTES

[1] See Prebisch (1950, 1959) and Singer (1950) on the terms of trade; Maddison (1994) on growth and industrialization.

[2] See Kaufman (1990) and Haggard (1990) for the political economy of this period.

[3] Ellis (1958) and Viner (1953) were early exceptions to this approach, each expressing more faith in market-based solutions.

[4] This section is based on Shapiro and Taylor (1990).

[5] The countries include China, India, Indonesia, South Korea, Malaysia, Taiwan, Thailand, Argentina, Brazil, Chile, Mexico, and Turkey. Argentina is the one exception with respect to government's role in capital formation.

[6] The comparative performance figures on industrialization and growth have been well documented. See World Bank (1993).

[7] For example, Brazil had a target program in place by 1970, which gave firms access to duty-free imports in exchange for exports. By 1990, as much as half of total exports were covered by this program. As early as the 1960s, India had an export program for textiles, which failed due to the lack of capital for restructuring. Similar incentives were offered to other industries in 1970, but the government failed to enforce the export requirements. Ironically, when trade was liberalized in the 1990s, similar programs were more effective (Amsden, 2001).

[8] Porter claims that import-substitution policies failed to create this type of environment and subsequently failed. It should be noted that this work was based primarily on firms in advanced, industrialized countries. Moreover, related work on developing countries generally addresses the challenge of creating competitive, domestically owned firms, as opposed to transnationals, which dominate manufacturing in Latin America. For more on this latter point, see Shapiro (2003).

9   See Nelson and Winter (1982), Best (2001), Lall 2001, Paus (2005), and Katz (1996).
10 Work by political scientists on Latin America also documents how economic liberalization does not eliminate incentives for rent-seeking but generates different ones. See Shamis (1999).
11 Data from Lall (2003) and Lall, Albeladejo and Moreira (2004).
12 This trend started in the 1970s, but accelerated in the 1980s and 1990. See Benavente and others (1996).
13 Lall, Albaladejo and Moreira (2004) suggest, but do not analyze, possible explanations for this gap.
14 For details on these programs, see Lall (2003), Amsden (2001), Wade (1990), and Rodrik (1995b).
15 In the UNDP's *Human Development Report 2003*, Stiglitz also points out that East Asia was slower to reduce trade barriers, liberalize capital accounts, and still used selective policies. Lall (2003: 9) points out that India also liberalized more slowly and selectively, and performed better in terms of growth in manufactured value added .
16 Porter's *The Competitive Advantage of Nations*, based primarily on firms in advanced, industrialized countries, deals almost exclusively with national firms. For a discussion of related works on developing countries, see Shapiro (2003).
17 The firm strategy literature criticizes import substitution and trade protection for creating weak supplier networks. Enright, Frances, and Scott Saavedra (1994) argued that import liberalization would both provide firms with access to the highest quality inputs and force domestic supplier industries to innovate. Instead, the speed of liberalization, in combination with foreign firms' access to global sources, forced out many domestic suppliers. See also Fairbanks and Lindsay (1997).
18 On Mexico, see also Dussel Peter (1996).
19 Miranda (2000), cited in Katz and Stumpo (2001).
20 See Meller (1995) and Ffrench-Davis (1997) on support to Chilean agriculture; see Bisang, Burachik and Katz (1995) and Stumpo (1995) on capital-intensive processing plants.
21 See Shapiro (2003). For a discussion on Turkey's export "miracle" of the 1980s, which was also based on a preexisting industrial based created during import substitution, see Boratav (1988).
22 See Katz and Stumpo (2001) for the role of industrial policy in revitalizing the Latin American auto industry in recent decades.
23 Amsden (2001: 173) elaborates on this point.
24 See Acemoglu, Johnson, and Robinson (2001), Engerman and Sokoloff (1997), and Ros (2001).
25 Katz and Stumpo (2001) also note the similarities to the debate over balance of payments in the 1950s.
26 See World Bank (2002) and Nolan and Pack (2003).

REFERENCES

Abramovitz, Moses (1952). Economics of growth. In B.F. Haley (ed.). *A Survey of Contemporary Economics*, Vol. II. Richard D. Irwin, Homewood, IL: 132-181.

Abreu, Marcelo de Paiva (2005). Which 'industrial policies' are meaningful for Latin America? Discussion paper no. 493, Department of Economics, PUC-Rio de Janeiro.

Acemoglu, Daron, Simon Johnson and James A. Robinson (2001). The colonial origins of comparative development: An empirical investigation. *American Economic Review* 91 (5): 1369–1401.

Amsden, Alice H. (2001). *The Rise of the Rest: Challenges to the West from Late-Industrializing Economies.* Oxford University Press, Oxford.

Amsden, Alice H. (1994). Why isn't the whole world experimenting with the East Asian model to develop?: Review of *The East Asian Miracle.* World *Development* 22 (4): 627–633.

Amsden, Alice H. (1989). *Asia's Next Giant: South Korea and Late Industrialization.* Oxford University Press, New York.

Balassa, Bela (1982). *Development Strategies in Semi-Industrial Economics.* Johns Hopkins University Press, Baltimore.

Bates, Robert H., and Anne O. Krueger (1993). *Political and Economic Interactions in Economy Policy Reform: Evidence from Eight Countries.* Blackwell, Oxford.

Benavente, Jose Miguel, Gustavo Crespi, Jorge Katz and Giovanni Stumpo (1996). Changes in the industrial development of Latin America. *CEPAL Review* 60.

Best, Michael (2001). *The New Competitive Advantage.* Oxford University Press, Oxford.

Bielschowsky, Ricardo A., and Giovanni Stumpo (1995). Transnational corporations and structural changes in industry in Argentina, Brazil, Chile, and Mexico. *CEPAL Review* 55: 143–169.

Bisang, Roberto, Gustavo Burachik and Jorge Katz (eds) (1995). *Hacia un nuevo modelo de organizacion industrial. El sector industrial argentino en los anos 90.* CEPAL y Alianza Editorial, Buenos Aires.

Boratav, Korkut (1988). Turkey. Stabilization and adjustment policies and programmes country study no. 5, WIDER, Helsinki.

Bruton, Henry J. (1998). A reconsideration of import substitution. *Journal of Economic Literature* 36 (2): 903–936.

Chenery, H.B., Sherman Robinson and Moshe Syrquin (1986). *Industrialization and Growth.* Oxford University Press, New York.

Ciccone, Antonio, and Kiminori Matsuyama (1996). Start-up costs and pecuniary externalities as barriers to economic development. *Journal of Development Economics* 49 (1): 33–59.

De Fontenay, Catherine C. (2004). The dual role of market power in the big push: from evidence to theory. *Journal of Development Economics* 75 (1): 221–238.

Diaz-Alejandro, Carlos F. (1965). On the intensity of import substitution. *Kyklos* 18 (3): 495–511.

Dussel Peter, Enrique (1996). From export-oriented to import-oriented industrialization: Changes in Mexico's manufacturing sector 1998–1994. In Gerardo Otero (ed.). *Neoliberalism Revisited.* Westview Press, Boulder.

Ellis, Howard S. (1958). Accelerated investment as a force in economic development. *Quarterly Journal of Economics* 72 (4): 485–495.

Engerman, Stanley L., and Kenneth L. Sokoloff (1997). Factor endowments, institutions, and differential paths of growth among new world economies. In S.H. Haber (ed.). *How Latin America Fell Behind.* Stanford University Press, Stanford.

Enright, Michael, Antonio Frances and Edith Scott Saavedra (1994). *Venezuela: El Reto de la Competitividad.* Editiones IESA, Caracas.

Evans, Peter (1995). *Embedded Autonomy: States and Industrial Transformation.* Princeton University Press, Princeton.

Fairbanks, Michael, and Stace Lindsay (1997). *Plowing the Sea: Nurturing the Hidden Sources of Growth in the Developing World.* Harvard Business School Press, Boston.

Fishlow, Albert, Catherine Gwin, Stephan Haggard, and Dani Rodrik (1994). *Miracle or Design? Lessons from the East Asian Experience.* Overseas Development Council, Washington, DC.

Ffrench-Davis, Ricardo (1997). *La Industrializacion Chilena Durante el Proteccionismo y Despues (1940–95).* Inter-American Development Bank, Washington, DC.

Garrido, Celso, and Wilson Peres (1998). Las grandes empresa y grupos industriales latinoamericanos en los anos noventa. In Wilson Peres (ed.). *Grandes Empresas y Grupos Industriales Latinoamericanos.* Siglo Ventiuno Editores and CEPAL, Mexico.

Gerschenkron, Alexander (1966). *Economic Backwardness in Historical Perspective.* Harvard University Press, Cambridge.

Haggard, Stephan (1990). *Pathways from the Periphery.* Cornell University Press, Ithaca.

Hausmann, Ricardo, and Dani Rodrik (2003). Economic development as self-discovery. *Journal of Development Economics* 72: 603–633.

Hirschman, Albert O. (1968). The political economy of import substituting industrialization in Latin America. *Quarterly Journal of Economics* 82 (1): 1–32.

Hirschman, Albert O. (1958). *The Strategy of Economic Development.* Yale University Press, New Haven.

Hofman, André (2000). Economic growth and performance in Latin America. Serie reformas economicas no. 53, CEPAL, Santiago.

Katz, Jorge, M. (ed.) (1996). *Establizacion macroeconomica, reforma estructural y comportamiento industrial.* CEPAL and Alianza Editorial S.A., Santiago and Buenos Aires.

Katz, Jorge, and Giovanni Stumpo (2001). Sectoral regimes, productivity and international competitiveness. *CEPAL Review* 75.

Kaufman, Robert (1990). How societies change developmental models or keep them: Reflections on the Latin American experience in the 1930s and the postwar world. In Gary Gereffi and Donald Wyman (eds). *Manufacturing Miracles.* Princeton University Press, Princeton.

Kosacoff, Bernardo (ed.) (2000). *Corporate Strategies under Structural Adjustment in Argentina.* St Martin's Press, New York.

Krueger, Anne (1974). The political economy of the rent-seeking society. *American Economic Review* 64 (3): 291–303.

Kuczynski, Pedro-Pablo, and John Williamson (eds) (2003). *After the Washington Consensus.* Institute for International Economics, Washington, DC.

Lall, Sanjaya (2003). Reinventing industrial strategy: The role of government policy in building industrial competitiveness. Paper prepared for The Intergovernmental Group on Monetary Affairs and Development (G-24), UNCTAD, Geneva.

Lall, Sanjaya (2001). *Competitiveness, Technology and Skills.* Edward Elgar, Cheltenham.

Lall, Sanjaya, Manuel Albaladejo, and Mauricio Mesquita Moreira (2004). Latin American industrial competitiveness and the challenge of globalization. INTAL-ITD Occasional Paper-SITI-05, Inter-American Development Bank, Washington, DC.

Lewis, W. Arthur (1955). *The Theory of Economic Growth.* R.D. Irwin, Homewood, IL.

Little, Ian M.D., Tibor Scitovsky and Maurice Scott (1970). *Industry and Trade in Some Developing Countries: A Comparative Study.* Oxford University Press, London.

Maddison, Angus (1994). Explaining the economic performance of nations. In William Baumol, Richard Nelson and Edward Wolff (eds). *Convergence of Productivity.* Oxford University Press, Oxford.

Maloney, William, and Rodrigo Azevedo (1995). Trade reform, uncertainty and export promotion: Mexico 1982-1988. *Journal of Development Economics* 48 (1): 67–89.

Meller, Patricio (1995). Chilean export growth, 1970-90: An assessment. In G.K. Helleiner (ed.). *Manufacturing for Export in the Developing World.* Routledge, London: 21–53.

Miranda, J.C. (2000). Abertura comercial, reestruturacao industrial exportacoes brasileiras: Avaliacao de potencial exportador das 500 maiores empresas industrias brasileiras. Proyecto CLA/99-1671, Universidade Geral de Rio de Janeiro, Rio de Janeiro.

Moreno Brid, Juan Carlos (2000). Essays on the balance of payments constraint with special reference to Mexico. Ph.D. dissertation, Faculty of Economics and Politics, Cambridge University, Cambridge.

Moreno Brid, Juan Carlos, Esteban Perez Caldentey and Pablo Ruiz Napoles (2004-5). The Washington consensus: A Latin American perspective fifteen years later. *Journal of Post-Keynesian Economics* 27 (2): 345–365.

Murphy, Kevin M., Andrei Shleifer, and Robert W. Vishny (1989). Industrialization and the big push. *Journal of Political Economy* 97 (5): 1003–1026.

Nelson, R.R., and S. J. Winter (1982). *An Evolutionary Theory of Economic Change.* Harvard University Press, Cambridge.

Nolan, Marcus, and Howard Pack (2003). *Industrial Policy in an Era of Globalization: Lessons from Asia.* Institute for International Economics, Washington, DC.

Nurkse, Ragnar (1961). *Problems of Capital Formation in Underdeveloped Countries.* Oxford University Press, Oxford.

Ocampo, José Antonio (2004-5). Beyond the Washington consensus: What do we mean? *Journal of Post Keynesian Economics* 27 (2): 293–314.

Paus, Eva (2005). *Foreign Investment, Development, and Globalization: Can Costa Rica Become Ireland?* Palgrave Macmillan, New York.

Peres,Wilson (ed.) (1998). *Grandes empresas y grupos industriales latinoamericanos.* Siglo ventiuno editores and CEPAL, Mexico.

Prebish, Raul (1959). Commercial policy in the underdeveloped countries. *American Economic Review* 49: 257–269.

Prebish, Raul (1950). *The Economic Development of Latin America and Its Principal Problems.* United Nations, Lake Success, NY.

Roberts, Mark J., and James R. Tybout (1995). An empirical model of sunk costs and the decision to export. Policy research working paper no. 1436, International Economics Department, International Trade Division, The World Bank, Washington, DC.

Rodrik, Dani (2004). Industrial policy for the twenty-first century. John F. Kennedy School of Government faculty research working papers series no. RWP04-047, Harvard University, Cambridge.

Rodrik, Dani (1995a). Trade and industrial policy reform. In Jere Behrman and T.N. Srinivasan (eds.). *Handbook of Development Economics*, volume III. North Holland, Amsterdam.

Rodrik Dani (1995b). Getting interventions right: How South Korea and Taiwan grew rich. *Economic Policy* 10 (20): 53–107.

Romer, Paul, 1994. New goods, old theory, and the welfare costs of trade restrictions. *Journal of Development Economics* 43 (1): 5–38.

Romer, Paul (1990). Endogenous technological change. *Journal of Political Economy* 98 (5): 71–102.

Romer, Paul (1986). Increasing returns and long-run growth. *Journal of Political Economy* 94 (5): 1002–1037.

Ros, Jaime (2001). Industrial policy, comparative advantages, and growth. *CEPAL Review*, 73.

Ros, Jaime (2000). *Development Theory and the Economics of Growth*. University of Michigan Press, Ann Arbor.

Rosenstein-Rodan, Paul N. (1943). Problems of industrialization of Eastern and South-Eastern Europe. *Economic Journal*, June-September.

Rosenstein-Rodan, Paul N. (1961). Notes on the theory of the 'Big Push'. In Howard S. Ellis (ed.). *Economic Development for Latin America*. St. Martins Press, New York.

Scitovsky, Tibor (1954). Two concepts of external economics. *Journal of Political Economy* 62 (2): 143–151.

Shamis, Hector E. (1999). Distributional coalitions and the politics of economic reforms in Latin America. *World Politics* 51 (2): 236–268.

Shapiro, Helen (2003). Bringing the firm back in. In A.K. Dutt and Jaime Ros (eds). *Development Economics and Structuralist Macroeconomics*. Edward Elgar, Cheltenham, UK.

Shapiro, Helen (1994). *Engines of Growth*. Cambridge University Press, Cambridge.

Shapiro, Helen (1993). Automobiles: from import substitution to export promotion in Brazil and Mexico. In David Yoffie (ed.). *Beyond Free Trade: Firms, Governments and Global Competition*. Harvard Business School Press, Boston.

Shapiro, Helen, and Lance Taylor (1990). The state and industrial strategy. *World Development* 18 (6): 861–878.

Singer, Hans (1950). The distribution of gains between investing and borrowing countries. *American Economic Review*, 40 (2): 473–485.

Stallings, Barbara, and Wilson Peres (2000). *Growth, Employment and Equity: The Impact of the Economic Reforms in Latin America and the Caribbean*. CEPAL, Santiago, and Brookings Institution, Washington, DC.

Streeten, Paul (1963). Balance versus unbalanced growth. *The Economic Weekly*, 20 April.

Stumpo, G. (1995). El sector de celulosa y papel en Chile: un caso exitoso de reestructuracion hacia los *commodities* industriales. LC/R.1521, CEPAL, Santiago.

Taylor, Lance (ed.) (1993). *The Rocky Road to Reform: Adjustment, Income Distribution, and Growth in the Developing World*. MIT Press, Cambridge.

Traca, Daniel A. (2002). Imports as competitive discipline: the role of the productivity gap. *Journal of Development Economics* 69 (1): 1–21.

UNCTAD (2003). *Trade and Development Report, 2003*. UNCTAD, Geneva.

UNDP (2003). *Human Development Report, 2003*. United Nations, New York.

UNIDO (2003). *Industrial Development Report, 2002/2003*. United Nations, Vienna.

Viner, Jacob (1952). *International Trade and Economic Development*. Free Press, Glencoe, IL.

Wade, Robert (1990). *Governing the Market: Economic Theory and the Role of Government in East Asian Industrialization*. Princeton University Press, Princeton.

World Bank (1993). *The East Asian Miracle*. Oxford University Press, New York.

World Bank (2002). *World Development Report*. Oxford University Press, New York.

7

Openness and Growth: What Have We Learned?

FRANCISCO RODRÍGUEZ[*]

The period since 1990 has been one of trade policy reform. According to the World Bank's *World Development Indicators*, the average tariff rate in the world went down from 10.5 per cent to 6.0 per cent between 1990 and 2002 and the ratio of imports plus exports in GDP rose from 75.2 per cent to 86.8 per cent. In 1990, the General Agreement on Tariffs and Trade had been signed by 96 countries: between 1990 and 2005, 65 countries joined it either as the GATT or in its most recent incarnation as the WTO.

The trade policy reform of the nineties was spurred by a broad coincidence among a significant proportion of highly-trained economists regarding the benefits of greater economic integration. Anne Krueger's words in her 1997 Presidential Address at the American Economic Association capture the state of thinking at the time:

> "It is now widely accepted that growth prospects for developing countries are greatly enhanced through an outer-oriented trade regime and fairly uniform incentives (primarily through the exchange rate) for production across exporting and import-competing goods... It is generally believed that import substitution at a minimum outlived its usefulness and that liberalization of trade and payments is crucial for both industrialization and economic development . . . the current consensus represents a distinct advance over the old one, in terms both of knowledge and of the prospects it offers for rapid economic growth" (Krueger, 1997: 1)

Krueger's statement is indeed a reflection of the state of academic debate at the time. In a citations count of the most cited papers dealing with openness and growth published after 1992 that Dani Rodrik and

I carried out (Rodríguez and Rodrik, 2001, henceforth RR), the four most cited papers were concerned with cross-national statistical evidence linking trade and growth, and all claimed to find a positive association between economic integration and growth or convergence.

In RR, we carried out a systematic critique of this evidence. We argued that the results in these papers either derived from the fact that the openness indicators used were *not* appropriately measuring openness (while more appropriate indicators in fact failed to deliver a significant association) or that the papers in question had made questionable methodological choices. Using the same data than the authors of these papers, we showed that correcting for these shortcomings in measurement and methods made the significance of the results go away.

Reactions to RR were varied. As was to be expected, a number of the authors whose work we surveyed responded to our objections. In his comment on our paper in the 2000 NBER Macroeconomics Annual Conference, Charles Jones (2001) staked out a position that would be followed by a number of researchers. He distinguished between a narrow and a broad interpretation of our results. The narrow interpretation was that the results of the studies that we surveyed were not as strong as their authors had indicated. The broad interpretation would be that trade policy is not very important for growth. Jones agreed with the narrow interpretation of our results, but disagreed with the broad one. A number of researchers have followed this line, attempting to remedy the faults that we had found in earlier research and to provide methodologically sounder strategies for estimating the relationship between trade and growth. One interesting result of a number of these studies appears to be the confirmation of our finding that there was no significant statistical association between trade *policy* and growth, but at the same time the identification of a strong positive partial correlation between trade *volumes* and growth. Questions about the causality behind this partial association remain. I will discuss the results of this research in the next section.

Meanwhile, the world did not stop in its tracks to wait for the results of these more careful studies. The trend towards liberalization continued into the twenty-first century, with only some signs of what political scientists and commentators have dubbed "reform fatigue" in recent years. Therefore, the evidence on trade and growth today is not the same as it was in the early nineties. Most of the studies that we surveyed at the time used the Mark 5.6 version of the Penn World Tables (Heston and others, 1995), which covered the 1950–1992 period (for many countries, the data only went up to the late eighties). Recent studies have used data ranging up to 1998 and in some cases up to 2000. Given that we now have data available up to 2003 from World Bank (2005), it is worth taking a closer look at the data to see what, if anything, has changed.

The second part of this paper looks at the results of growth experiences around the world during the 1990–2003 period and their implications for hypotheses of the growth-openness link. As I show, this period did not confirm the predictions of liberalization enthusiasts. As a rule, more open economies did not fare better than less open economies during this period, and according to some measures of openness, tariff restrictions are actually negatively associated with growth (though never significantly so). The list of star performers from this period includes some economies that are commonly perceived as being highly restrictive of international trade, such as Lebanon and Lesotho, whereas some of the worst growth performances have been in economies that made substantial efforts to liberalize their trade regimes, such as Ukraine and Mongolia. This evidence is discussed in greater detail in the third section.

In the penultimate section, I take up the issue of the meaning and significance of these weak correlations. There are at least two positions that can be taken with respect to these results. In one interpretation, these results show that there is no evidence linking greater openness and economic growth. In an alternative interpretation, they emerge from the inherent coarseness of the cross-country data and the limitations of using regression-based analysis to study phenomena of such complexity. I discuss these interpretations in the concluding section.

A Review of Recent Contributions

RR started out from a simple observation: If we look at the correlation between growth and the most straightforward indicators of trade policies, such as tariffs or non-tariff barriers, it is very hard to find a significant negative correlation between them and economic growth. Most studies that claimed to find a negative association between barriers to trade and economic growth for not use these simple indicators but rather rely on the construction of complex indices whose relation to trade policy was open to question.

Thus, Sachs and Warner (1995) constructed an indicator of openness that enters very robustly in most growth specifications. The Sachs-Warner dummy put together information on average tariffs, non-tariff barriers, adoption of central planning, state monopolies of exports, and the black-market premium. Whereas we found the rationale for including these variables jointly into an index reasonable, we also found that the explanatory power of this variable in growth regressions came almost exclusively from its use of the state monopoly of exports and black-market premium variable. This fact in itself was preoccupying since it implied that the robustness of these variables in cross-country growth regressions derived from the two components of the index whose link to trade policy was most tenuous. But what was more worrying was the fact that both of these variables were not proxying for trade policy, but were rather bringing in measurement errors that tended to bias the coefficients in favor of finding a growth-openness link. For example, the export-marketing board dummy was based on a 1994 World Bank (1994) study called *Adjustment in Africa* that covered only 29 African economies undergoing adjustment programs during the eighties. The use of this study, for example, led to the incorrect exclusion of Mauritius and Indonesia from the group of closed economies. Given that these were two of the ten fastest growing economies in their sample, this exclusion by itself substantially biased the Sachs-Warner result.

A particularly influential paper in the literature had been Jeffrey Frankel and David Romer's 1999 *American Economic Review* paper "Does Trade Cause Growth?" That paper used an ingenious device for disentangling causality links in the estimation of the trade-growth relationship. It constructed an indisputably exogenous variable – the amount of trade caused by geographical factors – to use as an instrument for trade/GDP ratios in a regression in which income levels are the dependent variable. Their results showed that, when instrumented with this predicted trade share, trade ratios maintain a strongly significant coefficient in these regressions. Our objection to the Frankel and Romer argument was that this predicted trade share could be acting as a proxy for geography's direct effect on growth which could work through the effect of climate on disease, international transmission of technology and institutions or patterns of specialization. Normally, this would be handled through a traditional exclusion restrictions test, but the nature of Frankel and Romer's just identified model precluded them from carrying out such a test. RR showed, however, that if one introduces several measures of geography such as distance from the equator into the Frankel and Romer regressions, the coefficient on trade becomes statistically insignificant.

Naturally, some of the authors of the work we surveyed did not agree with our conclusions. Some of these reactions were initially captured by Jones (2001), who contacted some of these authors in order to write his comment on our paper. Sebastian Edwards, for example, pointed to conceptual concerns about our use of White-robust standard errors to control for heteroskedasticity and defended his strategy of weighting by the level of GDP instead of the log of GDP, as we did. Dan Ben-David pointed to the convergence observed in per capita GDP between the US and Canada after the Kennedy Round reduction in tariffs and discounted the relevance of Nazi Germany's pre-war economic growth during a period of military buildup.

Warner (2003)

Andrew Warner (2003) provided a more extensive reply. In that paper, he contrasted our argument that simple correlations tended to show no relationship between tariffs and GDP with the fact that the un-weighted average tariff rate on capital and intermediate goods did display such a simple negative correlation (at least after dropping India from the sample). He also argued that most African countries that were catalogued as closed because of the export marketing board variable would indeed be classified as closed in any reasonable analysis. Furthermore, Warner recalled the relevance of export marketing boards and exchange controls in limiting access to international trade.

Let us look at Warner's arguments in turn. First, Warner shows a number of regression results displaying a negative significant effect of the un-weighted average tariff rate on capital and intermediate goods from Lee (1993) on growth. Warner (2003: 7) is incorrect in asserting that "Rodriguez and Rodrik never show the reader results using this average tariff data". Indeed, it is used several times in our Table 3, in regressions which have the same controls as Sachs and Warner (1995) but attempt to identify the individual significance of the coefficients: there we show that it displays a t-statistic of –0.18 when introduced together with other openness indicators (whereas the black market premium and the state monopoly of exports variable remain strongly significant), and that when it is combined into a 0–1 indicator variable together with non-tariff barriers and the socialism indicator, the resulting index fails to attain conventional significance levels. It is also used in Tables IV.1 and IV.3 of our working paper version (Rodríguez and Rodrik, 1999), where we show that its simple partial correlation with growth is –.048 and that when it is used to construct alternative indicators of openness with the other four components of the Sachs-Warner index, it is consistently outperformed by those indicators from which it is excluded. Indeed, most of our results in these tables use the Sachs-Warner threshold of a 40 per cent tariff rate to distinguish between economies that are closed and open only on the tariff dimension, thus avoiding the capacity of outliers in average tariff rates like India to have an inordinately high leverage on the results.

Regrettably, I have been unable to reproduce Warner's (2003) results using the Barro-Lee data. Table 7.1 shows the results of running a regression of growth of 1970–1990 growth from the Barro-Lee data set on the Lee measure of tariffs. The coefficient, –1.51 (t-stat=–1.24), is not too different from Warner's reported coefficient of –1.53 (t-stat=-1.23), so that the results could be due to approximation errors. The same thing is true when one excludes India from the regression; the estimated coefficient of –3.67 (t-stat=–2.38) which is similar (though not identical) to his –3.84 (–2.22). The differences start when one controls for the log of GDP: the estimated coefficient is now –3.38 (t-stat=–1.33), whereas he reports –4.70 (t-stat=–2.43) and when one adds schooling rates, making the estimated coefficient –3.96 (t-stat=–1.06) versus his reported –7.45 (t-stat=–3.43). In order to test whether the differences refer to differences in the data set used, Table 7.2 reproduces the last equation (where controls for log of initial GDP and secondary schooling are introduced) with alternative data sources. In column 1, I combine the 1970–1990 growth rate with the 1970–1989 growth rate for countries that did not have an observation in 1990. In column 2, I use simply the 1970–1989 growth rate. In columns 3 and 4, I use the Penn World Tables version 5.6 and 6.1 respectively (Heston and others, 1995, Heston, Summers and Aten, 2002), which are updated in comparison to that used by Barro and Lee (5.0). In no case was I able to replicate Warner's results; only for the case of version 5.6 of the Penn World Tables can one derive a coefficient that is significant (at 10 per cent). The results in these tables are consistent with the idea that there is a weak, insignificant statistical relationship between tariffs and growth.[1]

TABLE 7.1
Replication attempts of Warner (2003) results: Barro-Lee Data

Dependent Variable: Barro-Lee (PWT 5.0)	(1)	(2)	(3)	(4)
Growth, 1970–1990				
Constant	2.006665	2.322868	1.805165	2.748851
	(6.37)***	(6.96)***	(0.61)	(0.78)
Lee (1993) Tariffs	–1.514296	–3.672483	–3.381879	–3.068279
	(1.24)	(2.38)**	(1.33)	(1.06)
Log of 1970 GDP			0.0600999	–0.1201777
			(0.19)	(0.30)
Secondary enrolment				0.0240136
				(1.80)*
R-squared	0.0201	0.0541	0.0547	0.0808
# of Obs	74	73	73	65
Reported Warner Coefficient on Lee (1993) Tariffs	–1.53	–3.84	–4.7	–7.45
	(1.23)	(2.22)	(2.43)	(3.43)

Note: T-Statistics based on White-Robust Standard Errors in parenthesis *–10%, **–5%, ***–1%.

TABLE 7.2

Replication attempts of Warner (2003) results: Alternative Growth Data

Dependent Variable	1970–90, 1970–89 for missing values, PWT 5.0	1970–89, PWT 5.0	PWT 5.6	PWT 6.1
Constant	3.508661	3.553547	4.757151	3.055499
	(1.12)	(1.17)	(1.47)	(1.11)
Log of 1970 GDP	−0.2380782	0.2552282	0.4029782	−0.2232623
	(0.65)	(0.72)	(1.07)	(0.70)
Lee (1993) Tariffs	−3.725361	−3.477662	−4.616517	−2.371624
	(1.47)	(1.45)	(1.79)	(0.97)
Secondary enrolment	0.0346897	0.0349804	0.043706	0.0444808
	(2.33)**	(2.41)**	(2.36)**	(2.67)***
R-squared	0.1097	0.1116	0.1384	0.1288
# of Obs	76	76	74	75
Reported Warner Coefficient on Lee (1993) Tariffs	−7.45	−7.45	−7.45	−7.45
	(3.43)	(3.43)	(3.43)	(3.43)

Note: T-Statistics based on White-Robust Standard Errors in parenthesis *−10%, **−5%, ***−1%.

Even if we were to trust Warner's results and accept that the own-weighted average tariff rate on capital goods and intermediates had a negative effect on growth, where would that leave us? Warner does not dispute the result that the weighted average tariff rate does not have a significant coefficient in a growth regression; what he argues is that the tariff rate on intermediate inputs and capital goods does. Taking his analysis at face value, we would be led to conclude that a policy of protecting consumer goods industries is not harmful for growth but that protecting the intermediate and capital goods industry is. This would be an interesting conclusion, but it would be quite distinct and much more nuanced than the Sachs and Warner claim to have found a significant linear effect of openness on growth.

Warner asserts that a measure of average import-duties is "known to be inferior due to the fact that high tariffs may depress imports and therefore tariff revenue and make tariffs seem small." This may be true, but it is just as true of the measure that he uses, which is Lee's (1993) own-import weighted tariff rate, as incorporated into the Barro-Lee (1994) data set. This fact is evident when one reads Lee's own discussion abut the shortcomings of his data, where he recognizes that "tariff rates for each country are weighted by their own import value. Thus, an import-weighted average of sectoral tariff rates has a problem of downward bias because imports become smaller in a sector with a higher tariff rate" (Lee, 1993: 320).

It is probable, however, that differences between the variable used by Warner and the World Bank data do not reflect a difference between the effects of imports on intermediates and capital goods *vis-à-vis* consumer goods. Lee's data was constructed combining three different data sets: Lee and Swagel (1992), GATT (1980) and Greenaway (1983) which cover different time periods and different groups of products (see Lee (1993: 319) for a description). Our preferred tariff indicator, the weighted tariff rate derived from the *WDI*, has thus three distinct advantages over the Lee data: (i) it corresponds to the average level over the period of interest in our regressions, 1974–1995, and not just over the 1985–88 period (ii) it is built according to a consistent methodology for all countries, and (iii) it refers to the tariff rate on all goods and not just imported and intermediate goods.

Warner's second objection to RR is that we ask readers "to focus only on the tariffs and quotas of textbook trade policy, ignoring inconvertible currencies and a wide range of other barriers." In section 3 of his paper, Warner (2003: 8) lays out a set of arguments why exchange restrictions and state monopolies of exports can have effects similar to those of conventional trade barriers, and criticizes RR for "advocat[ing] a radical narrowing of the evidence". It is difficult to read this criticism without feeling that the thrust of our argument has not gotten across. Our basic argument was that the statistical significance of the Sachs-Warner variable comes not from the more direct measures of trade policy such as tariffs and quotas, but from those whose link to trade policy is most tenuous, such as the Black Market Premium and the Export Marketing Variable. The fact that the former is correlated with a number of macroeconomic distortions – as one would expect it to be on theoretical grounds – and that the latter is biased against classifying well-performing economies as closed because it is derived from a study of African economies under adjustment, produces a negative correlation between the Sachs-Warner index and economic growth which is completely uninformative about the growth effect of trade policies.

Warner's third argument relies on the presentation of a set of robustness tests in which he progressively modifies the original Sachs-Warner variable in ways similar to those suggested by us. In particular, his equation (3) excludes from the sample the set of countries that are rated as closed according to the Black Market Premium or Export Marketing Board criteria. This would appear to be a similar test to our construction of a variable with the other three criteria (although instead of reclassifying them, Warner simply drops them from the sample). But the coefficient on the openness variable here remains significant, leading Warner to claim that "it is hard to argue that this result is due to a special way in which closed and open are defined because it survives alterations to the definition."

The regressions that Warner uses to support this claim, however, are different from those of the original Sachs-Warner paper. In these regressions he also includes an interaction term between openness and initial GDP. He neglects to take this term into account when evaluating the statistical significance of the openness effect. Quite simply, under the specification

$$\gamma_y = \alpha_1 * open + \alpha_2 * \ln(gdp) * open + \beta X ,$$

the marginal effect of openness on growth is $\alpha_1 + \alpha_2 \ln(gdp)$ and *not* α_1. Any significance test for this coefficient will depend on the value of per capita GDP. Figure 7.1 plots the point estimates of this marginal effect (as well as their associated confidence intervals) that can be derived from Warner's estimates. Note that the coefficient turns negative at a per capita GDP of just above $7,800. Note also that the point estimate becomes not significantly different from zero at a per capita GDP of just over $4,500, roughly equal to Hong Kong's 1970 per capita GDP.

FIGURE 7.1
Confidence Intervals for estimates of openness effect by levels of income, Warner (2003) estimates

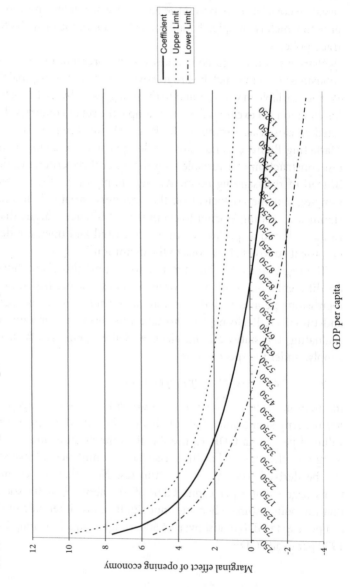

The possibility that openness may be beneficial to very poor countries but not for middle-income economies, as well as the idea that tariffs on intermediate and capital goods (but not tariffs on consumer goods) are detrimental to growth are interesting and merit further exploration. They are very much in the spirit of the call to look for contingent relationships which RR close with. They are also very far from Sachs and Warner's (1995: 35–36) original claim to have found "a strong association between openness and growth, both within the group of developing and the group of developed countries".

Dollar and Kraay (2002)

In their paper "Trade, Growth and Poverty", David Dollar and Aart Kraay attempt to deal with some of the measurement and robustness issues that had been raised in the discussion by looking at differences in openness over time and its correlation with changes in growth rates. Dollar and Kraay argue that many of the reasons for which we could be skeptical of cross-sectional results on openness and growth have to do with omitted variable and simultaneity problems that can be significantly diminished in a first-difference analysis. The main problem with a first-difference approach would be that it throws away valuable information and may increase measurement error. The attenuation bias that comes from increased measurement error, however, will tend to bias coefficients downward, making it all the more striking if significant results are found.

Dollar and Kraay's findings can be summarized in two key facts. First, they find that countries that have increased their exposure to international trade – which they label "globalizers" – have increased their growth rates from 2.9 per cent in the 1970s to 5.0 per cent in the 1980s, while those that have not have seen their growth rate decline from 3.3 per cent to 1.4 per cent over the same period. Second, they find that trade shares have a significant effect on growth in a first-differences instrumental variables regression that is presumed to reduce simultaneity and omitted variable biases.

Rodrik (2000) and Nye, Reddy and Watkins (2002) have criticized Dollar and Kraay on several grounds. Rodrik, who commented on an early version of the paper, criticized the way in which the groups of globalizers and non-globalizers had been built and pointed to a number of arbitrary criteria that Dollar and Kraay had adopted in order to build these groups. He provided, using Dollar and Kraay's data, a "no-tricks" classification of globalizers and non-globalizers: to find countries that are in the top 40 in terms of growth in Trade/GDP ratios and proportionate reduction in tariffs and select countries that make it to the list. He finds that the countries in this list (as well as an alternative list built only with tariff reductions) have had undistinguished growth performances and have seen decelerations in their growth rates since the 70s.

Nye, Reddy and Watkins (2002) point to several shortcomings of the Dollar and Kraay approach. They point out that, if one uses the criteria of tariff reductions to distinguish globalizers from non-globalizers, one find that non-globalizers actually outperform globalizers: non-globalizers saw an acceleration of 1.7 percentage points in their growth rates between 1985–89 and 1995–97, whereas globalizers saw an increase of 1.3 percentage points. How do Dollar and Kraay claim the exact opposite? By comparing tariff reductions between the late eighties and the nineties with growth rates between the late *seventies* and nineties. Obviously, such a comparison is not meaningful. Nye, Reddy and Watkins also bring up the interesting observation that the set of "globalizers" in the Dollar-Kraay categorization are invariably more *closed* economies according both to the Trade/GDP criterion and the tariff criterion. These are indeed economies that are increasing their exposure to international trade from a position of being relatively closed. Therefore, if we are to take Dollar and Kraay's evidence at face value and accept that countries that saw greater increases in their trade also saw their growth rates accelerate, we would have to accept that less open economies experienced greater accelerations in their growth rates.

It is indeed striking that in their published version Dollar and Kraay produce two criteria for constructing groups of globalizers and non-globalizers, one based on trade/GDP ratios and the other one based on tariff rates, but when they turn to regression analysis they only produce results with trade/GDP ratios. One cannot help but ask what the regressions with tariff rates looked like.

In any case, the Dollar and Kraay evidence is consistent with the Frankel and Romer (1999) findings discussed above. The data appears to display a strong correlation between trade *volumes* and growth rates, both in levels as well as in first-differences. Whether this correlation is spurious or not is an open question: Dollar and Kraay's solution to the identification problem, which is to instrument the first differences with lagged levels, is far from perfect. If shocks are persistent over time, this will not be an appropriate solution to simultaneity problems; it also leaves open the problem of omitted variables such as institutions.[2]

Wacziarg and Welch (2003)

Romain Wacziarg and Karen Welch's 2003 paper "Trade Liberalization and Growth: New Evidence" constitutes an attempt to correct some of the problems with the Sachs-Warner variable while retaining their basic approach. The authors revised the Sachs-Warner criteria in order to correct for the biases pointed out by RR and others (see Harrison and Hanson, 1999) and have extended their data to cover the 1990s. They summarize their results as follows:

"We revisited the evidence on the cross-country effects of SW's simple dichotomous indicator of outward orientation on economic growth, confirming the pitfalls of this indicator first underlined by RR. Additionally, we showed that the partitioning of countries according to the SW dichotomous indicator, while it effectively separates fast growing countries from slow growing ones in the 1980s and to a lesser extent in the 1970s, fails to do so in the 1990s" (Wacziarg and Welch 2003: 28).

Wacziarg and Welch do not stop here, however. They go on to build a time-dependent index of liberalization based on a country's date of trade liberalization. This exercise uses as its starting point Sachs and Warner's (1995) liberalization dates, a somewhat different exercise that did not play such a central role in their original analysis. These dates are in principle built according to the same criteria as the dichotomous variable, but given the lack of yearly data availability the criteria are necessarily less strictly applied and there is substantial room for subjective judgment. Using these dates, the authors produce estimates that show liberalization having significant effects on growth, investment, and openness.

In order to understand the full implication of Wacziarg and Welch's work, it is important to understand what their exercise consists in. Wacziarg and Welch consistently apply the same criteria used by Sachs and Warner (tariffs or quotas above 40 per cent, black market premium above 20 per cent, state monopoly of exports and socialist economic system) to determine the date in which countries liberalized. Thus, in essence, this is the Sachs-Warner exercise carried out at the within-country level. Is it still open to the criticisms made by RR?

Remember that the key objections that RR made to the Sachs-Warner variable were that: (i) the variable relied heavily on the black market premium and export marketing board variables to classify countries as open and closed. (ii) The black market premium variable is likely to capture the effects of a number of macroeconomic distortions, and the export marketing board variable acted as a proxy for being an African country undergoing structural adjustment in the eighties. Both of these variables thereby introduced trade-unrelated information that was likely to bias the estimates of openness's growth effect.

A look at the Wacziarg and Welch data indicates a heavy reliance on the black market premium and export marketing boards to rate economies as open or closed. Out of 31 economies that they classify as closed at the end of 2001, 27 are deemed closed exclusively because of their black market premium or state monopoly of exports. Only in 3 cases (Angola, China and India) is information provided that would lead to classifying these countries as closed because of their tariffs, quotas or state socialist system. In one remaining case (Republic of Congo) an IMF assessment of its "insufficient progress" in economic reforms was used to classify it as closed. The average growth rates of the countries that are rated as closed *exclusively* because of their black market premium or state monopoly of exports during the 1990–2003 period is –0.1 per cent, considerably below the world average of 1.1 per cent. While dropping these observations would not affect their results given their use of fixed effects and the fact that these economies remain closed throughout the sample, reclassifying some of them as having liberalized in the late eighties /early nineties could have a significant effect, given the precipitous decline in growth rates suffered by many of them.

Despite Wacziarg and Welch's attempt to correct some of the biases in the Sachs-Warner data by comprehensively revising their ratings, a close examination of their revisions show a number of preoccupying inconsistencies. Gabon is rated as closed because of state ownership of the petroleum industry, but Mexico and Indonesia are not. Ukraine and Venezuela are rated as closed in periods in which they adopt exchange controls despite having maintained relatively liberal trade regimes; Malaysia, which did the same thing at the end of the nineties, is not.

It is also hard to look at this data and not conclude that the excessive reliance on the black market premium is causing a number of economies to be misclassified. Most specialists would agree that Russia is today, by and large, a free market economy with a liberalized trade regime (see, e.g., Shleifer and Treisman, 2004), but Wacziarg and Welch classify it as closed due to its black market premium. In 1998, the final year used in Wacziarg and Welch's panel regressions, Estonia was among the five economies in the world to score the lowest possible score (1.0) in the Heritage Institution's index of trade restrictions (Heritage, 2005). Wacziarg and Welch nevertheless classify Estonia as closed, again due to its black market premium.[3]

Given that Wacziarg and Welch construct a time-dependent version of the Sachs-Warner dummy, it is not surprising that they are able to derive strong statistical effects of openness on growth in this exercise. Their classification is, as in the original Sachs and Warner data, heavily dependent on the black market premium and export marketing board variables. They are thus open to the same objections that were leveled against Sachs and Warner: they have provided us with a measure of trade liberalization that is negatively correlated with growth but that is at the same time so contaminated by non-trade information so as to leave room for considerable skepticism as to the appropriate interpretation of their results.[4]

Recent Advances

One of the main reasons why it is so hard to reach definitive conclusions regarding the trade-growth link is the complex web of interrelationships that is involved in the determination of a nation's income. Trade can have a significant impact on GDP, but so can many factors that can be related to trade. As highlighted in the discussion of Frankel and Romer's work, geography can have effects on trade but also have direct effects on growth. Geography could in turn also be related to the institutions that an economy can develop. Trade itself could affect institutions directly. Disentangling the effects of trade on growth from the effects of geography and policies would appear to be an unmanageable task.

Rodrik, Subramanian and Trebbi (2004) and Rigobón and Rodrik (2005) constitute two recent attempts to tackle these issues. The first of these papers uses the instruments derived by Frankel and Romer as well as the instrument for institutions suggested by Acemoglu, Johnson and Robinson (2001) – the European settler mortality rate, to run a horse race between geography, trade and institutions. The authors show that the institutions variable consistently comes out with a significant coefficient in these regressions, whereas geography displays an insignificantly positive coefficient and the coefficient on the trade/GDP ratio actually turns negative. Rigobon and Rodrik (2005) take this experiment one step further, relying not on instrumental variable methods but on the novel technique of identification through heteroskedasticity proposed by Rigobón (2003). Their results confirm the relevance of institutions: both political and economic institutions are estimated to have positive effects on growth, although the effects of the latter are much more important. In contrast, openness is estimated to negatively affect income levels and democracy, although it appears to reinforce the rule of law.

An alternative set of authors have attempted to use advances in panel data methodology to combine the information on changes in growth, as proposed by Dollar and Kraay, without paying the efficiency cost of sacrificing information in levels. Of particular note are Chang, Kaltani and Loayza (2005) and DeJong and Ripoll (2006). Both of these papers use the Blundell and Bond (1997) GMM estimator, which combines information from a regression in levels and a regression in first-differences, to produce a more efficient estimation. The difference between the two approaches is that the former paper uses trade ratios while the latter uses tariff rates, as originally suggested by RR. Both papers reach similar conclusions: the effect of openness on growth is conditional on the level of income. In particular, DeJong and Ripoli (2005) fail to find any evidence that openness has an effect on growth in developing economies.[5]

Discussion

If the adoption of protectionist policies took the life out of growth prospects in the developing world during the postwar period, it managed to leave no smoking gun behind. Growth displays no significant correlation with the most direct measures of trade policy. The case against trade policy necessarily hinges on the interpretation of particular pieces of circumstantial evidence: Growth is negatively correlated with policy measures with some theoretical link to trade, such as the black market premium; income levels and growth rates are negatively correlated with trade shares, an imperfect and highly endogenous measure of trade policy. As is commonly the case with circumstantial evidence, alternative interpretations can be offered to explain these facts. The black market premium can pick up the effect of alternative macroeconomic distortions. State monopolies of exports have yet to be consistently measured. And different methodologies to control for causality give widely divergent results with respect to the identification of the direct effect of trade volumes on growth.

The existence of gains from trade is one of the main tenets of modern economic theory. Even authors who have shown how these results can be reversed in theory shy away from questioning them in practice. It is thus not surprising to see economists devote substantial intellectual resources to try to find such a link. Perhaps the fact that the link is so hard to find can serve as intellectual stimulus to uncover techniques that will allow us to confirm the intuitions of basic trade theory. Or perhaps the link is so difficult to find because it does not exist.

TRADE AND GROWTH IN THE NINETIES

During the time that the academic debate on the merits of openness was going on, a large number of countries was implementing economic reforms with a substantial trade liberalization component. Indeed, by 1998, not a single country in the world had an average tariff rata above 40 per cent, the level that Sachs and Warner had deemed sufficient to determine that an economy was closed. This increase in economic integration was not accompanied by an evident increase in world growth rates: average growth during the 1990–2003 period was 1.07 per cent, actually lower than the 1.42 per cent average growth rate of the 1975–1990 period.[6]

TABLE 7.3
Average Growth Rates by level of Openness, 1990–2003

Category Variable	Open	Not Open	P-Value of Test for Equality of Means
Trade/GDP Ratio	1.14%	0.98%	0.68
Weighted Tariff Rate	1.19%	1.20%	0.97
Unweighted Tariff Rates	1.31%	1.25%	0.87
Sachs-Warner Openness (1)	1.25%	0.26%	0.03
Sachs-Warner Openness (2)	1.06%	0.89%	0.69
Changes in Trade Ratio	1.63%	0.74%	0.13

What does the post-1990 experience tell us about the link between trade and growth? Did open economies grow faster during this period? The evidence does not show significant differences between economies' growth rates based on their level of integration. Table 7.3 displays the average growth rates of open and not open economies, where we have used several common criteria to distinguish the restrictiveness of trade regimes: the Trade/GDP ratio, the import-weighted tariff rate calculated using import and export tax revenues from the *World Development Indicators*, Wacziarg and Welch's (2003) un-weighted tariff rate, two versions of the Wacziarg-Welch openness variable, as well as the changes in the trade ratios and tariff rates between the 1980–1990 and 1990–2003 periods. The difference between the two Wacziarg-Welch indicators is that the first one uses the original Sachs and Warner thresholds while the second one lowers the tariff and NTB thresholds to 20 per cent and he black market premium threshold to 10 per cent. As we can see there, when the *level* of trade restrictions is used to distinguish between open and closed economies, the growth rate of these two groups is undistinguishable. Indeed, when one uses the import-weighted tariff rate the group of economies that were not open slightly outperforms open economies. When one uses the Wacziarg-Welch indicator that we have discussed in section 2, one does find a significant difference between open and not open economies, but this difference vanishes if one lowers the threshold for tariff rates. When we turn to a measure of changes in trade shares, as do Dollar and Kraay, we find that economies that saw greater increases in trade shares do seem to have outperformed those that did not. However, this difference is not significant at conventional levels (p-value=0.13).

Table 7.4(a)
10 Fastest Growing Economies, 1990–2003

Rank	Country	Growth Rate, 1990–2003	Trade/ GDP Ratio	Average Tariff Rate	Openness (Trade/ GDP)	Openness (Tariffs)
1	China	8.3%	37.2806	3.3%	Not Open	Open
2	Ireland	6.5%	134.158	0.0%	Open	Open
3	Lebanon	6.1%	57.1125	8.2%	Not Open	Not Open
4	Vietnam	5.1%	75.3637	8.7%	Open	Not Open
5	Luxembourg	4.8%	227.215	0.0%	Open	Open
6	Lesotho	4.8%	129.826	19.7%	Open	Not Open
7	Korea	4.7%	57.414	3.8%	Not Open	Open
8	Chile	3.9%	53.9963	*	Not Open	*
9	Mozambique	3.9%	51.6874	*	Not Open	*
10	Mauritius	3.8%	133.795	11.5%	Open	Not Open

TABLE 7.4(B)
10 Slowest Growing Economies, 1990–2003

Rank	Country	Growth Rate, 1990–2003	Trade/ GDP Ratio	Average Tariff Rate	Openness (Trade/ GDP)	Openness (Tariffs)
140	Burundi	–2.8%	32.9722	23.1%	Not Open	Not Open
141	Kyrgyz Republic	–3.0%	81.0445	*	Open	*
142	Mongolia	–3.0%	91.4524	2.7%	Open	Open
143	Haiti	–3.1%	42.7533	*	Not Open	*
144	Ukraine	–3.8%	68.1068	1.8%	Open	Open
145	Sierra Leone	–5.1%	52.5972	17.0%	Not Open	Not Open
146	Georgia	–5.5%	35.9498	2.0%	Not Open	Open
147	Tajikistan	–6.1%	125.279	*	Open	*
148	Congo, Dem. Rep.	–6.9%	50.8966	*	Not Open	*
149	Moldova	–7.4%	107.057	1.3%	Open	Open

*- Revenues from Import Taxes npt reported in World Bank (2005)

Tables 7.4A and 7.4B help us get some insight as to why there is no simple link between trade and openness (at least in levels) in this data. Both lists of the fastest growing and the slowest growing economies in the world are populated by open and closed economies. According to the trade ratio and tariff criteria, Lebanon cannot be classified as an open economy, but it has the third highest growth rate in the world for the 1990–2003 period. Lesotho has one of the highest remaining levels of tariffs in the world, 19.7 per cent, more than twice the world average of 7.05 per cent, but has the sixth highest growth rate of per capita incomes in the world. At the same time, there are obvious cases of unquestionably open economies, such as Ireland and Luxembourg, on this list. Similarly, the list of slowest growing economies displays some clearly restrictive economies such as Sierra

Leone and Burundi, but is also integrated by open economies such as Moldova and Mongolia. Similarly, Tables 7.5A and 7.5B display the growth performance of the most closed economies according to the tariff and trade ratio criteria. The message is the same: some closed economies do badly, but some (India, Lesotho, Ghana and Botswana) appear to do pretty well.

TABLE 7.5(A)
Growth Performance of 10 Most Restrictive Economies in the World (Tariff Criteria), 1990–2003

Rank	Country	Growth Rate, 1990–2003	Average Tariff Rate
1	Guinea	0.87%	32.21%
2	Rwanda	−0.05%	25.71%
3	Côte d'Ivoire	−2.07%	25.01%
4	India	3.64%	23.21%
5	Burundi	−2.82%	23.15%
6	Vanuatu	1.04%	20.24%
7	Lesotho	4.76%	19.69%
8	Ghana	1.98%	19.14%
9	Ethiopia	0.61%	18.88%
10	Botswana	2.79%	18.52%
	Average, 10 most restrictive economies	1.07%	22.58%
	World Average	1.07%	7.23%

TABLE 7.5(B)

Growth Performance of 10 Most Restrictive Economies in the World (Trade Ratio Criteria), 1990–2003

Rank	Country	Growth, 1990–2003	Trade/GDP Ratio
1	Brazil	0.99%	14.71
2	Japan	0.99%	17.64
3	Argentina	1.95%	19.90
4	India	3.64%	21.90
5	United States	1.69%	22.41
6	Bangladesh	2.73%	25.21
7	Peru	1.92%	26.28
8	Colombia	0.52%	30.09
9	Uganda	3.46%	30.81
10	Burundi	–2.82%	32.97
	Average, 10 most restrictive economies	1.51%	24.19
	World Average	1.07%	78.57

Tables 7.6 to 7.10 present the result of cross-sectional regressions that attempt to account for growth in per capita GDP as a function of the alternative openness indicators and a set of common controls. The Trade/GDP ratio has a positive albeit far from significant effect on growth, which actually becomes negative (always insignificant) as more controls are added to the regression. When measured by import-weighted tariffs or un-weighted tariffs, the coefficient of openness on growth is actually negative though not significant (tariffs are multiplied by –1 to make interpretation of these coefficients as effects of openness simple). Consistent with the results of Wacziarg and Welch (2003), we find that the Sachs-Warner-Wacziarg-Welch indicator has a positive but insignificant effect on growth when the original thresholds are used, but a negative insignificant coefficient with the lower thresholds. Additional tests, reported in the working

paper version of this paper (Rodríguez, 2006), show no relationship between changes in growth and changes in the trade/GDP ratio, regardless of whether the latter is instrumented or not on lagged openness.

TABLE 7.6
Cross-Sectional Growth Regressions 1990–2003, Trade/GDP Ratio as Indicator of Openness

	(1)	(2)	(3)	(4)
Constant	0.0168	0.0265	0.0457	0.0816
	(1.17)	(0.91)	(1.75)	(2.68)***
Log(1990 GDP)	0.0029	−0.0039	−0.0074	−0.0223
	(1.83)*	(0.96)	(1.98)*	(3.47)***
Trade/GDP Ratio	0.0000	0.0000	0.0000	0.0000
	(1.16)	(1.65)	(0.04)	(0.21)
Years of Schooling		0.0030	0.0017	0.0002
		(2.07)**	(1.55)	(0.2)
Investment Rate			0.0014	0.0009
			(4.33)***	(2.39)**
Life Expectancy				0.0012
				(2.17)**
Rule of Law				0.0081
				(2.46)**
Population Growth Rate				−0.0034
				(1.48)
n	141	93	93	82
R2	2.46	3.42	6.99	4.2

Note: T-Statistics based on White-Robust Standard Errors in parenthesis *–10%, **–5%, ***–1%.

TABLE 7.7

Cross-Sectional Growth Regressions 1990–2003, Weighted Tariffs as Indicator of Openness

	(1)	(2)	(3)	(4)
Constant	−0.0680	0.0243	0.0146	0.0270
	(0.84)	(0.25)	(0.17)	(0.28)
Log(1990 GDP)	0.0050	−0.0030	−0.0058	−0.0214
	(1.4)	(0.55)	(1.17)	(2.85)***
Weighted Tariffs	−0.0347	−0.0023	−0.0199	−0.0379
	(0.7)	(0.04)	(0.39)	(0.63)
Years of Schooling		0.0024	0.0012	0.0004
		(1.75)*	(1.14)	(0.45)
Investment Rate			0.0014	0.0008
			(4.14)***	(2.06)**
Life Expectancy				0.0014
				(2.09)**
Rule of Law				0.0070
				(1.96)*
Population Growth Rate				−0.0032
				(1.25)
n	114	81	81	71
R2	0.0274	0.0427	0.2069	0.4087

Note: T-Statistics based on White-Robust Standard Errors in parenthesis *–10%, **–5%, ***–1%.

TABLE 7.8
Cross-Sectional Growth Regressions 1990–03, Unweighted Tariffs as Indicator of Openness

	(1)	(2)	(3)	(4)
Constant	−0.0413	0.0103	0.0228	0.0740
	(2.27)**	(0.36)	(0.9)	(1.98)*
Log (1990 GDP)	0.0056	0.0025	−0.0056	−0.0215
	(3.04)***	(0.64)	(1.6)	(2.93)***
Weighted Tariffs	−0.0005	−0.0004	−0.0004	−0.0001
	(1.83)*	(1.42)	(1.74)*	(0.49)
Years of Schooling		0.0034	0.0018	0.0004
		(2.34)**	(1.68)*	(0.38)
Investment Rate			0.0014	0.0008
			(5.03)***	(2.55)**
Life Expectancy				0.0012
				(2.04)**
Rule of Law				0.0081
				(2.45)**
Population Growth Rate				−0.0032
				(1.42)
n	115	91	91	80
R2	0.0611	0.0987	0.2681	0.4313

Note: T-Statistics based on White-Robust Standard Errors in parenthesis *– 10%, **–5%, ***–1%.

TABLE 7.9

Cross-Sectional Growth Regressions 1990–2003, Sachs-Warner-Wacziarg-Welch (Original Thresholds) as Indicator of Openness

	(1)	(2)	(3)	(4)
Constant	0.0195	0.0371	0.0510	0.0912
	(1.38)	(1.39)	(2.14)**	(2.99)***
Log(1990 GDP)	0.0029	−0.0058	−0.0087	−0.0234
	(1.71)*	(1.48)	(2.48)**	(3.59)***
SWWW Dummy	0.0071	0.0108	0.0089	0.0076
	(1.33)	(1.4)	(1.29)	(1.25)
Years of Schooling		0.0030	0.0015	0.0003
		(2.03)**	(1.36)	(0.3)
Investment Rate			0.0013	0.0008
			(4.71)***	(2.73)***
Life Expectancy				0.0012
				(2.11)**
Rule of Law				0.0078
				(2.47)**
Population Growth Rate				−0.0042
				(1.98)*
n	129	93	93	82
R2	0.0518	0.1104	0.2665	0.4443

Note: T-Statistics based on White-Robust Standard Errors in parenthesis *–10%, **–5%, ***–1%.

TABLE 7.10
Cross-Sectional Growth Regressions 1990–2003, Sachs-Warner-Wacziarg-Welch (New Thresholds) as Indicator of Openness

	(1)	(2)	(3)	(4)
Constant	−0.0272	0.0267	0.0413	0.0809
	(1.67)*	(0.93)	(1.66)*	(2.46)**
Log(1990 GDP)	0.0046	−0.0035	−0.0067	−0.0222
	(2.29)**	(0.84)	(1.81)*	(3.26)***
SWWW Dummy	−0.0030	−0.0025	−0.0036	−0.0004
	(0.6)	(0.48)	(0.76)	(0.08)
Years of Schooling		0.0032	0.0017	0.0002
		(2.15)**	(1.46)	(0.22)
Investment Rate			0.0014	0.0008
			(4.91)***	(2.66)***
Life Expectancy				0.0012
				(2.19)**
Rule of Law				0.0081
				(2.47)**
Population Growth Rate				−0.0034
				(1.46)
n	129	93	93	82
R2	0.0393	0.0783	0.2481	0.4292

Note: T-Statistics based on White-Robust Standard Errors in parenthesis *–10%, **–5%, ***–1%.

If there was a relationship between openness and growth in the data, it seems to have disappeared during the period since 1990. In this section, I have looked at the effects of six measures of openness that have been widely used in the literature. A fair summary of the evidence previous to 1990 is that some of these measures (tariffs, non-tariff barriers) displayed a negative correlation with growth, while others (trade shares, changes in trade shares, Sachs-Warner dummy) portrayed a positive correlation. The results above show that over the 1990–2003 period, *none* of these measures have been significantly associated with growth.

Concluding Comments

In the preceding pages, I have discussed recent empirical research regarding the link between openness and growth in cross-country data. I have argued that a close reading of the evidence presented in the latest contributions does not alter the conclusion that standard measures of trade policy are basically uncorrelated with growth. It is only by adding information with a tenuous link to trade policies that these papers are able to derive such a correlation. And, while the data does display a correlation between income (both in levels and growth rates) and trade shares, recent attempts at disentangling the complex set of links of causality and endogeneity among geography, trade shares and institutions do not point to a strong effect of integration on economic growth.

The experience of the 1990s reaffirms the conclusion that emerged from this discussion of the literature. In the third section I examined how growth rates between 1990 and 2003 correlated with several measures of openness. Recent data again fails to display a self-evident link between greater integration and economic growth. Some of the fastest growing economies since 1990, such as Lebanon and Lesotho, have applied restrictive trade policies, whereas some of the most open economies in the world, such as Moldova and Mongolia, have experienced considerable growth collapses. If there ever was a negative relationship between trade and growth, it fell apart in the nineties.

New developments in growth theory, however, have given reasons to suspect that the growth regression framework is inappropriate for dealing with complex relationships like the one that may characterize the openness-growth nexus. Recent contributions by Hausmann, Rodrik and Velasco (2004) and Aghion and Griffith (2005), among others, have pointed to the relevance of strong non-linearities and non-separabilities in the growth process. In particular, it may well be the case that the effect of openness on growth depends on a country's structural or institutional conditions. Some recent papers, such as Chang, Kaltani and Loayza (2005) and DeJong and Ripoll (2006), have attempted to take into account these contingencies. Elsewhere in this volume, I discuss in further detail the reasons why these approaches may be inadequate for dealing with the truly complex relationships that appear to characterize the data. The conclusions of that chapter reaffirm the conclusion that there is little in the cross-national data that can be used as evidence of a strong link between openness and growth.

NOTES

* This chapter was originally prepared as a background paper for the United Nations' *2006 World Economic and Social Survey*. The author is grateful to the Department of Economic and Social Affairs of the United Nations for its financial support. Jomo K.S., Sanjay Reddy, and Romain Wacziarg provided valuable comments, while William López provided excellent research assistance. The author is completely responsible for any flaws and errors.

1 At the time of writing, we had yet to receive a reply from Andrew Warner regarding these differences in our estimates.

2 One solution to the problem of persistent shocks is to use the Blundell and Bond (1997) estimator, which combines information from the regression in levels with the first-differenced regression. Dollar and Kraay eschew this solution, claiming that it is inappropriate to measure the effects of changes in openness. See the discussion below for recent contributions that have used this method.

3 Again, dropping these observations would not change Wacziarg and Welch's results, but reclassifying them as having liberalized during the late 1980s and early 1990s could have a significant effect. Wacziarg (personal communication) has noted that, even if these economies were reclassified, it would be very difficult to obtain GDP data for them prior to 1990 as many of them did not exist as nations. While this is correct, it implies that an important piece of information regarding the relationship between openness and growth, which is the precipitous decline in per capita GDP levels of many Eastern European nations which aggressively liberalized, is not taken into account in the statistical estimates presented by the paper.

4 Wacziarg and Welch recognize that the RR critique is valid "not only in terms of countries' statuses based on the OPEN90-99 dummy, but also to some extent in terms of trade liberalization dates." (p.10), but claim, based on their analysis of a number of case studies, that liberalizations of exchange controls and eliminations of state monopolies of exports were also accompanied by more comprehensive liberalizations. However, this would occur naturally if there was a worldwide tendency to liberalize trade, as there has been during the nineties: since virtually all counties in the world now have tariffs and NTBs below the Sachs-Warner thresholds, it will obviously be true that countries that eliminated their black market premia and export marketing boards would also sooner or later end up with lower tariffs. As I have argued above, there is a significant number of countries that have liberalized their trade regimes but that retain high black market premia and state monopolies of exports, shedding doubt on whether the latter are good proxies for trade policies.

5 A drawback of the Blundell and Bond (1997) approach is that it relies on the questionable assumption that there be no unconditional correlation between the unobserved heterogeneity and growth rates. In other words, the Blundell and Bond approach rules

out unconditional divergence! DeJong and Ripoll do show that their results are not sensitive to choice of specification.

[6] The comparisons and regressions in this section use the World Bank's (2005) PPP adjusted per capita GDP, which at the time of writing was available up to 1993.

REFERENCES

Acemoglu, Daron, Simon Johnson and James A. Robinson (2001). The colonial origins of comparative development: An empirical investigation. *American Economic Review* 91 (5): 1369–1401.

Aghion, Phillipe, and Stephanie Griffith (2005). *Competition and Growth: Reconciling Theory and Evidence.* MIT Press, Cambridge.

Barro, Robert, and Jhong-Wha Lee (1994). Data set for a panel of 138 countries. National Bureau of Economic Research, Cambridge, Massachusetts.

Ben-David, Dan (1993). Equalizing exchange: Trade liberalization and income convergence. *Quarterly Journal of Economics* 108 (3): 653–679.

Blundell, R., and S. Bond (1997). Initial conditions and moment restrictions in dynamic panel data models. Discussion papers in economics, 97/07. University College, London, July.

Chang, Roberto, Linda Kaltani, and Norman Loayza (2005). Openness can be good for growth: The role of policy complementarities. Processed, World Bank, Washington DC.

DeJong, D.N., and M. Ripoll (2006). Tariffs and growth: An empirical exploration of contingent relationships. *Review of Economics and Statistics*, forthcoming.

Dollar, David, and Aart Kraay (2002). Trade, growth, and poverty. *Economic Journal* 114 (493): F22-F49.

Edwards, Sebastian (1998). Openness, productivity and growth: What do we really know? *Economic Journal* 108 (447): 383–398.

Frankel, Jeffrey, and David Romer (1999). Does trade cause growth? *American Economic Review* 89 (3): 379–399.

GATT (1980). *The Tokyo Round of Multilateral Trade Negotiations.* General Agreement on Tariffs and Trade, Geneva.

Greenaway, David (1983). *Trade Policy and the New Protectionism.* St. Martin's Press, New York.

Harrison, Ann, and Gordon Hanson (1999). Who gains from trade reform? Some remaining puzzles. *Journal of Development Economics* 50 (1): 125–154.

Hausmann, Ricardo, Dani Rodrik, and Andrés Velasco (2004). Growth diagnostics. Processed, Harvard University, Cambridge, MA.

Heston, Alan, Robert Summers, Daniel Nuxoll, and Bettina Aten (1995). Penn World Table Version 5.6. Processed, University of Pennsylvania (Computer File).

Heston, Alan, Robert Summers, and Bettina Aten (2002). Penn World Table Version 6.1, Center for International Comparisons at the University of Pennsylvania, October (Computer File).

Heritage Foundation (2005). *Economic Freedom Index Database.* Heritage Foundation, Washington DC.

Jones, Charles (2001). Comment. In Ben S. Bernanke and Kenneth Rogoff (eds). *NBER Macroeconomics Annual 2000*. National Bureau of Economic Research, Cambridge, MA. p. 330–337.

Krueger, Anne (1997). Trade policy and development: How we learn. *American Economic Review* 87 (1): 1–22.

Lee, Jhong-Wha (1993). International trade, distortions, and long-run economic growth. *International Monetary Fund Staff Papers* 40 (2): 299–328.

Lee, Jhong-Wha, and Phil Swagel (1992). Measuring trade distortions. Processed, Harvard University, Cambridge, MA.

Nye, Howard L.M., Sanjay Reddy, and Kevin Watkins (2002). Dollar and Kraay on trade, growth and poverty: A critique. Processed, Columbia University, New York.

Rigobón, Roberto (2003). Identification through heteroskedasticity. *Review of Economics and Statistics*, 85 (4). pp. 777–792.

Rigobón, Roberto, and Dani Rodrik (2005). Rule of law, democracy, openness and income: Estimating the interrelationships. *Economics of Transition* 13 (3): 533–564.

Rodríguez, Francisco (2006). Openness and growth: What have we learned? Wesleyan economics working papers, 2006–011. Department of Economics, Wesleyan University.

Rodríguez, Francisco, and Dani Rodrik (1999). Trade policy and economic growth: A skeptic's guide to the cross-national evidence. NBER working paper, #7081. National Bureau of Economic Research, Cambridge, MA.

Rodríguez, Francisco, and Dani Rodrik (2001). Trade policy and economic growth: A skeptic's guide to the cross-national evidence. In Ben S. Bernanke and Kenneth Rogoff (eds). *NBER Macroeconomics Annual 2000*. National Bureau of Economic Research, Cambridge, MA. pp. 261–325.

Rodrik, Dani (2000). Comments on trade, growth, and poverty by D. Dollar and A. Kraay. Processed, Harvard University, Cambridge, MA.

Rodrik, Dani, Arvind Subramanian, and Francesco Trebbi (2004). Institutions rule: The primacy of institutions over geography and integration in economic development. *Journal of Economic Growth* 9 (2): 131–165.

Sachs, Jeffrey D., and Andrew Warner (1995). Economic reform and the process of global integration. *Brookings Papers on Economic Activity 1995* (1): 1–118.

Shleifer, Andrei, and Daniel Treisman (2004). A normal country. *Foreign Affairs* 83: 20–38.

Wacziarg, Romain, and Karen H. Welch (2003). Trade liberalization and growth: New evidence. NBER working paper, no. 10152. National Bureau of Economic Research, Cambridge, MA.

Warner, Andrew (2003). Once more into the breach: Economic reform and global integration. Processed, Center for Global Development, Washington DC.

World Bank (2005). *World Development Indicators, 2005*. World Bank, Washington DC.

World Bank (1994). *Adjustment in Africa: Reforms, Results, and the Road Ahead*. Oxford University Press, Oxford.

8

Financial Development and Economic Growth: A Critical View

E. V. K. FITZGERALD

Long-term sustainable economic growth depends on the ability to raise the rates of accumulation of physical and human capital, to use the resulting productive assets more efficiently, and to ensure the access of the whole population to these assets.

Financial intermediation supports this investment process by mobilizing household and foreign savings for investment by firms; ensuring that these funds are allocated to the most productive use; and spreading risk and providing liquidity so that firms can operate the new capacity efficiently.

Financial development thus involves the establishment and expansion of institutions, instruments and markets that support this investment and growth process. Historically, the role of banks and non-bank financial intermediaries ranging from pension funds to stock markets, has been to translate household savings into enterprise investment, monitor investments and allocate funds, and to price and spread risk. Yet, financial intermediation has strong externalities in this context, which are generally positive (such as information and liquidity provision), but can also be negative in the systemic financial crises which are endemic to market systems.

Financial development and economic growth are very clearly related, and this relationship has occupied the minds of economists from Smith to Schumpeter, although the channels and even the direction of causality have remained unresolved in both theory and empirics. Moreover, the wide range of organizational forms involved precluded any clear conclusion as to what kind of financial institutions might maximize economic growth.

Nonetheless, strong causality from particular forms of organization of financial institutions towards rapid economic growth has recently become a central axiom of economic theory, strengthened by apparent support from empirical cross-country studies of the relationship between indicators of financial development and observed rates of growth. The core argument is neatly summarized by Table 8.1, from which two key conclusions are commonly drawn. First, that greater financial *depth* (that is, higher ratios of total financial assets to national income or output) is associated with higher levels of productivity and thus income per capita. Second, that the latter are also associated with a more 'advanced' financial *structure*, that is: the move from banks towards non-bank financial intermediaries, and from both of these towards stock markets.

TABLE 8.1

Financial Development by Income group, 1990s (asset capitalization as percent of GDP)

	Banks	NBFIs	Stock markets	Total
High income countries	81	41	33	155
Upper middle income countries	40	21	11	72
Lower middle income countries	34	12	12	58
Low income countries	23	5	4	32

Source: World Bank (2001)

The dismantling of the traditional development finance model (based on bank-based systems, directed credit, public development banks, closed capital accounts, capped interest rates, and active monetary intervention) that had been established in developing countries in the post-War decades has become a core element of the economic reform and structural adjustment process led by the international financial institutions. The new standard model of financial structure was held to reflect the imperatives of 'financial development' based both on research in developing countries and the concurrent process of financial market liberalization under way in the advanced economies which were moving away from national bank-based systems towards open capital markets. These reforms were expected to raise savings and investment levels, increase the rate of growth and reduce macroeconomic instability. However, it is far from clear that these objectives have been achieved. Most debated have been the series of financial crises that have erupted since the mid-1990s; but the decline of funding for large firms in productive sectors, and SMEs in general, is also a major problem and is probably even more significant for sustainable growth and poverty reduction in the long run.

This chapter has the following structure. The next section sets out the theory and empirics on the relationship between financial development and economic growth, which underpin the 'new standard model' of financial reform in developing countries. The following section examines the growing empirical evidence that suggests that this relationship is not so close or as unidirectional as is usually supposed, and does not provide a sound evidential basis for the prescriptions of the new standard model. I then turn to two central issues in more detail: the effect of financial reform on savings and investment in the next section; and the consequences for macroeconomic stability in the penultimate section. The final section concludes with the policy implications of the arguments and evidence presented in this chapter.

THE IMPACT OF FINANCIAL DEVELOPMENT ON ECONOMIC GROWTH

According to McKinnon (1973), liberalization of financial markets allows financial deepening which reflects an increasing use of financial intermediation by savers and investors and the monetization of the economy, and allows efficient flow of resources among people and institutions over time. This encourages savings and reduces constraint on capital accumulation and improves allocative efficiency of investment by transferring capital from less productive to more productive sectors.

The efficiency as well as the level of investment is thus expected to rise with the financial development that liberalization promotes. These benefits include a decrease in firms' in self-investment at low and even negative rates of return, allocation of credit by capital markets rather than by public authorities and commercial banks, a shift away from capital-intensive investments due to the higher cost of capital reflecting its scarcity, the lengthening of financial maturities, and the elimination of fragmented and inefficient curb markets (Balassa, 1993). Development of the financial system facilitates portfolio diversification for savers reducing risk, and offers more choices to investors increasing returns. Another important function of financial system is to collect and process information on (productivity-enhancing) investment projects in a cost effective manner, which reduces cost of investment for individual investors (King and Levine, 1993b). The productive capacity of the economy is determined by the quality as well as by the quantity of investment and capacity utilization is as important as the installed capacity. Easing credit constraints, particularly working capital, is expected to improve the efficiency of resource allocation and thereby reduce the gap between actual and potential output.

Lack of clarity persists as to what institutional forms should in fact replace the previous system, which was clearly inefficient but did directly support strategic investment and growth objectives. In fact, financial systems serve five broad functions. First, they produce information ex ante about possible investments. Second, they mobilize and pool savings and allocate capital. Third, they monitor investments and exert corporate governance after providing finance. Fourth, they facilitate the trading, diversification and management of risk. Fifth, they ease the exchange of goods and services. While all financial systems provide these financial functions, and each of these functions can be expected to have an impact on economic growth, there are large differences in how well they are provided. There are three basic characteristics of financial systems that are now regarded as capturing the impact of these five functions on economic growth: (i) the level of financial intermediation; (ii) the efficiency of financial intermediation; and (iii) the composition of financial intermediation.

First, the level of financial intermediation: the size of a financial system relative to an economy is important for each of the functions listed above. A larger financial system allows the exploitation of economies of scale, as there are significant fixed costs in the operation of financial intermediaries. As more individuals join financial intermediaries, the latter can produce better information with positive implications (and externalities) for growth, a channel emphasized in some of the earlier theoretical models of the finance-growth literature (e.g., Greenwood and Jovanovic, 1990; Bencivenga and Smith, 1991). A larger financial system can also ease credit constraints: the greater the ability of firms to borrow, the more likely that profitable investment opportunities will not be by-passed because of credit rationing.

A large financial system should also be more effective at allocating capital and monitoring the use of funds as there are significant economies of scale in this function – and thus by implication it is difficult for 'small' economies (in terms of wealth per capita as well as population size) to sustain a modern financial sector. There may be no upper limit to these scale economies in the sense that global banks are clearly efficient in any financial services. Greater availability of financing can also increase the resilience of the economy to external shocks, helping to smooth consumption and investment patterns. More generally, a financial system plays an important function in transforming and reallocating risk in an economy. Besides cross-sectional risk diversification, a larger financial system may improve inter-temporal risk sharing (Allen and Gale, 1997). By expanding a financial system to more individuals there will be a better allocation of risks, which can, in turn, boost investment activity in both physical and human capital, leading to higher growth rates.

Second, the efficiency of financial intermediation: the channels linking the size of the financial system and growth implicitly assume a high quality of financial intermediation. The efficiency of financial systems, however, cannot be taken for granted, especially as information gathering is one of their key functions. Asymmetric information, externalities in financial markets (Stiglitz and Weiss, 1992) and imperfect competition (for example, as a result of fixed costs) can lead to sub-optimal levels of financing and investment, an inefficient allocation of capital, or have other undesirable consequences such as bank runs, fraud or illiquidity which are detrimental for economic growth. Some of these market imperfections may be best addressed through appropriate oversight by a public body but the legal and institutional background (including competition policy) may also foster the efficiency of financial markets and hence contribute to economic growth.

Third, the composition of financial intermediation: two important shifts in the composition of financial intermediation relate to the maturity of financing available and the growth of capital markets and institutional investors such as pension funds and insurance companies. The maturity of loans and bonds may affect the extent to which certain investments may be profitably exploited. On the other hand, the replacement of banks by markets appears to be a result of changes in the cost of intermediation. As noted by Jacklin (1987), there is no specific advantage to banks. If liquid equity markets exist, all agents will save through equities as they offer higher long-term returns. Indeed, the earliest corporate finance models even suggested the irrelevance of the choice of financing for company's investment decisions (Modigliani and Miller, 1958).

One potential channel for the composition of financial intermediation to affect the efficiency with which firms allocate resources is through its impact on corporate governance. There are however no theoretical models that assess the role of markets as opposed to banks in boosting steady-state growth through their impact on corporate governance. Indeed, starting with Berle and Means in 1932 many researchers have observed the limited corporate governance capability afforded by markets, either because of diffused shareholdings – which leads to managerial discretion - or because of the excessive power often exerted by controlling owners – which can distort corporate decisions (Shleifer and Vishny, 1997).

The pioneering study by King and Levine (1993a) and subsequent work by Levine and Zervos (1998), Levine (2000), and Levine, Loayza and Beck (2000) have provided new evidence in an attempt to resolve this debate. They identify three indicators of financial sector development that are best at explaining differences in economic growth between countries over long periods: bank credit to the private sector, stock market activity (proxied by the turnover rate or the ratio of traded value to GDP), and features of the legal system such as the extent of shareholder and creditor protection[1]. Levine (2000) further shows that the impact of financial development on growth acts mainly through total factor productivity rather than through capital accumulation or savings rates. He concludes, therefore, that 'maybe Schumpeter was right'. A somewhat different conclusion, albeit supportive for the general direction of the argument is that of Aghion and others (2005) who claim that financial development explains whether there is convergence or not but it does not exert a direct effect on steady-state growth.

Other studies have shown further light on the transmission channel between bank credit and growth. Gavin and Haussmann (1996) have found that high ratios of bank credit to GDP in Latin America are associated with smaller detrimental effects of volatility on long-run growth. A study by Aghion, Howitt and Mayer-Foulkes (2005) has confirmed this relationship for a cross-section of 70 OECD and non-OECD countries. They surmise that mitigating the response to volatility and exogenous shocks may be the most important transmission channel for the effects of deeper credit markets.

Finally, a related empirical literature has also started to look at the impact of financial development on income inequality and poverty. Li, Squire and Zou (1998) found that financial depth (proxied by private sector credit) entered strongly and significantly as a contributor to lower inequality and raise the average income of the lower 80 percent of the population. Honohan (2004) presents initial evidence suggesting that private sector credit reduced absolute poverty rates in a sample of 70 countries. On the other hand, adding stock market capitalization and/or market turnover to the equation did not significantly alter fit or other coefficients, while the new variables were not significant. Beck, Demirguc-Kunt and Levine (2004) also provide empirical evidence showing that financial development reduces income inequality and absolute poverty levels. However, as the effect of economic growth itself on income distribution is still hotly debated, and (as I argue here) the contribution of financial development to growth is also unclear, it is not possible to conclude that financial development has an unambiguously positive effect on income inequality or poverty.

EMPIRICAL EVIDENCE ON FINANCIAL DEVELOPMENT AND ECONOMIC GROWTH

We now turn to a closer examination of the empirical evidence on the linkage between financial development and economic growth. As a canonical example, King and Levine (1993a) regress growth in 1960–89 for seventy-seven OECD and developing countries as a cross-section on *previous* financial depth (M_2/Y in 1960) in order to avoid endogeneity of the contemporary M_2/Y variable. However, the statistical significance of their financial depth variable is almost entirely eliminated by highly significant regional dummies.[2] Moreover, when contemporary correlation between financial depth and growth is accounted for the predictive power of the model fails completely (Arestis and Panicos, 1997).

This is not just a technical issue. In fact, the widely used M_2/Y is not a really reliable indicator of financial depth at all. It varies enormously over time as well as across countries, and responds to changing monetary policy stances – indeed it is as likely to be associated with asset bubbles as with financial development proper. Figure 8.1 uses King and Levine [1993a, b] measure of financial depth applied to the UK over the long run. While the increase in the measure during the 1980s does clearly reflect the major financial liberalization and modernization of that decade, did the UK really become *less* financially developed between 1950 and 1980, or during the early 1990s?

This problem is brought out even more starkly by the case of Mexico, where the M_2/Y measure in fact shows relatively little variance over the long run despite major changes in Mexico's financial system; while the short-run shifts are clearly related to shifts in monetary stance related to fiscal or external shocks. As in the case of the UK, therefore, cross-section studies including Mexico are liable to be misleading as the specific choice of base year will clearly affect the results substantially. Indeed, if we take this measure literally, Mexico had the same financial depth (a key measure of financial development as we have seen) as the UK in the mid-seventies (Figure 8.2)!

FIGURE 8.1

King and Levine [1993a, b] measure of financial depth applied to the UK over the long run

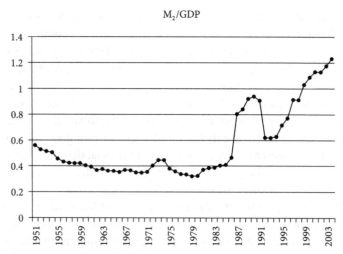

Source: IMF, International Financial Statistics.

In case it might be thought that a broader measure of financial assets than the M_2 used in these cross-section studies would yield more reassuring results, we can look at the long-run evolution of total financial claims on the private sector. Figure 8.3 shows this measure (as a proportion of GDP) for the UK over the past fifty years. The trend is certainly more stable, and the major step-change in the 1980s is much more evident, yet there are also shorter-term movements which clearly reflect asset bubbles and shifting monetary policy stances.

However, in the case of Mexico, this broader measure still exhibits considerable instability over the long run as Figure 8.4 shows. The increase of the early 1990s has been claimed as evidence of the positive effects of financial liberalization; but by the same token the second half of that decade reflects the collapse of the asset bubble and thus the decade as a whole corresponds to a cycle of external capital flows. Taking the whole five decades, by this measure there has been no financial deepening at all!

FIGURE 8.2

King and Levine measure of financial depth applied to Mexico over the long run

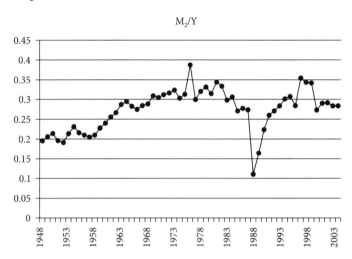

M_2/Y

Source: IMF, *International Financial Statistics.*

FIGURE 8.3

Claims on the private sector, UK

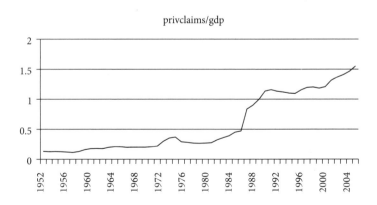

privclaims/gdp

Source: IMF, *International Financial Statistics*

FIGURE 8.4

Claims on the private sector, Mexico

claims/gdp Mexico

Source: IMF/IFS

It is important to note that the different indicators of financial development that have a significant impact on growth reflect different characteristics of financial development. Bank credit to the private sector. The ratio of GDP ratio shown in Figure 8.4 is a better measure of the level of financial intermediation (first characteristic of financial development) than the M_2 /Y measure discussed above, but still has significant shortcomings that are revealed by time series but obscured by cross-section studies. The second and third measures in Table 8.2 (stock market liquidity and legal rules), on the other hand, are measures of the efficiency of financial intermediation (second characteristic of financial development).

TABLE 8.2

Summary of characteristics and indicators of financial development used in empirical studies

Characteristic of financial development	Indicator of financial development
Level of financial intermediation	Size of bank credit relative to GDP
Efficiency of financial intermediation	Stock market turnover rate / stock market traded value relative to GDP; legal rules and corporate governance activism
Composition of financial intermediation	Maturity of bank credit and fixed income securities

Further, King and Levine [1993a, b] and the other studies surveyed in the previous section do not find any explanatory power in the ratio of stock market capitalization to GDP or in the size of stock markets relative to that of banks. The large fixed costs of a stock market listing may explain why in countries with few large companies the balance between bank financing and capital markets is tilted towards the former. Moreover, firm-level evidence shows that there are complementarities between banks and markets in developing countries (Demirgüç-Kunt and Maksimovic, 1996). Another possible indicator of financial development that has not been used in cross-country studies, probably because of lack of data availability, is the duration of bank loans and fixed income securities, which corresponds to the third characteristic of financial development described above. Caprio and Demirgüç-Kunt (1997) show that companies grow faster and are more productive when more long-term finance is available to them. We return to this point in the next two sections.

De Gregorio and Guidotti (1995) find that the high level of bank credit to GDP ratios in Latin America during the 1970s and 1980s was actually negatively correlated with growth. They attribute this result to the inadequate regulation and deposit insurance policies of the time, which led to an unwarranted over-expansion in credit and subsequent banking crises. Loayza and Rancière (2004) have also found evidence of a negative relationship between short-term (temporary) changes in bank credit and growth in those countries that present high levels of financial fragility (proxied by credit volatility and frequency of banking crises). Periods of financial fragility in turn have coincided in many countries with financial liberalization. They claim that these temporary effects are compatible with the positive impact that permanent increases in bank credit have on economic growth over the long term, however.

Previous studies have tended to pool developed and developing countries when examining the relationship between financial development and economic growth. Yet it is quite likely that the impact of financial development will differ depending on the stage of economic development of a country. Furthermore, each of the mechanisms may differ in importance at different developmental stages. The level of financial intermediation may be most important for economic growth at initial stages of development, while for richer countries, the efficiency and composition of financial intermediation may be a more relevant determinant of economic growth. We are not aware of any study that has tried to shed light on this specific conjecture. The original study by King and Levine (1993a) and later ones by Andrés, Hernando and Lópes-Salido (1999) and Leahy and others (2001), however, are consistent with this view, as they were unable to find significant links between bank credit to GDP ratios and subsequent economic growth rates in OECD countries. On the other hand, the other studies mentioned include developing countries for which there is a robust relationship between these two variables, even though in many cases their financial systems are far from efficient.

FIGURE 8.5
Private Credit/GDP and GDP per capita, 2000

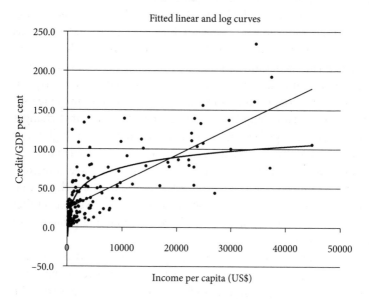

Fitted linear and log curves

Source: World Bank, World Development Indicators 2005.

The reason for this result is evident from Figure 8.5, which shows that not only is there an enormous dispersion around the fitted linear trend, but also that the logged relationship shows much less variation above a per capita income level of $10,000.

The large differences are evident in Table 8.3, both within the OECD and between developing regions in the level of financial market capitalization, but these are not clearly related to economic development or efficiency. In fact, corporate investment finance patterns differ due to evolution of ownership and regulation: they cannot be seen as a steady 'progression' towards a single US/UK model (Mayer, 1990). Banks remain the key element in the system, especially when we take into account the fact that they own most of the non-bank financial

TABLE 8.3
Financial Depth Worldwide, 2003

As shares of GDP	Stock Market	Debt Sector			Bank Assets	Total Capital
		Public	Private	Total		
World	0.86	0.56	0.88	1.44	1.12	3.42
EMU*	0.60	0.67	0.97	1.64	1.60	3.84
US	1.30	0.46	1.46	1.91	0.52	3.73
Japan	1.14	1.43	0.53	1.96	1.45	4.54
UK	0.37	0.29	1.05	1.34	2.22	4.93
* of which						
Germany	0.45	0.48	1.20	1.68	1.20	3.33
France	0.71	0.60	0.88	1.47	1.99	4.17
Spain	0.86	0.53	0.74	1.27	1.09	3.22
Portugal	0.42	0.72	0.81	1.53	1.18	3.14
Greece	0.60	1.29	0.12	1.41	1.02	3.03
EMs	0.47	0.23	0.15	0.37	0.78	1.63
LA	0.76	0.21	0.24	0.45	1.12	2.33
Asia	0.35	0.37	0.12	0.49	0.45	1.29
ME	0.12	0.01	0.02	0.03	0.85	1.00
Africa	0.30	0.13	0.05	0.18	0.60	1.08
Europe	0.09	0.27	0.03	0.30	0.27	0.67

Source: IMF Financial Stability Report 2005

intermediaries. Pension and insurance funds emerge as major players in securitization very late in economic development.

In effect, specific financial functions are carried out by different institutional forms with remarkably similar outcomes. A very good example of this diversity is the institutional form of housing finance (mortgage provision): in the US this is done by securitization under government guarantee; in the UK by building society and bank loans; in Germany by insurance companies; in Spain by savings and loans associations (*cajas de ahorro*); and in Mexico by construction companies.

In consequence, financial structures appear to be very different across the world, as Table 8.4 demonstrates. It is not possible to claim

TABLE 8.4
Financial structure worldwide

As shares of total assets	Stock Market	Debt Sector			Bank Assets	Total Capital
		Public	Private	Total		
World	0.25	0.16	0.26	0.42	0.33	1.00
EMU*	0.16	0.17	0.25	0.43	0.42	1.00
US	0.35	0.12	0.39	0.51	0.14	1.00
Japan	0.25	0.31	0.12	0.43	0.32	1.00
UK	0.28	0.06	0.21	0.27	0.45	1.00
* of which						
Germany	0.13	0.15	0.36	0.50	0.36	1.00
France	0.17	0.14	0.21	0.35	0.48	1.00
Spain	0.27	0.16	0.23	0.39	0.34	1.00
Portugal	0.13	0.23	0.26	0.49	0.38	1.00
Greece	0.20	0.43	0.04	0.47	0.34	1.00
EMs	0.29	0.14	0.09	0.23	0.48	1.00
LA	0.33	0.09	0.10	0.19	0.48	1.00
Asia	0.27	0.28	0.10	0.38	0.35	1.00
ME	0.12	0.01	0.02	0.03	0.85	1.00
Africa	0.28	0.12	0.04	0.16	0.56	1.00
Europe	0.14	0.40	0.04	0.45	0.41	1.00

Source: IMF *Financial Stability Report 2005*

that there is a unique relationship between financial structure and either levels of, or growth in, income per capita. It is also clear that banks remain central to the financial intermediation process in all countries other than the US – and even there most of the non-bank financial intermediaries in fact form part of bank holding groups and are thus closely associated with a particular bank.

FINANCIAL LIBERALIZATION, SAVINGS AND INVESTMENT

The proponents of financial liberalization as leading to financial development have emphasized two main channels through which private investment is expected to rise. The first channel is through an increase in the availability of credit that would follow the removal of interest rate ceiling due to increased private saving; and the second is through the enhanced screening of investment projects due to the higher cost of capital, thereby increasing the marginal productivity of investment (McKinnon, 1973). Ending financial repression would also improve bank efficiency by ensuring positive real interest rates, eliminating excessive reserve requirements and removing mandated credit allocations (McKinnon, 1989). Supporters of the basic McKinnon-Shaw hypothesis have extended these ideas, by focussing on investment levels (Kapur, 1976; Mathieson, 1980) or investment quality (Galbis, 1977; Fry, 1988) as lending shifts from curb markets into the banking system.

Critics of this model such as van Wijnbergen (1983) or Taylor (1983) are sceptical that increased financial intermediation will result from liberalization, because of shifts from curb markets that were not subject to the reserve requirement that apply to banks. Hence, if substitution takes place between time deposit and curb market, total supply of funds available to the business sector will decline. Moreover, if banks then lend to the public sector (e.g., by investing in Treasury bills), the diversion of funds away from the curb market may result in a net decline in the availability of private sector credit. Due to limited access of the small and medium firms to bank credit, a shift of funds from curb market to the banking system may reduce the availability of credit for these types of firms unless the liberalization of banking system reduces bias against small borrower.

The experience of financial liberalization across countries suggests that the process of liberalization varied widely, as did the outcome. Moreover, in most developing countries where both market and non-market imperfections exist within broader liberalized macroeconomic framework, there is a host of factors other than the volume and cost of credit that influence firms' investment decisions. For instance, evidence from four African countries (Uganda, Kenya, Malawi and Lesotho) does not support the hypothesis that increase in financial depth increases the volume of savings or access to credit of the commercial banks in rural areas, except for those who already have collateral (Mosley, 1999). Conventional financial institutions are biased against small borrowers due to the high unit costs of loan administration and lack of effective collateral, which translate into low returns and high risk. This is a major problem for all developing countries as small firms account for the bulk of production and the great majority of employment. This 'gap' has traditionally been addressed by public sector development banks and extension schemes; but these have generally been dismantled as part of financial reforms, and not effectively replaced by micro-credit schemes, which are systemically limited in their coverage and scope.

There is a general agreement that financial liberalization has led to greater allocative efficiency from the point of view of commercial profitability, but the predicted boost in saving as predicted by McKinnon and Shaw has not been observed (Williamson and Mahar, 1998). Studies by the World Bank (1989), Fry (1997), Ghani (1992) and King and Levine (1993b) revealed positive and significant cross-section relationship between average economic growth and real interest rate. However, Fry (1997) observed an inverted U shaped relation between national savings and real interest rates in his study on 16 developing countries: national savings declines at both very high and low real interest rates through the effects of these rates on output growth.[3]

In the case of Uruguay, de Melo and Tybout (1986) found that reform induced structural shift in savings and investment behaviour 'although these shifts were not entirely as envisioned by proponents of financial deregulation'. In particular the savings constraint for investment in the presence of repression during pre-reform period was not found. Nevertheless, a positive effect on investment efficiency for Uruguay is reported by Noya, Casacuberta and Lorenzo (1998). For Argentina no strong relationship between real interest rate and quantity of investment was reported (Morisset, 1993), although an increase in financial deepening was observed (Fanelli, Rozenwurcel and Simpson, 1998).

Again, the Mexican experience shows little evidence that movement in real interest rates significantly affected economic performance. While financial saving is positively correlated with real interest rates, total domestic saving appears to be unrelated to the rate of interest, which may imply some substitution of domestic non-financial assets into domestic financial savings (Warman & Thirlwall, 1994). The net effect of interest rates on Mexican investment is thus negative. Gunçavdi, Bleaney and McKay (1998) observed structural change in the aggregate investment equation after financial liberalization in Turkey: as expected, the credit variable became much less important although cost of capital did not become significant.

In sum, there is little evidence that financial liberalization has in fact resulted in higher savings rates, which was supposed to be the main contribution to higher investment and thus growth. There are two reasons for this outcome. First, financial reform has the effect of shifting savings out of assets such as precious metals, property or currency into bank deposits and marketable securities. This will raise the recorded financial 'depth' without raising savings rates. Second, financial liberalization expands access to consumer credit in the form of factoring systems, credit cards and personal loans. These in turn *reduce* aggregate household saving because this is simply the difference between the increase in household financial assets and the increase in household financial liabilities. In many emerging markets, this effect was compounded by simultaneous trade liberalization and real exchange rate liberalization which cheapened imported luxury goods (Calderon and FitzGerald, 1997).

In consequence, as Figure 8.6 illustrates, there is no robust evidence that financial deepening (measured by the widest possible measure

– total market capitalization) increases the rate of saving and thus investment or growth. In fact, savings rates appear to depend on other factors such as demographic and tax influences on pension provision, funding of health and education, and the ownership structure of corporations or even family organization.

FIGURE 8.6
Financial market capitalization and savings rates (shares of GDP), 2003

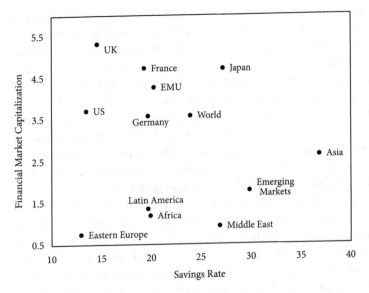

Source: IMF *Financial Stability Report, 2005*. Note: 'Financial market capitalization' refers to the sum of stock market capitalization, outstanding debt securities and bank assets as a share of GDP. The 'savings rate' refers to gross national savings as a percentage of GDP.

Of course, the effect of financial development and liberalization might still be positive through the quality of investment improving due to the monitoring and discipline exercised by financial markets, even if absolute investment levels do not rise. Rajan and Zingales (1998) thus attempt to establish whether industrial sectors that are relatively more in need of external finance develop disproportionately faster in countries with more-developed financial markets. They use the ratio of credit to (claims on) the private sector to GDP as the financial depth indicator, but adds an indicator of compliance with international accounting standards to reflect the quality of that finance. They get significant results from a panel of 55 countries over 1980–1990, indicating that financial development does have a positive effect on growth through the corporate finance channel. However, there are serious shortcoming in this method: first, the unreliability of the financial depth indicator, as we have noted above; second, the degree of financial dependence used for all countries is that for the US in the corresponding industrial sector; and third, the index of compliance with international accounting standards does not seem to be reliable.[4]

The solution may be to look at corporate finance in more detail in order to establish the link between financial development and firms' investment. However, as is well known, corporate investment even in advanced economies is largely self-financed out of retained profits. The analysis of net sources of finance for physical investment in Germany, Japan, the UK and the US reveal not only the predominance of retained profits to be higher in the UK and the US despite their more developed financial markets, but the key role of banks in all cases among external sources (Corbett and Jenkinson, 1997). Only in the case of the US are bonds a significant source of corporate investment finance, and even here it should be recalled that a considerable share of these bonds are held by banks. We should not expect, therefore, to find a large effect on aggregate investment levels from financial liberalization.

Indeed, great expectations were raised by the prospect of stock markets as a new source of corporate finance in developing countries in the early 1990s. However, this boom was closely associated with capital inflows, producing an apparent correlation with economic growth (e.g. Levine and Zevos, 1998). However, these markets have since shrunk dramatically, and turn out to have low liquidity (i.e. turnover) with volatile and pro-cyclical returns. Further, after the initial flotation of state enterprises, new issues have declined markedly because large domestic firms can access global capital markets and the costs of listing are too high for SMEs.

TABLE 8.5
Net sources of finance, 1970–1994 (% of physical investment)

	Germany	Japan	UK	US
Internal	78.9	69.9	93.3	96.1
Bank finance	11.9	26.7	14.6	11.1
Bonds	–1.0	4.0	4.2	15.4
New equity	0.1	3.5	–4.6	–7.6
Trade credit	–1.2	–5.0	–0.9	–2.4
Capital transfers	8.7	–	1.7	–
Other	1.4	1.0	0.0	–4.4
Statistical adjustment	1.2	0.0	–8.4	–8.3

Source: Corbett and Jenkinson, 1997.

FINANCIAL LIBERALIZATION AND ECONOMIC INSTABILITY

Improvements in the efficiency of resource allocation efficiency depends, to a great extent, on minimizing emerging capital market imperfections such as moral hazard and adverse selection (Watson, 1993). Stiglitz and Weiss (1981) show that an equilibrium loan market rate is characterized by credit rationing; and Mankiw (1986) shows that there may not exist any equilibrium at all (i.e., a 'collapsed market' with no lending). Asymmetric informational problems prevent banks from adequately measuring the risk associated with their lending; to compensate for this risk banks push their lending rates up leading to deterioration of the creditworthiness of borrowers. The bank thus turns down safe borrowers with a high interest rates, while new firms with no past credit record (and/or little collateral) find funding difficult to obtain at any price. Moreover, much the same happens in capital markets.

This constrains the desired level of investment to that fundable by cash flow and trade credit resulting in a sub-optimal level of investment with consequences for over all economic growth. Further, the higher cost of capital induces the borrower to choose riskier projects, as higher risk is associated with high returns on favourable outcomes. This may result in higher probability of default. A small increase in the risk of some potential borrowers can cause the credit market to collapse even though there may not be any change in the expected return of investment projects. Hence, the market equilibrium, if any, will be very fragile. Small changes in the exogenous risk free interest rate or a monetary contraction can have a large impact on the efficiency of the market allocation of credit. In such a situation, government intervention (in the form of a tax subsidy or a loan guarantee) can improve the situation even if the government has no informational advantage over lenders characterized by unobservable heterogeneity, as long as the return exceeds opportunity cost. Market failure in a liberalized financial regime may thus call for some *selective* public intervention. Stiglitz and others (2006) can thus suggest that a delay in capital market liberalization, and thus a degree of continued financial repression, may be beneficial until a very advanced stage of the development process.

Macroeconomic instability increases the variance in project returns and also adverse selection possibility by the banks, thus making banks risk averse. The real benefit of macroeconomic stability comes not only from increased financial savings and greater availability of credit, but also from its favourable impact on the risk-sharing relationship between borrowers and lenders (Villanueva & Mirakhor, 1990). The pace of liberalization itself is thus crucial in the sense that sudden increase in lending rate resulting from freeing of interest rate may render some firms unprofitable as they need to pay a higher price for their funds borrowed earlier at a lower rate. This will in turn result in non-repayment of loans. Mathieson (1980) warned that this leads to widespread bankruptcies in the banking system and a programme of gradual interest rate decontrol is necessary rather than sudden decontrol. Moreover, such decontrol should not be attempted until a sufficient degree of fiscal and macroeconomic stability has been achieved – financial liberalization has not been effective as a means of achieving stability in itself.

Moreover, since information collected through monitoring the financial institutions regarding their solvency and management practices by individuals is costly and a public good, there would be sub-optimal expenditure by depositors on monitoring them (Fry, 1997). As financial institutions know that depositors do not adequately monitor them, they have incentives to take greater risks with their deposits. However, as long as central bank plays its role of supervision and monitoring and makes the information public this cost could be minimized. Nevertheless, the non-existence of markets does not necessarily imply that public intervention would result in a superior outcome. There may be other markets dealing with the problem (e.g., higher equity participation to tackle uncertainty problems, specialized institutions/banks for industrial credit, leasing companies). So the pertinent question is why those contingent-markets are absent. Public intervention as a substitute for market failure can suffer from exactly the same problems of unobservable outcomes (e.g., contractual default), unobservable behaviour (e.g., moral hazard) or unobservable characteristics (e.g., adverse selection) (see Obstfeld and Rogoff, 1996).

A major problem for developing countries in this context is the absence of a domestic market for treasury or corporate bonds. This means that it is difficult to fund public infrastructure investment and major private modernization projects on the one hand. On the other hand, it becomes impossible for firms to hedge against exchange rate changes, further destabilizing foreign currency markets and monetary intervention in order to counteract external shocks becomes very difficult. Financial liberalization has not led to this important outcome, for at least two reasons. First, fiscal reform has been geared to reducing budget deficits, and to avoiding monetization (i.e., inflation targeting) from issuance of short-term T-bills, rather than developing a long bond market. Second, the absence of institutional market makers in these securities persists if no special facilities (such as rediscount facilities or tax incentives) are extended to pension and insurance funds to encourage demand for these assets.

With the deregulation of interest rates, banks gamble for higher profit by lending to the booming sector, such as real estate. This leads to an asset price boom that "can exacerbate the adverse incentive on banks to take risk, increased interest rates, increased macroeconomic instability and, if bank's portfolios are concentrated on particular sectors, increased covariance in the returns to banks' borrowers" (Brownbridge and Kirkpatrick, 1999). The booms and slumps in the asset prices – where banks play a crucial role through credit expansion during the upswing in the business cycle and thus raising value of collateral and stimulating more borrowing, leading to over indebtedness and making borrowers vulnerable to any macroeconomic changes (e.g., interest rate increases) and ultimately rendering them insolvent – frequently result in banking crises. Moreover, personnel in the banking sector in the developing countries often lack the skill required for evaluating risky investment projects and monitoring borrowers. Indeed the liberalized environment itself causes a moral hazard problem and induces the banks to take on risks: "a further factor contributing to moral hazard is the erosion of bank franchise values as ceilings on deposit interest rates are lifted and barriers to entry reduced" (Brownbridge and Kirkpatrick, 1999). Last, but not least, in many developing countries, due to liberalization and consequently few entry of new banks and other financial institutions, demand for supervisory activities has increased at a higher rate than the supervisory capacity – itself undermined by budget constraints and competition from private sector for skilled staff.

Financial liberalization is usually associated with integration to global capital market. In principle, this should make an international pool of liquidity available to the domestic financial system, which should then be more stable. However, in practice, the high degree of volatility of international capital inflows combined with the narrow and thin nature of host markets subjects the recipient countries to shocks and crises, which can be both large and frequent. The quantity effect of these flows is exacerbated by the fact that arbitrage leads to the domestic interest rate being set by the world interest rate, plus expected devaluation plus the perceived default risk premium. This uncovered interest rate parity principle leads to very high real rates of interest in emerging markets. Analysing the impact of exogenous changes in short-term capital flows on real sector of the economy, FitzGerald (1997) suggests that "the impact on the firms sector is mainly through the supply of working capital, which generates asymmetric responses in terms of investment and output due to the impact on firms' balance sheets; the volatility of expected profits resulting from this has a strong depressive effect on private investment." Moreover, while an increase in the real rates of interest hardly stimulates aggregate savings, it clearly discourages private investment, worsens public debt service burden and in this context, attracts volatile capital flows which increasing the budgetary cost and also the vulnerability of domestic firms. Although the inflow of funds takes place over a period of time, the outflow occurs suddenly with its impact on the real sector and the economy as a whole. The orthodox policy response to these crises can further worsen the situation as firms are forced into bankruptcy by high real interest rates and large devaluations with asymmetric effects on balance sheets.

Domestic investment financed by foreign savings leads to a temporary increase in real income and perceived wealth and relaxation of lending standard by banks as current trends are expected to continue (Reisen, 1999). With the increase in both consumption and the investment balance of payment deteriorates which remains unnoticed at initial stage. Overvaluation of the exchange rate can sustain this sense of optimism – and thus exacerbate the asset bubble. Hence, for most of the developing countries the question of exchange rate policy is also crucial to the success of financial liberalization. From the point of view of firms, faced by irreversible investment decisions, macroeconomic stability and policy credibility may be much more important than tax incentives or freedom from regulation (Pindyck and Solimano, 1993).

In sum, the *process*, rather than the *objectives* of financial liberalization has emerged as the central problem, and whether the 'big bang' is appropriate or clearly dangerous. Clarke (1996) suggests that the concept of an 'equilibrium' interest rate may be undefined or at least unobtainable through the process of competition since the rate required to balance financial markets differs from that required to equilibrate savings and investment. In this process an increase in repression (or control) in some areas of financial markets is essential in order to ensure that the whole process does not go out of hand during the transitional period (Fanelli and Medhora, 1998).

Theoretically, there are potential gains from the deregulation of financial institutions in the form of increasing growth and social welfare. But much of these depend on proper sequencing and if poorly sequenced, deregulation can be counterproductive. The literature on sequencing of financial liberalization seek to determine the optimal order for liberalizing the domestic real sector, the domestic financial sector, the external real sector and the external financial sector. Studies on this aspect further examine the issue of synchronizing the order of liberalization with macroeconomic stabilization. It is generally agreed that domestic financial liberalization should come after domestic real and before external financial sector liberalization. However, it is not very clear whether domestic financial liberalization should come before or after external liberalization, e.g. trade liberalization (Gibson and Tsakalotos, 1994). Institutional factors such as the legal infrastructure, bankruptcy code, accounting norms, disclosure rules and prudential regulations, are all important for fostering the operation of financial markets and capturing any ensuing efficiency gains, and are central elements in successful financial liberalization (Aivazian, 1998).

Sikorski (1996) points out that financial liberalization theory was predicated on an unashamed faith in markets and the widespread belief that 'government failure' was best combated by removing the government. But this belief conflicts with what actually happens in any real economy where social institutions play a crucial role in gathering information and reducing uncertainty (Gibson & Tsakalotos, 1994; Soskice, 1991). Thus, deliberate institutional design is essential in order to develop the long-term, high trust relations between market participants that determine how well a country can compete in international markets and hence for economic performance.

Conclusions

In this chapter, four main points have been made:
1. The potential contribution of financial development to economic growth is considerable, but cannot be taken for granted since it depends on the construction of the appropriate institutional structure.
2. Conventional measures of financial 'depth' (in terms of private assets) and financial 'development' (defined as moving

from banks towards capital markets) are not associated with higher rates of economic growth.

3. Financial liberalization leads to more efficient and liquid financial intermediation, but does not appear to raise the rates of domestic savings or investment in the aggregate.

4. The efficiency gains from the standard model of financial liberalization in terms of investment allocation and corporate governance can be outweighed by new instability from short-term foreign capital flows.

The implications of these findings are substantial:

i. First, it is necessary to reappraise the role of commercial banks in developing countries, which have been the traditional intermediaries between saving households and investing firms, but have more recently moved into asset management and fee-based services. The move away from the financing of productive investment in general, and SMEs in particular, has been encouraged by regulators concerned for bank liquidity.

ii. Second, the decision to close public sector development banks was justified by their heavy losses (and vulnerability to political pressure) but the financing gap for long-term investment in key sectors such as exports and infrastructure remains. Public intervention is still needed to correct this market failure – although this could take the form of risk insurance, support for debt securitization and market making, rather than traditional bank credit.

iii. Third, the relaxation of regulatory restrictions (e.g. deregulation of interest rates, removal of controls on bank credit allocation, removal of entry prohibitions into banking, increased competition in the financial sector, deregulation of stock markets, and full convertibility of currencies) without adequate institutional provision (plus fiscal reform and balance of payments stability) can engender serious financial crises and create systemic risks. Greater rather than less public intervention is thus needed in emerging markets, geared to raising levels of productive investment and thus growth.

iv. Fourth, the irreversible nature of productive investment means that monetary policy (including exchange rates) should be geared towards providing credible stability for firms: specifically a low and stable real interest rate and a competitive real exchange rate, supported by appropriate tax incentives.

v. Fifth, effective liberalization requires the removal of restrictions on market transactions at one level and the simultaneous imposition of new regulatory and legal provisions on financial intermediaries at another level: these should aim to not only to prevent bank fragility but also to contain shocks to corporate balance sheets.

vi. Sixth, the development of a long term bond market should be a priority, as this would not only provide long-term capital for growth at reasonable real cost but also stabilize exchange rate expectations and enable the monetary authorities to intervene effectively to damp macroeconomic cycles caused by external shocks.

NOTES

[1] Levine, Loayza and Beck (2000) and Beck and Levine (2001) also correct some methodological problems in Levine and Zervos (1998). The latter analysis does not account for potential simultaneity bias nor does it control explicitly for country fixed effects. Levine, Loayza and Beck (2000) use the La Porta and others (1998) measures of legal origin as instrumental variables to demonstrate causality.

[2] This point on regional differences in financial structure is taken up again in the penultimate section below.

[3] Indeed, even at the theoretical level, the net effect of interest rates on saving is ambiguous because the wealth effect and the relative price effect have negative and positive effects respectively. See FitzGerald (2006).

[4] Specifically, Rajan and Zingales (1998) give the following index values (implicitly set for US = 100) among others: Austria (54), Mexico (60), Germany (62), Netherlands (64), Philippines (65), New Zealand (70), Malaysia (76), UK (78)!

REFERENCES

Aghion, P., P. Howitt, and D. Mayer-Foulkes (2005). The effect of financial development on convergence: Theory and evidence. *Quarterly Journal of Economics* 120 (1): 173–222.

Aivazian, V.A. (1998). Microeconomic elements and perspectives from finance theory. In J.M. Fanelli and R. Medhora (eds). *Financial Reform in Developing Countries*. International Development Research Centre, Canada.

Allen, F., and D. Gale (1997). Financial markets, intermediaries and intertemporal smoothing. *Journal of Political Economy* 105: 523–546.

Andrés, J., I. Hernando, and J.D. Lópes-Salido (1999). The role of the financial system in the growth inflation link: the OECD experience. Banco de España working paper, October. Banco de España, Madrid.

Arestis, Philip, and Demetriades Panicos (1997). Financial development and economic growth: Assessing the evidence. *Economic Journal* 107 (442): 783–799.

Bailliu, Jeanine, and Helmut Reisen (1997). Do funded pensions contribute to higher aggregate savings? A cross country analysis. OECD Development Centre working paper no. 130. Organisation for Economic Co-operation and Development, Paris.

Balassa, B. (1993). *Policy Choices in the 1990s*. Macmillan, London.

Beck, T. and R. Levine (2001). Stock markets, banks and growth correlation or causality? Policy Research Working Paper Series No 2670. World Bank, Washington, DC

Beck, Thorsten, Asli Demirguc-Kunt and Ross Levine (2004). Finance, inequality and poverty: Cross-country evidence. NBER working paper no. 10979. National Bureau of Economic Research, Cambridge, MA.

Bencivenga, V.R., and B.D. Smith (1991). Financial intermediation and endogenous growth. *The Review of Economic Studies* 58 (2): 196–209.

Berle, A.A., and G.C. Means (1932). *The Modern Corporation and Private Property*. Harcourt Brace Jovanovich, New York.

Financial regulation in developing countries: A critical survey. Paper presented at the Finance and Development Research Programme Workshop, 9–10 July, Manchester.

Calderon, A. and V. FitzGerald (1997). Incomplete adjustment: Fiscal policy, private savings and current account deficits in Mexico since 1982. In K. Jansen and R. Vos (eds). *External Finance and Adjustment: Failure and Success in the Developing World*. Macmillan, Basingstoke, 121–156.

Caprio, G. and A. Demirgüç-Kunt (1997). The Role of Long-Term Finance: Theory and Evidence. *World Bank Research Observer*, 13(2): 171-89, August.

Clarke, R. (1996). Equilibrium exchange rates and financial liberalization in developing countries. *Journal of Development Studies* 32 (3).

Corbett, J., and T. Jenkinson (1997). How is investment financed? A study of Germany, Japan, the United Kingdom and the United States. *The Manchester School (Supplement)* 65(i): 69–93.

De Gregorio, José and Pablo E. Guidotti (1995). Financial development and economic growth, World Development, 23(3): 433-48, March.

de Melo, J. and J. Tybout (1986). The Effects of Financial Liberalization on Savings and Investment in Uruguay, *Economic Development and Cultural Change*, 34(3): 561–87, April.

Demirguc-Kunt, A., and V. Maksimovic (1996). Stock market development and firm financing choices. *World Bank Economic Review* 10: 341–370.

Fanelli, J.M., and R. Medhora (1998). Financial reform in developing countries: An overview. In J.M. Farnelli and R. Medhora (eds). *Financial Reform in Developing Countries*. International Development Research Centre, Canada. [pp. nos.?]

Fanelli, J.M., G. Rozenwurcel, and L.M. Simpson (1998). Country case studies: Argentina. In J.M. Fanelli and R. Medhora (eds). *Financial Reform in Developing Countries*. International Development Research Centre, Canada. [pp. nos.?]

FitzGerald, V. (1997). Short-term capital flows, the real economy and income distribution in the developing countries. In W. Mahmud (ed). *Adjustment and Beyond: The Reform Experience of South Asia*. Macmillan for International Economic Association, Basingstoke and Paris.

FitzGerald, V. (2006). Models of saving, income and the macroeconomics of developing countries in the Post-Keynesian tradition. In P. Arestis, J. McCombie and R. Vickerman (eds). *Growth and Economic Development: Essays in Honour of AP Thirlwall*. Edward Elgar, Cheltenham: 247–262.

Fry, M.J. (1988). *Money, Interest and Banking in Economic Development*. 2nd edition in 1995. John Hopkins University Press, Baltimore.

Fry, M.J. (1997). In favour of financial liberalization. *The Economic Journal* 107 (May): 754–770.

Galbis, V. (1977). Financial intermediation and economic growth in less-developed countries: A theoretical approach. *Journal of Development Studies* 13(2) January: 58–72.

Ghani, E. (1992). How financial markets affect long-run growth: A cross-country study. PR working paper no. WPS 843, January. Country Economic Operations, World Bank, Washington DC.

Gibson, H.D., and E. Tsakalotos (1994). The scope and limits of financial liberalization in developing countries: A critical survey. *Journal of Development Studies* 30 (3), April: 578–628.

Greenwood, J., and B. Jovanovic (1990). Financial development, growth, and the distribution of income. *Journal of Political Economy* 98 (5): 1076–1107.

Günçavdi, O., M. Bleaney, and A. McKay (1998). Financial liberalization and private investment: Evidence from Turkey. *Journal of Development Economics* 57 (2): 443–455.

Honohan, Patrick (2004). Financial development, growth, and poverty: how close are the links? Policy Research Working Paper Series 3203, World Bank, Washington D.C.

IMF (2005) *Financial Stability Report 2005*. Cited p. 11

Jacklin, C. (1987). Demand deposits, trading restrictions, and risk sharing. In E.D. Prescott and N. Wallace (eds). *Contractual Arrangements for Intertemporal Trade*. University of Minnesota Press, Minneapolis: 26–47.

Kapur, B.K. (1976). Alternative stabilization policies for less-developed economies. *Journal of Political Economy* 84(4), August: 777–795.

King, R.G., and R. Levine (1993a). Finance and growth: Schumpeter might be right. *Quarterly Journal of Economics* 108 (3): 717–737.

King, R.G., and R. Levine (1993b). Finance, entrepreneurship, and growth: Theory and evidence. *Journal of Monetary Economics* 32: 513–542.

La Porta, Rafael and others (1998) Law and finance. *Journal of Political Economy*, 106 (4), December: 1136–55.

Leahy, M., S. Schich, G. Wehinger, F. Pelgrin, T. Thorgeirsson (2001). Contributions of financial systems to growth in OECD Countries. OECD Economics Department working papers no. 280. Organisation for Economic Co-operation and Development, Paris.

Levine, R. (2000). Bank-based or market-based financial systems: Which is better? University of Minnesota, Processed, January.

Levine, R., and S. Zervos (1998). Stock markets, banks, and economic growth. *American Economic Review* 88(2), June: 537–558.

Levine, R., N. Loayza, and T. Beck (2000). Financial intermediation and growth: Causality and causes. *Journal of Monetary Economics* 46 (1): 31–77.

Li, H., L. Squire, and H. Zou (1998). Explaining international and intertemporal variations in income inequality. *Economic Journal* 108 (1): 26–43.

Loayza, N., and R. Rancière (2004). Financial development, financial fragility and growth. World Bank, Washington, DC. Mimeo.

Mankiw, N.G. (1986). The allocation of credit and financial collapse. *Quarterly Journal of Economics* 101 (3): 455–470.

Mathieson, R.J. (1980). Financial reform and stabilization policy in a developing economy. *Journal of Development Economics* 7(3) September: 359–395.

Mayer, C. (1990). Financial systems, corporate finance and corporate finance. In H.R.G. Hubbard (ed.) *Asymmetric Information, Corporate Finance and Investment.* University of Chicago Press, Chicago

McKinnon, R.I. (1973). *Money and Capital in Economic Development.* Brookings Institutions, Washington DC.

McKinnon, R.I. (1989). Financial liberalization and economic development: A reassessment of interest rate policies in Asia and Latin America. *Oxford Review of Economic Policy* 5 (4): 29–54.

Modigliani, F., and M.H. Miller (1958). The cost of capital, corporate finance, and the theory of investment. *American Economic Review* 48 (2): 261–297.

Morisset, Jacques (1993). Does Financial Liberalisation really Improve Private Investment in Developing Countries"? *Journal of Development Economics*, 40 (1), February: 133–150.

Mosley, P. (1999). Micro-macro linkages in financial markets: The impact of financial liberalization on access to rural credit in four African countries. Finance and Development Research Programme working paper series, no. 4. Institute for Development Policy and Management, University of Manchester.

Noya, N., C. Casacuberta, and F. Lorenzo (1998). Country case studies: Uruguay. In J.M. Fanelli and R. Medhora (eds). *Financial Reform in Developing Countries.* International Development Research Centre, Canada.

Obstfeld, M., and K. Rogoff (1996). *Foundation of International Macroeconomics.* MIT Press, Cambridge MA.

Pindyck, R.S., and A. Solimano (1993). Economic stability and aggregate investment. NBER working paper no. 4380. National Bureau of Economic Research, Cambridge, MA.

Rajan, R.G., and L. Zingales (1998). Financial dependence and growth. *American Economic Review* 88: 559–586.

Reisen, H. (1999). Domestic causes of currency crisis: Policy lessons for crisis avoidance. *IDS Bulletin* 30 (1): 120–133.

Shleifer, A., and R.W. Vishny (1997). A survey of corporate governance. *Journal of Finance* 52 (2): 737–783.

Sikorsky, M.T. (1996). *Financial Liberalization in Developing Countries.* Edward Elgar, Cheltenham.

Soskice, David (1991). The institutional infrastructure for international competitiveness: A comparative analysis of the UK and Germany. In A.B. Atkinson and R. Brunetta (eds.), *Economics of the New Europe.* London, Macmillan.

Stiglitz, Joseph E. and A. Weiss (1981). Credit rationing in markets with imperfect information. *American Economic Review* 71 (2): 393–410.

Stiglitz, Joseph E. and Andrew Weiss (1992). Asymmetric Information in Credit Markets and Its Implications for Macro-economics, *Oxford Economic Papers*, 44 (4): 694–724.

Stiglitz, Joseph E., J.A. Ocampo, S. Speigel, R. Ffrench-Davis, and D. Nayyar (2006). *Stability with Growth: Macroeconomics, Liberalization and Development.* Oxford University Press, New York.

Taylor, L. (1983). *Structuralist Macroeconomics: Applicable Models for the Third World.* Basic Books, New York.

Villanueva, D., and A. Mirakhor (1990). Strategies for financial reforms. IMF Staff Papers. 37(3): 509–536

Warman, F., and A.P. Thirlwall (1994). Interest rate, savings, investment and growth in Mexico, 1960–90: Tests of financial liberalization hypothesis. *Journal of Development Studies* 30 (3): 629–649.

Watson C.M. (1993). Financial liberalization and the economic adjustment process. Development Studies working papers, no. 61. Queen Elizabeth House, University of Oxford.

van Wijnbergen, S. (1983). Interest rate management in LDCs. *Journal of Monetary Economics* 12(3): 433–452.

Williamson, J., and M. Mahar (1998). A survey of financial liberalization. *Essays in International Finance* no. 211. Princeton University, Princeton

World Bank (1989). *World Development Report 1989.* Oxford University Press for the World Bank, New York.

World Bank (2001). *Finance for Growth: Policy Choices in a Volatile World.* Oxford University Press for the World Bank, New York.

9

Aid Does Matter After All: Revisiting the Relationship between Aid and Growth[*]

CAMELIA MINOIU AND SANJAY G. REDDY

The effectiveness of Official Development Assistance (ODA) to developing countries has been fiercely debated. Analyses of the average effect of aid on growth have long yielded contradictory answers to the question of whether aid spurs economic growth. Despite the abundance of studies that have attempted to investigate the aid-growth relationship, a consensus is yet to emerge. In the recent words of the former IMF chief economist, *"the debate about aid effectiveness is one where little is settled"* (Rajan, 2005).

Early protagonists in the debate on aid focused on case studies.[1] More recent work has evaluated the available data using increasingly complex econometric techniques. In our view, these studies – many of which have come to pessimistic conclusions concerning the impact of aid – have failed adequately to assess the relationship between aid and growth. None of the studies has asked whether aid directed toward developmental purposes spurs economic growth over time periods sufficiently lengthy to produce results. In other words, none has asked the question, what is the *long-term* impact of developmental aid? Furthermore, few studies have attempted to disentangle the effects of different components of aid (such as developmental versus geopolitical aid, multilateral versus bilateral aid or tied versus untied aid) on economic growth. In this chapter, we report the results of an effort to do both of these things together. Our conclusion – at variance with the recent "aid pessimistic" literature – is that developmental aid has a large impact on subsequent economic growth.

We use a large cross-section of recipient countries spanning the period 1960–2000, and explore the impact of developmental aid (as opposed to total aid) on economic growth over periods of upto several decades. In addition to our central finding that developmental aid (appropriately defined) appears to have a large effect on growth, we find (contrary to an important strand of the recent literature) that the quality of the domestic policy environment does not affect the growth-effectiveness of aid, and that there is no evidence of diminishing returns to aid or that the effect of aid on growth depends on whether the recipient country is a low or lower middle income country. Our results are robust to the choice of a wide variety of different specifications of the model and the application of alternative proxies for the explanatory variables (in particular, developmental and geopolitical aid).

This study has important policy implications. For aid to spur economic growth, it must be developmental in nature. Furthermore, the effects of developmental aid can only be observed over long periods of time, sometimes decades, as having translated into growth outcomes. Increased aid flows of the right sort can have substantial growth impact, if donors and recipients are patient.

PREVIOUS STUDIES AND OUR CONTRIBUTION

The Recent Cross-Country Aid-Effectiveness Literature

Two major assumptions have been made in the recent aid effectiveness literature, and in particular that using econometric methods. The first assumption is that total aid has a *contemporaneous* (rather than a lagged) effect on economic growth. The second assumption is that *all* components of aid have the *same* impact on average growth. In this section, we first review selected influential studies, highlighting the consequences of these assumptions for coefficient estimates of the marginal effect of growth in econometric models. Next, we challenge these assumptions and propose new ways of addressing the aid effectiveness question.

As noted, the first assumption underlying empirical studies in the aid effectiveness literature is that *present* aid has a causal effect on *present* growth. The difficulty in estimating the causal impact of present aid on present growth has to do with its possibly endogenous nature: aid may be extended in expectation of good growth performance (rendering aid a determinant of economic growth), or a poor expected growth performance may trigger higher aid flows. To address this issue, an instrumentation approach has been undertaken in most studies. The approach is based on the idea that exogenous variation in aid can be isolated using variation in so-called *friends of the donors* variables (Easterly, 2005) which capture geopolitical influences on the extension of aid. Examples of such variables include dummies for common signatories to ententes or alliances, the size of the recipient countries as measured by their population, indicator variables for Egypt and for oil producing countries (with which to reflect the increase in US aid to these countries after the 1977 Camp David accord), dummy variables for former French, Spanish, Portuguese, and other colonies, and common language dummies. A second frequently used instrument for current aid is past aid. The former approach to instrumentation has been implemented for example, by Boone (1994, 1996), Burnside and Dollar (2000), Easterly (2003, 2005) and Rajan and Subramanian (2005). In contrast, Daalgard, Hansen and Tarp (2004) have taken the second approach. It should be noted, in relation to this choice of instruments, that an important requirement for variables to serve as instruments (in our case, either lagged aid or geopolitical variables) is that they satify the exclusion restriction, i.e., they do not have a direct causal impact on growth. If one believes, as we do, that both lagged aid and the geopolitical variables that are used to predict exogenous variation in aid have a direct causal effect on growth (i.e., that they belong to the true model of the determinants of growth), then this untestable restriction fails and the models proposed in the literature suffer from misspecification.

Burnside and Dollar (2000) influentially examined the growth-effectiveness of aid in a panel of 56 countries over the period 1970–1993. They claimed to find little evidence that aid is a determinant of growth in countries with poor domestic fiscal, monetary and trade policies. The authors reported that aid is effective only in countries where the 'quality' of policies is high, but that aid itself does not play a role in producing policies. Burnside and Dollar (2000) argued that reallocating aid towards countries with 'good' policies would result in a substantial improvement in those countries' growth performance.

A study that builds on the original Burnside-Dollar approach is that by Collier and Dollar (2002). The authors assess the effect of aid on growth as a function of the quality of the policy environment for the time period 1990–1996 in a cross section of 86 countries. Collier and Dollar (2002) argue in favor of a proxy for the policy environment that is different from the weighted average of budget surplus, inflation and trade openness used by Burnside and Dollar (2000). Specifically, Collier and Dollar (2002) use the World Bank's Country Policy and Institutional Assessment index. The authors claim that the Burnside-Dollar results are robust to uses of alternative samples and time periods. In contrast to that study, however, they do not find evidence of diminishing returns to aid. Other successors to the Burnside-Dollar study include the comment by Easterly, Levine and Roodman (2004) and the reply by Burnside and Dollar (2004). Easterly, Levine and Roodman (2004) enrich the original database by adding four more years (to cover 1970–1997) and find that Burnside and Dollar's initial findings do not hold up to this extension of the original dataset. While the authors do not explicitly argue that aid is ineffective at all, they find no evidence that it works better in 'good' policy environments.

More recently, Dalgaard, Hansen and Tarp (2004), employing a sample of 65 countries, find evidence that aid has been less effective in countries located in tropical areas, but that it is in general growth promoting. The authors argue against the use of the World Bank's Country Policy and Institutional Assessment index (CPIA) as an indicator of countries' policy environment (due to its possible endogeneity to growth and because its use in aid allocation across countries may result in systematic correlation with unobserved unfavorable initial conditions). Rajan and Subramanian (2005) is the most recent study to re-assesses the aid-growth relationship in a cross-country setting (using a sample of 107 countries). As before, the authors rely on an instrumentation strategy to identify the effect of present (total) aid on present economic growth, and find "*little robust evidence of a positive (or negative) relationship between aid inflows into a country and its economic growth"* (Rajan and Subramanian, 2005, p.1).

Although the aid effectiveness literature is vast, few studies have attempted to identify the impact of different components of aid on growth. The working hypothesis in these studies has been that all aid has the same effect on growth, regardless of the sector to which it is allocated (e.g., general budgetary support or emergency assistance, technical cooperation or health and education). A notable exception is Clemens, Radelet and Bhavnani (2004), who look at the short-run impact of aid allocated to support budget and balance of payments, investments in infrastructure, agriculture and industry (amounting to fifty-three percent of total aid receipts). The authors argue that aid allocated to these sectors is likely to have a discernable impact on growth within the subsequent four years. They find strong evidence that this is the case, with estimates suggesting that $1 increase in short-impact aid raises income, on average, by $1.64 (in present value). The authors suggest that aid which is aimed at supporting democracy, the environment, health and education is likely to have a long-term impact on growth, but do not attempt to identify its effect.

Rajan and Subramanian (2005) also investigate the relationship between different components of aid and growth. They distinguish between multilateral and bilateral aid, economic, social and food aid, long-impact and short-impact aid as defined by Clemens, Radelet and Bhavnani (2004), as well as aid originating from Scandinavian countries. In all these cases, the authors attempt to uncover the *contemporaneous* effect of distinct components of aid on average growth, use *friends of the donors variables* as instruments, and find no evidence that the type of aid matters in explaining growth performance. In a similar vein, Miquel-Florensa (2006) disentangles the growth effectiveness of tied aid versus untied aid. Using the dataset of Easterly, Levine and Roodman (2004), the author finds that tied aid is negatively and statistically significantly associated with average growth. However, the result is not robust to the use of different samples. The overall conclusion is that untied aid is more growth-effective than tied aid in countries with more 'favourable' policy environments.

An explanation as to why previous studies had failed to uncover an effect of aggregate aid on growth is offered by Headey (2005) which argued that bilateral aid (amounting to 70 percent of total aid) did not have an impact on growth prior to 1990 (during the Cold War) primarily because it served – at the global level – the donors' geopolitical interests. It is thus not surprising, according to the author, that aggregate aid does not seem to have influenced average growth between 1970–2001. Headey (2005) uses a dataset of 56 countries spanning the 1970–2001 period and finds evidence that multilateral aid flows were more effective than bilateral aid flows during the pre-Cold War period, a finding explained by the fact that bilateral aid was dominated by largely geostrategically-driven contributions from a few large donors. In contrast, using the post-Cold War sample, the author identifies a large positive effect of bilateral aid on growth, and concludes that the pooling of the two samples might serve as an explanation of why earlier studies (often covering precisely the Cold War period) often found that aggregate aid was growth-ineffective.

Challenging the Assumptions

As noted, many of the previous studies assume that all components of aid have the same impact on economic growth. Furthermore, they frequently assumed that ODA solely has a *contemporaneous* or nearly contemporaneous effect on growth. These two working hypotheses lead to the following model being typically estimated in a cross-country context:

$$Growth_{it} = \beta(Total\_Aid/GDP)_t + \delta(Controls)_t + \varepsilon_t \qquad (1)$$

where i is an index for recipient countries, t is the time index, and ε_{it} is a composite error term comprised of fixed effects, time-specific shocks, and random error. The control variables usually account of the possibly confounding effect of other growth determinants, such as initial conditions, the quality of institutions (governance), geographical factors (e.g., frost days or share of land in tropical areas), the quality of the policy environment (in particular, a measure of trade openness or a policy index appropriately defined), inflation (as a measure of domestic monetary policies), political and social stability. The model is usually estimated in the cross-sectional setting using Ordinary Least Squares (OLS) or Two Stage Least Squares. In the latter case, total aid is usually instrumented for with either past values of aid, or with geostrategic variables from the *friends of the donors* class. In a panel setting, the model is estimated using Fixed Effects or Generalized Method of Moments (GMM) techniques.

In the work summarized in this chapter, we depart from (1) in two major ways. We assume that (a) different components of aid have a distinct effect on growth, and (b) that aid has a discernible impact on economic growth over the long-term. In relation to the first point, we argue that aid expended in a manner that can reasonably be anticipated to promote development (e.g., aid aimed at and/or spent on building growth-promoting infrastructure such as roads, bridges or ports or on health and education) can be expected to have a different effect on growth than aid that could not reasonably be anticipated to have this effect (e.g., aid spent on strengthening a military or reinforcing a political alliance).[2] For this reason, we distinguish between aid spent in a manner that could reasonably be anticipated to promote development and aid of all other kinds. We refer to the former type of aid as *developmental aid*, and to the latter type of aid as *geopolitical aid*. Of course, it may be the case that geopolitical aid, thus defined, ultimately has an effect on development. The definitions we offer are "expenditure side" definitions, which do not directly hinge on the *motives* for providing aid. Of course, there may be an empirical tendency for aid that is motivated by geopolitical considerations to be non-developmental according to the expenditure side definition we provide here, which we may rely on in our efforts to differentiate these econometrically. The heart of this distinction between different types of aid is a view that total aid contains a developmental, possibly growth-enhancing expenditure component (*developmental aid*), in addition to a growth-neutral or possibly growth-depressing expenditure component (*geopolitical aid*).

Our second departure from the standard model derives from the belief that developmentally-oriented aid takes longer to translate into development outcomes than the periods of one or four years that have been assumed in the recent literature. Our definition of developmental aid is therefore closest to that of *long-impact aid* proposed by Clemens,

Radelet and Bhavnan (2004) and Rajan and Subramanian (2005). Since it is natural to expect that investments in infrastructure, health and education should affect economic growth over the long-run, we allow for various possible lags of developmental aid to enter the model as distinct determinants of present average growth. There is no reason to treat geopolitical aid differently (unless one believes that it has no effect on growth, which is an empirical question), and multiple lags of geopolitical aid are also included in the model. We are thus specifying a very broad model that allows each component of aid to have a distinct, long-term effect on growth. As will be explained in the next section, data limitations will place a restriction on the model we can estimate.

To illustrate the departure in this chapter from the consensus in the literature, we specify the following model:

$$Growth = \beta_{1k} \sum_{k \neq 0} (Developmental\_Aid/GDP)_{i,t-k}$$
$$\beta_{2k} \sum_{k \neq 0} (Geopolitical\_Aid/GDP)_{i,t-k} + (Controls)_{it} + \varepsilon_{it}$$

where lags up to k periods have been specified as entering the model directly for the two distinct components of aid.

A direct comparison between Equations 1 and 2 can help to explain why previous studies of the effect of aid on economic growth might have failed to uncover a systematic relationship between the two. Specifically, in Equation 1, isolating the exogenous variation in total aid with geostrategic variables (such as colonial dummies) may result in only the geopolitically-motivated portion of aid being captured by the fitted second-stage regressor. In that case, it is hardly surprising that total aid is unable to explain the growth performance of recipient countries, since geopolitical aid may well have either zero or a negative impact on growth. Similarly, restricting developmental and geopolitical aid to have the same marginal effect on growth (represented by β in Equation 1) leads to a downward bias in the estimator for β under the assumption that one component of aid has a positive effect on growth, and the other operates in the opposite direction. If geopolitical aid has a negative (or zero) effect on economic growth, any positive effect on growth from developmental aid will be 'buried' by the effect of geopolitical aid. (For technical details, see

Reddy and Minoiu (2006: Appendix 1A and 1B)). Since our aim is to identify the growth-impact of developmental aid without interference from that of geopolitical aid, we allow for the two components of aid to have distinct effects on growth. Whether or not this is the case can be determined empirically. Our results are outlined in the next section.

EMPIRICAL FINDINGS

The Sample

We use information on aid disbursements (representing net loans and grants) from the Organization for Economic Co-operation and Development – Development Assistance Committee database (DAC, 2006) and Gross Domestic Product (GDP) data from the World Bank's World Development Indicators (2006) for 107 countries between 1960 and 2000. All other variables are from Rajan and Subramanian's (2005) and were made available to us by courtesy of the authors. Reddy and Minoiu (2006: Appendix 2) contains a complete list of the variables and their sources. Since we wish to assess the long-term impact of aid on growth, we focus on the determinants of average growth in the 1990s. All control variables represent averages over 1990–2000, while developmental aid enters the specifications in lagged form. Depending on data availability, the sample varies between a minimum of 64 and a maximum of 77 countries. Summary statistics for selected variables used in the regressions are reported in Reddy and Minoiu (2006: Appendix 3).

Proxies for Developmental Aid

We face several challenges in defining proxies for developmental aid. The ideal procedure for isolating the developmental component of total aid would entail classifying aid by type of expenditure, and classifying expenditures by their expected effect on economic growth. For example, aid that is spent on infrastructure (e.g., for building roads, irrigation systems, water and electricity delivery systems, housing, etc.) and aid spent on health, education and population policies, would fall under the category of developmental aid since such expenditures are expected to have a positive impact on development and economic growth. In contrast, aid covering the administrative costs of donors or aimed at emergency relief would not be classified as developmental in nature. However, data on aid by type of expenditure only goes back to 1990 (for disbursements) and to 1973 (for commitments). It is thus not appropriate for purposes of our analysis.

To arrive at proxies for developmental aid, we take another approach. First, we treat all multilateral aid as developmental in nature, since, as the definition for multilateral aid from the Development Assistance Committee database reads, *"multilateral transactions are those made to a recipient institution which conducts all or part of its activities in favor of development"* (DAC, 2006[3]) and multilateral aid channeled through international organizations is less likely to have a geopolitical rationale. Furthermore, we take total bilateral aid from the Nordic countries to be a proxy for development aid, since Nordic countries are reputed to have aid programs that are more developmentally-oriented than other donor countries. Total bilateral aid from Denmark, Finland, Norway, Sweden, and Iceland (comprising group G1 of donors) is the first proxy for developmental aid that we consider. Since this proxy of developmental aid may be subject to the claim that bilateral aid from other donors also contains development components (which would otherwise remain unaccounted for in our analysis), we extend the list of G1 donor countries by adding five more donors (comprising group G2 of donors). The additional countries are Austria, Canada, Luxembourg, the Netherlands, and Switzerland. The choice of countries is, admittedly, based on a subjective judgement of the development-orientation of these donor countries' aid programmes.

A second proxy that reduces this subjectivity, is based on the aid-quality ranking according to the Commitment to Development Index (for aid) developed by Roodman (2006). A donor country is ranked higher according to the index if the country offers a larger proportion of grants rather than loans, if its aid is less likely to be tied, if it channels aid towards poorer and less 'corrupt' governments, and if its aid programmes consist of fewer projects (not to place a strain on a recipient country government's administrative capacity). According to the Commitment to Development Index (for 2005), the highest ranked 5 donor countries (defined as group G3 of donor countries) are Denmark, Norway, Sweden, the Netherlands, and Switzerland. Finally, the highest ranked 10 donor countries form group G4 of development-friendly donor countries, and include the donors from G3 as well as Ireland, UK, Belgium, Finland, and France. Notably, one shortcoming of our approach is that the 2005 aid quality ranking of donors may not be representative of the quality of aid of the same donors in the past. Despite this possible source of concern, and in light of lack of alternative feasible approaches to identifying proxies for developmental aid, we use cumulative bilateral aid from donor groups G1, G2, G3, and G4, in turn, as proxies for development aid to estimate Equation (2).

Proxies for Geopolitical Aid

A possible proxy for geopolitical aid is the share of total aid predicted by geostrategic variables. Another possible proxy is cumulative bilateral aid from donor countries that extend aid for geostrategic reasons (computed as total aid minus total bilateral aid from the each of the four groups of development-friendly donor countries). Since our main results are similar for the two proxies, we present findings in this chapter based on the former proxy. Thus, geopolitical aid in our empirical model represents the share of total aid predicted by the following set of geostrategic variables: a dummy for common membership in the Entente Alliance, a dummy for Egypt and Israel after the Camp David accord, past and present colonial relationship dummies (with France, UK, Spain and Portugal), as well as a common language indicator variable. The variable is taken from the Rajan and Subramanian (2005) database, and had been constructed by the authors with the aim of isolating the component of total aid that is exogenous to countries' growth performance. Since we believe that this instrument does not satisfy the restriction of not having a direct causal effect on growth, we include it as an independent variable in the empirical model, and interpret it as a proxy for geopolitical aid. Summary statistics for developmental and geopolitical aid are presented in Reddy and Minoiu (2006: Appendix 3).

The Estimated Model

Our proxy for geopolitical aid represents the component of total aid that is predicted by geostrategic variables. Since it is only available for our regression analysis as an average over several decades, we estimate a version of the model that slightly differs from Equation 2 as it only considers the *contemporaneous* effect of geopolitical aid. First, we write the model in panel form:

$$Growth_{it} = \beta_{1k} \sum_{k \neq 0} (Developmental\_Aid/GDP)_{i,t-k} +$$
$$\beta_2 (Geopolitical\_Aid/GDP)_{it} + \delta\,(Controls)_{it} + \varepsilon_{it}$$

To estimate cross-sectional regressions using OLS, averages are taken for all variables over the relevant time periods, as follows: the dependent variable is average growth in the 1990s, (lagged) developmental aid is averaged over 1960–1990, while geopolitical aid is averaged over 1990–2000. The other covariates also represent averages over 1990–2000. The set of covariates includes the following determinants of average growth: initial per capita GDP, initial level of life expectancy, institutional quality (proxied by an index of institutional quality equal to the average of the following six Institutional Country Risk Guide governance indicators: corruption, rule of law, repudiation risk of government contracts, bureaucratic quality, ethic tensions, and expropriation risk), a measure of geography (representing the average of frost days and tropical land area), initial government consumption, a measure of social and political unrest (namely, the number of revolutions and coups over the period), the average and standard deviation of the terms of trade, initial level of a policy variable (namely, the Sachs-Warner (1995) trade openness indicator variable updated by Wacziarg and Welch (2003)), and East Asia and sub-Saharan Africa dummies.

The estimated model is given below:

$$Growth_i = \beta_1 (Developmental\_Aid/GDP_i) +$$
$$\beta_2 (Geopolitical\_Aid/GDP_i) + \delta Controls_i + \varepsilon_i$$

Partial Correlations and Cross-Sectional Regression Results

We present partial scatterplots that illustrate the conditional relationships between the variables of interest, namely our proxies for developmental and geopolitical aid, and average growth in the 1990s. At the same time, we discuss regression results presented in Reddy and Minoiu (2006). Figure 9.1 below depicts the conditional relationship between lagged developmental aid (averaged over 1960–1990) and growth in the 1990s when the sole proxy for developmental aid is aid extended by multilateral institutions.

FIGURE 9.1

Conditional scatterplot of lagged development aid (proxied by lagged Multilateral Aid) against average growth

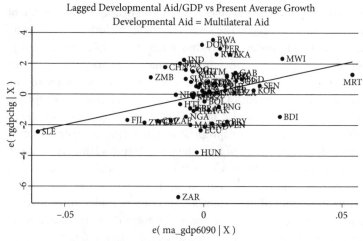

Lagged Developmental Aid/GDP vs Present Average Growth
Developmental Aid = Multilateral Aid

coef = 39.913968, (robust) se = 11.815067, t = 3.38
Multilateral Aid is averaged over 1960–1990 || Growth is averaged over 1990–2000

As expected, there is a positive and statistically significant relationship between past multilateral aid and current growth. The result is also evident in the regression analyses outlined in Reddy and Minoiu (2006: Appendix 5, Table 5A). Lagged multilateral aid has a large subsequent effect on average growth. Average growth in the

1990s is higher by one third of a percentage point on average when the share of multilateral aid in GDP increases by 1 percentage point. At the same time, geopolitical aid appears to have a negative and statistically significant, yet smaller effect on average growth. Despite our attempt to control for possible confounding factors, these results should be interpreted with caution. It may be the case that growth-enhancing elements of aid have been omitted from this specification. For example, since our proxies for developmental and geopolitical aid do not add up to total aid (by construction), we cannot ensure that all forms of aid (productive or unproductive) have been accounted for in this specification. For this reason, in subsequent specifications we use richer proxies for developmental aid.

Next, we illustrate the conditional scatterplots of lagged developmental aid against average growth (Figure 9.2). We focus on two proxies for developmental aid, representing total bilateral aid from

FIGURE 9.2
Conditional scatterplots of lagged development aid (proxied by lagged Total Bilateral Aid from groups G2 and G4 of development-friendly donor countries) against average growth

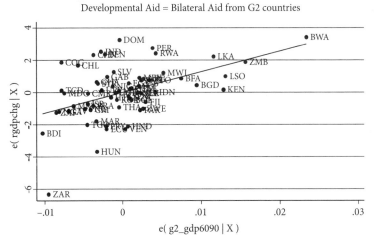

Lagged Developmental Aid/GDP vs Present Average Growth
Developmental Aid = Bilateral Aid from G2 countries

coef = 128.25029, (robust) se = 32.617775, t = 3.93
Bilateral Aid from G2 countries is averaged over 1960–1990 || Growth: 1990–2000

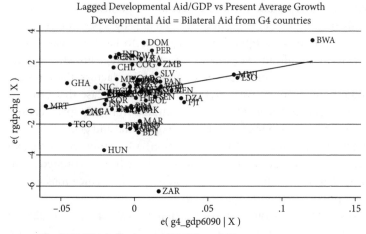

Lagged Developmental Aid/GDP vs Present Average Growth
Developmental Aid = Bilateral Aid from G4 countries

coef = 17.186354, (robust) se = 6.4831388, t = 2.65
Bilateral Aid from G4 countries is averaged over 1960–1990 || Growth: 1990–2000

groups G2 to G4 of development-friendly donor countries. In each specification underlying the conditional scatterplot, the share of multilateral aid in GDP is included as a control variable to attenuate the possible bias in the coefficients on bilateral aid that might arise if multilateral aid were omitted. The remaining sources of bias in these coefficient estimates are those developmental components of total aid (if any) that have not been accounted for by our proxies for developmental aid. An example would be bilateral aid from donor countries that are not included in groups G2 and G4.

The two diagrams speak for themselves. Our proxies for lagged developmental aid (averaged over 1960–1990) are strongly positively correlated with average growth in the 1990s, conditional on the set of covariates. The regression results corresponding to this figure are shown in Reddy and Minoiu (2006: Appendix 5, Tables 5C and 5E, first column of lowermost panel). The coefficient estimates throughout these specifications are large and statistically significant at the 1 percent level of significance. The magnitude of the coefficients on total bilateral aid from groups G2 and G4 is remarkable: an increase in the share of total bilateral aid in GDP from the G2 group of donor countries by 1 percent (between 1960–1990) is associated with an increase in average per capita GDP growth rate in the 1990s by 1.28

percentage points. Similarly, for the group of donor countries G4, the analogous coefficient estimate is 0.17 percentage points.

As shown in the remaining tables in Reddy and Minoiu (2006: Appendix 5, Tables 5B-5E), this positive and statistically significant relationship is robust to the use of alternative proxies for developmental aid (namely, total bilateral aid from groups G1 to G4 of donor countries), as well as alternative time-periods over which the developmental aid is lagged and averaged. Developmental aid averaged over periods such as 1960–1970, 1960–1975, 1960–1980, 1960–1985, 1960–1990, 1970–1980, 1970–1990, and 1980–1990, is always accompanied by a statistically significant and large marginal effect on subsequent growth (in the 1990s). This is a consequence of the high degree of correlation of aid across the time periods considered. For this reason, we believe that the best specification among those shown is that in which aid is lagged over 1960–1990, i.e., the entire period for which data are available. In that model, the possibility of omitted variables such as lagged aid from other time periods is minimal. We decided not to include several lags of aid as explanatory variables in any given model due to the small sample size (between 64 and 77 countries) and the relatively large number of covariates.

We find that the proxy for geopolitical aid is consistently negatively correlated with growth, but that its coefficient estimate is not always statistically significantly different from zero. Insofar as geostrategical aid is endogenous to the growth performance of a country (for example, since strategic alliances may be formed in anticipation of higher aid flows of the richer partners in those alliances), this finding should be interpreted with caution. However, the presumption in the literature has been that geopolitically-motivated aid is exogenous to growth, and for this reason it has been considered an appropriate instrument for total aid. Under this assumption, the inclusion of present geopolitical aid as an explanatory variable would not give rise to misspecification (unless one believes that *past* geopolitical aid is likely to affect current growth, and has been omitted). In our models, present geopolitical aid (expressed as the share of total aid predicted by *friends of the donors* variables) is often negatively correlated with growth. As shown in Reddy and Minoiu (2006: Appendix 5, Tables 5B-5E), the coefficients reach a magnitude of -10.6. This means that an increase in the ratio of geopolitical aid to GDP by 1 percentage point (in the 1990s) is associated with an average growth rate (in the 1990s) lower by 0.1 percentage point. The negative (contemporaneous) relation between geopolitical aid and average growth is depicted in Figure 9.3.

FIGURE 9.3
Conditional scatterplot of present geopolitical aid (proxied by the share of total aid explained by geostrategic variables) against average growth. The regression corresponds to Reddy and Minoiu (2006: Appendix 5, Table 5E, lowermost panel, column 1).

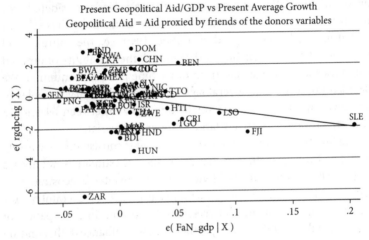

Present Geopolitical Aid/GDP vs Present Average Growth
Geopolitical Aid = Aid proxied by friends of the donors variables

coef = -10.07069, (robust) se = 3.7460525, t = -2.69
Geopolitical Aid is averaged over 1990–2000 || Growth is averaged over 1990–2000

Panel Regression Results

The coefficient estimates from our cross-country regressions involving averaged variables may be biased due to the omission of time-invariant country unobserved characteristics which might be correlated with the covariates. For this reason, we estimate our model in a panel setting as well, using a GMM estimation procedure. We use the 'system GMM' estimator developed by Blundell and Bond (1998) which specifies a rich set of moment conditions likely to be valid for the type of data often used in cross country growth-regressions (see, for example, Bond, Hoeffler and Temple, 2001). The sample consists of 71 recipient countries, the variables are five-year averages from 1960 to 2000, and the specifications include a full set of time dummies. The results are reported in Reddy and Minoiu (2006: Appendix 7, Table 7).

Our main findings from the cross-sectional setting are replicated in the panel framework. We find that developmental aid has a large and statistically significant effect on growth after approximately twenty-five years. An increase in total bilateral aid in GDP from group G1 of donor countries by 1 percentage point, leads to an increase by 1.75 percentage points in average growth rate 2.5 decades later. The same coefficient magnitude is found for developmental aid proxied by total bilateral aid from group G3. The coefficient corresponding to G1 is of almost 1 percentage point. Furthermore, the coefficient estimates for lagged multilateral aid and geopolitical aid are not statistically significantly different from zero. In the GMM specifications, we fail to reject the Hansen test of over-identifying restrictions, which indicates that the instruments used by the GMM estimator are valid.

Robustness Checks

Alternative Proxies for Developmental Aid

We subjected our main results to a series of robustness checks. First, we identify an alternative proxy for developmental aid. Developmental aid is defined as the share of total aid predicted by National Rainfall Index (NRI), developed by the Food and Agriculture Organization, Environment and Natural Resource Service (FAO-SDRN). In developing this proxy, our premise is that the level of developmental aid offered to recipient countries is related to their agricultural productivity. Since the NRI serves as an indicator of the quality of the agricultural season, we use its exogenous variation to predict the (exogenous) part of total aid which can be interpreted as developmental in nature. More precisely, we create a variable that represents the share of total aid in GDP predicted by NRI lagged one period. Then we use that variable as a proxy of developmental aid alongside that for geopolitical aid. The results in a cross-sectional setting are reported in Reddy and Minoiu (2006: Appendix 8, Table 8B).

We find that the previously uncovered positive and statistically significant relationship between lagged developmental aid and average growth in the 1990s holds up when this alternative proxy for developmental aid is used. However, the magnitude of the coefficient estimates is lower. A one percentage point increase in the developmental aid to GDP ratio (over 1960–1990) is associated with an almost one quarter of a percentage point increase in average growth (in the 1990s). In this model, the coefficient on geopolitical aid is not statistically significant, which suggests that geopolitically-motivated aid may well have a neutral impact (as contrasted with our previous finding of a possibly depressing effect on economic growth).

Alternative Specifications

Three other propositions have been central to the recent aid effectiveness literature. The first is that a big push in aid is needed by countries caught in a 'poverty trap' (Sachs et al, 2004) in order to set themselves on a trajectory of sustained economic growth. The hypothesis is that geopolitics, geography, disease, lack of infrastructure, and low levels of technology, produce income levels that are too low to allow for capital investment sufficient to trigger and sustain growth. We tested this premise by evaluating whether the impact of aid on growth depends on the income level of the country (in particular, whether they are low or lower middle income countries). Our results indicated that there were no income thresholds affecting countries' ability to use aid productively. The interaction terms between developmental aid and income levels had statistically insignificant coefficient estimates. However, developmental aid continued to display a high level of positive conditional correlation with subsequent average growth.

Second, a number of studies have advanced the conclusion that there are diminishing returns to aid. Again, this finding was not evident using our data and specifications. Our models suggested that there are either no diminishing returns to aid or small negative effects.

However, these results were not robust across multiple specifications and time periods, so a definite conclusion could not be reached.

Third, a number of authors, including Burnside and Dollar (2000) and Collier and Dollar (2002) have asserted that aid is effective only in 'good' policy environments. Using a number of proxies for the quality of the policy environment, we re-estimated our specifications including interaction terms between the components of aid and the policy variables. These proxies included: the Sachs-Warner (1995) openness indicator variable, the updated Sachs-Warner variable (Wacziarg and Welch, 2003), the World Bank CPIA ratings (used by Collier and Dollar, 2002), and the policy index representing a weighted average of budget surplus, inflation and openness (constructed by Burnside and Dollar, 2000). We found no evidence that developmental aid is more growth-effective in countries with 'better' domestic policies. Again, developmental aid appeared to spur growth regardless of the quality of policy environment as captured by these variables.

CONCLUSIONS

We offer new evidence that aid 'matters' for growth and indeed that it can matter a great deal. However, only certain kinds of aid have a statistically and economically discernible impact on average growth, and only over the *long-term*. This chapter contributes to the aid effectiveness literature by disentangling the *distinct* effects of developmental and geopolitical aid on growth. Furthermore, it reports evidence that aid assistance to developing countries translates into development outcomes with a lag, sometimes involving several decades.

Using a variety of proxies for developmental aid and numerous specifications, we found that developmental aid has a positive, large, and statistically significant effect on subsequent growth. These proxies included total bilateral aid from Nordic countries, as well as countries that rank high on a widely-used aid-quality index. Furthermore, developmental aid predicted as the share of total aid explained by the quality of the agricultural season also had a statistically significant effect on subsequent growth. In contrast, geopolitical aid was found to either have a negative or zero effect on average growth. In a series of robustness checks, we did not find evidence that aid is more growth-effective in 'better' policy environments, that there are diminishing returns to aid, or that there are income thresholds in the ability of countries to utilize aid productively.

In conclusion, recent judgments regarding the growth ineffectiveness of aid are not supported by the data. Aid matters for growth. However, it is *developmental* aid rather than *geopolitical* aid that matters. The policy implications of this study stand in contrast to those of previous studies. A change in the composition of total aid that favors developmental aid, as well as an increase in the total volume of ODA extended to developing countries, are policy measures likely to have a substantial and large effect on the future growth of those countries. To validate and improve these results, we believe that further research should aim at identifying the growth impact of distinct categories of aid over the medium and long-term, using more fine-grained data. This appears to be a promising area for research aimed at moving beyond the debate on whether aid is effective and shedding light on the now pertinent question of *what* makes aid effective.

Notes

[*] Based on Reddy and Minoiu (2006). We would like to thank the Department of Economic and Social Affairs of the United Nations for supporting this research. We are grateful to Kathleen Apltauer for her help in editing this chapter.
[1] See, e.g., the work on this subject by Peter Bauer (1959, 1971, 1981) and the review of Bauer (1981) by Sen (1982).
[2] Clearly, there is a need for a threshold with which to undertake such differentiation. We note this requirement without explicitly specifying such a threshold.
[3] More specifically, DAC Glossary on Aid Statistics, 2006. URL: http://www.oecd.org/glossary/0,2586,en_2649_34447_1965693_1_1_1_1,00.html

References

Bauer, Peter Thomas (1959). *United States Aid and Indian Economic Development*. American Enterprise Association: Washingon, D.C.
Bauer, Peter Thomas (1971). *Dissent on Development: Studies and Debates in Development Economics*. Weidenfeld and Nicolson: London, and Harvard University Press: Cambridge, MA.

Bauer, Peter Thomas (1981). *Equality, the Third World and Economic Delusion.* Weidenfeld and Nicolson: London, and Harvard University Press: Cambridge, MA.

Blundell, Richard and Stephen Bond (1998). Initial conditions and moment restrictions in dynamic panel data models. *Journal of Econometrics* 87: 115–143.

Blundell, Richard, Anke Hoeffler and Jonathan Temple (2001).GMM estimation of empirical growth models, Discussion paper 3048, Center for Economic Policy Research, London.

Boone, Peter (1994). The impact of foreign aid on savings and growth. Working paper 1265, Centre for Economic Performance, London School of Economics, London.

Boone, Peter (1996). Politics and the effectiveness of foreign aid. *European Economic Review* 40(2): 289–329.

Burnside, Craig and David Dollar (2000). Aid, policies and growth. *American Economic Review* 90 (4): 847–869.

Burnside, Craig and David Dollar (2004). Aid, policies and growth: Reply. *American Economic Review* 94 (3): 781–784.

Clemens, Michael A., Steven Radelet and Rikhil Bhavnani (2004). Counting chickens when they hatch: The short-term effect of aid on growth. CGD working paper no. 44, Center for Global Development, Washington, DC.

Collier, Paul and David Dollar (2002). Aid allocation and poverty reduction. *European Economic Review* 46 (8): 1475–1500.

Dalgaard, Carl-Johan, Henrik Hansen and Finn Tarp (2004). On the empirics of foreign aid and growth. *The Economic Journal* 114 (496): 191-216.

Development Assistance Committee Online database (2006). Paris, Development Assistance Committee (DAC). URL: www.oecd.org/dac/stats/idsonline

Easterly, William (2003). Can foreign aid buy growth? *Journal of Economic Perspectives* 17 (3): 23–48.

Easterly, William (2005). What did structural adjustment adjust? The association of policies and growth with repeated IMF and World Bank adjustment loans. *Journal of Development Economics* 76 (1): 1–22.

Easterly, William, Ross Levine and David Roodman (2004). New data, new doubts: A comment on Burnside and Dollar's "Aid, Policies and Growth". *American Economic Review* 94 (3): 774–780.

Headey, Derek (2005). Foreign aid and foreign policy: how donor undermine the effectiveness of overseas development assistance. Centre for Efficiency and Productivity Analysis Working paper 05, School of Economics, University of Queensland, Australia.

Miquel-Florensa, Josepa (2006). Aid effectiveness: A comparison of tied and untied aid. Unpublished manuscript, Columbia University.

Rajan, Raghuram (2005). Aid and growth: The policy challenge. *Finance and Development* 42 (4). URL: http://www.imf.org/external/pubs/ft/fandd/2005/12/straight.htm

Rajan, Raghuram and Arvind Subramanian (2005). Aid and growth: What does the cross-country evidence really show? IMF Working paper WP/05/127, International Monetary Fund, Washington, DC.

Reddy, Sanjay and Camelia Minoiu (2006). Development aid and economic growth: a positive long-run relation. Working paper 29, Department of Economic and Social Affairs, United Nations, New York.

Roodman, David (2006). Building and running an effective policy index: Lessons from the commitment to development index. Essay, Center for Global Development, Washington, DC.

Sachs, Jeffrey D. and Andrew M. Warner (1995). Economic reform and the process of global integration. *Brookings Papers on Economic Activity* 1: 1–118.

Sachs, Jeffrey D., John W. McArthur, Guido Schmidt-Traub, Margaret Kruk, Chandrika Bahadur, Michael Faye, and Gordon McCord (2004). Ending Africa's poverty trap. *Brookings Papers on Economic Activity* 1: 117–240.

Sen, Amartya (1982). Just Deserts. *The New York Review of Books* 29 (3). URL: http://finance.sauder.ubc.ca/~bhatta/BookReview/sen_on_bauer.html

Wacziarg, Romain, and Karen Horn Welch (2003). Trade liberalization and growth: New evidence. NBER working paper 10152, National Bureau of Economic Research, Cambridge, MA.

World Bank (2006). World Development Indicators online. World Bank Group, Washington, DC. URL: http://devdata.worldbank.org/dataonline/old-default.htm

10

Have Collapses in Infrastructure Spending led to Cross-Country Divergence in Per Capita GDP?

FRANCISCO RODRÍGUEZ*

One of the most striking facts of post-war economic history is the continuously increasing trend of growing disparities between poor and rich countries. Even though some developing countries, primarily located in the East Asian region, managed during this period to close their gap with the developed world, this was an exception to the broader trend. As Figure 10.1 shows, the standard deviation of log per capita incomes has been growing continuously since the early sixties, and now stands 31 per cent higher than in 1960. The advent of market-oriented reforms during the eighties and nineties appears to have done little to reverse this trend: dispersion has grown faster during the 1990s than in any other decade since the sixties.

This chapter explores one possible explanation for this great divergence: the decline in the provision of infrastructure that has occurred in many developing countries since the eighties. In their recent work, Easterly and Servén (2003) have shown that there were significant declines in public infrastructure investment in a number of Latin American economies since the eighties. These authors have argued that the growing divergence between East Asia and Latin America can be accounted for in part in terms of their differing investments in public infrastructure. In this chapter, we will attempt to understand whether this explanation can be taken further to help account for the growing disparities in living standards across the world.

The argument is simple. Infrastructure is a public good that produces positive externalities for production. Investment in infrastructure raises production as well as the marginal product of private capital,

FIGURE 10.1
Standard Deviation of log per capita incomes, 1960–2001

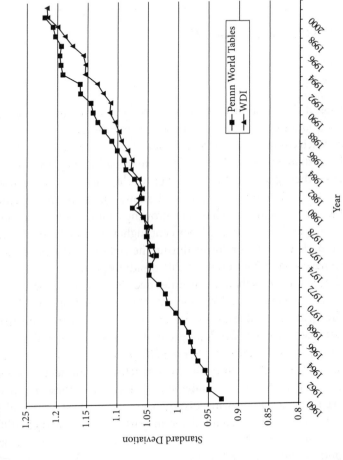

thus raising the incentive to invest. If poor and middle-income countries cut back investment in infrastructure, it would lead to a decline in their steady-state levels of income. If the stocks of developed countries do not change, it will also lead to an increase in world dispersion of incomes.

The argument is indeed simple, but is it true? Is there evidence of substantial effects of infrastructure investment on productivity and growth? Can the decline in infrastructure investment in less-developed countries account for a significant fraction of growing world disparities? The rest of the chapter will attempt to answer these questions. I begin by discussing the existing empirical evidence. As in many fields of applied economics, the evidence regarding the effects of infrastructure on productivity and growth is open to multiple interpretations, with existing estimates ranging from very large to nonexistent. The next section will attempt to make sense of this debate and to understand why there is so much disagreement. The following section will then use a simple aggregate production function framework, together with the range of estimates derived from our survey of the literature, to understand the quantitative magnitude of the possible links between infrastructure and growth.

The conclusions of this empirical exercise imply that at most changes in public investment have been a minor contributor to the gap between rich and poor countries, accounting for no more than 12 per cent of the increase, and possibly much less. However, the majority of estimates do point towards a positive contribution of infrastructure trends to growing dispersion, suggesting that it may be part of the explanation, though far from being the primary factor.

IS PUBLIC INVESTMENT IN INFRASTRUCTURE RELEVANT FOR PRIVATE SECTOR PRODUCTIVITY?

Any attempt to link trends in infrastructure provision with broader trends in per capita incomes must start out from a discussion of the vast amount of empirical research linking these two forces. Theoretically, the idea that public capital can have an effect on productivity growth and capital accumulation goes back at least as far as the theoretical models of Arrow and Kurz (1970) and Ogura and Yohe (1977), and introduced to the study of growth in the work of Barro (1990). Consider a production function of the form

$$Y = F(G, K, L), \tag{1}$$

where Y is aggregate output, G is the public capital stock, K is the private capital stock, and L aggregate employment. Two key questions emerge from this framework that are of relevance to our study. The first one refers to the magnitude of F_G: how large is the expected effect on aggregate output from increasing the provision of public capital? The second one is about the magnitude of the cross-derivatives F_{KG} and F_{LG}, which will tell us how strong are the complementarities between public capital and private capital or employment. To the extent that private capital accumulation is endogenous, as it is in most growth models, then F_{KG} will influence the subsequent growth rate of the economy. Since a positive value of F_{KG} raises incentives for the accumulation of physical capital, studies of its magnitude are often framed within the context of disentangling the existence of crowding-out versus crowding-in effects.

Evidence from the United States

Empirical studies of the relationship between public investment and productivity growth were rare before the late eighties. A series of studies by David Aschauer (1989a, 1989b, 1990) changed this. Using a production function like (1), Aschauer argued that fully 57 per cent of the post-1970 US productivity slowdown could be explained by the decline of infrastructure investment during the same period, spurring talk of the deficit in infrastructure provision as "America's Third Deficit"

Aschauer's evidence was three-fold. In his first paper on this topic, Aschauer (1989a) presented time-series evidence linking productivity growth between 1949 and 1985 and different types of public capital. He found that a measure of "core infrastructure" which included highways, mass transit, airports, electrical and gas facilities, water, and sewers had a highly significant effect on both labour and multifactor productivity. The decline in US infrastructure investment after 1970 had led, according to Aschauer's calculations, to a decline in TFP growth of 0.8 per cent a year – a very large effect.

Aschauer's second and third papers (1989b, 1989c) complemented this evidence with cross-sectional evidence from US states and with panel data from 7 OECD economies. Alicia Munnell (1990a, 1990b) expanded on Aschauer's studies in two directions: she refined Aschauer's calculation by adjusting labour inputs to take account of changes in the age/sex composition of the labour force, and proceeded to build state-level estimates of the public and private capital stock. She used this data to estimate state-level production functions, finding again a significant effect of public investment on productivity growth, albeit with somewhat smaller quantitative effects. She also estimated the effect of public investment on private investment, to test whether the former crowded-out the latter or not, concluding that the complementarities in the estimated production function were large enough to generate "crowding-in" effects through which the provision of greater public capital led to greater private productivity and greater public investment.

The results of Aschauer and Munnell's research generated considerable excitement and immediately spilled over into discussions in the policy arena. Almost simultaneously, however, a number of economists started questioning the Aschauer and Munnell results. A first objection was raised by Gramlich (1994), who noted that the Aschauer elasticity estimates implied rates of return on public investment as high as 100 per cent. In this logic, public investment would basically pay for itself. But if this was true, asked Gramlich, would private investors not "be clamouring to have the public sector impose taxes or float bonds to build roads, highways, and sewers to generate these high net benefits?" Gramlich argued that if anything what could be observed was quite the contrary: private investors were more often heard arguing that tax rates were, if anything, too high.

Another set of authors pointed out that Aschauer's results could be due to spurious correlation between non-stationary time series. This point paralleled a general preoccupation with the pervasiveness of spurious trends in econometrics that followed on Granger and Newbold's (1974) article pointing out the invalidity of standard t-tests to evaluate the relationship between non-stationary variables.

Aaron (1990), Hulten and Schwab (1991), Jorgenson (1991) and Tatom (1991) all made this point. Hulten and Schwab (1991) and Tatom (1991) also argued that if one first-differenced the data, thus doing away with any common trends that could cause a spurious relationship, Aschauer's estimated positive and significant effect of public investment on productivity disappeared. Tatom (1991, 1993) went one step further and tried to discern whether there was indeed a long-run relationship between public capital and productivity using cointegration tests designed to identify such relationships between non-stationary variables. He found no evidence that such a long-run relationship existed. He also used Granger causality tests to discern whether changes in the public capital stock preceded changes in productivity, with the results pointing to reverse causation.

A third objection was raised by Holtz-Eakin (1994), who revisited the Aschauer-Munnell results on a panel of US states. The key distinction between Holtz-Eakin (1994) and previous studies is that the latter controlled for state-specific effects. Holtz-Eakin (1994) showed that Hausmann specification tests reject the hypothesis that the state-effects are uncorrelated with the regressors, making OLS or random-effects estimates of the productivity-infrastructure link biased and inconsistent. Once one controls for state-specific effects, Holtz-Eakin showed, the productivity-infrastructure link disappears and in some specifications actually turns insignificantly negative.

By the mid-nineties, the pendulum had swung back and the critics of the infrastructure-productivity link appeared to have gained the upper hand. In a review article in the *National Tax Journal*, Hulten and Schwab (1993: 271) argued that

> the link between infrastructure and economic performance is, at the margin, *very weak*. Much of the research that followed David Aschauer's work provides little support for the hypothesis that the slowdown in infrastructure spending caused the economy to perform poorly over the last 20 years (emphasis in original).

But did these criticisms really demonstrate that infrastructure had no effect on private sector productivity? Let us look at them in turn. First, there is the argument that a high return to infrastructure should lead to substantial political pressures for public investment which we do not observe. This argument relies on the belief that high social returns produce political actions from private agents calling for their realization. Such a simplistic argument is at odds with most of the political economy literature on the provision of public goods. The same reasons that make public infrastructure a pure public good – its non-rivalrous and non-excludable nature – also make it extremely difficult for potential beneficiaries to organize in order to pressure for its provision. This point was originally made by Olson (1971) and has recently been revisited – in the context of the US electoral system – by Lizzeri and Persico (2001). The basic idea is that there is a distinction between socially preferred outcomes and the outcomes that one will see agents defending in the midst of the political process. Because of the implicit free-rider problems in public goods provision, agents will tend to misrepresent their desire for public goods, in the hope that the cost of their provision will be borne by others. Inferring that private agents do not want infrastructure because they don't pressure for it is rather like deducing that the suspects that confessed their guilt in the Prisoner's Dilemma game had no interest in being set free.

In contrast, the objection that Aschauer's results are due to spurious correlations is certainly correct: it is by now broadly recognized that one has little to learn from time-series regressions between non-stationary variables. At best, the Aschauer findings can be characterized as one data point: the coincidence of an increase in infrastructure spending and increasing productivity in the US time series, but not much more. The problem with this objection is that it is very hard to infer *anything* (either the existence of a relationship or its absence) from this type of data. Suppose for example that there is a link between infrastructure and productivity, but that it has an uncertain and variable timing. It could take time for firms to learn how to take advantage of infrastructure improvements, and such timing may depend on the precise type of project and sectors that it affects. Estimating this complex relationship would require a correct specification of the underlying project and sector-specific relationships, which may be much more than can be achieved with aggregate time-series data. In this case, a prolonged period of infrastructure improvements should be followed by a trend of growing productivity, and a collapse of infrastructure spending, if maintained over time, would lead to a decline in productivity. A simple time-series regression such as Aschauer's would capture this. But one should not be surprised if a first-differenced regression such as that run by Hulten and Schwab (1991), which tests whether increases in infrastructure provision lead to increases in productivity *in the same year*, yields insignificant estimates.

In principle, the hypothesis of a long-run relationship between infrastructure and productivity could be appropriately dealt with by searching for a cointegration relationship as done by Tatom (1991), who used the Stock-Watson (1988) procedure and failed to find a significant effect of public investment in infrastructure on productivity. Does this imply that there is no long-run relationship between infrastructure and productivity? Not necessarily. One of the characteristics of conventional unit root and cointegration tests is that they tend to have very low power to reject alternative hypotheses under small samples (Christiano and Eichenbaum, 1990; Rudebusch, 1993). In other words, these tests will yield few mistakes when there is a unit root (or when there is no cointegration) but can be mistaken with considerable frequency when there is no unit root (or when there *is* a cointegrating relationship). Since the traditional methods require first evaluating whether the variables in question have unit roots or not and then testing for a cointegrating relationship, they are prone to making two types of mistakes: finding that the variables in question are non-stationary when they are not (and thus leading to conclude that correlations among them are spurious) and finding that there is no cointegrating relationship between the variables when one exists.

These low power properties of tests for non-stationarity tend to emerge in short samples. As sample length is increased, one often finds evidence for stationarity where the tests had previously tended to point towards non-stationarity (Perron and Shiller, 1984; Hakkio and Rush, 1991). Given that Tatom used a 32-year period for his tests, it may be the case that the time period was simply too short to uncover existing relationships. Indeed, Kocherlakota and Yi (1996) use a longer data set going back to 1925 and do find a robust significant effect of public investment in structures on economic growth.

The third objection, based on the finding that existing correlations disappear when one controls for state-level fixed effects, is actually not rare in panel data studies of economic performance. Cross-national studies of economic performance often find that the introduction of fixed effects specifications tends to produce very weak statistical results (Caselli, Esquivel and Lefort, 1999). The reason is that most of the variation in these data sets tends to come from the cross-sectional dimension. Therefore, it can well be the case that one gets insignificant parameter estimates not because the relationship does not exist, but because eliminating all the cross-sectional information leaves us with very little variation.

The use of state-specific effects in panel data studies reflects a preoccupation with omitted variables that might be correlated with the right-hand side variables. It is important to understand that if one wants to understand the *total* (as opposed to the partial) effect of infrastructure spending on economic growth, omitted variable bias is only a problem if one is worried that infrastructure spending is endogenous. To see why, suppose that we were sure that infrastructure spending is exogenous and we believed that increases in the provision of infrastructure led to higher degrees of innovation (perhaps by facilitating communication of ideas). If we were to control for innovation activity and were to find that the effect of infrastructure on productivity growth disappeared, that would only reinforce the evidence that there is a significant effect of infrastructure on productivity growth, and that it runs through the innovation channel. It is only if we believe that infrastructure could be caused by innovation activity, or if we thought that both of them were caused by a third variable, that we would be worried about the bias arising from omitting innovation.[1]

Therefore, it appears that concentrating directly on the issue of causality may have high payoffs if one wants to disentangle the possible channels operating in the infrastructure-productivity relationship. Fernald (1999) constitutes one of the most careful attempts to carefully estimate reverse causation effects in the study of the US growth-infrastructure link. Fernald starts out from a simple observation: if infrastructure were a significant force behind productivity growth, then we would expect the link between productivity growth and public capital to be greater for industries that use roads intensively. If the building of infrastructure were simply a reaction to income growth or if both were caused by a third factor, in contrast, the effect of road growth on productivity would be uncorrelated with road-intensity. Indeed, Fernald finds that when growth in the stock of roads increases, productivity increases disproportionately in industries that are intensive in the use of vehicles. Fernald's estimates indicate that the growth of infrastructure provision in the United States from 1953 to 1973 had an average rate of return of 104 per cent, quite in line with Aschauer's original estimate. However, Fernald also finds that the rate of return decreased dramatically and became insignificant after 1973.

The most logical interpretation of Fernald's results appears to be related to the construction of the interstate highway network in the fifties and sixties. This network was largely completed by 1973, after which the productivity effect of further road building was likely to be negligible. An important implication of this interpretation is that governments in less developed economies in which a network of national roads is lacking may have substantial gains from undertaking such a project. The fact that the US now has very low returns from infrastructure investment at the margin may be a reflection of the fact that it has invested a lot in the past, with substantial realized payoffs. From the standpoint of a poor country that does not have a national highway system, the relevant elasticity estimates would be the pre-1973 estimates, and the lack of such a system may be an important reason for its inability to converge to the level of income of rich countries.

Another paper worth mentioning is Shioji (2001). This paper estimates conditional convergence growth regressions á la Barro and Sala-i-Martin (1991) on a panel of US regions. The key distinction between his approach and Holtz-Eakin (1994) is that Shioji uses growth as the dependent variable and initial per capita income and the public capital stock as right-hand side variables. The convergence approach, however, allows for estimation of the effect of a public capital stocks on the steady-state level of income, thus taking into account not only its effect on productivity, but also its induced effect on GDP via higher private capital accumulation. What is interesting is that *despite controlling for regional fixed effects*, Shioji obtains significant effects of infrastructure spending on productivity growth, shedding doubt on the robustness of Hotz-Eakin's (1994) result to changes in specification.

As this literature evolved towards a more nuanced understanding of the relationship between infrastructure and productivity growth, the very facts that Aschauer had set out to attempt to explain changed. From 1995 to 2000, output per hour in non-farm business grew at an average annual rate of about 2½ per cent compared with increases of only about 1½ per cent per year from 1973 to 1995. Oliner and Sichel (2003) find that advances in information technology as well as the greater use of IT capital more than account for this increase in productivity. The coincidence of these increments in productivity with the massive investment in the development of the internet, which had its origin as a government project in the US Department of Defence underscores the potentially high payoffs to public infrastructure projects (Blinder, 2000). While it may be true that it would make little sense to build another interstate highway system, that does not mean that the public sector has run out of socially productive infrastructure projects. In the words of Berkeley Lab's Tsu Loken (cited in Kahn, 1993), "The federal government has a long history of investment in the nation's infrastructure. It built canals in the 18th century, railroads in the 19th century, and interstate highways in the 20th century. Then, about 10 years ago, it began the construction of high-speed computer networks. These networks are the highways of the Information Age."

Cross-National Evidence

In contrast to the US literature, cross-national studies of infrastructure and growth often tend to find positive rates of return to infrastructure investment whatever the methodology used. Debate in this literature has centred on other issues such as the magnitude of the return and the wisdom of investing in infrastructure vis-à-vis other choices that may be faced by the government. The first and most common reference in this literature is Easterly and Rebelo's (1993) cross-national analysis of the relationship between economic growth and fiscal policy for the 1970–1988 period. Easterly and Rebelo found a positive correlation between public transport and communication investment and growth. The coefficient was very high and remained positive and significant in instrumental variables estimation, with an estimated elasticity of 0.16. The authors were somewhat puzzled by this high coefficient but mentioned that World Bank studies often found similarly high rates of return for transport and communications projects.

A contrasting view was proposed by Devarajan, Swaroop and Zou (1996). These authors start out from the observation that the finding of a positive coefficient for infrastructure in a production function or growth regression does not by itself imply that raising infrastructure investment is an optimal policy. As long as infrastructure is imperfectly substitutable for other public goods, it may be the case that the government is already over-investing in infrastructure. The authors address this point by looking at the effect of changing the composition of spending from infrastructure to current expenditures. Somewhat surprisingly, they find that this generally has a positive effect on growth, implying that infrastructure may be overprovided.

Both the Easterly and Rebelo (1993) and the Devarajan, Swaroop and Zou (1996) findings related the growth rate to public investment rates. More recent work has concentrated on the relationship between growth and stocks of infrastructure. Sanchez-Robles (1998) found a significant effect on growth of a principal-components index of infrastructure stocks. Easterly (2001) finds a similar effect for telephone lines. Demetriades and Mamuneas (2000) specialize in the analysis of OECD economies. Instead of estimating a reduced form growth equation they estimate a multi-equation model including a profit function, factor demand functions and accelerator equations. The estimated short-run rates of return range from 11 per cent in the United States to 27 per cent in Italy, whereas the long-run rates are much higher, ranging from 29 per cent in the United States to 38 per cent in Italy. Röller and Waverman (2001) take a similar approach but concentrate on the effect of telecommunications infrastructure in OECD countries. They also find significant effects, particularly after a basic threshold of infrastructure provision is achieved.

Although most estimates of production functions or growth regressions at the cross-national level deliver positive effects of public infrastructure provision, the relevant policy question may not be whether infrastructure enters positively into the production function, but rather whether the return from increasing it outweighs its cost of provision. For example, Canning (1999) estimated the return to electricity generation and transportation routes to be no different from the private returns (although he did find that telephones per worker had a substantially higher return). He argues that this result raises doubts about the wisdom of financing infrastructure provision with distortionary taxation.

The evidence here appears to be somewhat mixed. Esfahani and Ramírez (2003) estimate a multi-equation model of growth and infrastructure investments with separate equations for GDP growth and infrastructure capital accumulation. They find significant effects of infrastructure services to GDP growth which, in general, exceed the cost of provision of those services. The elasticity estimates are particularly robust and stable and imply elasticities between 0.08–0.10 for telephones and 0.13–0.16 for electricity generation. Calderón and Servén (2005) use a data set measuring infrastructure stocks and the quality of infrastructure services to evaluate the effect of infrastructure provision on growth. They find statistically and economically significant effects of infrastructure provision on economic growth.

On the other hand, Canning (1999) and Canning and Pedroni (2004) have argued that there is evidence of overprovision of infrastructure in many developing countries. In both cases, cointegration methods are used to distinguish the effect of infrastructure on growth from the reverse causation effect. For example, Canning and Pedroni use an error-correction model to estimate the bidirectional causation effects, which is tantamount to identifying temporal precedence with causality – in the style of Granger causality tests. They find no effect of infrastructure on long-term growth on average, although they do find that this is not true for all countries and that in some there is evidence of overprovision while in others there is evidence of under-provision.

Thus the evidence on infrastructure stocks parallels the earlier work on investment flows. On the one hand, there are a number of reduced form estimates that imply a positive effect of infrastructure provision on growth. On the other hand, a set of studies argue that infrastructure may be overprovided. Is there a way to make sense of these conflicting results?

The key source of differences in these results is that while the bulk of researchers have attempted to estimate the direct effect of increasing infrastructure provision, holding everything else fixed, on economic growth, Devarajan, Swaroop and Zou (1996), Canning (1999) and Canning and Pedroni (2004) actually carry out a different exercise: to calculate the effect of reducing other types of expenditure to increase infrastructure investments. In the case of Devarajan, Swaroop and Zou (1996), the experiment is to reduce other types of public expenditures which include education and health spending. This is obviously a much higher hurdle than that of simply evaluating whether public infrastructure spending is productive. The Canning (1999) and Canning and Pedroni (2004) exercises are different: they imply studying the effect of an increase in public capital *holding total investment constant*. In other words, they assume that any increase in the public capital stock is accompanied by an identical decline in the private capital stock. In Canning and Pedroni (2004), for example, this feature is built into the model by assuming a constant national savings rate, an element which is not a characteristic of the Barro (1990) model.

This gets back to the issue of crowding-out. Canning (1999) and Canning and Pedroni (2004) basically build crowding-out into their models. It is hard to see why this would be a sensible modelling assumption, particularly when evidence for such an effect is hard to find. If public and private capital are complements, an increase in infrastructure will raise the rate of return on private capital and thus induce an increase in the stock of private capital. This effect could be substantial, particularly in an open economy. But even in a closed economy, if one were to use the simple assumption that the private (as opposed to the *national*) savings rate is constant, a tax-financed increase in public investment would lead to a reduction in private investment equal to the marginal propensity to save times the increase in public investment.

Although all of these studies attempt to deal with endogeneity, none of the solutions that they adopt are immune to criticism. Esfahani and Ramírez (2003) and Calderón and Servén (2005) address the issue through the use of IV and systems estimators, but many of their exclusion restrictions appear quite arbitrary from a theoretical point of view. Canning and Pedroni's (2004) method for identification, while apparently novel, relies on associating temporal variations with causality, even though the long gestation lags associated with many infrastructure projects would appear to imply that these are likely to have significant effects on expectations even before they are constructed.

Truly exogenous and excludable instruments are difficult to find in cross-country work in general, and it is hard to think of an exogenous source of cross-country variations in infrastructure stocks. Furthermore, even with appropriate instruments, the pervasive non-linearities which appear to be present in the cross-national data can wreak havoc with instrumental variables estimates. Finding successful answers to the endogeneity problem in these estimations may require shifting to careful analysis of the within-country evidence. In a recent paper, José Pineda and I (Pineda and Rodríguez, 2005) have attempted to address the endogeneity issue through the use of firm-level data from the Venezuelan *Encuesta Industrial*. We take advantage of the 1994 creation of the Intergovernmental Decentralization Fund which allocated a portion of VAT revenues for infrastructure investment to state and local governments based on their initial development levels, total populations and land area. As this rule was held fixed over time, it generated variations in transfers to regions that depended on the interaction between the parameters of the rule and national VAT collection, both of which can be taken to be exogenous at the state level. This exogenous source of variation allowed us to estimate the effect of state infrastructure investments on firm-level productivity growth in Venezuelan manufacturing. Our elasticity estimates of 0.33–0.35 are substantial. Curiously, they are remarkably similar to Fernald's estimate of .38 for the manufacturing industry in the US data.

Discussion

Empirical work on US and cross-country data is subject to multiple interpretations. Many well-known studies have obtained positive and significant effects of infrastructure on productivity. On the other hand, most of those studies have been the subject of extensive criticism, a great deal of which has been technically right. In my view, however, there are too many pieces of evidence that point towards significant effects that it is difficult to ignore them. While it is true that one time series correlation is not much evidence of anything, the fact that the positive relationship emerges in many cross-sections, both within the US and at the cross-country level, could only be discounted with a very convincing endogeneity argument. I have yet to see that argument, and the attempts that have been made to take the case for endogeneity seriously, such as Fernald (1999) or my recent work with José Pineda (2005), have not found substantial evidence that reverse causation is driving the relationship. Ultimately, however, the reading of the evidence must also rely on our basic understanding of the world and a fair bit of common sense. If it were true that public infrastructure were unproductive, one should be able to imagine a world with substantially lower levels of public infrastructure (e.g., the US without an interstate highway system) and argue that private capital would yield the same returns under those conditions than it does now. Personally, I find that kind of world very hard to imagine.

Per Capita Divergence and Infrastructure Stocks

Did the post-1980s' collapse in infrastructure investment generate an increase in divergence of per capita income across countries? The discussion of the previous section has made clear that there are theoretical reasons to believe that the two events are connected. I now turn to examining whether the cross-national evidence lends support to this hypothesis. I approach this question by calculating the extent of per capita income dispersion that could have been caused by changes in the distribution of infrastructure stocks across countries. Obviously, these calculations will depend on the magnitude of the elasticity of production with respect to infrastructure. The purpose of this section is to explore whether the range of estimates presented in the literature, which go from this lower bound of zero to values around 0.3, would help in attributing an important role to infrastructure stocks in divergence of per capita incomes.

Figure 10.2 shows a first stumbling block for this line of argument. Despite the prevalence of fiscal adjustments that emphasized retrenchments in government investment in middle and low-income economies, the dispersion of per-worker infrastructure stocks across

FIGURE 10.2
Dispersion in Infrastructure Stocks

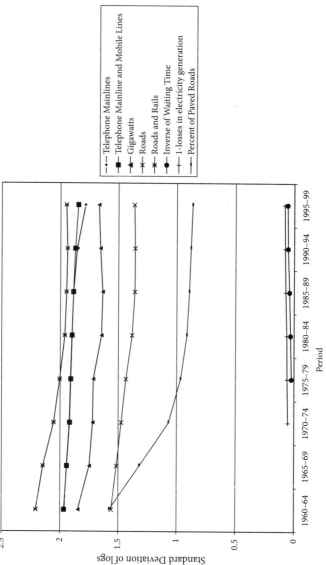
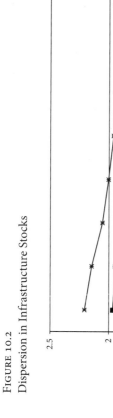

the world has not increased since the sixties. On the contrary, as we show in Figure 10.2, for most indicators of infrastructure stocks, inter-country dispersion has been declining substantially. It would thus appear on first sight that growing inequalities in infrastructure provision cannot be a cause behind growing inequalities in world incomes because the distribution of infrastructure provision has actually been growing *less* unequal.

Figure 10.3 gives an illustration of why this is the case. It plots the length of roads per square kilometre in six developing countries that experienced substantial decelerations in their growth of road infrastructure, together with the United States. As one can observe from the graph, while the group of developing countries saw its stock of infrastructure stagnate after the mid-eighties, so did the United States, so that the dispersion between these economies did not increase. Recall that the decline in infrastructure investment in the US was precisely what spurred Aschauer's original research on the productivity slowdown. This declining rate of infrastructure growth in developed countries is a more general feature: while the average annual growth rate of the stock of roads was 1.18 per cent between 1960 and 1980, it fell to 0.87 per cent between 1980 and 1995.

Is this fact the nail in the coffin of an infrastructure-based explanation of increasing divergence? Not quite. A lower dispersion of infrastructure stocks does not necessarily lead to a lower dispersion of per capita incomes. The reason is that if the dispersion is reduced by increases in the provision of infrastructure in high-income countries that happened to start out with low infrastructure provision, then it could lead to higher inequalities in the world distribution of per capita incomes. In order to make this argument clear, it is useful to look at it more formally.

Let us start out from a Cobb-Douglas production function expanded to include the external effects generated by infrastructure:

$$Y = AG^\beta K^\alpha L^{1-\gamma} \qquad (2)$$

where Y is GDP, G denotes the stock of public infrastructure capital, K the private capital stock, and L the labour force. Let us use as our measure of dispersion the standard deviation of logarithms:

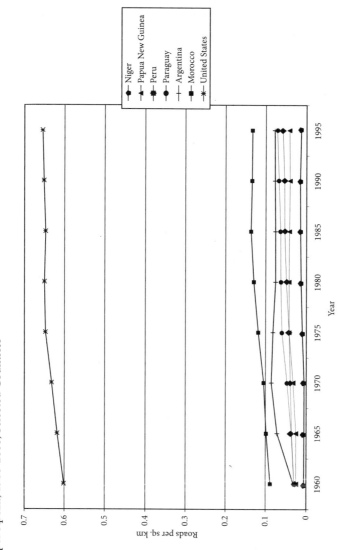

FIGURE 10.3
Roads per sq. km, 1960-2000, Selected Countries

$$s_y = \frac{\sum_i (y - \bar{y})^2}{N} \tag{3}$$

where we have let lower cases denote natural logarithms. Substituting (2) into (3) and deriving with respect to time gives us an expression for the evolution over time of s_y:

$$\frac{ds_y}{dt} = \beta^2 \frac{s_g}{s_y} \frac{ds_g}{dt} + \beta\alpha \frac{1}{2s_y} \frac{d\,\mathrm{cov}(g,k)}{dt} + \beta\gamma \frac{1}{2s_y} \frac{d\,\mathrm{cov}(g,l)}{dt} +$$

$$\alpha^2 \frac{s_k}{s_y} \frac{ds_k}{dt} + \gamma^2 \frac{s_l}{s_y} \frac{ds_l}{dt} + \alpha\gamma \frac{1}{2s_y} \frac{d\,\mathrm{cov}(k,l)}{dt} \tag{4}$$

where $cov(i,j)$ denotes the square root of the empirical covariance between i and j. Dispersion of incomes across countries will be influenced by changes in infrastructure provision through two effects: a direct effect – captured by the first term on the right-hand side of equation (4) - that works through changes in the dispersion of infrastructure stocks, and an indirect effect – captured in the second and third terms - that depends on changes in the empirical covariances between infrastructure and other capital stocks.[2]

Note that an increase in the correlation between infrastructure and other factors of production will lead, *ceteris paribus*, to an increase in dispersions of pre capita incomes. To understand the intuition for this, imagine that there were high levels of inequality in infrastructure stocks but that countries with lower physical capital stocks tended to have greater levels of infrastructure. This would mean that countries that would tend to be poorer than average due to their capital stocks would be less poor because of their high levels of infrastructure. In the same way, declines in the correlation between capital stocks and infrastructure stocks imply that one is more likely to find cases of capital-poor countries with high infrastructure stocks, and thus to observe decreasing dispersion.

Are these offsetting forces enough to counteract the direct effect of falling dispersion? Columns 2 and 3 of Table 10.1 show our estimates of the indirect effect terms $(\beta\alpha \frac{1}{2s_y} \frac{d\,\mathrm{cov}(g,k)}{dt}$ and $\beta\gamma \frac{1}{2s_y} \frac{d\,\mathrm{cov}(g,l)}{dt})$ for the 1965–94 period. These are almost uniformly positive and often quantitatively greater than the direct effect of infrastructure dispersion. Table 10.1 also shows our overall calculation of the estimated effect of changes in the distribution of infrastructure from the first three terms on the right-hand side of equation (4). We set α = γ = 1/3, as is standard practice, though reported results tend to be robust to different values of the capital and labour share. Given our review of existing empirical estimates of β, we expect it to be between 0 and 0.3, so that we use 0.10, 0.20 and 0.30 for our simulation (β=0 simply leads to zero effect as infrastructure becomes irrelevant for production). We consider six indicators of infrastructure stocks: telephone mainlines per 1000 workers, telephone mainlines and mobile lines per 1000 workers, Gigawatts per 1000 workers, kilometres of roads per square kilometre, kilometres of roads and railroads per square kilometre, and the percentage of paved roads. The data are taken from Calderón and Servén (2005).[4] Capital stock estimates are from Crego and others (2003) and labour force, population and per capita PPP GDP are taken from World Bank (2005).

As shown in Table 10.1, the direct effect is always negative. This simply reflects the fact that, as shown in Figure 10.2, the dispersion of infrastructure stocks has been decreasing over time. The contribution of this direct effect ranges from between –0.16 per cent and –0.41 per cent for $\beta\beta$=0.1 to between –1.12 per cent and –3.73 per cent for β=0.3. However, this is offset by the indirect effects $\beta\alpha \frac{1}{2s_y} \frac{d\operatorname{cov}(g,k)}{dt}$ and $\beta\gamma \frac{1}{2s_y} \frac{d\operatorname{cov}(g,l)}{dt}$, which are increasing in all but one case. For five of the six indicators, the total result is to predict an increase in dispersion between 1964 and 1994 when $\beta\beta$=0.10 or 0.20. The picture is a bit more mixed as $\beta\beta$=0.30 because the magnitude of the direct effect becomes much larger, so that in that case three of the six indicators actually predict a *decrease* in dispersion of per capita GDP levels arising from changes in the distribution of infrastructure stocks.[4]

Even though many of the estimates point towards a positive contribution of changes in infrastructure stocks towards growing world dispersion of per capita incomes, all of the estimated effects are quantitatively small, usually not exceeding one percentage point in the standard deviation of log incomes, with the highest estimate being only 2.38 percentage points, or approximately one-tenth of changes in the world dispersion of incomes.

TABLE 10.1

Estimated Effects of Dispersion in Infrastructure Stocks on World Dispersion of per capita incomes, 1965–94

Calibrated Change	Divergence in Infrastructure	Corelation with Capital Stocks	Correlation with Labor Force Participation	Total Effect	Increase in World Dispersion	Percentage Attributable to Infrastructure
Beta=0.10						
Telephone Mainlines	-0.16%	0.68%	0.43%	0.95%	21.59%	4.39%
Telephone Mainlines + Mobile Lines	-0.12%	0.73%	0.44%	1.04%	21.59%	4.84%
Gigawatts	-0.15%	0.38%	0.23%	0.46%	21.59%	2.15%
Roads	-0.21%	-0.01%	0.13%	-0.09%	21.59%	-0.41%
Roads and Rails	-0.39%	0.59%	0.26%	0.46%	21.59%	2.12%
Paved Roads	-0.41%	0.83%	0.29%	0.71%	21.59%	3.30%
Beta=0.20						
Telephone Mainlines	-0.62%	1.35%	0.85%	1.58%	21.59%	7.33%
Telephone Mainlines + Mobile Lines	-0.50%	1.47%	0.87%	1.84%	21.59%	8.51%
Gigawatts	-0.59%	0.77%	0.45%	0.63%	21.59%	2.94%
Roads	-0.84%	-0.02%	0.26%	-0.60%	21.59%	-2.77%
Roads and Rails	-1.55%	1.17%	0.52%	0.14%	21.59%	0.64%
Paved Roads	-1.66%	1.66%	0.59%	0.60%	21.59%	2.76%
Beta=0.30						
Telephone Mainlines	-1.40%	2.03%	1.28%	1.91%	21.59%	8.83%
Telephone Mainlines + Mobile Lines	-1.12%	2.20%	1.31%	2.38%	21.59%	11.03%
Gigawatts	-1.32%	1.15%	0.68%	0.51%	21.59%	2.36%
Roads	-1.90%	-0.03%	0.39%	-1.53%	21.59%	-7.09%
Roads and Rails	-3.49%	1.76%	0.78%	-0.96%	21.59%	-4.43%
Paved Roads	-3.73%	2.50%	0.88%	-0.35%	21.59%	-1.61%

Conclusions

This chapter has reviewed the empirical evidence supporting the assertion that the collapses in infrastructure investment that occurred during the eighties and nineties in many developing countries are a major force behind growing disparities in world incomes. While we have argued that the empirical evidence supports the existence of a positive effect of infrastructure provision on productivity and growth, we find little evidence that the retrenchments in infrastructure provision have played a major role in growing disparities. The basic reason is that most developed countries also experienced a deceleration in their accumulation of infrastructure stocks during this period, allowing some developing countries to catch up and others not to fall behind in terms of infrastructure provision. Our calculations indicate that at best infrastructure has been a minor contributor to the growing divergence in living standards across the world.

These results should not be taken to imply that developing countries ought to view investment in infrastructure as unimportant in a strategy for catching up with richer economies. We have argued that a balanced reading of the empirical evidence leads to the conclusion that infrastructure provision does have a significant effect on living standards and productivity. Even if decelerations in the rate of accumulation of infrastructure stocks have not been the culprit of growing dispersions, policies centred on infrastructure provision could play a major role in reversing this tendency.

Notes

* This chapter is based on a background paper prepared for the 2006 *World Economic and Social Survey* of the United Nations Department of Economic and Social Affairs. The author is grateful for that institution's financial support and to Rob Vos, Jomo K. S., Codrina Rada and Pingfan Hong for useful comments and suggestions. All errors are my own responsibility.
1 In marginally more technical language, omitted variable bias emerges only if there is a correlation between the omitted variable and the included variable. But if the included variable is truly exogenous, this correlation can only reflect a causal effect of it on the omitted variable, and thus form part of the total (as opposed to the partial) effect of it on the dependent variable.

282 • Growth Divergences

² The remaining terms reflect the effects of the distribution of physical capital and labour.
³ We do not use waiting time nor generation and distribution losses because they are not available for all of our period.
⁴ The preceding argument has assumed that changes in the dispersion of the public capital stock have no effect on the dispersion of private capital stocks. However, as we have argued before, it is likely that changes in g induce changes in k so that we may be excluding an important source of variation in our calculations. How relevant this effect is will depend on the relative importance of changes in g in determining variations in k. If g is the only source of variations in k (as would occur in a model with a constant private savings rate in which government spending is financed by a tax on consumption), allowing for induced accumulation actually lowers the predicted increase in dispersion, thus only heightening the puzzle.

References

Aaron, H.J. (1990). Why is infrastructure important? In A. H. Munnell (ed.). *Is There a Shortfall in Public Capital Investment?* Federal Reserve Bank of Boston, Boston: 51–63.

Arrow, K. J., and Mordecai Kurz (1970). *Public Investment, the Rate of Return and Optimal Fiscal Policy.* Johns Hopkins University Press, Baltimore.

Aschauer, D.A. (1989a). Does public capital crowd out private capital? *Journal of Monetary Economics* 24 (2): 171–188.

Aschauer, D.A. (1989b). Is public expenditure productive? *Journal of Monetary Economics* 23: 177–200.

Aschauer, D.A. (1989c). Public investment and productivity growth in the Group of Seven. *Economic Perspectives* 13 (5): 17–25.

Aschauer, D.A. (1990). *Public Investment and Private Sector Growth.* Economic Policy Institute, Washington, DC.

Barro, R.J. (1990). Government spending in a simple model of endogenous growth. *Journal of Political Economy* 98: 103–125.

Barro, Robert J., and Xavier Sala-i-Martin (1991). *Economic Growth.* MIT Press, Cambridge, MA.

Blinder, A.S. (2000). The Internet and the new economy. Policy Brief 60, Brookings Institution, Washington, DC.

Calderón, C. A., and Luis Servén (2005). *The Effects of Infrastructure Development on Growth and Income Distribution.* World Bank, Washington, DC.

Canning, David (1999). The contribution of infrastructure to aggregate output. Policy Research working paper, World Bank, Washington, DC.

Canning, David, and P. Pedroni (2004). The effect of infrastructure on long-run economic growth. Processed, Harvard University, Cambridge, MA.

Caselli, Francesco, Gerardo Esquivel, and Fernando Lefort (1999). Reopening the convergence debate: A new look at cross-country growth empirics. *Journal of Economic Growth* 1 (3): 363–389.

Christiano, L.J., and M.S. Eichenbaum (1990). Unit roots in real GNP – Do we know and do we care? *Carnegie Rochester Conference Series on Public Policy* 32: 7–61.

Crego, Al, Donald Larson, Rita Butzer, and Yair Mundlak (2003). A cross-country database for sector investment and capital. Electronic file, World Bank, Washington, DC.

Demetriades, Panicos, and T.P. Mamuneas (2000). Intertemporal output and employment effects of public infrastructure capital: Evidence from 12 OECD economies. *The Economic Journal* 110: 687–712.

Devarajan, Shantayanan, Vinaya Swaroop, and Zou Heng-fu (1996). The composition of public expenditure and economic growth. *Journal of Monetary Economics* 37: 313–344.

Easterly, William (2001). The lost decades: Explaining developing countries' stagnation in spite of policy reform, 1980–1998. *Journal of Economic Growth* 6 (2), June: 135–157.

Easterly, William, and Sergio Rebelo (1993). Fiscal policy and economic growth: An empirical investigation. *Journal of Monetary Economics* 32, December: 417–458.

Easterly, William, and Luis Servén (2003). *The Limits of Stabilization: Infrastructure, Public Deficits and Growth in Latin America.* World Bank, Washington, DC.

Esfahani, H.S., and M.T. Ramírez (2003). Institutions, infrastructure and economic growth. *Journal of Development Economics* 70: 443–477.

Fernald, J.G. (1999). Roads to prosperity? Assessing the link between public capital and productivity. *American Economic Review* 89 (3): 619–638.

Gramlich, E.M. (1994). Infrastructure investment: A review essay. *Journal of Economic Literature* 32 (September): 1176–1196.

Granger, C.W.J., and P. Newbold (1974). Spurious regressions in econometrics. *Journal of Econometrics* 2: 111–120.

Hakkio, C.S., and Mark Rush (1991). Cointegration: How short is the long run? *Journal of International Money and Finance* 10: 571–581.

Holtz-Eakin, Douglas (1994). Public sector capital and the productivity puzzle. *Review of Economics and Statistics* 76: 12–21.

Hulten, Charles R., and Robert M. Schwab (1991). *Is There Too Little Public Capital? Infrastructure and Economic Growth.* American Enterprise Institute for Public Policy Research, Washington, DC.

Hulten, Charles R., and Robert M. Schwab (1993). Infrastructure spending: Where do we go from here? *National Tax Journal* 46 (3): 261–273.

Jorgenson, Dale W. (1991). *Fragile Statistical Foundations: The Macroeconomics of Public Infrastructure Investment.* American Enterprise Institute for Public Policy Research, Washington, DC.

Kahn, Jeffery (1993). Building and rescuing the Information Superhighway. *LBL Research Review.* http://www.lbl.gov/Science-Articles/Archive/information-superhighway.html, accessed 20 November 2005.

Kocherlakota, Narayana, and Yi Kei-mu (1996). A simple time series test of endogenous vs. exogenous growth models: An application to the United States. *Review of Economics and Statistics* 78 (1): 126–134.

Lizzeri, Alessandro, and Nicola Persico (2001). The provision of public goods under alternative electoral incentives. *American Economic Review* 91 (1): 225–239.

Munnell, A.H. (1990a). Why has productivity growth declined? Productivity and public investment. *New England Economic Review* (Jan/Feb): 3–22.

Munnell, A.H. (1990b). How does public infrastructure affect regional economic performance? *New England Economic Review*, Sept./Oct, pp. 11–32.

Ogura, Seititsu, and Gary Yohe (1977). The complementarity of public and private capital and the optimal rate of return. *Quarterly Journal of Economics* 91 (4): 651–662.

Oliner, Stephen D., and Daniel E. Sichel (2003). Information technology and productivity: Where are we now and where are we going? *Journal of Policy Modeling* 25 (5), July: 477–503.

Olson, Mancur (1971). *The Logic of Collective Action*. Harvard University Press, Cambridge, MA.

Perron, Pierre, and Robert J. Shiller (1984). Testing the Random Walk hypothesis: Power vs. frequency of observation. Discussion paper no. CFDP732. Cowles Foundation for Research in Economics, Yale University, New Haven, CT.

Pineda, José, and Francisco Rodríguez (2005). Public investment in infrastructure and productivity growth: Evidence from the Venezuelan manufacturing sector. Processed, Wesleyan University, Middletown, CT.

Röller, Lars-Hendrik, and Leonard Waverman (2001). Telecommunications infrastructure and economic development: A simultaneous approach. *American Economic Review* 91: 909–923.

Rudebusch, G.D. (1993). The uncertain unit root in real GNP. *American Economic Review* 83 (1): 264–272.

Sanchez-Robles, Blanca (1998). Infrastructure investment and growth: Some empirical evidence. *Contemporary Economic Policy* 16: 98–108.

Shioji, Etsuro (2001). Public capital and economic growth: A convergence approach. *Journal of Economic Growth* 6: 205–227.

Stock, J.H., and M.W. Watson (1988). Testing for common trends. *Journal of the American Statistical Association* 83 (404): 1097–1107.

Tatom, J.A. (1991). Should government spending on capital goods be raised? *Federal Reserve Bank of St. Louis Review* March/April: 3–15.

Tatom, J.A. (1993). Is an infrastructure crisis lowering the nation's productivity. *Federal Reserve Bank of St. Louis Review* November-December: 3–21.

World Bank (2005). *World Development Indicators*. World Bank, Washington, DC.

11

Governance, Economic Growth and Development since the 1960s

MUSHTAQ H. KHAN

Economists agree that governance is one of the critical factors explaining the divergence in performance across developing countries. The differences of view between economists regarding governance are to do first, with the types of state capacities that constitute the critical governance capacities necessary for the acceleration of development, and secondly, with the importance of governance relative to other factors at early stages of development.

On the first issue, there is an important empirical and theoretical controversy between liberal economists, who constitute the mainstream consensus on good governance, and statist and heterodox institutional economists, who agree that governance is critical for economic development, but argue that theory and evidence shows that the governance capacities required for successful development are substantially different from those identified by the good governance analysis. The economists in favour of good governance argue that the critical state capacities are those that maintain efficient markets and restrict the activities of states to the provision of necessary public goods to minimize rent seeking and government failure. The relative failure of many developing country states are explained by the attempts of their states to do too much, resulting in the unleashing of unproductive rent seeking activities and the crowding out of productive market ones. The empirical support for this argument typically comes from cross-sectional data on governance in developing countries that shows that in general, countries with better governance defined in these terms performed better.

In contrast, heterodox institutional economists base their argument on case studies of rapid growth in the last fifty years. This evidence suggests that rapid growth was associated with governance capacities quite different from those identified in the good governance model. States that did best in terms of achieving convergence with advanced countries had the capacity to achieve and sustain high rates of investment and to implement policies that encouraged the acquisition and learning of new technologies rapidly. The institutions and strategies that achieved these varied from country to country, depending on their initial conditions and political constraints, but all successful states had governance capacities that could achieve these functions. This diversity in governance capacities in successful developers means that we cannot necessarily identify simple patterns in the governance capacities of successful states, but nevertheless, we can identify broad patterns in the *functions* that successful states performed, and this can provide useful insights for reform policy in the next tier of developers. The empirical and theoretical issues involved here clearly have critical policy implications for reform efforts in developing countries.

The second area of disagreement concerns the relative importance of governance reforms in accelerating development in countries at low levels of development. An important challenge to the mainstream good governance approach to reform in Africa has come from Sachs and others (2004) who argue that at the levels of development seen in Africa and given the development constraints faced by that continent, a focus on governance reforms is misguided. They support their argument with an empirical analysis that shows that the differences in performance between African countries is not explained by differences in their quality of governance (measured according to the criteria of good governance) once differences in their levels of development have been accounted for. The important policy conclusion that they derive is that in Africa the emphasis has to be on a big push based on aid-supported investment in infrastructure and disease control. While Sachs is right to emphasize the necessity of a big push in Africa (and their arguments in favour of such a strategy should hold true for other poorly performing countries in the developing world), the downgrading of governance capacities is probably misguided even for Africa. Our review of theory and evidence will address these two major questions and debates in the contemporary literature on the role of governance in explaining differences in performance in development since 1960, with particular emphasis on the period after 1980.

MARKET-ENHANCING VERSUS GROWTH-ENHANCING GOVERNANCE

To highlight the differences between the different economic approaches to governance, we will make a distinction between what we will call 'market-enhancing' and 'growth-enhancing' governance. The good governance argument that is frequently referred to in the governance literature and in policy discussions essentially identifies the importance of governance capacities that are necessary for ensuring the efficiency of markets. The assumption is that if states can ensure efficient markets (in particular by enforcing property rights, a rule of law, reducing corruption and committing not to expropriate), private investors will drive economic development. This approach is one that implicitly stresses the priority of developing market-enhancing governance, and is currently the dominant paradigm supported by international development and financial agencies.

The importance of markets in fostering and enabling economic development is not in question. Economic development is likely to be more rapid if markets mediating resource allocation (in any country) become more efficient. The development debate has rather been about the *extent* to which markets *can* be made efficient in developing countries, and whether maximizing the efficiency of markets (and certainly maximizing their efficiency to the degree that is achievable in developing countries) is *sufficient* to maximize the pace of development. Heterodox approaches to governance have argued that markets are inherently inefficient in developing countries and even with the best political will, structural characteristics of the economy ensure that market efficiency will remain low till a substantial degree of development is achieved. Given the structural limitations of markets in developing countries, successful development requires critical governance capacities of states to accelerate accumulation (in both the private and public sectors) and ensure productivity growth (again in both sectors). In support of these arguments, they point to the evidence of the successful East Asian developers of the last five decades, where state governance capacities typically amounted to a lot more than the capacities necessary for ensuring conditions for efficient markets. In fact, in terms of the market-enhancing conditions prioritized by the good governance approach, East Asian states often performed rather poorly. Instead, they had effective institutions that could accelerate growth in conditions of technological backwardness and high transaction costs. This approach identifies the importance of a different set of governance capabilities that can be described as growth-enhancing governance.

While a sharp distinction between these two approaches need not exist, it has been unfortunate for policy-making in poor countries that a somewhat artificial chasm emerged between these positions with the growing dominance of the liberal economic consensus of the 1980s. The new consensus was responding to the failure of many state-led industrialization policies in developing countries that had resulted in large non-performing industrial sectors in many of these countries by the 1970s. Instead of examining what was different about these cases compared to the successful developers, the new consensus argued that economic problems in these countries were mainly due to their attempt to correct market failures through state interventions. It concluded that the costs of state failure were significantly greater than the costs of market failure and so government policy should only focus on making markets more efficient (Krueger, 1990). The contribution of the New Institutional Economics that emerged at about the same time was to point out that efficient markets in turn require elaborate *governance* structures. From this emerged an analysis of the governance requirements for development based on the underlying assumption that efficient markets were the most important contribution that states could make to the development process. The goal of governance should therefore be to enhance what we describe as *market-enhancing* conditions (North, 1990; Kauffman, Kraay and Zoido-Lobatón, 1999).

In contrast to this view, an alternative body of economic theory and considerable historical evidence supports a different view of the governance capabilities required for accelerating economic development in poor countries. This theory and evidence identifies the importance of governance capabilities that can directly accelerate growth in a context of structurally weak markets and very specific 'catching-up problems' faced by developing countries. Specific governance capacities are required for assisting the allocation of assets and resources to higher productivity and higher growth sectors using both market and non-market mechanisms, and that can accelerate productivity growth by assisting the absorption and learning of new technologies. While the consensus development orthodoxy of the 1950s and 1960s recognized many of these functions as important in the context of significant market failures in developing countries, it did not adequately recognize that the successful implementation of these strategies required a complementary set of governance capabilities. This is why the failure of these strategies in many countries and their dramatic success in a small number of East Asian countries could not be satisfactorily explained at the time. These governance capabilities required for ensuring the effective implementation of growth-enhancing strategies are what we describe as *growth-enhancing governance capabilities.*

According to this view, the role of governance reform is to achieve these critical growth-enhancing governance capabilities. These governance capabilities are substantially different from those identified in the market-enhancing view. The two sets of governance capabilities are not necessarily mutually exclusive, but the distinction between them is important, particularly if an exclusive focus on market-enhancing governance diminishes the capacity of states to accelerate development. Box 11.1 summarizes the main characteristics of governance emphasized in each. The remainder of the section discusses these characteristics in greater detail. The section after that summarizes the empirical evidence.

Box 11.1 *Market-Enhancing* versus *Growth-Enhancing*
Governance
Market-enhancing governance focuses on the role of governance in reducing transaction costs to make markets more efficient. The key governance goals are:

- Achieving and Maintaining Stable Property Rights
- Maintaining a Good Rule of Law and Effective Contract Enforcement
- Minimizing Expropriation Risk
- Minimizing Rent Seeking and Corruption
- Achieving the Transparent and Accountable Provision of Public Goods in line with Democratically Expressed Preferences

Growth-enhancing governance focuses on the role of governance in enabling catching up by developing countries in a context of high-transaction cost developing country markets. In particular, it focuses on the effectiveness of institutions for accelerating the transfer of assets and resources to more productive sectors, and accelerating the absorption and learning of potentially high-productivity technologies. The key governance goals are:

- Achieving Market *and* Non-Market Transfers of Assets and Resources to More Productive Sectors
- Managing Incentives and Compulsions for achieving Rapid Technology Acquisition and Productivity Enhancement
- Maintaining Political Stability in a context of rapid social transformation

In the market-enhancing view, the governance capabilities that are critical include the state's capability to maintain stable property rights, since contested or unclear property rights raise the transaction costs of buyers and sellers and prevent potential market transactions and investments taking place. For property rights to be stable, the state in particular has to constrain itself from expropriating the fruits of private investment, so another critical governance condition in this analysis is the credibility of government in assuring investors of low expropriation risk. Efficient markets also require governance capabilities to ensure efficient and low-cost contracting and dispute resolution. This requires in turn a good legal system. The same economic theory tells us that markets require low corruption as corruption increases transaction costs as well as allowing the disruption of contracts and property rights. Corruption as a form of rent seeking can also result in the creation and maintenance of damaging rents. Finally, efficient markets require that the state will deliver public goods that the private sector cannot provide, and theory says that this requires an accountable and transparent government to convert a collective willingness to pay into efficient delivery of public goods and services. In theory, these governance capabilities should together ensure the efficiency of markets and from this stems much of the 'good governance' analysis of the role of governance in economic development. Efficient markets in turn will ensure the maximization of investments and the attraction of advanced technologies to the developing country, thereby maximizing growth and development. Thus, by enhancing the efficiency of markets, good governance drives economic development. The prediction of the theory is that differences in the quality of governance measured by these characteristics will correlate with performance in economic development. We will see that the evidence provides at best very weak support for this prediction.

There are at two related theoretical problems with this view of market-led development that are stressed in the growth-enhancing view. First, the historical evidence (some of it discussed below) shows that it is extremely difficult if not impossible to achieve these governance conditions in poor countries. In terms of economic theory, this observation is not surprising. Each of these goals, such as the reduction of corruption, the achievement of stable property rights and of an effective rule of law requires significant expenditures of public resources. Poor economies do not have the required fiscal resources and requiring them to achieve these goals *before* economic development takes off faces a serious problem of sequencing (Khan, 2005). It is not surprising that developing countries do not generally satisfy the market-enhancing governance criteria at early stages of development even in the high-growth cases. Thus, critically important resource re-allocations that are required at early stages of development are unlikely to happen through the market mechanism alone.

Not surprisingly, a significant part of the asset and resource re-allocations necessary for accelerating development in developing countries have taken place through semi-market or entirely non-market processes. These processes have been very diverse. Examples include the English Enclosures from the 16th to the 18th century; the creation of the chaebol in South Korea in the 1960s using public resources; the creation of the Chinese TVEs using public resources in the 1980s and their privatization in the 1990s; and the allocation and appropriation of public land and resources for development in Thailand. Successful developers have displayed a range of institutional and political capacities that enabled semi-market and non-market asset and property right re-allocations that were growth enhancing. In contrast, in less successful developers, the absence of necessary governance capabilities meant that non-market transfers descended more frequently into predatory expropriation that impeded development.

Secondly, even reasonably efficient markets face significant market failures in the process of organizing learning to overcome low productivity in late developers (Khan, 2000b). Growth in developing countries requires catching up through the acquisition of new technologies and learning to use these new technologies rapidly. Relying only on efficient markets to attract capital and new technologies is inadequate given that efficient markets will attract capital and technology to countries where these technologies are already profitable because the requirement skills of workers and managers already exist. Developing countries have lower technological capabilities and therefore lower labour productivity in most sectors compared to advanced countries, but as against this, they also have lower wages. If markets are efficient, capital will flow to sectors and countries where the wage advantage outweighs the productivity disadvantage. However, for many mid to high-technology sectors in developing countries, the productivity gap remains larger than the wage gap. This explains why most developing countries specialize in low technology sectors and why this specialization would not change rapidly if markets became somewhat more efficient. However, if developing countries could accelerate learning, and therefore productivity growth in mid to high-technology sectors, this would amount to an acceleration of the pace of development.

Rapid catching up therefore typically requires *some* strategy of targeted technology acquisition that allows the follower country to catch up rapidly with leader countries. However, technology-acquisition strategies have been remarkably diverse and high-growth countries have used very different variants of growth-enhancing governance that allowed the acceleration of social productivity growth. Thus, not only are markets unlikely to become very efficient in developing countries, even relatively efficient markets would not necessarily help overcome some of the critical problems constraining rapid catching up in developing countries.

To the extent that productivity growth depends on better resource allocation, improving market efficiency is clearly desirable. But sustained productivity growth depends on the creation of new technologies or (in the case of developing countries), learning to use existing technologies effectively. Markets by themselves are not sufficient to ensure that productivity growth will be rapid unless appropriate incentives and compulsions exist to induce the creation of new technologies or the learning of old ones. While technical progress is possible along the trajectory set by a market-driven strategy, the climb up the technology ladder is likely to be slower through diffusion and spontaneous learning compared to an active technology acquisition and learning strategy.

But to achieve growth faster than that possible through spontaneous learning and technology diffusion, states have to possess the appropriate *governance capabilities* both to create additional incentives (rents) for investments in advanced technologies that would not otherwise have taken place but also to ensure that non-performers in these sectors do not succeed in retaining the implicit rents. The creation and management of incentives by states in developing countries has been very diverse. In many developing countries, import-substituting industrialization attempted to leapfrog technological levels by protecting domestic private or public sector enterprises. But the absence of credible commitments to withdraw support in case of failure and of adequate institutions to assist technology acquisition and learning meant that in most cases, the results were inefficient public and private sector firms that never grew up. Successful countries used many policies that appear superficially similar, including tariff protection (in virtually every case), direct subsidies (in particular in South Korea), subsidized and prioritized infrastructure for priority sectors (in China and Malaysia), and subsidizing the licensing of advanced foreign technologies (in Taiwan). But while the mechanisms used in many less successful developers appear similar to the ones on this list, there were significant differences in the governance capacities for successfully implementing growth-enhancing strategies. In particular, they typically failed to deal with the moral hazard of inefficiency that easily emerges with such strategies (Khan, 2000b).

The sharp distinction that has emerged in policy between market-enhancing and growth-enhancing governance is to some extent also due to the fact that growth-enhancing governance has some effects that appear to contradict the requirements of market-enhancing governance. For instance, growth-enhancing governance can increase the chances of corruption and other forms of rent seeking as it creates rents for the beneficiaries of these policies. In countries where the enforcement of growth strategies is effective and productivity growth is high, the inevitable rent-seeking costs have to be set against the gains. But in countries where enforcement fails and productivity growth is low, the costs of rent seeking involved in any strategy of growth-enhancement appear to be the main problem. Indeed, in most developing countries where strategies of growth-enhancement was attempted, the results were poor, resulting in a growing consensus that such strategies had inbuilt adverse incentives that doomed them to failure. Box 11.2 summarizes the shift in consensus opinion away from a position that was very sympathetic to the growth-enhancing goals of intervention to a new consensus that stresses only market-enhancement.

Box 11.2. The Switch from Growth-Enhancement to Market-Enhancement

From roughly 1950 to 1980, the dominant view within development institutions was broadly sympathetic to a *growth-enhancement* approach to development. The consensus was that market failures were serious and state intervention was required to improve resource and asset allocation through non-market mechanisms. State intervention was also required to accelerate technology acquisition. This led to a broad degree of support for strategies of import-substituting industrialization, indicative planning and licensing the use and allocation of scarce resources like land and foreign exchange.

However, there was little attention given to the *governance capabilities* that states needed to have to implement these strategies and overcome the moral hazard problems of assisting some sectors and firms. Because of this, in most developing countries, the results of these strategies were poor. By the 1970s, a few developing countries had done spectacularly well but in most, the large protected sectors were performing poorly, many suffered from unsustainable fiscal deficits and debt, and the countries achieved low growth. A broad coalition of forces, including civil society groups and NGOs, the World Bank and IMF, international economists and even some bureaucrats and politicians within these states began to criticize these strategies and demand reform.

At this juncture, growing support for *market-enhancing* policies and the market-enhancing approach to governance emerged. The emerging consensus explained the poor performance of these countries in terms of their states trying to do what was unachievable and ignoring what was essential. The new consensus eventually accepted that the successful East Asian states did not fit this model, but it argued that their success was due to pre-existing state capacities that did not exist elsewhere (World Bank, 1993). But instead of focusing governance reforms to attain at least some of these capacities, reform focused on achieving market-enhancing governance. The problem remains that while growth-enhancing governance capacities may be difficult to achieve, market-enhancing capacities are not necessarily any easier to attain in poor countries. And even if markets became somewhat more efficient, it is not clear this would be sufficient to spur development in poor countries (see text).

As Box 11.2 suggests, the abandonment of growth-enhancing strategies by the 1980s had a lot to do with the lack of attention given to the *governance capabilities* that states needed to have to implement these strategies effectively. The problem is that these governance capabilities can vary from country to country depending on the type of growth-enhancing strategy attempted. When states intervene in markets to accelerate resource allocation in particular directions or assist technology acquisition, they create new incentives and opportunities, and the market on its own is not likely to suffice as a disciplining mechanism for the resources now allocated through non-market or part-market mechanisms. As a result, the effective implementation of growth-enhancing strategies typically also requires effective growth-enhancing governance systems of compulsion and discipline to supplement the discipline imposed by the market. But the precise nature of the governance capabilities required depends on the specific mechanisms through which the state attempts to accelerate technology acquisition and investment. The diversity of the experience of successful catching up in Asia tells us the importance of the *compatibility* of the governance capabilities that states have and growth-enhancement strategies they are attempting to implement.

The learning strategy that is most likely to be effectively implemented in a country can depend amongst other things on the internal power structure that can determine if a particular strategy is likely to be effectively enforced. If a strategy requires disciplining powerful individuals or groups who can by-pass disciplining given the internal organization of power, effective implementation is very unlikely. Reform should then focus on developing a different strategy that requires incentives and compulsion for groups who might be easier to discipline, or an improvement in the governance capabilities of the state to monitor and discipline the current beneficiaries. Doing neither and simply sticking with the existing strategy *may* deliver worse outcomes than depending on the market to allocate resources according to existing productive capabilities. This explains why abandoning growth-enhancement strategies in some developing countries can result for a time in better growth performance. The growth performance with liberalization is likely to be particularly strong (as in the Indian subcontinent), if growth-enhancing strategies had built up technological capacities that could not be profitably used given the failure of effective growth-enhancing governance, but which could be redeployed in a market regime to provide a spurt of growth.

THE EMPIRICAL EVIDENCE

The market-enhancing view of governance appears to explain the observation of *poor* performance in many developing countries attempting import-substituting industrialization in the 1960s and 1970s. Market-enhancing governance capabilities were poor in these countries, as was their long-term economic performance. However, the test that is required is to see if countries that scored higher in terms of market-enhancing governance characteristics actually did better in terms of convergence with advanced countries. When we conduct such a test we find that the evidence supporting the market-enhancing view of governance is weak. While poorly performing developing countries failed to meet the governance conditions identified in the market-enhancing view of governance, so did high-growth developing countries. This observation suggests that it is difficult for *any* developing country, regardless of its growth performance, to achieve the governance conditions required for efficient markets. This does not mean that market-enhancing conditions are irrelevant, but it does mean that we need to qualify some of the claims made for prioritizing market-enhancing governance reforms in developing countries.

Testing the relevance of the growth-enhancing view of governance is more complicated because we expect the relevant governance requirements will vary with the asset allocation and learning strategies followed by the country. Nevertheless, we suggest a typology of factors that can explain relative success and failure in a sample of countries that suggests that an alternative set of governance characteristics may have played a role in explaining differences in performance across countries. This approach can explain why there have been many *different* strategies of growth-enhancement in the successful countries of East Asia, each with different governance capabilities, and why some countries like India have apparently done better by abandoning strategies of growth-enhancement. There is some evidence of a similar experience in Latin America, with some countries achieving growth in new sectors following liberalization, sometimes using technological capabilities developed in the past.

Market-Enhancing Governance and Economic Growth

An extensive academic literature has tested the relationship between what we have described as market-enhancing governance conditions and economic performance. This literature typically finds a positive relationship between the two, supporting the hypothesis that an improvement in market-enhancing governance conditions will promote growth and accelerate convergence with advanced countries. This literature uses a number of indices of market-enhancing governance. In particular, it uses data provided by Stephen Knack and the IRIS centre at Maryland University (IRIS-3, 2000), as well as more recent data provided by Kaufmann's team and available on the World Bank's website (Kaufmann, Kraay and Mastruzzi, 2005). If market-enhancing governance were relevant for explaining economic growth, we would expect the quality of market-enhancing governance at the beginning of a period (of say ten years) to have an effect on the economic growth achieved during that period. However, the Knack-IRIS data set is only available for most countries from 1984 and the Kaufmann-World Bank data set only from 1996 onwards. We have to be careful to test the role of market-enhancing governance by using the governance index at the *beginning* of a period of economic performance to see if differences in market-enhancing governance explain the subsequent difference in performance between countries. This is important, as a correlation between governance indicators at the *end* of a period and economic performance during that period could be picking up the reverse direction of causality, where rising per capita incomes result in an improvement in market-enhancing governance conditions.

There are good theoretical reasons to expect market-enhancing governance to improve as per capita incomes increase (as more resources become available in the budget for securing property rights, running democratic systems, policing human rights and so on). This reverses the direction of causality between growth and governance. Thus, for the Knack-IRIS data, the earliest decade of growth that we can examine would be 1980–1990, and even here we have to be careful to remember that the governance data that we have is for a year almost halfway through the growth period. We do, however, have the Knack-IRIS indices for testing the significance of governance for economic growth during 1990–2003. The World Bank data on governance begins in 1996, and therefore these can at best be used for examining growth during 1990–2003, keeping in mind once again that these indices are for a year halfway through the period of growth being considered.

Stephen Knack's IRIS team at the University of Maryland compile their indices using country risk assessments based on the responses of relevant constituencies and expert opinion (IRIS-3, 2000). These provide measures of market-enhancing governance quality for a wide set of countries from the early 1980s onwards. This data set provides indices for a number of key variables that measure the performance of states in providing market-enhancing governance. The five relevant indices in this data set are for 'corruption in government', 'rule of law', 'bureaucratic quality', 'repudiation of government contracts', and 'expropriation risk'. These indices provide a measure of the degree to which governance is capable of reducing the relevant transaction costs that are considered necessary for efficient markets. The IRIS data set then aggregates these indices into a single 'property rights index' that ranges from 0 (the poorest conditions for market efficiency) to 50 (the best conditions). This index therefore measures a range of market-enhancing governance conditions and is very useful (within the standard limitations of all subjective data sets) for testing the significance of market-enhancing governance conditions for economic development. Annual data for the index are available from 1984 for most countries.

A second data set that has become very important for testing the role of market-enhancing governance comes from Kaufmann's team (Kaufmann, Kraay and Mastruzzi, 2005) and is available on the World Bank's website (World Bank, 2005a). This data aggregates a large number of indices available in other data sources into six broad governance indicators. These are:

1. *Voice and Accountability* – measuring political, civil and human rights
2. *Political Instability and Violence* – measuring the likelihood of violent threats to, or changes in, government, including terrorism

3. *Government Effectiveness* – measuring the competence of the bureaucracy and the quality of public service delivery
4. *Regulatory Burden* – measuring the incidence of market-unfriendly policies
5. *Rule of Law* – measuring the quality of contract enforcement, the police, and the courts, as well as the likelihood of crime and violence
6. *Control of Corruption* – measuring the exercise of public power for private gain, including both petty and grand corruption and state capture.

We have divided the countries for which data are available into three groups. "Advanced countries" are high-income countries using the World Bank's classification with the exception of two small oil economies (Kuwait and the UAE), which we classify as developing countries. This is because although they have high levels of per capita income from oil sales, they have achieved lower levels of industrial and agricultural development than other high-income countries. We also divide the group of developing countries into a group of "diverging developing countries" whose per capita GDP growth is lower than the median growth rate of the advanced country group, and a group of "converging developing countries" whose per capita GDP growth rate is higher than the median advanced country rate.

Table 11.1 summarizes the available data for the 1980s from the Knack-IRIS dataset. For the decade of the 1980s, the earliest property right index available in this dataset for most countries is for 1984. Table 11.2 shows data from the same source for the 1990s. Tables 11.3 to 11.8 summarize the data for the 1990s using the six governance indices from the Kaufmann-World Bank data set. Figures 11.1 to 11.8 show the same data in graphical form. The tables and plots demonstrate that the role of market-enhancing governance conditions in explaining differences in growth rates in developing countries is at best very weak.

FIGURE 11.1

Market-Enhancing Governance: Composite Property Rights Index and Growth (using Knack-IRIS data) 1980–1990

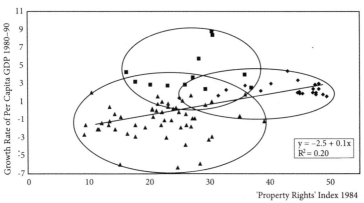

$$y = -2.5 + 0.1x$$
$$R^2 = 0.20$$

• Advanced Countries   ■ Converging Developing Countries   ▲ Diverging Developing Countries

FIGURE 11.2

Market-Enhancing Governance: Composite Property Rights Index and Growth (using Knack- IRIS data) 1990–2003

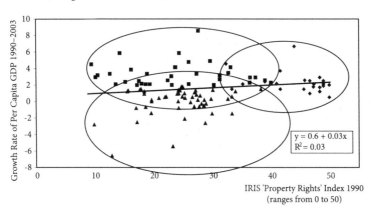

$$y = 0.6 + 0.03x$$
$$R^2 = 0.03$$

• Advanced Countries   ■ Converging Developing Countries   ▲ Diverging Developing Countries

FIGURE 11.3

Governance and Growth 1990–2003 using World Bank Voice and Accountability Index (World Bank/Kaufmann et. al. data)

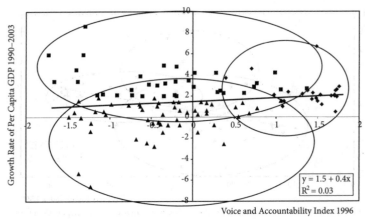

◆ Advanced Countries   ▲ Diverging Developing Countries   ■ Converging Developing Countries

FIGURE 11.4

Governance and Growth 1990–2003 using World Bank Political Instability and Violence Index (World Bank/Kaufmann et. al. data)

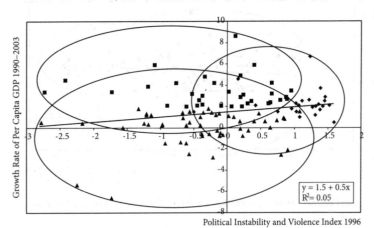

◆ Advanced Countries   ▲ Diverging Developing Countries   ■ Converging Developing Countries

FIGURE 11.5

Governance and Growth 1990–2003 using World Bank Government effectiveness Index (World Bank/Kaufmann et. al. data)

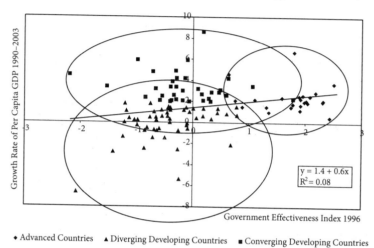

• Advanced Countries   ▲ Diverging Developing Countries   ■ Converging Developing Countries

FIGURE 11.6

Governance and Growth 1990–2003 using World Bank Regulatory Quality Index (World Bank/Kaufmann et. al. data)

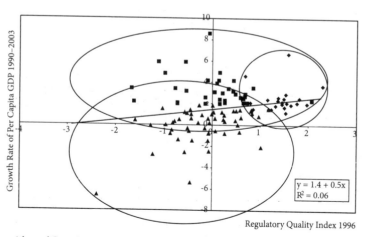

• Advanced Countries   ▲ Diverging Developing Countries   ■ Converging Developing Countries

FIGURE 11.7

Governance and Growth 1990–2003 using World Bank Rule of Law Index
(World Bank/Kaufmann et. al. data)

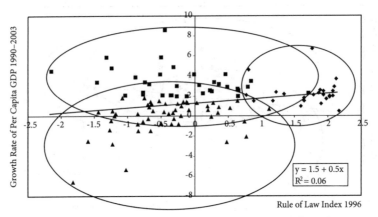

Advanced Countries ▲ Diverging Developing Countries ■ Converging Developing Countries

FIGURE 11.8

Governance and Growth 1990–2003 using World Bank Control of Corruption
Index (World Bank/Kaufmann et. al. data)

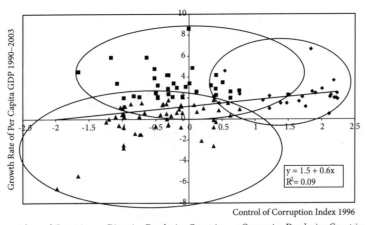

Advanced Countries ▲ Diverging Developing Countries ■ Converging Developing Countries

First, there is virtually no difference between the median property rights index between converging and diverging developing countries (particularly given the relative coarseness of this index and that for most of our data the governance indicators are for a year halfway through the growth period). Secondly, the range of variation of this index for converging and diverging countries almost entirely overlaps. The absence of any clear separation between converging and diverging developing countries in terms of market-enhancing governance conditions casts doubt on the robustness of the econometric results of a large number of studies that find market-enhancing governance conditions have a significant effect on economic growth (Knack and Keefer, 1995, 1997; Hall and Jones, 1999; Kauffman, Kraay and Zoido-Lobatón, 1999).

Third, for all the indices of governance we have available, the data suggest a *very weak* positive relationship between the quality of governance and economic growth. The sign of the relationship is as the market-enhancing governance view requires but the weakness of the relationship demands a closer look at the underlying data. This demonstrates that the positive relationship depends to a great extent on a large number of advanced countries having high scores on market-enhancing governance and the bulk of developing countries being low-growth and low scoring on market-enhancing governance. However, if we only look at these countries, we are unable to say anything about the direction of causality as we have good theoretical reasons to expect market-enhancing governance to improve in countries with high per capita incomes. The critical countries for establishing the direction of causality are the converging developing countries. By and large, these countries do not have significantly better market-enhancing governance scores than diverging developing countries. In the 1980s' data set, there are relatively very few converging countries, and so the relationship between market-enhancing governance and growth *appears* to be relatively strong using the Knack-IRIS data set. However, in the 1990s' data set, the number of converging countries in terms of our arithmetic definition is now greater and it is very significant that the strength of the relationship becomes much weaker both visually and using measures of goodness of fit despite the bias created by the governance indicators only being available from around

1994 for the Kaufmann-World Bank data set. This examination of the data therefore suggests to us that even the weak positive relationship between market-enhancing governance and growth could be largely based on the reverse direction of causality, with richer countries having better scores in terms of market-enhancing governance.

Finally, the policy implications of these observations are rather important. Given the large degree of overlap in the market-enhancing governance scores achieved by converging and diverging developing countries, we need to significantly qualify the claim made in much of the governance literature that an improvement in market-enhancing governance quality in diverging countries will lead to a significant improvement in their growth performance. Nevertheless, the significant differences in their growth rates suggest significant differences in the efficiency of resource allocation and use between these countries, and these differences are very likely to be related to significant differences in governance. The data suggests that since differences in market-enhancing governance capabilities are not significant between converging and diverging countries, we need to examine other dimensions of governance capabilities that could explain differences in growth performance.

TABLE 11.1

Market-Enhancing Governance: Composite Property Rights Index (Knack-IRIS dataset) and Economic Growth, 1980–90

	Advanced Countries	Diverging Developing Countries	Converging Developing Countries
Number of Countries	21	52	12
Median Property Rights Index, 1984	45.1	22.5	27.8
Observed range of Property Rights Index	25.1 – 49.6	9.4 – 39.2	16.4 – 37.0
Median Per Capita GDP Growth Rate, 1980–90	2.2	-1.0	3.5

The IRIS Property Rights Index can range from a low of 0 for the worst governance conditions to a high of 50 for the best conditions.
Sources: IRIS-3 (2000), World Bank (2005b).

TABLE 11.2

Market-Enhancing Governance: Composite Property Rights Index (Knack-IRIS dataset) and Economic Growth, 1990–2003

	Advanced Countries	Diverging Developing Countries	Converging Developing Countries
Number of Countries	24	53	35
Median Property Rights Index, 1990	47.0	25.0	23.7
Observed range of Property Rights Index	32.3 – 50.0	10 – 38.3	9.5 – 40.0
Median Per Capita GDP Growth Rate, 1990-2003	2.1	0.4	3.0

The IRIS Property Rights Index can range from a low of 0 for the worst governance conditions to a high of 50 for the best conditions.
Sources: IRIS-3 (2000), World Bank (2005b).

TABLE 11.3

Market-Enhancing Governance: Voice and Accountability (Kaufmann-World Bank dataset) and Economic Growth, 1990–2003

	Advanced Countries	Diverging Developing Countries	Converging Developing Countries
Number of Countries	24	53	35
Median Voice and Accountability Index, 1996	1.5	−0.4	−0.3
Observed range of Voice and Accountability Index	0.4 – 1.8	−1.5 – 1.1	−1.7 – 1.4
Median Per Capita GDP Growth Rate, 1990–2003	2.1	0.4	3.0

The Kaufmann-World Bank index has a normal distribution with mean 0 and standard deviation 1. Sources: World Bank (2005a), World Bank (2005b).

TABLE 11.4

Market-Enhancing Governance: Political Instability and Violence (Kaufmann-World Bank dataset) and Economic Growth, 1990–2003

	Advanced Countries	Diverging Developing Countries	Converging Developing Countries
Number of Countries	24	53	35
Median Political Instability and Violence Index, 1996	1.2	−0.4	0.0
Observed range of Instability and Violence Index	−0.5 – 1.6	−2.8 – 1.1	−2.7 – 1.0
Median Per Capita GDP Growth Rate, 1990–2003	2.1	0.4	3.0

The Kaufmann-World Bank index has a normal distribution with mean 0 and standard deviation 1. Sources: World Bank (2005a), World Bank (2005b).

TABLE 11.5

Market-Enhancing Governance: Government Effectiveness (Kaufmann-World Bank dataset) and Economic Growth, 1990–2003

	Advanced Countries	Diverging Developing Countries	Converging Developing Countries
Number of Countries	24	53	35
Median Government Effectiveness Index, 1996	1.9	−0.5	−0.2
Observed range of Govt Effectiveness Index	0.6 – 2.5	−2.1 – 0.8	−2.2 – 1.8
Median Per Capita GDP Growth Rate, 1990–2003	2.1	0.4	3.0

The Kaufmann-World Bank index has a normal distribution with mean 0 and standard deviation 1. Sources: World Bank (2005a), World Bank (2005b).

TABLE 11.6

Market-Enhancing Governance: Regulatory Quality (Kaufmann-World Bank dataset) and Economic Growth, 1990–2003

	Advanced Countries	Diverging Developing Countries	Converging Developing Countries
Number of Countries	24	53	35
Median Regulatory Quality Index, 1996	1.5	−0.1	0.2
Observed range of Regulatory Quality Index	0.8 – 2.3	−2.4 – 1.2	−2.9 – 2.1
Median Per Capita GDP Growth Rate, 1990–2003	2.1	0.4	3.0

The Kaufmann-World Bank index has a normal distribution with mean 0 and standard deviation 1. Sources: World Bank (2005a), World Bank (2005b).

TABLE 11.7

Market-Enhancing Governance: Rule of Law (Kaufmann-World Bank dataset) and Economic Growth, 1990–2003

	Advanced Countries	Diverging Developing Countries	Converging Developing Countries
Number of Countries	24	53	35
Median Rule of Law Index, 1996	1.9	−0.4	−0.3
Observed range of Rule of Law Index	0.8 – 2.2	−1.8 – 1.1	−2.2 – 1.7
Median Per Capita GDP Growth Rate, 1990–2003	2.1	0.4	3.0

The Kaufmann-World Bank index has a normal distribution with mean 0 and standard deviation 1. Sources: World Bank (2005a), World Bank (2005b).

TABLE 11.8

Market-Enhancing Governance: Control of Corruption (Kaufmann-World Bank dataset) and Economic Growth, 1990–2003

	Advanced Countries	Diverging Developing Countries	Converging Developing Countries
Number of Countries	24	53	35
Median Control of Corruption Index, 1996	1.8	–0.4	–0.3
Observed range of Control of Corruption Index	0.4 – 2.2	–2.0 – 0.8	–1.7 – 1.5
Median Per Capita GDP Growth Rate, 1990-2003	2.1	0.4	3.0

The Kaufmann-World Bank index has a normal distribution with mean 0 and standard deviation 1. Sources: World Bank (2005a), World Bank (2005b).

Studies that find a significant positive relationship between market-enhancing governance and growth usually do so by pooling advanced and developing countries together. Our examination of the data suggests that these studies can be misleading because we expect advanced countries to have better market governance capabilities. Pooling can thus confuse cause and effect. When developing countries are looked at separately, the relationship is much weaker if it exists at all. And even in this case, we need to be aware of sample selection problems if we pool relatively advanced and poor developing countries.

Our analysis is supported by the analysis of growth in African countries by Sachs and his collaborators (Sachs and others, 2004). In their study of African countries, they address the problem that countries with higher per capita incomes are expected to have better market-enhancing governance quality and so their better governance indicators should not be used to explain their higher incomes. They do this by not using market-enhancing governance indicators directly as explanatory variables, but instead by using the deviation of the governance indicator (in this case, the Kaufmann-World Bank index) from the predicted value of the indicator given the country's per capita income at the beginning of the period. This approach is a more sophisticated way of dealing with the two-way causation between governance and growth. If market-enhancing governance matters for growth, we would expect countries that had better governance than would be expected for their per capita incomes to do better in subsequent periods compared to countries that only achieved average or below average governance for their per capita incomes. By making this correction, the Sachs study finds that when adjusted in this way, market-enhancing governance has no effect on the growth performance of African countries. This result is entirely consistent with our observations of the global growth data recorded above.

However, we do not entirely agree with Sachs and his colleagues when they conclude that these results show that governance reforms are not an immediate priority for African countries. They argue that to trigger growth in Africa, what is required instead is a big push in the form of a massive injection of investment in infrastructure and disease control. While the case for a big push in Africa is strong, this does not mean that African countries have the minimum necessary governance conditions to ensure that a viable economic and social transformation will be unleashed by such an investment push. This is because the evidence of big push experiments in many countries has demonstrated that growth is only sustainable if resources are used to enhance productive capacity and new producers are able to achieve rapid productivity growth. These outcomes are not likely in the absence of institutional support and regulation from state structures possessing the appropriate governance capabilities given the reasons discussed earlier. The powerful econometric results reported by Sachs and others (2004) do not actually show that all types of governance are irrelevant for growth, only that the market-enhancing governance that is measured by available governance indicators clearly has less significance in explaining differences in performance between developing countries than is widely believed. Other forms of governance may be very important, but indices measuring these governance capacities are not readily available. In the next section, we look at the evidence suggesting the importance of growth-enhancing governance capabilities.

Growth-Enhancing Governance and Economic Growth

The argument for market-enhancing governance that we have examined so far is that if efficient markets can be constructed, they will attract the most profitable technologies to a developing country. In contrast, the case for growth-enhancing governance argues that the most efficient markets that developing countries can construct will, at best, be relatively inefficient in transferring assets and resources to growth sectors. In addition, they are also likely to attract low technology and low value-added activities into the developing country, as these are the only activities that are currently profitable given the technological capabilities of the typical developing country. If technological capacity development can be accelerated, very high returns are likely in the future. But projects that aim to enhance technological capacity involve learning how to use new technologies and new methods of organizing work practices. This involves potentially long periods of losses with the promise of high profitability in the future, but only if there is very rapid and disciplined learning. For private investors in developing countries, the uncertainty involved in investing in this type of learning is typically too high to be worth the risk given that alternative investment opportunities are less risky and immediately profitable. Rapid catching up therefore requires complementary growth-enhancing interventions by states and the governance capabilities to ensure that they are effectively implemented (Aoki, Kim and Fujiwara, 1997; Khan and Jomo, 2000).

The problem for growth-enhancing strategies is that while there is a credible theoretical case for intervention in late developers to assist them to move rapidly up the technology ladder, the effective implementation of such strategies typically also requires very effective governance capabilities to supplement the discipline imposed by the market. When states create incentives and opportunities to assist resource allocation or technology acquisition, the market on its own may well not suffice as a disciplining mechanism. Governance capacities are now required to ensure that moral hazard problems do not subvert the growth-enhancing strategy. The precise governance requirements depend on the specific mechanisms through which the state attempts to accelerate technology acquisition and investment.

The diversity of the policy mechanisms through which Asian countries accelerated catching up demonstrate that while there is clearly no single set of governance requirements to ensure that interventions for catching up are effective, the governance capabilities have to be *appropriate* for ensuring that the growth-enhancing interventions are effectively implemented and enforced.

If the requisite governance capacities are missing, a growth-enhancing strategy may deliver worse outcomes than a market-led strategy, as poorly implemented interventions may worsen resource allocation as well as induce high rent-seeking costs. But even a failed growth strategy can sometimes have unintended consequences that are potentially useful if it develops human capital, even though it fails to profitably employ these resources. If human resources are developed, these can often be exploited in new ways, even if the growth strategy fails. The interactive relationship between growth strategies, governance capabilities and technological capabilities of producers can help to explain (a) why many *different* strategies of industrial catching up were successful in East Asia, (b) why, at the same time, apparently *similar* growth-enhancing strategies have worked in some countries and failed dismally in others, (c) why some countries like India have done reasonably *well* with liberalization by using some of the capacities developed by previous growth strategies in new ways, and (d) why some countries in Latin America have fared rather *less well* in terms of growth after liberalization when they allowed markets to significantly guide resource allocation to areas of current comparative advantage. In Latin American countries, liberalization has often resulted in a shift towards lower technology manufacturing and commodity production.

While a full treatment of this diversity can only be done through a series of case studies, Table 11.9 summarizes these experiences for a selection of countries showing the type of growth-enhancing strategies that they followed and the associated governance capabilities that either supported or obstructed the implementation of these strategies. During the 1960s, 1970s and part of the 1980s, most developing countries followed growth-enhancing strategies that had many common elements, even though they often differed quite significantly in their detail. In all countries, two primary goals of developmental interventions were (a) to accelerate resource allocation to growth sectors and (b) to accelerate technology acquisition in these sectors through a combination of incentives and compulsions. To achieve the first, a variety of policy mechanisms were used, including bureaucratic allocation of land (including land reform), the licensing of land use, the licensing of foreign exchange use, and the licensing or bureaucratic allocation of bank credit. In some cases, price controls and fiscal transfers were also used to accelerate the transfer of resources to particular sectors. To achieve the second, incentives for technology acquisition included targeted tax breaks or subsidies, protection of particular sectors for domestic producers engaged in setting up infant industries, licensing of foreign technologies and subcontracting these to domestic producers, setting up investment zones for high technology industries and subsidizing infrastructure for them and so on. For both types of policies, growth-enhancing governance required monitoring resource use and withdrawing resources or support from sectors or firms that proved to be making inadequate progress. Monitoring progress is less complex than it may appear, particularly in countries that are well inside the technology frontier as export performance or the rate of import substitution (in the presence of competition between domestic producers) can provide very good indirect information about the rate of productivity growth and quality improvement achieved by individual producers. The difficult part of growth-enhancing governance is to implement and enforce difficult decisions about resource withdrawal when performance is poor.

These and other available case-study evidence suggest that success in growth-enhancing governance depends on a number of institutional and political factors that enable the effective implementation of the underlying growth-enhancing strategies. The institutional requirements include the requirement that the agencies involved in monitoring and enforcement are sufficiently centralized to be able to internalize all the costs and benefits of implementing the strategy (Shleifer and Vishny, 1993; Khan, 2000a). This is to ensure that failing industries or sectors are not able to offer inducements to monitoring agencies to allow them to continue to receive their rents without delivering performance. Just as important, if not more, is the political requirement that the governance agencies are able to enforce difficult decisions about rent and resource withdrawal from non-performing sectors and firms when required. This, in turn, requires a compatibility of the required governance tasks with the internal power structures of the country. Table 11.9 also summarizes how the internal power structures of these countries played an important role in explaining why particular strategies of governance could or could not be effectively implemented.

Growth-enhancing governance is helped if political factions are too weak to protect non-performing industries and sectors. If political factions are strong and there are many of them, it becomes relatively easy for failing firms to buy themselves protection by offering to share a part of their rents with factions that offer to protect them. The South Korean experience with industrial policy during the 1960s and 1970s demonstrates how the absence of strong political factions can have very beneficial effects for a particular strategy of growth-enhancing governance. In contrast, the South Asian experience during the same decades (like that of many other parts of the developing world) shows how fragmented political factions can prevent effective growth-enhancing governance. But growth-enhancing governance can be moderately effective, even in the presence of strong political factions, provided there is a political settlement that allows the political demands of factions to be satisfied through centralized transfers. This can reduce the incentive of factions to capture rents by protecting rent-recipients willing to pay. The Malaysian growth strategy of the 1980s and 1990s provides some support for this hypothesis.

These possibilities can explain why successful countries appear to have very different growth-enhancing strategies when we look at the details of the instruments and mechanisms through which they set out to achieve rapid development. Strategies that can be effectively implemented in one context may be much more difficult to implement somewhere else. Different policy instruments may be more effective in other contexts if governance capabilities are more appropriate for enforcing these alternative strategies. This can explain why we can observe different combinations of policies and growth-enhancing governance capabilities delivering good, if not equally good results in different countries. So, for instance, a strategy of subsidizing credit for

TABLE 11.9
Growth-Enhancing Governance in Selected Countries, 1960–2000

	Critical Components of Growth-Enhancing Strategy	Supportive or Obstructive Governance Capabilities	Economic Outcomes
South Korea 1960s to early 1980s	Non-market asset allocations (consolidations, mergers and restructuring of *chaebol*) Targeted conditional subsidies for *chaebol* to accelerate catching-up	Centralized and effective governance of interventions by agencies with long-term stake in development Effective power to implement assisted by weakness of political factions so that inefficient subsidy recipients are unable to buy protection from them	Very rapid growth and capitalist transformation
Malaysia 1980s 1990s	Public sector technology acquisition strategies using public enterprises with subcontracting for domestic firms. Targeted infrastructure and incentives for MNCs with conditions on technology transfer	Moderately effective centralized governance of interventions Assisted by centralized transfers to intermediate classes which reduced incentives of political factions to seek rents by protecting inefficient firms	Rapid growth and capitalist transformation
Indian subcontinent 1960s 1970s (With some variations these characteristics describe many developing countries of that period)	Targeted subsidies to accelerate catching up in critical sectors (using protection, licensing of foreign exchange, price controls and other mechanisms). Public sector technology acquisition in subsidized public enterprises. Resource transfers to growth sectors using licensing and pricing policy.	Moderate to weak governance capacities to discipline non-performing rent recipients. Agencies often have contradictory goals defined by different constituencies Fragmented political factions help to protect the rents of the inefficient for a share of these rents. State capacities decline as committed and intelligent individuals leave	Public and private sector infant industries often fail to grow up. Rent seeking costs are often the most visible effects of intervention. Moderate to low growth and slow transformation

TABLE 11.9 (Contd.)

	Critical Components of Growth-Enhancing Strategy	Supportive or Obstructive Governance Capabilities	Economic Outcomes
Indian subcontinent 1980s 1990s	Liberalization primarily in the form of a withdrawal of implicit targeted subsidies, in particular through the relaxation of licensing for capital goods imports. Much more gradual withdrawal of protection across the board for domestic markets.	Moderate to weak governance capacities to implement remain but do less damage as the scope of growth enhancing policies decline. Fragmented political factions continue to have an effect on market-enhancng governance by restricting tax revenues and making it difficult to construct adequate infrastructure.	Growth led by investments in sectors that already have comparative advantage. Higher growth but limited to a few sectors.
Latin America 1950s to 1970s	Domestic capacity building through selective tariffs and selective credit allocation.	Governance effective in directing resources to import-substituting industries but weak in disciplining poor performers. Weakness linked to "corporatist" alliances that constrained disciplining powerful sectors	Initial rapid growth slows down Many infant industries fail to grow up.
Latin America 1980s onwards	Rapid liberalization across the board	Focus on market-enhancing governance Breakdown of corporatist alliances allows rapid liberalization to be implemented	Output growth in sectors that already have comparative advantage, in particular in commodities

large conglomerates, as in South Korea, may have provided very poor results in a country like Malaysia where the enforcement capacities for such a strategy would have been much weaker. In contrast, the Malaysian strategy of creating incentives for multinational companies to bring in high technology industries and subcontract to local companies proved much more successful because this strategy was more consistent with Malaysian governance capabilities. Thus, while Malaysian economic performance was a little poorer than that of South Korea, given Malaysia's internal institutional and political structure and growth-enhancing governance capabilities, Malaysia's growth was probably higher than if Malaysia had tried to follow South Korean economic strategies precisely. An analysis of the types of growth-enhancing strategies that can be effectively implemented in particular developing countries could therefore identify somewhat different growth strategies in different countries, even though they address similar problems (of accelerating resource allocation to growth sectors and accelerating technology acquisition). The importance of such an analysis is not only to identify the growth strategies appropriate for the country, given its growth-enhancing governance capabilities. In many countries, growth-enhancing governance capabilities may be so poor that no growth strategy can be implemented. In these cases, the policy response should not necessarily be to abandon growth strategies and shift to market-enhancing strategies. It should rather be to examine the type of growth-enhancing governance capabilities that can feasibly be achieved in that country through a process of governance reform.

As our analysis suggests that growth outcomes depend on the compatibility of a growth strategy with growth-enhancing governance capabilities, it is also possible to explain why many developing countries performed so poorly with growth strategies that appear similar to the ones followed by successful East Asian countries. A growth strategy that cannot be implemented could well provide worse results than if there were no growth strategy at all because any growth strategy overrides some allocations that would otherwise have happened through the existing market system, thereby creating rents and rent seeking opportunities. If these rents fail to accelerate learning and instead result in large rent seeking costs, the economy would be worse off trying to implement these strategies. However, this is clearly not necessarily a failure of the policy as such, but rather an indication of its inappropriateness in a particular country, or the failure of the country to address the necessary governance requirements that would be required to accelerate growth and achieve more rapid development.

Another feature of the growth experience of the 1960s and 1970s was that many developing countries performed very well with growth-enhancing strategies that required minimal enforcement at the early stages when new resources were being made available to emerging infant industries. But their performance declined when the new industries demonstrated inadequate effort at learning and productivity growth and it turned out that states lacked the governance capacities to impose discipline or re-allocate resources. While the institutional and political features that led to this result were different in different countries, the overall story is common to very many countries in Asia, Africa and Latin America that began to perform very poorly in the latter half of the 1970s and beyond.

The liberalization that began in the late 1980s and 1990s in many developing countries has also produced very different results. This diversity of experience can also be addressed by an analytical approach that looks at the interdependence of growth strategies, growth-enhancing governance capabilities and technological capabilities. In countries where technological capabilities were already strong or were being continuously developed, partial liberalization produced strong results. At one end, China has emerged as the fastest growing economy in recorded economic history in a context of gradual and measured liberalization because previous growth-enhancing strategies had produced widespread technological capabilities within China to move into medium-tech manufacturing. Many aspects of the successful growth-enhancing strategies of the past continue to be effectively implemented, and appropriate growth-enhancing governance capabilities exist to implement them effectively. These strategies include the strategies of local and central governments in China to make land and infrastructure available on a priority basis to investors in critical sectors, and to offer fiscal incentives and attractive terms to both foreign and overseas Chinese investors engaging in investments critical for economic progress (Qian and Weingast, 1997). Thus, while compared to the earlier generation of East Asian developers, the Chinese state appears to be doing less in terms of actively supporting technology upgrading, it still has very strong governance capacities to ensure the allocation of land, resources and infrastructure to critical investors. With its vast internal market and the broad-based technological capabilities it has already achieved, Chinese manufacturing has been able to acquire scale economies that enable it to compete in price almost without challenge in the low to medium-technology manufacturing industries.

In contrast, the countries of the Indian subcontinent have had a different experience with liberalization. Here, previous growth-enhancing strategies had succeeded in creating technological capabilities that were less broad based than in China. Political fragmentation was much greater, and the governance capabilities of states to direct resources to investors were significantly lower than in China. As in China, liberalization proceeded at a very slow pace, opening up opportunities without precipitately destroying too much existing capacity by exposing inefficient industries to excessive competition in the local market. Growth has been led by sectors that had already achieved the minimum technological capability for international competition, taking the opportunity to start producing aggressively for domestic and international markets. The results were higher growth rates than in the past, led by a small number of sectors that had acquired enough technological capability to enjoy comparative advantage in international markets. These sectors differed across South Asia, ranging from the garments industry and shrimps in Bangladesh, low-end textiles in Pakistan to diamond polishing, call centres and software in India. The growth of internal demand has also sparked off investment in a range of industries that still have not acquired international competitiveness. While South Asia does not have the broad-based manufacturing growth we see in China, and has a much bigger and faster growing service sector, it too has been a beneficiary of very gradual liberalization of this type. However, while attempts at improving market-enhancing governance have not occupied too much time in China, the greater exposure of South Asian countries to the development discourse in multilateral agencies has resulted in much greater interest in and concern with improving performance in market-enhancing governance.

Our analysis suggests that while it is desirable, over time, to improve market-enhancing governance, the comparison of liberalization in China and India suggests that market-enhancing governance cannot explain their relative performance. Case studies of China and India do not suggest that China performs much better than India (if at all) along critical dimensions of market-enhancing governance such as the stability of property rights, corruption or the rule of law. Where it does do better is in having governance capacities for accelerating resource allocation to growth sectors, prioritizing infrastructure for these sectors, and in making credible and attractive terms available to investors bringing in advanced technologies, capabilities that we have described as growth-enhancing governance capabilities.

Latin America provides even more compelling evidence that a focus on market-enhancing governance alone cannot provide adequate policy levers for governments interested in accelerating growth and development. Compared to China and the Indian subcontinent, liberalization in Latin America has been more thoroughgoing and has extended, in many cases, to the liberalization of the capital account and much freer entry conditions for imports into the domestic market. In terms of market-enhancing governance, Latin America, on average, scores highly, compared to other areas of the developing world. This is not surprising given its higher initial per capita incomes, much longer history of development, and relatively old institutions of political democracy (even though, in many cases, these institutions were, for a while, subverted by military governments). Yet, the combination of more developed market-enhancing governance capabilities and a more thoroughgoing liberalization did not help Latin America beat Asia in terms of economic development in the 1990s and beyond. In fact, its relative performance was exactly the opposite of what we would expect from the relative depth of its liberalization strategy and its relative governance indicators. But in fact, the rapid liberalization of Latin America and its greater reliance on market-enhancing governance achieved results that should not be entirely surprising given our analysis. Latin American countries shifted even more rapidly to producing according to their comparative advantage, and in most Latin American countries, this meant a shift to lower technology industries and to commodity production. This has produced respectable output growth in some countries, but productivity growth has been low and living standards have yet to fully recover from the collapse suffered in the 1990s.

The distinction between market-enhancing and growth-enhancing governance can thus allow us to make sense of the complex comparative economic performance of countries since 1960. It also allows us to reassert the importance of governance even though the types of governance that many institutional economists have focused on do not correlate very well with comparative economic performance. From a policy perspective our analysis points out the limitations of the current governance agenda that focuses almost exclusively on market-enhancing governance. The danger of such an exclusive focus on market-enhancing governance is that we may lose opportunities for carrying out critical reforms more likely to produce results. We may also create disillusionment with governance reforms and the emergence of the false perception that governance does not matter that much for economic development.

REFERENCES

Aoki, Masahiko, Kim Hyung-Ki, and Masahiro Okuno-Fujiwara (eds) (1997). *The Role of Government in East Asian Economic Development: Comparative Institutional Analysis.* Clarendon Press, Oxford.

Hall, Robert, and Charles Jones (1999). Why do some countries produce so much more output per worker than others? *Quarterly Journal of Economics* 114 (1): 83-116.

IRIS-3 (2000). *File of International Country Risk Guide (ICRG) Data.* Edited by Stephen Knack and the IRIS Center, University of Maryland, College Park.

Kauffman, Daniel, Aart Kraay, and Pablo Zoido-Lobatón (1999). Governance matters. World Bank policy working paper no. 2196, World Bank, Washington, DC.

Kaufmann, Daniel, Aart Kraay, and Massimo Mastruzzi (2005). *Governance Matters IV: Governance Indicators for 1996–2004.* Available http://www.worldbank.org/wbt/wbi/governance/pubs/govmatters4.html

Khan, Mushtaq H. (2000a). Rent-seeking as process. In Mushtaq H. Khan and Jomo K.S. (eds). *Rents, Rent-Seeking and Economic Development: Theory and Evidence in Asia.* Cambridge University Press, Cambridge.

Khan, Mushtaq H. (2000b). Rents, efficiency and growth. In Mushtaq H. Khan and Jomo K.S. (eds). *Rents, Rent-Seeking and Economic Development: Theory and Evidence in Asia.* Cambridge University Press, Cambridge.

Khan, Mushtaq H. (2005). Review of DFID's governance target strategy paper. Commissioned paper submitted to DFID. Department for International Development Department, London.

Khan, Mushtaq H., and Jomo K.S. (eds) (2000). *Rents, Rent-Seeking and Economic Development: Theory and Evidence in Asia*. Cambridge University Press, Cambridge.

Knack, Stephen, and Philip Keefer (1995). Institutions and economic performance: Cross-country tests using alternative institutional measures. *Economics and Politics* 7 (3): 207–227.

Knack, Stephen, and Philip Keefer (1997). Why don't poor countries catch up? A cross-national test of an institutional explanation. *Economic Inquiry* 35 (3): 590–602.

Krueger, Anne O. (1990). Government failures in development. *Journal of Economic Perspectives* 4 (3): 9–23.

North, Douglass C. (1990). *Institutions, Institutional Change and Economic Performance*. Cambridge University Press, Cambridge.

Qian, Yingyi, and Barry R. Weingast (1997). Institutions, state activism, and economic development: A comparison of state-owned and township-village enterprises in China. In Masahiko Aoki, Hyung-Ki Kim and Masahiro Okuno-Fujiwara (eds). *The Role of Government in East Asian Economic Development: Comparative Institutional Analysis*. Clarendon Press, Oxford.

Sachs, Jeffrey D., John W. McArthur, Guido Schmidt-Traub, Margaret Kruk, Chandrika Bahadur, Michael Faye, and Gordon McCord (2004). Ending Africa's poverty trap. *Brookings Papers on Economic Activity* 1: 117–240.

Shleifer, Andrei, and Robert W. Vishny (1993). Corruption, *Quarterly Journal of Economics* 108 (3): 599–617.

World Bank (1993). *The East Asian Miracle: Economic Growth and Public Policy*. Oxford University Press, Oxford.

World Bank (2005a). *Governance Indicators: 1996–2004*. World Bank, Washington, DC. Available http://info.worldbank.org/governance/kkz2004/tables.asp

World Bank (2005b). *World Development Indicators 2005*. CD-ROM. World Bank, Washington, DC.

12

The Conflict-Growth Nexus and the Poverty of Nations

SYED MANSOOB MURSHED

A fifth of humanity lives in abject poverty.[1] This is something that should be unacceptable to the more affluent for two related reasons. First of all, it affronts our sense of common humanity. Secondly, it undermines international security, as poverty eventually engenders violence and revolt. Enlightened self-interest therefore dictates that poverty should be alleviated. In short, it is difficult to separate the development and security agenda. The reduction of absolute poverty yields a double dividend by simultaneously addressing security considerations and developmental concerns. Thus, the achievement of the millennium development goals (MDGs) regarding poverty reduction is twice blessed: it serves both the altruistic and security minded motives of the donor community.

Most wars nowadays are intra-state or civil wars. The overwhelming majority of these civil wars occur in developing countries. Ultimately, wars are irrational when compared to negotiated settlements, because wars destroy part of the initial endowment of belligerents, no matter what the final outcome. But the logic of bounded or myopic rationality can sometimes make war rational. Furthermore, there is an intimate link between poverty and conflict. On the one hand, war prevents the achievement of the MDGs, perpetuating poverty, under-development and the lack of growth. On the other hand, poverty provides fertile grounds for conflict entrepreneurs, as potential combatants have less to lose from death and destruction on account of their own poverty. For all of these reasons, ending conflict, or reducing its intensity, must be a high policy imperative in the development, poverty reduction and international security agenda.

Despite the reservations of some, economic growth constitutes the principal avenue by which sustainable poverty reduction can be attained in low-income developing countries. Redistributing income, without making the cake bigger, only serves to make the already poor more equal. Thus, growth is a necessary condition for poverty reduction in low-income countries. Growth can reduce poverty if some of the benefits of growth trickle down to the poor, even if its principal beneficiaries are the wealthy. This is where other notions of pro-poor growth, such as those advocated by Kakwani and Pernia (2000), become relevant. According to this view, in order for growth to be truly pro-poor, it must disproportionately benefit the poorer segments of society; thus requiring an improvement in the distribution of income. Additionally, such pro-poor growth can also serve to stem the seeds (poverty and inequality) of conflict. Moreover, there are similarities between conflict prevention and the deep determinants of growth in the long-run because of factors common to both: institutions, inequality, endowments and so on. Despite our concern with poverty reduction, we cannot ignore the consequences of inequality, within and between nations, because of the insecurity that high inequality engenders. The lack of growth creates more inequality, and inequality breeds human insecurity. Thus an important growth-conflict nexus does exist, and the purpose of this chapter is to explore that link.

The rest of the chapter is organized as follows. The second section describes the growth record (recent and historical) of developing countries. The third section is concerned with conflict. It describes the stylised facts of civil war and summarises and synthesises the causes of civil war (greed versus grievance). The penultimate section sketches the empirical associations among endowment, growth, polity and conflict. The final section concludes with some policy recommendations for post-conflict reconstruction.

Long-Run Determinants of Growth

The economic history of the world in the last two centuries is a sorry tale of widening disparities between rich and poor nations; see Maddison (2001). As Table 12.1 indicates, the average income gap, measured in 1990 purchasing power parity (PPP) dollars between rich and poor nations was 1.97: 1 during the early stages of the industrial revolution in 1820. In a 178 year period to 1998, this gap widened to 6.92. The increase in the average disparity between rich and poor nations was approximately 350 per cent during this period. Table 12.1 clearly shows that the present-day disparities between rich and poor states are a consequence of the lower growth rates in poor countries.

TABLE 12.1
Long-Run Patterns of Growth in the World Economy

Per-Capita GDP levels in 1820 and 1998 (1990 PPP), and growth rates.	1820	1998	1820–1998 (% annual growth rates)
Western Europe	1232	17,921	1.51
Western offshoots	1201	26,146	1.75
Japan	669	20,413	1.93
Average-rich	**1130**	**21,470**	**1.67**
Latin America	665	5795	1.22
Asia	575	2936	0.92
Africa	418	1368	0.67
Average-poor	**573**	**3102**	**0.95**

Source: Maddison (2001), Western offshoots refer to North America, and Australia and New Zealand.

One of the precepts of neoclassical growth theory is that poorer regions should grow faster than richer countries, eventually catching up with the higher living standards of affluent nations. The relative gap between rich and poor nations should become narrower over time, a phenomenon known as 'convergence'. This has not occurred, despite the fact that a handful of poor countries have joined the club of affluent nations. Consider Table 12.2, based on Milanovic (2005), describing the number of countries in transition from poor to middle-income to rich and so on, since 1960. Rich refers to a typical OECD country (minus Turkey and other new entrants to the OECD). Upper middle refers to countries with at least two-thirds of the average per-capita income in the poorest OECD country. Lower-middle refers to those with between a third and two-thirds of the average income in the poorest OECD country. Poor refers to the number of nations with less a third of the average income in the poorest rich country.

TABLE 12.2

The Number of Countries Going from Rich to Poor and vice versa, 1960–2000

Type	1960	2000
Rich (OECD)	41	31
Upper-Middle	22	8
Lower-Middle	39	25
Poor	25	67

Source: Milanovic (2005)

Between 1960 and 2000 the Western share of rich countries has been increasing; to be affluent has almost become an exclusive Western prerogative – 16 out of 19 non-Western nations who were rich in 1960 traversed into less affluent categories by 2000 (for example, Algeria, Angola and Argentina). Against that four Asian non-rich countries moved into the first group.[2] Most non-western rich nations in 1960 joined the second income-group by 2000, and most non-Western upper-middle income countries in 1960 had fallen into the third and fourth income categories by 2000. Of 22 upper-middle income nations in 1960, 20 had declined into the third and fourth income categories, among them the Democratic Republic of the Congo (DRC), also known recently as Zaire, and Ghana. Most nations in the third group in 1960 descended into the lowest income category by 2000. Only Botswana moved to the third group from the fourth category, while Egypt remains in the third category. We seem to inhabit a downwardly mobile world with a vanishing middle-class;

by 2000 most countries were *either rich or poor*, in contrast to 1960 when most nations were in the middle-income groups.

Table 12.3 also illustrates that the growth rates for developing countries as a whole were greater in the 1960s and 1970s compared to the more globalized era of the 1980s or 1990s. For Africa and Latin America, the last two decades of the twentieth century were lost decades in terms of growth and other human development indicators. Many of the countries that have experienced this downward spiral have been affected by conflict (Angola, Algeria and the DRC), besides having negative or very low growth rates in the 1965–2000 period (see Murshed, 2006).

TABLE 12.3
GDP per capita (1995 constant US$) growth rates, 1960–2000

Area/Country	Annual average GDP growth %			
	1960–1970	1970–1980	1980–1990	1990–2000
All developing countries	3.1	3.3	1.2	1.9
East Asia & Pacific	2.9	4.5	5.9	6.0
South Asia	1.8	0.7	3.5	3.2
Latin America & Caribbean	2.6	3.4	–0.8	1.7
Sub-Saharan Africa	2.6	0.8	–1.1	–0.4

Source: World Bank *World Development Indicators 2002.*

The lack of growth in many parts of the developing world is a major cause of concern because it simultaneously prevents poverty reduction and increases conflict risk. Institutional quality has been identified as a major long-term cause of growth or its absence (see, for example, Rodrik, Subramanian and Trebbi, 2004). But what determines institutional functioning?

Murshed (2004) presents evidence that developing countries with a large mineral type natural resource endowment have tended to have low growth rates, compared to resource poor countries, since the 1970s, notwithstanding a handful of success stories like Botswana. Natural resource rents can make corruption, predation and rent-seeking more attractive. The incentive is greater, the weaker the environment of law and contract enforcement. A rich mineral type natural resource endowment, where ownership and production are concentrated may therefore produce poor institutions and even outright conflict. Hence, *endowments* may be key in determining institutional quality.

Malfunctioning institutions may thus retard growth and increase the risk of war. Easterly and Levine (2003) present evidence, based on cross-country regressions, that a mineral natural resource endowment, a poor geographical (tropical) location and an excessive mortality rate (disease burden) retard economic development, but via *institutional quality*, as proxied by governance data. Similarly, bad economic policy choices also hinder economic development via institutions. Consequently, institutions and institutional functioning are the crucial link between resource endowments, geography, and policies on the one hand and economic outcomes on the other. Can democracy 'capture' institutional quality? Most developing countries are imperfect democracies, having the characteristics of both democracies and autocracies (anocracy), because they combine weak checks on the executive and imperfect rule of law with regular elections.[3]

Lipset's (1960) famous *modernisation* hypothesis gives us an endogenous view of democracy. According to this theory, democracy is an inevitable outcome of economic progress. At high levels of income, the demand for democracy is unstoppable. Similarly, at high levels of income, the risk of societal conflict and civil war is less likely, as people have more to lose (relative to their prospects for gain) from violent struggles over resources.

CONFLICT

Definitions & Stylised Facts

The quantitatively minded conflict research community has increasingly placed its faith in the Uppsala data set (see Harbom and Wallensteen (2005) for recent descriptions).[4] The Uppsala data set defines several types of conflict: inter-state (between nation states), intra-state (civil wars), intra-state internationalised (where foreign powers are involved) and extra-state (wars of national independence, which mostly ended in the 1970s). A conflict is defined as minor if there are no more than battle-related deaths per year for every year in the period. It is intermediate when 26 to 1000 battle-related deaths occur per year for every year in the conflict period. War as to describe situations with more than a thousand battle-related deaths in each year of the conflict. Any particular conflict can slip between these categories as the war escalates and wanes over time.

The salient stylized facts regarding recent civil wars are:

1. According to Harbom and Wallensteen (2005), reporting on the Uppsala data-set, there have been 118 conflicts in 80 locations since 1989. In 2004, there were 30 armed conflicts in 22 different locations.

2. Since 1946, the peak in the number of armed conflicts was either in 1991 or 1992, according to the above source. It does seem that the number of intra-state wars has been declining since the mid-1990s, a point repeatedly stressed in the *Human Security Report* (2005). This may be more due to conflict terminations, rather than a fall in the start of new civil wars (Hegre, 2004). This does not, however, provide grounds for complacency regarding the dangers of civil war; the world, especially Western powers and aid donors, need to be vigilant regarding conflict risk and its consequences for poverty.

3. The 2005 *Human Security Report* also reports the total incidence of conflict in different countries. Bearing in mind that there may be more than one conflict inside a single nation-state, which leads to more than one conflict in a single calendar year, the list is led by Burma, with 232 conflict years since 1946. India follows with 156 years; Ethiopia has the third highest incidence of conflict with 88 years, and the UK, with 77 years, is in sixth position just behind Israel (79 years).[5]

4. The 2005 *Human Security Report* also reports a downward trend in the number of battle related deaths because of the nature of low-intensity warfare and smart weapons. The figures for total war deaths post 1998, as reported in the 2005 *Human Security Report* is, however, disputed by the World Health Organisation, who put them much higher.

5. As far as duration or the number of years a civil war lasts is concerned, the average may be showing an upward trend (see Fearon 2004). He puts the average duration of a civil war at 16 years in 1999. He also argues that civil wars with 'sons of the soil' dynamics (mainly wars of secession) last longer, as do wars where a lootable commodity, such as alluvial diamonds or illicit drugs (cocaine or heroin), or an obstructable commodity, such as oil, is involved; Also see Ross (2004).

Causes of Conflict

In broad terms, the contemporary 'rational choice' economics literature offers two explanations for the origin of conflict. I will first summarise the role of relative deprivation (*grievance*), then go on to contests for resource wealth (*greed*), before synthesising these arguments.

Relative Deprivation

Relative deprivation – the perception by one or more parties that they are being unjustly treated – is a major cause of civil war. Many conflict societies are characterised by large inequalities in access to the productive assets necessary for livelihoods and in public spending on economic and social infrastructure and services. Research on conflict has emphasized the importance of *horizontal* inequalities between groups, distinguished by ethnicity, religion, linguistic differences, tribal affiliations, etc., as sources of conflict; see Stewart (2000), for example. This concept should be distinguished from *vertical* inequality, which is inequality within a homogenous group. Three dimensions of horizontal inequality are discussed below:

○ *Discrimination in Public Spending and Taxation.* Perceived discrimination in the allocation of public spending on unfair tax burdens lead to serious unrest. Grossman (1991) develops a theoretical model of insurrection against the state by the peasantry reacting to over-taxation, where the state is a tax-farmer interested in maximizing the income of the rentier class. Discrimination in the allocation of public employment is particularly resented in societies in which public employment represents the principal avenue for personal advancement, as in Burundi. In addition, the over taxation of smallholders encourages insurrection, and indigenous peoples often face discrimination in access to schooling, health care, and public-sector jobs; many of these factors are present in Nepal's current civil war, e.g., see Murshed and Gates (2005). Where there are inter-group fiscal transfers, which may take the form of spending on education and health for disadvantaged groups or including them in government employment, commitment to the transfer by those in power may be imperfect. This lack of credibility of the transfer can eventually lead to civil war.

o *High Asset Inequality.* Agrarian societies with high income inequality—for example, El Salvador, Guatemala, Nepal, the Philippines, and Zimbabwe—have high asset inequality, and are very prone to conflict. In these societies, agrarian elites use their collateral to further leverage their existing wealth through a financial system that they control by means of family/business cross-holdings. Asset redistribution, such as land reform to lessen inequality, is more difficult than public finance reform.

o *Economic Mismanagement and Recession.* Africa, Latin America and the former Soviet Union, and other conflict-ridden countries have also suffered prolonged economic mismanagement and growth collapse. Also, as Rodrik (1999) emphasizes, countries with weak institutions of conflict management as well as high income inequality, are less able to withstand economic shocks and experience growth failure. They are also prone to the risk of civil strife and war, since their weak institutions, further weakened by shocks and lower growth, are unable to contain the resulting social pressures and distributional conflicts.

The measurement of horizontal inequality presents a number of challenges, as no consensus exists in this regard in the literature. It is a relatively new concept, and the associated measures have not been properly worked out. For example, the use of Gini coefficients to measure between group horizontal inequality is hugely problematic, because different cultural or ethnic groups are not homogenous in size, and have rich and poor strata within each group, making it difficult to array equally sized population groups on the basis of income or some other socio-economic indicator. Horizontal inequality is best measured as a gap with the national average; from Murshed and Gates (2005) pioneered this concept, with Nepal data.[6] For example, the group's human development index (HDI) gap compared to the national HDI or the HDI for the capital city, which can be regarded as the reference for national achievement.[7] Within a country, disaggregated data for the human development index is collected for many countries in Asia and Latin America. This data is usually available spatially – across provinces or districts. But we can impute group inequalities from spatial data because certain ethnic groups chiefly reside in certain areas. In a few instances, household surveys explicitly ask questions about the ethnicity or religion of households. If that is the case, we can compute differences (gaps) in income, poverty incidence, educational and health status across ethnic or religious groups, for example, in Indonesia.

Two further points are worth emphasizing at this juncture. First, horizontal inequality must be measured at the level of the nation state. We are interested in cross-sectional variation *within* a specific country. It does not really lend itself to cross-country comparisons, unlike the impact of natural resource rents on conflict risk, as populations across countries are not homogenous in this regard. The data in different countries on horizontal inequality is embryonic, subject to methodological differences, while no single universal measure for horizontal inequality exists as yet. Even if that were to eventually emerge, horizontal inequality will essentially remain a gap measure, and that will limit cross-country (as opposed to within country) comparisons. The study of horizontal inequality is likely to continue at the level of detailed quantitative country-case studies, where such data are available. Secondly, most nation states do not keep systematic or detailed data on group inequalities (say between Catholics and Protestants, Hutus and Tutsis, Muslims and Christians, etc.) because of the obvious political sensitivities. However, an ethnic question in household surveys will go a long way in generating data on inter-group differences in socio-economic achievement. Horizontal inequalities have been found to significantly affect conflict in Nepal, to cite one example; see Murshed and Gates (2005).

Contest for Natural Resource Rents

Collier and Hoeffler (2002, 2004) find empirical evidence from cross-country regression analysis showing a relatively high dependence on primary commodity exports is highly correlated with the risk of civil war. This result has had immense influence in the media and policy community, including Ministries for Overseas Development (and among the relevant ministers). Natural resources constitute 'booty' and this fact has been used to emphasize the greed or *criminal* motivation for civil war. Certain resources are more easily captured: they may be lootable, such as alluvial diamonds (in Sierra Leone, Angola) available in river beds by using artisanal techniques; or obstructable like an oil pipe line; see Ross (2003) on these issues. Belligerents in the wars of natural-resource rich countries act in ways closer to what Mancur Olson (1996) called 'roving bandits' – who have no interest in preserving the state or its people, but are simply intent on loot – a contrast to 'stationary' bandits who take control of the state and seek to maximise their own income by encouraging stability and growth in their new domain. Civil wars, motivated by the desire to control natural resource rents, are also akin to "warlord competition" – a term that owes its origins to the violent competition between leaders attempting to control economic resources in medieval European cities (Skaperdas 2002).

How empirically valid is the simple version of the greed hypothesis? Ross (2004) and Fearon (2005), among others, point out that the widely accepted Collier and Hoeffler (2002) – finding that the share of primary commodity exports as a proportion of national income significantly contributes to the risk of conflict (in a logistic regression) – is not econometrically robust. In other words, this cross-country result will not withstand variation in sample and data coverage.

There is also a problem with the variable definition itself. The term *primary* commodity includes both agricultural commodities and minerals/fuels, but crucially excludes illegal substances (cocaine and heroin) as well as illegal alluvial diamonds. Illicit gemstones and drugs are arguably more crucial to financing rogue conflict entrepreneurs in a greed based conflict; their omission is a serious flaw. But even before we begin to search for more appropriate natural resource rent data for conflict analysis, it is important to understand that the famous Collier-Hoeffler pronouncement about civil wars being mainly 'greed thinly masked as grievance' does not survive serious scrutiny. Lootable or obstructable mineral resources may not be the initial cause of civil wars, but once started, these wars tend to persist for a long time, as the rents from these commodities help to finance war besides being a source of profit (Fearon, 2004; Ross, 2004).

Lujala, Gleditsch and Gilmore (2005) go a step further in refining the *lootable* natural resource rent data. They focus on data on the production and deposits of alluvial or secondary diamonds, sometimes referred to as conflict diamonds. They find that these types of diamonds significantly increase the risk of civil war and their duration. This risk has been greater since the end of the Cold War. Non-lootable deep mine shaft diamonds, however, has a lower risk of civil war onset. In the same vein, Humphreys (2005) argues that, in some instances, it is better to utilise data on oil deposits, rather than oil exports, to study the resource-civil war nexus.

There may be mechanisms that exist between natural resource endowments and the risk of civil war, and help explain why an abundance of certain types of resources actually lead to war. Two promising explanations, among a plethora proposed in Humphreys (2005), include an undiversified economy (sparse economic interactions imply less economic interdependence and greater scope for conflict, meaning low growth along the lines of Lipset's modernization theory) and weak state capacity (kleptocracy versus relative benevolence).

Snyder and Bhavnani (2005) argue that the causal mechanism between conflict and lootable resources is, broadly speaking, a government *revenue* effect. This implies examining how the state obtains its revenues: e.g., whether or not taxing the mineral sector (which may or may not be lootable) is important to the state. Even if a lootable sector exists, it may not be important for state revenues if other revenue sources exists side-by-side. Additionally, the mode of extraction matters: whether it is artisanal or industrial. Only the former makes resources lootable. Finally, and most importantly, how governments spend their revenue matters: if the state spends its revenues on social welfare, military expenditure and growth enhancing investment, conflict is less likely than if it appropriates revenues for factional and kleptocratic purposes, e.g. Sierra Leone. Prior to 1985, its alluvial diamonds were extracted in an industrial fashion, rather than by artisans, making it non-lootable. It did not collapse into civil war until after that.

Dunning (2005) compares Mobutu's Zaire (1965–1997) to Suharto's Indonesia (1965–1998) and Botswana during the same period. In Indonesia and Zaire, resource flows were volatile. In one case, the dictator (Suharto) chose diversification and high growth rendering policies, as well as policies aimed at equalisation and poverty reduction to contain political opposition. In the other case (Zaire, now DRC), Mobutu did not, because he felt that diversification and investment in infrastructure would loosen his grip on power and strengthen political opposition to him based on ethnicity. In East Asia, perhaps greater fears of communism strengthened developmental initiatives by dictators (South Korea, Taiwan Singapore and Indonesia), whereas in Africa, a certain type of factionalism dominated policies and politics, retarding growth-enhancing economic diversification and infrastructural development.

The greed versus grievance dichotomy is a useful entry point into the debate about the causes of conflict. But for these forces to take the form of large-scale violence, there must be other factors at work, specifically a weakening of what Addison and Murshed (2002a) call the 'social contract' (see also Murshed, 2002). This is similar to the state capacity arguments made above. Therefore, while rents from capturable resources constitute a sizeable 'prize', violent conflict is unlikely to take hold if a country has a framework of widely-agreed rules, both formal and informal, that govern the allocation of resources, including resource rents, and the peaceful settlement of grievances. Such a viable social contract can be sufficient to restrain, if not eliminate, opportunistic behaviour such as large-scale theft of resource rents and the violent expression of grievance. Conflict-affected nations have histories of weak social contracts (or a once strong social contract that has degraded).

Hegre and others (2001) point out that the risk of conflict is lower in both well established democracies and autocracies, perhaps because of greater state capacity. It suggests that conflict risk is at its highest during transitions to and from democracy, when state capacity is weak, and also in fledgling and imperfect democracies (anocracies). A final complexity in fatally weakening social contracts was the interaction of these 'domestic' factors with external events, notably the Cold War, which provided finance and ideological succour to ruling elites and rebels (notably in Central America, Central Africa, and the Horn of Africa). The net result of these processes is the accumulation of grievances within the context of a disintegrating social contract that would otherwise have provided the rules of the game to govern the distribution of the social pie and to achieve peaceful conflict resolution.

Greed is rarely the sole cause of conflict. Addison, Le Billon, and Murshed (2002) construct a game-theoretic model of contemporary conflict involving competition for resources combined with historical grievances. In addition to resource rents, grievances also play their part in fuelling conflict by explaining inter-group non-cooperation and serving to lower the cost of participation in conflict. Conflict can increase because of heightened intrinsic grievances, or because there are more lootable resources. Additionally, they distinguish between two main types of resource exploitation: *point resources*, which mostly (but not exclusively) involve the *extraction* of non-renewable resources (minerals), require less labour input and are geographically concentrated; and *diffuse resources*, such as those which mostly involve the *production* of renewable resources (crops), require large amounts of labour, and are spread geographically (see also Murshed, 2004). Occasionally, coffee/cocoa exporting economies are also classified as point resource because coffee is often marketed like minerals, and coffee/cocoa based economies are characterised by a (rentier) political economy, similar to point-resource economies. The same argument could be applied to the production and export of illicit drugs (heroin, coca) where data for these exist.

In summary, the type of economy can matter in explaining either or both civil war onset and its duration. As far as the competing greed versus grievance hypotheses are concerned, they may be complementary explanations for conflict. The greed explanation for conflict duration and secessionist wars works in cross-sectional studies, but has to make way for grievance-based arguments in quantitative country-case studies. Grievances and horizontal inequalities may, after all, be better at explaining why conflicts begin, but not necessarily why they persist (greed). The empirical literature on the causes of conflict tells us that the most robust and significant predictor of conflict risk and its duration across all studies is some indicator of economic prosperity such as income per-capita within a cross-section (of countries or regions) where average income does vary. This is because at higher incomes, people have more to lose from the destructiveness of conflict (Lipset, 1960); and a higher per-capita income implies a better functioning social contract, institutions and state capacity.

GROWTH, POLITY, ENDOWMENTS AND CONFLICT

There are several obvious similarities between the causes of growth failure and the factors affecting the likelihood of conflict: a substantial point resource endowment being the most palpable feature. Also, analogies can be drawn between the coordination failure game that explains the absence of a big push in growth, and the game describing commitment failure to peace agreements. Additionally, stable democracies and autocracies lower conflict risk, just as democracy's impact on growth contains positive and negative channels. But more fundamentally, the lack of economic growth significantly contributes to the risk of conflict in low-income nations; by perpetuating poverty and increasing inequality they breed grievances and enhance horizontal inequality. Even the foremost exponents of the greed hypothesis (Collier and others, 2003) concede that poverty has an important part to play in engendering conflict. Institutional malfunctioning is hugely important in explaining both the lack of long-term growth and the emergence of conflict. Whether the cause of growth failure in the long-run is attributable to geography, culture, endowments or wrong policies they all impact on growth rates via institutional functioning. Similarly, irrespective of whether the causes of conflict are greed or grievance (or both), the outbreak of violent conflict requires institutional failure in conflict management, something referred to in the previous section as either poor state capacities or social contract failure.

To get an empirical feel for some of the channels mentioned above, a descriptive look at the data may be in order. We compare growth rates, the combined democracy and autocracy score, known as Polity 2, endowment type and conflict intensity or incidence in selected developing countries during the period 1965–2000. This is done selectively in Table 12.4, and more fully in Murshed (2006).

TABLE 12.4

Conflict Years, Growth, Polity and Economic Typology in Selected Countries

Country	Incidence conflict in years, 1960–2000	Most frequent regime type	Ann. Av. per capita income growth rate, 1965–1999	Economic Typology
Myanmar	177	1	1.5%	Diffuse, Point
India	104	3	2.4%	Manufacturing
Ethiopia	81	1	–0.3%	Coffee/Cocoa
Philippines	59	1;2;3	0.9%	Diffuse, Manufacturing
Iraq	57	1	–3.5%	Point
Angola	43	1	–2.1%	Point
Iran	41	1;2	–1.0%	Point
Algeria	37	1;2	1.0%	Point
Chad	36	1	–0.6%	Point
Colombia	35	3	2.1%	Coffee/Cocoa
Indonesia	32	1	4.8%	Point, Manufacturing
Guatemala	31	1;2	0.7%	Coffee/Cocoa
Sudan	31	1;2;3	0.5%	Diffuse, Point
South Africa	31	2	0%	Point
Mozambique	27	1	1.3%	Diffuse
Uganda	23	1;2	2.5%	Coffee/Cocoa
Sri Lanka	22	3	3.0%	Diffuse, Manufacturing

Sources: Conflict years at http://www.prio.no/cwp/ArmedConflict; UNCTAD data base and Murshed (2004) for the typology of the economy; Polity data at www.cidcm.umd.edu/inscr/polity; and *World Development Indicators* (2002) for growth rates.

The Polity score is a proxy for institutional capacity, which is coded 1 for autocracies (those with an autocracy score below -4), 3 for democracies (for democracy scores above 4) and 2 for anocracies that have both democratic and autocratic characteristics (with scores of between –4 and 4), and the endowment typology (based upon a country's principal exports, which is subject to change) integrates economic typology with institutional quality and conflict occurrence (measured by conflict incidence and intensity), and then, growth.[8]

Table 12.4 shows 17 countries with the highest conflict incidence since 1960[9], along with their average annual long-term growth rates of per-capita income accompanied by the typology of the economy and the most frequently occurring regime type. Note that countries can have more than one year of civil war in any given calendar year if there are several conflicts taking place within the nation simultaneously. Burma, India, Ethiopia, Philippines, Iraq, Angola and Israel had more than one conflict per annum in the 41 year period reported in Table 12.4. Note that incidence does not imply anything about conflict intensity, which is measured by fatalities, as defined above.

Only five of the high conflict incidence nations reported in Table 12.4 had a per-capita income growth rate in excess of 2 per cent per annum in the long-term: Indonesia, India, Sri Lanka, Colombia and Uganda. Generally speaking, poor growth performers had more conflict years in Table 12.4. Even in these cases, it might be possible to construct counter-factual analyses to demonstrate that conflict adversely affected growth. In Indonesia and India, conflicts have been highly localized in the context of vast populations, with little effect on the entire economy; also, Indian growth rates were very low prior to 1990. In Uganda, there was a sharp and remarkable growth recovery in the 1990s' post-conflict era, making up for the earlier lost years. Only four economies (India, Philippines, Sri Lanka and Mozambique) have not been point-source or coffee/cocoa economies (the Burmese conflicts are fuelled by trade in illegal substances which cannot be reported here, because of data paucity). This lends some support to the arguments made above regarding empirical regularities regarding conflict across a cross-section of countries.

Many point-sourced and coffee/cocoa economies that are growth failures (with long-term growth rates under 2 per cent per annum on average) have tended to fall into conflict, besides having polities that are not democracies. Only three point-sourced countries and four coffee/cocoa economies did not descend into some form of civil war; see Murshed (2006). Diffuse economies also have conflicts; examples of high incidence of civil wars occurring in diffuse economies are in South Asia, the Philippines and Burma, as well as Mozambique and Zimbabwe in Africa. In total, eight out of thirty diffuse economies have avoided civil war, a record better than for point-sourced and coffee/cocoa based economies. Notwithstanding India, manufacturing economies are least likely to experience outright civil war. Perhaps this is because they have the best growth rates and institutional quality. They also probably have the most diversified economies, and are able to withstand the commodity price and national income fluctuations associated with the staple trap (reliance on a single commodity), which make economies more prone to conflict

India, Sri Lanka and Colombia are the stable democracies in the post-1960 era that have had civil wars, including high intensity conflict. India, in particular, is interesting because of its very high democracy score, and having the highest number of total conflict years (due to the multiplicity of civil wars in India) after Burma, which has not been a democracy in the period under question. All the transitions in regime type from autocracy to anocracy to democracy (during 1960–2000) are described in Murshed (2006). It is clear that multiple switches in all directions are possible, and not just from autocracy to democracy. Nevertheless, only 5 out of the 17 nations with a high conflict incidence have ever been democracies with a democracy score over 4.

Three points about democratic transitions need to be reiterated here. First, most developing countries were not democracies before the end of the Cold War. The end of the Cold War heralded democratization due to outside pressures, but many of these countries descended into anocracy. Secondly, few developing countries are fully established and meaningful democracies, in the sense of having democracy scores of 8 or above. Costa Rica is the best example of a full democracy in the global South, followed by India. Even Colombia has sometimes slipped down to a score of 7. Finally, democracy, even stable democracy, does not guarantee the absence of armed conflict, both of the secessionist and rebel varieties, as the examples of India, Colombia, Sri Lanka, the Philippines and others indicate. Autocracies also fall into conflict, as Table 12.4 and Murshed (2006) point out. Nevertheless, stable autocracies, such as China and Singapore, have avoided civil war, as did Taiwan and South Korea which became democracies recently. Despite prominent outliers such as India, Colombia, and Saudi Arabia, most conflict prone countries are neither stable democracies nor autocracies, lending support to the Hegre and others (2001) finding that conflict risk is greatest when regime types are in transition. While we can never be sanguine about the true nature of the causes of conflict, it does seem to occur more frequently in non-manufacturing and non-diffuse economies, and there does seem to be a distinctive positive association between conflict and growth failure.

Conclusions and Policy Recommendations

The importance of the growth and intra-state conflict nexus cannot be overemphasized. The lack of growth prevents poverty reduction and achievement of the MDGs. Similarly, poverty and low growth help increase the risk of conflict, as individuals have less to lose from conflict in low income situations, and because poverty helps supply conflict warlords with ready recruits. Consequently, the security and development agendas can never be dichotomized. Also, recent economic history provides ample evidence of diverging average incomes between rich and poor countries. This rising inequality between rich and poor nations also adds to global insecurity.

As far as the causes of conflict are concerned, both the greed and grievance hypotheses can have some validity. But the operation of either or both these motivations for civil war require the breakdown of the institutions of conflict management, referred to as the break-down of the social contract. The greed explanation for conflict is mainly applied in cross-country econometric studies. Its validity as a direct causal mechanism of civil war onset has recently been brought into serious question. The relationship between conflict onset and natural resource revenues must work through other mechanisms, such as a weakening social contract and withering state capacity.

But the abundance of lootable mineral resources or illicit drugs can help to perpetuate existing civil wars, and the prevalence of conflict seems greater among mineral and coffee/cocoa exporters compared to other agricultural and manufactured goods exporters. The latter two categories of economies also seem to experience higher growth rates. This does not mean that undiversified agricultural economies are not at risk of conflict. The grievance explanation for contemporary civil war has been found to be dominant in detailed conflict case studies. Grievances can be historical, but it can have a measurable and quantitative counterpart in group inequalities in socio-economic achievement. Here, the neglected dimension of inter-group or horizontal inequality, measured by factors such as human development gaps, can have a great deal of explanatory power. It is useful to remind ourselves that the single most robust explanatory variable for conflict risk is (low) per-capita income (implying growth failure), as it acts as a proxy for institutional quality.

Finally, a number of policy recommendations:

o   Growth can reduce conflict risk in four ways. First of all, by lowering poverty, it provides fewer ready recruits for conflict entrepreneurs. Secondly, growth can ultimately lower inequality, and this can also reduce conflict producing inter-group or horizontal inequality. Thirdly, growth creates denser sets of interaction between economic agents, resulting in situations where there is much to lose from conflict. Fourthly, growth can improve institutional functioning, creating better chances of peaceful conflict resolution; even producing situations ripe for the emergence of high quality democracy.

o   By the same token, income poverty reduction and achieving the MDGs also lower conflict risk. For most low-income countries, meaningful poverty reduction will only come about through growth. Ideally, growth induced poverty reduction should be truly pro-poor (growth that also redistributes income towards the poor), not merely relying on trickle-down effects where the poor receive some crumbs of the larger cake.

o Development strategies based on poverty reduction alone are insufficient; attention has to be focussed on lessening inequality if sustainable pro-poor conflict-reducing growth is to take place. Also, the reduction of group or horizontal inequalities is important in outright conflict prevention in low-income countries characterized with lootable resources and weak institutions.

o Improvements in institutional quality and good governance are important for both growth and conflict prevention (or peaceful conflict resolution). Institutional malfunctioning, weakened state capacity and the breakdown of social contracts ultimately lie behind the emergence of open conflict, irrespective of the root causes of conflict. Also, as discussed above, institutional quality is an important long-term determinant of growth.

o Lessons can be learned from why some countries avoided conflict and others did not, despite having similar initial conditions. It is instructive to contrast cases of success such as Botswana and Malaysia after the 1970s on the one hand, against failures such as the Democratic Republic of Congo (Zaire) on the other hand. In the Malaysian case, the government: (a) ended up redistributing income, via government expenditure policies favouring ethnic Malays, who were poorer; and, (b) invested in infrastructure and human capital. Botswana avoided factionalism through political consensus.

o Failing peace agreements that characterize the conflict-ridden world at the moment deserve greater attention than superficial and patchy attempts to end war. Despite copious external intervention of both the peaceful (Norway, Finland) and forceful (UK and the USA) varieties, most peace agreements do not stand a very high chance of being sustainable and self-enforcing. To avoid this requires strengthening the anchors of commitment to an externally brokered peace treaty; on this, see Addison and Murshed (2002b). This requires the carrot of overseas development aid to be backed by the stick of effective military sanctions against spoiler groups.

Aid aimed at achieving peace can be misused for future belligerent activities; see Addison and Murshed (2003) on this. Effective military sanctions by outside powers against those who renege on peace agreements can be expensive, and donors may be more willing to finance this nearer home (Balkans), compared to costly interventions in distant lands (Africa).

o Some issues in post-conflict macroeconomic policies include:

- Conflict distorts the economy, making activities with short-term returns, such as services more attractive compared to those which require long-term investment such as agriculture or manufacturing, see Addison and Murshed (2005). Analytically, the effect is similar to Dutch disease problems that distort the economy towards greater non-traded, relative to traded, goods production. The post-conflict economic recovery may be similarly lop-sided. This can impose an unfortunate path-dependence on reconstruction and growth. One source of distortion is the sharp increase in transactions costs resulting from war, including the destruction of transport, the planting of land mines, and institutional collapse that drive a wedge between producer and consumer prices. Typically, production (especially agriculture) is more vulnerable compared to other sectors such as urban-based trade and services. Services and trade heavily dominate wartime economies and, because of the relative price effect, the collapse in production usually exceeds that due to destruction alone. In addition to raising transactions costs and production costs, conflict raises uncertainty about the future and the private discount rates of investors. To avoid these pitfalls, selective policies of subsidies to the productive sectors have to be followed, see Murshed (2001).

- But just as economic growth in general can broadly or narrowly distribute its benefits across society – depending upon the initial distribution of assets and skills – so too can reconstruction-led growth. Pre-war asset and skill distributions may have been highly unequal, with resulting grievances contributing to conflict, and can worsen dramatically during wartime. The already poor often lose the few assets they have, and looting adds to the number of poor. In contrast, warlords and their followers accumulate assets, and so, while the early years of peace may see quite rapid GDP growth, it can be very narrow in its benefits – unless policies are put in place to restore the productive assets and human capital of the poor. The immediate post-conflict situation may offer a golden opportunity for pro-poor asset redistribution as well, although this can be impeded when rich 'winners' from war block the necessary measures.

- Aid fatigue usually sets in after the first few years of donor involvement in post-conflict situations. In the early stages of donor involvement, relatively large sums are promised by donors. But these funds cannot always be absorbed by war torn economies in early 'post-conflict' phases. One idea is to create an aid trust fund, where unused aid monies can be lodged for future use.

- Conflict generally impacts negatively on financial development and deepening; see Addison and others (2005). In many countries, currency reform is necessary after war, sometimes via the introduction of a new monetary unit of account. To gain credibility for the new money, and build confidence in the new currency, a variety of strategies could be adopted. These include dollarization, where the domestic government surrenders the freedom to conduct independent monetary and exchange rate policies. Alternatively, currency boards, where changes in the monetary base are related to domestic reserves of a selected hard currency, is a less drastic means of gaining credibility. Reviving the banking system and introducing prudential regulation are also major challenges.

- It is important to rebuild a post-conflict nation's fiscal institutions. State capacity, including the public expenditure system, may be so weak that it is unable to use any revenue raised to deliver improved infrastructure and services. This will also affect the ability of governments to use aid and debt relief to make the fiscal transfers necessary to redress grievances, and achieve broad-based recovery. Further difficulties arise from the need in many countries to undertake the introduction of fiscal federalism to redress previous over-centralization of political and fiscal powers. Also, as formal (taxed) activity shrinks during conflicts, so the state loses its revenue base, and while resources at the disposal of resource rentiers and warlords may become greater than those of any legitimate post-war authority. Criminal resources can be used to thwart government attempts to collect revenues (for example, extensive rackets were run to evade excise duties on petrol, alcohol, and tobacco in the countries of the former Yugoslavia), and to corrupt and control the political process. However, countries that emerge out of conflict with higher levels of *non-criminal* social capital are in a better position to achieve post-war revenue mobilization for a shared sense of nation-building.

o   In connection with natural resource rents, particularly oil revenues in the context of the recent rise in crude oil prices, the notion of revenue management is important. Essentially, this involves the creation of a social trust fund, whose principal aim is to minimize the kleptocratic syphoning-off of revenues and windfalls for ruling elites. Several points deserve mention in this connection:

- Commodity price stabilization funds may be considered, as commodity prices are very volatile. Fluctuating national incomes, as a result of commodity price volatility, lead to government revenue and growth collapses in developing countries with conflict generating consequences.
- Monies in the trust fund should be mainly used for public investment, in activities such as education and infrastructural development, rather than consumption.

> This is of greater importance in resource-rich, post-conflict economies.

- The main aim should be to diversify the economy and to avoid the staple trap (reliance on a single commodity). A diversified economy is better able to withstand economic shocks, as not all sectors (prices and quantities) decline simultaneously. Ultimately, economic diversification emanates from general economic growth.

o Lastly, extractive industries should exercise greater corporate social responsibility in countries they operate in, at least seeing to it that natural resource rents do not become a source of the *increased* grievances and horizontal inequality that produce conflict. This, for example, is a major issue in the Niger delta region of Nigeria, where the oil multinational. Shell, operates. There, as elsewhere (such as in Aceh in Indonesia), the local population feels they have less than their fair share of the bounties that nature has bestowed on their regions. Local employment creation, infrastructural development and fiscal federalism help assuage these perceived injustices, but care has to be taken not to fall prey to the machinations of opportunistic local politicians.

Notes

1 Based upon the widely accepted purchasing power parity (PPP) concept of a dollar a day per person as the international absolute poverty line.
2 Hong Kong, Singapore, Taiwan and South Korea.
3 Many data sets on democracy exist. To give one example, the Polity data set gives a democracy score of between 0–10 (with Western democracies scoring 10). A truly meaningful democracy is only arrived at with a Polity score of 8. The autocracy data set gives an autocracy score of between –10 and 0. The Polity 2 score is a combination of both autocracy and democracy, and a reflection of a country's democratic or non-democratic status. See www.cidcm.umd.edu/insr/polity.
4 The data are available at http://www.ucdp.uu.se and at http://www.prio.no/cwp/ArmedConflict.
5 Interestingly, the UK is involved in the greatest number of inter-state wars (21) during the 1946-2003 period, ahead of France (19) and the USA (16).
6 Analogies with the poverty-gap measure are appropriate.
7 The human development index is an un-weighted average of income per-capita, educational status and longevity.

[8] I do not propose any *direct* econometric investigation, which would be fraught with endogeneity and reverse causality problems

[9] I have excluded Israel with 49 years, as it is a rich country when one excludes the Palestinian territories, as well as Cambodia (36 years) and Yemen (23 years) because of the paucity of economic data.

REFERENCES

Addison, Tony, Alemayehu Geda, Philippe Le Billon, and S Mansoob Murshed (2005). Reconstructing and reforming the financial system in conflict and 'post-conflict economies'. *Journal of Development Studies* 41 (4): 703–718.

Addison, Tony, Philippe Le Billon, and S Mansoob Murshed (2002). Conflict in Africa: The cost of peaceful behaviour. *Journal of African Economies* 11 (3): 365–386.

Addison, Tony, and S Mansoob Murshed (2002a). On the economic causes of contemporary civil wars. In S Mansoob Murshed (ed.). *Issues in Positive Political Economy*. Routledge, London: 22–38.

Addison Tony, and S. Mansoob Murshed (2002b). Credibility and reputation in peacemaking. *Journal of Peace Research* 39 (4): 487–501.

Addison, Tony, and S Mansoob Murshed (2003). Debt relief and civil war. *Journal of Peace Research* 40 (2): 159–176.

Addison, Tony, and S Mansoob Murshed (2005). Post-conflict reconstruction in Africa: Some analytical issues. In Paul Collier and Augustin Fosu (eds). *Post Conflict Reconstruction in Africa*. Palgrave, London: 3–17.

Collier, Paul, and Anke Hoeffler (2002). On the incidence of civil war in Africa. *Journal of Conflict Resolution* 46 (1): 13–28.

Collier, Paul, and Anke Hoeffler (2004). Greed and grievance in civil wars. *Oxford Economic Papers* 56 (4): 563–595.

Collier, Paul, Lani Elliot, Håvard Hegre, Anke Hoeffler, Marta Reynal-Querol, and Nicholas Sambanis (2003). *Breaking the Conflict Trap: Civil War and Development Policy*. Oxford University Press, New York, for World Bank, Washington, D.C.

Dunning, Thad (2005). Resource dependence, economic performance, and political stability. *Journal of Conflict Resolution* 49 (4): 451–482.

Easterly, William, and Ross Levine (2003). Tropics, germs and crops: How endowments influence economic development. *Journal of Monetary Economics* 50 (1): 3–39.

Fearon, James (2004). Why do some civil wars last so much longer than others. *Journal of Peace Research* 41 (3): 379–414.

Fearon, James (2005). Primary commodity exports and civil war. *Journal of Conflict Resolution* 49 (4): 483–507.

Grossman, Herschel I. (1991). A general equilibrium model of insurrections. *American Economic Review* 81: 912–921.

Harbom, Lotta, and Peter Wallensteen (2005). Armed conflict and its international dimensions, 1946-2004. *Journal of Peace Research* 42 (5): 623–635.

Hegre, Håvard (2004). The duration and termination of civil war. *Journal of Peace Research* 41 (3): 243–252.

Hegre, Håvard; Tanja Ellingsen, Scott Gates, and Nils Petter Gleditsch (2001). Towards a democratic civil peace? Democracy, civil change, and civil war 1816–1992. *American Political Science Review* 95: 17–33.

Human Security Report (2005). University of British Columbia, Vancouver, B.C., http://www.humansecurityreport.info/.

Humphreys, Macartan (2005). Natural resources, conflict, and conflict resolution: Uncovering the mechanisms. *Journal of Conflict Resolution* 49 (4): 508-537.

Kakwani, Nanak, and Edward Pernia (2000). What is pro-poor growth. *Asian Development Review* 16 (1): 1–16.

Lipset, Seymour (1960). *Political Man*. Doubleday, New York.

Lujala, Päivi, Nils Petter Gleditsch, and Elisabeth Gilmore (2005). A diamond curse? Civil war and a lootable resource. *Journal of Conflict Resolution* 49 (4): 538–562.

Maddison, Angus (2001). *The World Economy: A Millennial Perspective*. Organisation for Economic Co-operation and Development (OECD), Paris.

Milanovic, Branko (2005). *Worlds Apart: Measuring International and Global Inequality*. Princeton University Press, Princeton, New Jersey.

Murshed, S Mansoob (2001). Short-run models of natural resource endowment. In Richard M Auty (ed.). *Resource Abundance and Economic Development*. Oxford University Press, Oxford: 113-125.

Murshed, S Mansoob (2002). Civil war, conflict and underdevelopment. *Journal of Peace Research* 39 (4): 387–393.

Murshed, S Mansoob (2004). When does natural resource abundance lead to a resource curse. IIED-EEP working paper 04–01. International Institute for Environment and Development, London. http://www.iied.org.

Murshed, S Mansoob (2006). Turning swords into ploughshares and little acorns to tall trees: The conflict growth nexus and the poverty of nations. Background paper for the Department for Economic and Social Affairs, United Nations. *World Economic and Social Survey*, 2006. http://www.un.org/esa/policy/wess/.

Murshed, S Mansoob, and Scott Gates (2005). Spatial-horizontal inequality and the Maoist conflict in Nepal. *Review of Development Economics* 9 (1): 121–134.

Olson, Mancur (1996). Big bills left on the sidewalk: Why some nations are rich, and others poor. *Journal of Economic Perspectives* 10: 3–24.

Polity 4 Data Base, Center for International Development and conflict Management, University of Maryland, College Par, MD www.cidcm.umd.edu/inscr/polity

Rodrik, Dani (1999). Where did all the growth go? External shocks, social conflict, and growth collapses. *Journal of Economic Growth* 4: 385–412.

Rodrik, Dani, Arvind Subramanian, and Francesco Trebbi (2004). Institutions rule: The primacy of institutions over geography and integration in economic development. *Journal of Economic Growth* 9 (2): 131–165.

Ross, Michael L. (2003). Oil, drugs and diamonds: The varying role of natural resources in civil wars. In Karen Ballentine and Jake Sherman (eds). *The Political Economy of Armed Conflict: Beyond Greed and Grievance*. Lynne Rienner, Boulder CO: 47–70.

Ross, Michael L (2004). What do we know about natural resources and civil wars. *Journal of Peace Research* 41 (3): 337–356.

Skaperdas, Stergios (2002). Warlord competition. *Journal of Peace Research* 39 (4): 435–446.

Snyder, Richard, and Ravi Bhavnani (2005). Diamonds, blood and taxes: A revenue-centered framework for explaining political order. *Journal of Conflict Resolution* 49 (4): 563–597.

Stewart, Frances (2000). Crisis prevention: Tackling horizontal inequalities. *Oxford Development Studies* 28 (3): 245–62.

UNCTAD (2002). *Handbook of Statistics.* Online database, United Nations Conference on Trade and Development, Geneva.

Uppsala/Prio Armed Conflict Dataset, Center for the Study of Civil War, International Peace Research Institute, Oslo, Norway. http://www.prio.no/cwp/ArmedConflict

World Bank (2002). *World Development Indicators 2002.* World Bank, Washington D.C., CD-ROM.

Contributors

Valpy FitzGerald is Professor of International Economics and Finance at Oxford University, Professorial Fellow of St Antony's College Oxford, and Extraordinary Professor of Development Economics at the Institute of Social Studies, The Hague. He is also Director Designate of the Department of International Development, Oxford University. He has acted as adviser on issues of international development finance to various UN agencies, the OECD and the UK Government. His current research interests include capital flows to developing countries, long-run economic growth in Latin America, and global tax reform.

Jomo K. S. has been Assistant Secretary General for Economic Development in the United Nations' Department of Economic and Social Affairs (DESA) since January 2005. He was Professor in the University of Malaya until November 2004, and then Visiting Professor at the National University of Singapore. Jomo was Founder Chair of IDEAs, International Development Economics Associates (www.ideaswebsite.org), and has authored over 35 monographs, edited over 50 books and translated 12 volumes besides writing many academic papers and articles for the media. He is on the editorial boards of several learned journals.

Mushtaq Khan is Professor in the Economic Department at the School of Oriental and African Studies, University of London.

Richard Kozul-Wright, is a senior economist at the United Nations Conference on Trade and Development (UNCTAD), Geneva. He received his Ph.D in economics from Cambridge University, from where he went to work at the United Nations, first in New York on the

World Economic and Social Survey and subsequently in Geneva on the *World Investment Report*, the *Trade and Development Report* and the *Economic Development in Africa Report*. He has published articles on a wide range of development issues and on economic history in the *Economic Journal*, the *Cambridge Journal of Economics*, the *Oxford Review of Economic Policy* and the *Journal of Development Studies*. His forthcoming book on *The Resistible Rise of Market Fundamentalism* will be published this year by Zed Press.

Camelia Minoiu is a PhD Candidate in Economics at Columbia University. Her current research interests are in the area of density estimation methods used in assessing inequality and poverty based on grouped data. Her work also includes an analysis of the vulnerability of Romanian rural households to negative income shocks, which is forthcoming in the *Economics of Transition*.

Syed Mansoob Murshed is Professor of the Economics of Conflict and Peace at the Institute of Social Studies (ISS) in the Netherlands, and Professor of International Economics at the Birmingham Business School, University of Birmingham, UK. He is also affiliated to the Peace Research Institute in Oslo (PRIO). His research interests lie in conflict, growth, the resource curse, aid effectiveness and political economy.

José Antonio Ocampo was United Nations Under-Secretary-General of the Department of Economic and Social Affairs from September 2003 to June 2007. Prior to that, he served as Executive Secretary of the United Nations Economic Commission for Latin America and the Caribbean, Minister of Finance, Minister of Agriculture and in other portfolios in the Colombian Government. He holds a Ph.D. from Yale University, has taught in several universities and published extensively on economic and social issues. He is currently a Professor at Columbia University

Mariangela Parra is inter-regional advisor to the Under-Secretary-General for Economic and Social Affairs of the United Nations in New York. Until 2003, she was an advisor to the Executive Secretary of the Economic Commission for Latin America and the Caribbean (ECLAC) in Santiago. Currently she is doing her PhD in Economics at the New School University in New York. Her areas of interest are economic development, international trade and finance.

Codrina Rada was formerly an Associate Economic Officer with the United Nations Development Policy and Analysis Division working on issues related to economic growth and development. Codrina's main research interest is on structuralist macroeconomic models and what drives structural change in an economy and why some countries perform better than others in terms of expanding growth and employment.

Sanjay G. Reddy is an Assistant Professor of Economics at Barnard College, Columbia University, and also teaches Economics at the School of International and Public Affairs, Columbia University. He has research interests in development economics, political economy and economics and philosophy.

Francisco Rodriguez (Ph.d, Harvard 1998) is Assistant Professor of Economics and Latin American Studies at Wesleyan University. From 2000 to 2004 he served as Chief Economist of the Venezuelan National Assembly. He has published numerous academic articles on economic growth, openness, political economy, and income distribution.

Helen Shapiro is an Associate Professor at the University of California, Santa Cruz, where she teaches in the departments of Sociology, Latin American and Latino Studies, and Economics. She has published widely on Latin American economic development and industrial policy, including *Engines of Growth: The State and Transnational Auto Companies in Brazil* (Cambridge: Cambridge University Press, 1994). She previously taught at the Harvard Business School, and received her Ph.D. in economics from Yale University.

Lance Taylor is Arnhold Professor and Director of the Center for Economic Policy Analysis, New School for Social Research. He has written widely in macroeconomics and development economics, and has been a visiting scholar and policy advisor in numerous countries. His latest book is *Reconstructing Macroeconomics* (Harvard University Press, 2004).

Rob Vos is Director of the Development Policy and Analysis Division at the Department of Economic and Social Affairs of the United Nations and in that capacity responsible for, among others, the UN's annual flagship publications the World Economic Situation and Prospects and the World Economic and Social Survey, as well as for the secretariat of the Committee for Development Policy. He is also an affiliate Professor of Finance and Development at the Institute of Social Studies in The Hague and Professor of Development Economics at the Free University, Amsterdam. Previously, he was the Deputy Rector of the Institute of Social Studies and worked as senior economist at the Inter-American Development Bank. His most recent book is *Who gains from Free Trade? Export-led Growth and Poverty in Latin America* published by Routledge in 2006.

Index